WOMEN IN THE SEVENTEENTH-CENTURY
QUAKER COMMUNITY

Women and Gender in the Early Modern World

Series Editors: Allyson Poska and Abby Zanger

In the past decade, the study of women and gender has offered some of the most vital and innovative challenges to scholarship on the early modern period. Ashgate's new series of interdisciplinary and comparative studies, *Women and Gender in the Early Modern World*, takes up this challenge, reaching beyond geographical limitations to explore the experiences of early modern women and the nature of gender in Europe, the Americas, Asia, and Africa. Submissions of single-author studies and edited collections will be considered.

Titles in the series include:

Women in the Seventeenth-Century Quaker Community

A Literary Study of Political Identities, 1650–1700

CATIE GILL
Loughborough University, UK

ASHGATE

Published by
Ashgate Publishing Limited
Gower House
Croft Road
Aldershot
Hampshire GU11 3HR
England

Ashgate Publishing Company
Suite 420
101 Cherry Street
Burlington, VT 05401-4405
USA

Ashgate website: http://www.ashgate.com

British Library Cataloguing in Publication Data
Gill, Catherine
   Women in the seventeenth-century Quaker community : a
   literary study of political identities, 1650–1700. – (Women
   and gender in the early modern world)
   1. English literature – Early modern, 1500–1700 – History and criticism 2. English
   literature – Quaker authors – History and criticism 3. English literature – Women authors –
   History and criticism 4. Quaker women – England – History – 17th century 5. Sex role –
   Religious aspects – Quakers 6. Quakers in literature 7. Sex role in literature 8. Group
   identity in literature
   I. Title
   820.9'382896'09032

Library of Congress Cataloging-in-Publication Data
Gill, Catie.
   Women in the seventeenth-century Quaker community : a literary study of political
identities, 1650–1700 / Catie Gill.
      p. cm.—(Women and gender in the early modern world)
   Includes bibliographical references and index.
   ISBN 0-7546-3985-1 (alk. paper)
   1. Quaker women—England—History—17th century. 2. Christian literature, English—
Women authors—History and criticism. 3. Christian literature, English—Quaker
authors—History and criticism. 4. Women and literature—England—History—17th
century. I. Title. II. Series.

   BX7748.W64G55 2005
   289.6'42'082—dc22

                                                                2004008768

ISBN 0 7546 3985 1

Printed and bound in Great Britain by TJ International, Padstow, Cornwall

Contents

List of Illustrations

Illustrations 2.1, 3.1, 3.2, 3.3, 3.4, 4.1 and 4.3 are by permission of the British Library; E 884 (3), 4152f21 (5), E861 (14), 669f19 (73)

Cover illustration and illustrations 4.2 and 5.1 are by permission of the Society of Friends

Acknowledgements

Acknowledgements are an inadequate expression of thanks for all the support I have received from my extended family: Mum, Dad and Helen; their partners: David, Lynn and Matt; my favourite niece and nephew, Paige and Nathan; Gran; Barbara and Sue; and Mary Grouse. Thanks, also, to dear friends: Neil Burton, David Campling, Phoebe Mould, Andrea Peterson, Emma Whewell, Tim Wright, Womenspace – and, much loved, Ellen Grierson. Further thanks to the friends who directly or indirectly speeded my way.

I am extremely grateful to the financial support given to me by Loughborough University, firstly as a part-time research student, then, in my final year, full time. I am also indebted to Martyn Bennett, T.N. Corns, Mark Hyde, Bill Overton, Gillian Spraggs, and Nigel Wood. To the students in the Department of English and Drama, Loughborough, and, latterly, to the staff and students at University College Worcester: thanks.

I would also like to thank the staff at the following libraries: Loughborough University; The British Library; Woodbrooke Quaker Studies Centre and the kind and knowledgeable people at Friends' House, London.

Thanks to Ashgate's Erika Gaffney, and to the anonymous reader whose initial responses to the manuscript have made this a better book.

And then there's Elaine Hobby. I simply could not have done this without her. This book is for my supervisor and friend.

List of Abbreviations

i) Spelling and Punctuation:
Seventeenth-century spelling and punctuation has been retained, except where 'u' and 'v' have been silently altered.

ii) The Bible:
Quotations from the Bible within the text of this book are from the 1611 bible. Where biblical passages are referred to in parenthesis, the edition used has been *The Holy Bible: The New King James Version* (Nashville, Tennessee: Thomas Nelson Publishers, 1982).

iii) Footnotes and Bibliography:
References to seventeenth-century texts are given by name, short-title, place, printer and date. However, many of these texts are more complex than the norm described above; and my approach to multiply authored texts is as follows: the author of a multiply authored text is stated as the first person to sign their name in the tract. When providing footnotes in instances where the writer is a contributor, rather than the first person to have signed their name, the convention has been to treat the contributor as one would a modern critic writing for an edited volume of essays. In both the footnotes and the bibliography, the abbreviation 'Sigy' represents 'signatory': this is used to identify a named contributor to a text, or passage, with more than two named authors.

iv) Abbreviations:
Where Christian names are abbreviated in the Quaker text, they have been expanded only if the attribution of the text to a particular author is well established; these names have been checked against the bibliography of Friends' books by Joseph Smith, Rosemary Foxton's bibliography, and the *DQB*.[1] Where an abbreviated name cannot be authenticated, it has been left in its original form.

Where initials, rather than the full name, are used to signify authorship, two different approaches have been taken. Commonly known Quaker figures, whose authorial activities are certain, are identified by the full name rather than by their initials. G. F., for instance, has been automatically changed to George Fox.

---

[1] Joseph Smith, *A Descriptive Catalogue of Friends' Books*, 2 vols (London: R. Barrett & Sons, 1867); Rosemary Foxton, *'Hear the Word of the Lord': A Bibliographical Study of Quaker Women's Writing 1650-1700* (Melbourne: The Bibliographical Society of Australia and New Zealand, 1994); *DQB: The Dictionary of Quaker Biography* (Friends' House Library, London).

In cases where the attribution is less certain, a qualifying remark indicates that this is the case. In other instances, where the initial cannot be expanded to a full name because insufficient evidence exists, the original has been retained.

iv) Variant spellings of proper names:
Where the spelling of an author's name varies, either within the same text, or between texts, some attempt has been made at standardisation. Standard forms for some of the more inconsistently spelled names have been adopted: Judith Boulbie, Josiah Cole, Ruth Crouch, Margaret Killam, Barbara Patison, Edward Pyot, Thomas Simmonds, Martha Simmonds, Katherine Whitton, John Willsford. (The inconsistencies are often widespread, and in some instances it is just commonsense to standardise these names silently – for example Edward Burrough/Burroughs, and Richard Farnsworth/Farnworth).
Please refer to the bibliography for further information on the conventions adopted.

Primary and Secondary Sources: Abbreviations

i) Books
BQ William C. Braithwaite, *The Beginnings of Quakerism*, 2nd edn (York: William Sessions, 1981)
EQW Hugh Barbour and Arthur O. Roberts, *Early Quaker Writings 1650-1700* (William B. Eerdmans, 1973)
HPS Mary Garman (et al.) (eds), *Hidden in Plain Sight: Quaker Women's Writing 1650-1700* (Wallingford, Pennsylvania: Pendle Hill Publications, 1996)
SPQ William Braithwaite, *The Second Period of Quakerism*, 2nd edn (York: William Sessions, 1979)

ii) Journals
JFHS The Journal of the Friends' Historical Society
PMLA The Publications of the Modern Language Association

Introduction

'Who hath writ more than a Quaker?' asked a late seventeenth-century polemicist, Francis Bugg: 'whoever exposed the professors of Christianity more than they?'[1] Who indeed? If we indulgently make a few changes to Francis Bugg's quotation, accepting the fact that he had been engaged in a protracted print controversy with a female Quaker, Anne Docwra, his quotation might be even more apt for this book: 'who hath writ more than a Quaker woman?'[2] In seventeenth-century print culture, female Quakers had few rivals.

The Quaker corpus provides a signal point of interest for feminist scholars: a substantial number of texts by women. The aim of this book is to explore patterns of continuity and change within women's authorship. It is estimated that texts by women in the Quaker corpus form a significant part of the whole. Perhaps as many as 3,853 published Quaker texts exist for the period 1650-1699; David Runyan's statistical analysis provides this benchmark.[3] Quakers (or, Friends, as they called themselves) were keen interventionists in the public sphere of print, and the survival of their texts is high since Friends methodically archived their published writing, so preserving this large body of material. The corpus contains at least 220 texts where women wrote as the sole or main author.[4] Taking this figure as a marker, women contributed 5.7 per cent of the texts in the Quaker canon. Statistics are not an absolute guide to the source material, however, and empirical estimates will be returned to later in this introduction. In the meantime, it is possible to provisionally observe that female Friends contributed in significant numbers to Quaker print culture, and to assert that they have a visible presence in the corpus.

Quaker women writers were shaped by their religious context, but they were also active in the process of creating Quaker identities in print. The contention of this book is that women's contributions to both the Quaker movement, and its published writing, were significant. Of course, this is a judgement based not only on reading the past, but also on present (feminist) concerns to re-write history to include women. It places women within the context of their religious community not just to establish that women apprehended their relationship to it, but also to

---

[1] Cited in Luella M. Wright, *The Literary Life of Early Friends 1650-1725* (New York: Columbia University Press, 1932), p. 79.

[2] See Paula McDowell, *The Women of Grub Street: Press, Politics, and Gender in the London Literary Marketplace 1678-1730* (Oxford: Clarendon Press, 1998), pp. 145-153.

[3] David Runyan, 'Appendix: Types of Quaker Writings by Year – 1650-1699', in *EQW*, pp. 567-576.

[4] Hugh Barbour, 'Quaker Prophetesses and Mothers in Israel', in *Seeking the Light: Essays in Quaker History in Honour of Edwin B. Bronner*, ed. by William J. Frost and John M. Moore (Wallingford and Haverford: Pendle Hill Publication and Friends' Historical Association, 1896), pp. 41-60 (p. 46).

show that they had an integral role to play in the construction of collective understandings of what it meant to be a Friend. Women were not marginal figures in the development of Quakerism; they had a defining influence through their presence in the literature of the period.

Quakerism in the 1650s was characterised by a number of key features that explain why women were role players in this religious body. Quakerism sprang up in the culture of radical millenarianism and antinomian dissent that accompanied the civil wars in Britain. Its spiritual and political imperatives were reformist; Quakers sought, in Edward Burrough's words, 'a New Earth, as well as a New Heaven'.[5] They tended to believe in universal salvation and they had a sense that god inhabited the believer. These Quaker attitudes were significant for women in various ways. Firstly, the theological understanding of an 'indwelling' god in each believer meant that the particular experiences of each person were important. Sharon Achinstein has commented on this fundamental feature of the canon, noting that 'the Quaker doctrine of the inner light accessible to all promoted an extraordinary production of writing, by men and women who felt called to speak'.[6] Secondly, an antinomian disregard for earthly laws led Quakers to challenge churchmen, even though the practice frequently led to their imprisonment. Women figure extensively in the literature of 'suffering' that results. Hence, one of the earliest published Quaker texts shows women imprisoned alongside men; in *False Prophets* (1652) three men and three women signed a text written from York prison.[7] Moreover, Quakers refused to pay towards the financing of the state church (the tithe). Over 7,000 women protested against the tax during the 1650s, and it can legitimately be argued that they made the tithe a woman's issue. Early Quakerism reveals the extensive involvement of women in shaping a movement that was open to them.

The first four chapters of this book deal with contemporary perceptions of Quakerism in the 1650s by analysing women's roles, their representation in works by men, and their single authored and collectively written texts. Together, these chapters indicate that, across a relatively broad spectrum of texts, there can be agreement that women had an impact on the production of Quaker identities in print.

In its fifth chapter, this book traces the path from activism to what William Braithwaite described as the 'hermit-like' approach of later Quakerism.[8] The dominant context for Quaker women in the later seventeenth century was the home; their identities were constructed through familial depictions of women as wives, mothers and daughters. I analyse deathbed testimonies, writings from the

---

[5] Barry Reay, 'The Quakers, 1659, and the Restoration of Monarchy', *History*, 63 (1978), 193-213 (p. 194).
[6] Sharon Achinstein, 'Texts in Conflict: The Press and the Civil War', in *The Cambridge Companion to Writing of the English Revolution*, ed. by Neil Keeble (Cambridge: CUP, 2001), pp. 50-68 (p. 63).
[7] Thomas Aldam (et al.), *False Prophets* (n. pl.: n. pr., 1652). The signatories were Aldam, Mary Fisher, Jane Holmes, Elizabeth Hooton, Benjamin Nicholson, and William Pears.
[8] Braithwaite, *BQ*, p. 309.

women's meetings, and later seventeenth-century prophecy. This chapter largely concentrates on works published during the 1680s, because this decade produced substantial numbers of writings by women. Deathbed testimonies are memorialising writings that commemorate a deceased Friend. Some of the subjects of this discourse were women; hence dying in the faith shows their continued presence in the movement. Wives and daughters might also write testimonies to deceased husbands and fathers; memorialising literature gives a voice to women as writers. The post-Restoration period saw a decline in the prophetic activity that had characterised early Quakerism; 'Prophecy has and must cease', observed a Quaker testimony writer, Rebecca Travers, writing in 1680.[9] In the movement's later history, this decline is evident in the turning away from the radical sense of the indwelling god (the inner light) towards other forms of expression. Joan Whitrow, the 1680s prophet considered in this chapter, writes as an ex-Quaker, for instance. Post-restoration Quakerism also established duties and responsibilities for women to carry out in the separate women's meetings, and texts detailing their approach are also explored in chapter five.

This book's rationale is to explore paradigmatic relationships between the individual and the Quaker movement, largely through analysis of multiply-authored printed texts. It is beyond the scope of this book to consider manuscript culture, since the resources are too extensive to be assessed here alongside the already plentiful printed text. Sufferings narratives, the anti-tithe petition, deathbed testimonies, and statements from the women's meetings are multiply-authored works, typically. Prophecies, considered in chapter four, are commonly single-handed works, but because they are a major source for women's writing they are also assessed in detail. A full bibliography of the writers and signatories of works mentioned supplements the information provided in the chapters, since it exposes the collaborative efforts of Quakers. *Women in the Seventeenth-Century Quaker Community* goes some way towards establishing norms of Quaker authorship in the period 1650-1690.

The two genres that dominate Quaker women's writing are the prophecy (in the 1650s) and the deathbed testimony (in the post-Restoration period). The Quaker corpus is heavy with prophetic writing, and its preponderance as a leading genre is evident (see chapter four). However, bibliographies do not present a clear and consistent picture. This is principally because prophecy is a very imprecise genre, and some bibliographers avoid extensive use of the term, in recognition it seems of the problems of definition.[10] For our present purposes, however, David Runyan's approach will be adopted, since his categories also facilitate comparison

---

[9] Rebecca Travers, in Anne Martindall (et al.), *A Relation of the Labour, Travail and Suffering of [...] Alice Curwen* (n. pl.: n. pr., 1680), sig C4^v.

[10] Rosemary Foxton, *'Hear the Word': A Critical and Bibliographical Study of Quaker Women's Writing 1650-177* (Melbourne: The Bibliographical Society of Australia and New Zealand, 1994), avoids the term, preferring instead 'admonition', 'warning', and 'exhortation'. Rosemary Moore, *The Light in their Consciences* (Philadelphia: The Pennsylvania State University Press, 2000) also omits prophecy from her calculations. See, also, Moore's on-line bibliography http://www.qhpress.org/cgi-bin/rmoore/q1650s.html.

to the deathbed testimonies produced later in the seventeenth century. Runyan grouped together 'proclamation, prophetic judgement, and other preaching to non-Quakers', when assessing the corpus. He found that the years 1650-1660 produced 334 texts of this prophetical or proclamatory kind.[11] By contrast, the same period saw only one 'memoir or testimony' reach the Quaker press. Memorialising writing (see chapter five) is a far less unstable genre than prophecy. Sometimes, these testimonies act as a preface to posthumously issued collections of the deceased's works. In the period covered by this book, the primacy of 'prophecy' over 'memoir' that is evident in the early period is later overturned, since the years 1680-1690 find 45 texts of 'proclamation, prophetic judgement, and other preaching', in comparison to 99 tracts of remembrance. Runyan's figures, of course, relate to both male and female writing, yet the broad lesson from his survey is that 'prophecy' was over seven times less popular in the 1680s than it was in the 1650s, whilst 'memoir' was 99 times more popular. Bibliographical studies of Quaker publishing confirm the dominance of the two genres, and they also indicate that each belongs to a different historical period, broadly speaking.

Bibliographies of women's writing increasingly recognise the importance of multiple-authorship as a specific feature of the Quaker corpus. Maureen Bell (et al.) observes that 'later women's writing is often hidden as prefaces, testimonies, or contributions to memorial volumes issued to honour the first generation of respected Friends, recently dead', and *A Biographical Dictionary of English Women Writers 1580-1720* provides a full listing in recognition of this fact.[12] Rosemary Foxton likewise produced a bibliography counting every contribution as a mark of authorship, from extended prose accounts to a signature appended to a text: all are valued.[13] The only difficulty of such an approach is that it makes more tenuous the statistical comparison of women's writing (estimates of which now include multiple-authorship) to men's writing (which doesn't). Men's writing is also 'hidden' within such multiply-authored texts, and, if their work were categorised more fully, their presence in the Quaker corpus would surely be greater. According to Hugh Barbour's bibliographical estimate, 620 Quaker authors wrote for print in total, of whom 82 were women.[14] However, Foxton's analysis shows that 234 women wrote or signed texts (when multiple authorship is taken into account). Evidently, Foxton's total cannot be compared with Barbour's, because they calculate authorship according to different criteria. Because this book's bibliography lists both male contributors as well as female, it begins the process of re-calculation that is necessary for a fuller understanding of men's role in multiply-authored pamphleteering.

---

[11] Runyan, 'Appendix', in *EQW*, pp. 567-577 (pp. 568-569).

[12] Maureen Bell (et al.), *A Bibliographical Dictionary of English Women Writers 1580-1720* (New York: Harvester Wheatsheaf, 1990), p. 262. Maureen Bell first suggested to me that collaborative writing would be a fit subject for analysis; Elaine Hobby also noted its importance in *Virtue of Necessity: English Women's Writing 1649-88* (London: Virago, 1988), p. 206.

[13] Foxton, 'Hear the Word', *passim.*

[14] Barbour, 'Quaker Prophetesses', p. 46.

It seems clear, however, that Quaker women produced more texts than other female contemporaries writing with a clear religious allegiance. At least 20 per cent of the women writing for publication in the seventeenth century were Friends: possibly more.[15] In part, their prominence is due to the Quaker usage of multiple-authorship, since this does not place the same demands on individual authors as singly produced works. Their texts are often relatively brief entries in larger pamphlets. In a period when it was relatively rare for women to write for publication, Quaker women had comparatively more options when it came to print. Even at the high water mark of women's pamphleteering, other women's works struggled to constitute more than one per cent of the total press output. Joad Raymond's analysis makes this clear, when noting that 'the incidence of female authorship more than doubled after 1641', whilst still only reaching 'almost [...] 1 per cent'.[16] If Quaker women did write 5.7 per cent of the overall Quaker output, then their presence was greater than other women of the time.

Multiple-authorship is an understudied phenomenon in the field of seventeenth-century non-conformist writing. Before starting to explain my approaches to multiple-authorship, I need to indicate the variety of authorial positions within Quaker writing, sketching why this diversity is interesting. Quaker writing varies enormously, and the formal issues these different agencies present to the critic, can perhaps best be indicated in a list.

1. Single-handed writing
2. Two or more single-handed texts published in the same pamphlet or book
3. Single-handed writing subsumed, or embedded, within a larger work (usually by another author or authors)
4. Dual authorship
5. Multiple authorship by named contributors
6. Multiple authorship by unnamed contributors
7. Collective petitions
8. Anonymous writing

The first category, single-handed writing, is where creativity is most autonomous. An example would be Dorothy White's prophecies, all of which take this form and, therefore, produce an authorial presence of the kind that is most familiar in the study of writers and their work.[17]

The second category is a development of the first. It is where the published text is compound: two or more writers' works are yoked together, occasionally for

[15] Patricia Crawford, 'Women's Published Writings 1600-1700', in *Women in English Society 1500-1800*, ed. by Mary Prior (London: Methuen, 1985), pp. 211-244 (p. 213, p. 269). The compilers of *A Bibliographical Dictionary of English Women Writers 1580-1720* argue that one third of the women writers whose religious affiliations are known were Quakers. See Bell (et al.), p. 250.

[16] Joad Raymond, *Pamphlets and Pamphleteering in Early Modern Britain* (Cambridge: CUP, 2003), p. 300.

[17] See the bibliography for a list of White's texts.

no obvious reason. It is sometimes difficult to account for the relations between writers, and these texts need to be distinguished from the embedded texts that I will discuss next. An example of a text where the joint publication of two texts has no particular logic, for instance, is the tract containing work by Hester Biddle alongside writing by Thomas Woodrowe.[18]

On the other hand, the third category of writing – 'embedded' texts – arranges writers in relation to each other. This is the case, for instance, in Anne Audland's 'A Warning from the Spirit of the Lord' that, since it details her imprisonment in Banbury, is clearly connected to the depiction of Quaker persecution in this region – events that are conveyed in *The Saints Testimony*.[19] This 'embedding' of writers within a connected narrative is very common in two main genres of Quaker writing: the prison narrative (see chapter two), and the deathbed testimony (see chapter five).

The dual-authored text (my fourth category) is a collaborative endeavour between two people; the prophetic writings of Margaret Killam and Barbara Patison (jointly), and Priscilla Cotton and Mary Cole (also jointly), are key examples.[20] Here, issues of authorial propriety are of little importance; what emerges is a relational sense of Quaker identity where shared norms are commonly advanced.

The fifth distinction is named multiple authorship. This is where signatures appended to the end of the text identify more than two writers. The prisoners at York who wrote *False Prophets* provide an example of this approach.[21]

The other kind of multiple-authorship (unnamed; category six) is identified through study of anonymous texts to determine, from textual detail, whether the voice is solitary or multiple. One example that fits this model, and has already been referred to in the discussion of 'embedded' texts, is *The Saints Testimony*. Here, multiplicity is evident in the opening pages, where observers from 'Bristol, Glocestershire [sic], Barkshire [sic]' describe the trial of leading Quakers, including Anne Audland.[22]

Collective petitions are a separate category because clearly there is a difference between signing your name to a text by six or seven contributors and adding your name to a petition. In the case of *These Several Papers* – the Quaker women's petition against tithes of 1659 – approximately 7,500 women sign a protest to parliament. This petition will be examined in detail (in chapter three), since it manifests a public aspect of Quaker collective identities.

Anonymous texts (the last category) are fairly self-evidently texts to which authorial agency cannot be attributed. Other aspects of Quaker collaboration might

---

[18] Thomas Woodrowe (et al.), *A Brief Relation of the State of Man Before Transgression* (n. pl.: T. W. for Thomas Simmonds, 1659).
[19] Anne Audland (et al.), *The Saints Testimony* (London: Giles Calvert, 1655).
[20] Margaret Killam [Killin] and Barbara Patison, *A Warning from the Lord to the Teachers and People of Plymouth* (London: Giles Calvert, 1655); Priscilla Cotton and Mary Cole, *To the Priests* (London: Giles Calvert, 1655).
[21] Aldam (et al.), *False Prophets*; see above.
[22] Anne Audland (et al.), *The Saints Testimony*, p. 1.

be of interest – preface writing, for instance – but only brief consideration is given to such texts here. A further aspect of Quaker writing must be indicated: that the texts do not uncommonly contain more than one of the above categories simultaneously.

Through the collaborative efforts of Quakers writing multiply-authored texts, lines of horizontal alliance were drawn. In terms of their form, collectively authored texts produce an impression of community, since they implicitly unite Friends around an issue, or series of concerns, within a single work. The effect of such writing is that it offers a way to explore women's relationship to the wider Quaker body. I am interested in both singular and collective identities – the practice of writing *as women* and *as Friends*. In a recent article on Leveller women, Ann Hughes contended that the sectarian background of each female activist should be explored because 'there is some danger of misunderstanding the precise significance of particular interventions by women if we stress only that they were women, and not also recognize that they were Levellers, or supporters of peace, or Quakers'.[23] The focus on collectivity, here, is one of the ways of assessing the significance of sectarian membership for women. Luella M. Wright observes of Friends' writing that 'group consciousness characterises the entire Quaker literary contribution'; her comments suggest that authors wrote with a sense of their identities *as Quakers.*[24] The identification of collectively maintained norms and values is a key aim of this book. It confirms Margaret Ezell's sense that '[early modern] women joined together to write for pressing political reasons'.[25] These texts as well as others show how shared accounts produce a sense of community through print.

This twin focus – on selfhood and community – demonstrates that, in part because of its collective principles, the Quaker movement created positive roles for women. But, whilst recognising the egalitarianism of early Quakerism, this study also establishes that Friends reproduced some traditional arguments attesting to the weakness and domestication of women. Through close study of multiply-authored texts, the factors that either restricted or liberated Quaker women emerge. What becomes clear, when the various different aspects of Quaker identity are considered as a whole, is that the Religious Society of Friends produced varied, and sometimes contradictory roles for women. Quaker identity was multifarious, not uniform: fluid, not static.

Women's sense of what it meant to write *as Quakers,* I will argue, was not constant; this study contends that even within the movement's first decade, contrasting and contradictory beliefs about the group's goals and identity are

---

[23] Ann Hughes, 'Gender and Politics in Leveller Literature', in *Political Culture and Cultural Politics in Early Modern England: Essays Presented to David Underdown,* ed. by Susan D. Amussen and Mark A. Kishlansky (Manchester: MUP, 1995), pp. 162-188 (p. 164).

[24] Wright, *The Literary Life of the Early Friends,* p. 10.

[25] Margaret J. M. Ezell, 'Women and Writing', in *A Companion to Early Modern Women's Writing,* ed. by Anita Pacheco (Oxford: Blackwell, 2002), pp. 77-94 (p. 87).

evident. At the ideological level, Quaker writers participated in the moulding of collective priorities, political and religious. This doctrine of the inner light, so central to Quaker figurations of the believer's inner relationship with God, serves as an example of ideological diversity (see chapter 4). Women's works evidence that even the most central aspects of Quaker belief were malleable. Hence, this book indicates that the foundation of Quaker religiousness was demonstrably unstable.

The exploration of self/society paradigms in this study indicates that there were solid connections between the writer and the religious community. Many of the prophets writing single-handed works, for instance, repeatedly use their pamphlets to foreground their sense of being part of a collective effort. When writers such as Hester Biddle, Dorothy White, and Rebecca Travers wrote about their experiences, they defined themselves as spokespeople for the Quaker cause (see chapters 2 and 4). As a result of finding expressions of collective beliefs across a wide spectrum of Quaker texts, this book argues that the shared sectarian allegiance makes these works manifest twin identities: female and Quaker, individualised and collective. It is perhaps no wonder that neither of these identities were constant.

This study traces the development from political radicalism to the relative quietism of the Restoration period, and it explains these developments with reference to gender. Examining how the movement responded to women's commitment to Quakerism shows how the movement's identity was constructed within gender paradigms. I will demonstrate that the four principal genres of Quaker writing – prophecy, sufferings narratives, petitions, and deathbed testimonies – give form to gender issues. In doing so, I aim to indicate how central to the movement's development were these attitudes to gender. Collectivity appears to have led to an embracing of women's commitment, whilst establishing boundaries at the same time. Quakerism can both be egalitarian in its approach to women, and also restrictive. Examining how boundaries were produced helps show the contradictions about gender that shaped seventeenth-century Quakerism.

To begin with, though, the first chapter shows how 1650s attitudes to organisation, funding, and discipline began to establish formal structures within Quakerism. An historical chapter and literature survey, this section is concerned to sketch Friends' religious and social backgrounds. Key events in early Quaker history are also briefly examined: one of these is the circumstances that led James Nayler and others to re-enact Christ's entry into Jerusalem in a 'sign' delivered to the people of Bristol (1656). Nayler was subsequently tried for blasphemy, and his actions brought the Quakers to national prominence. The early 'enthusiasm' of Quaker pamphlets is given context here, as well as the role of women within the movement. The Quaker Martha Simmonds, who was amongst the number accompanying Nayler, was partly blamed for these events that drew so much hostility in Friends' direction. Quaker reactions to 'turbulent' women therefore emerge when considering the Nayler case.[26]

This book will consider the numerous functions for print within the period whilst assessing community writing. It assesses the works of prisoners (chapter two), petitioners (chapter three), prophets (chapter four), and (in chapter five) testimony writers, statements from the women's meetings, and prophecy. Through close attention to individually and collectively written texts, Quaker identities become manifest.

---

[26] George Whitehead termed the women around Nayler 'turbulent', cit. in Leo Damrosch, *The Sorrows of the Quaker Jesus: James Nayler and the Puritan Crackdown on the Free Spirit* (Cambridge, Massachusetts and London: Harvard University Press, 1996), p. 117.

Chapter 1

Quakerism in the 1650s

A dual authored tract of 1655, by two female Quakers, enthusiastically defines the
religious community's sense of unity:

> For he [God] hath fulfilled this Scripture in many thousands this day whom he hath
> gathered out of Anti-Christs Opinions to worship one God in one way; if you speak
> with ten thousand of them, they all agree, having one King, one Law giver.[1]

Their understanding was overly optimistic. Quakerism in the 1650s – the main
period dealt with in this book – was in the process of creating its identity, its
organizational structures, and its internal leadership, even as it was rapidly altering
to changing circumstances. Early Quakerism (1650-1660) presents a shifting sense
of what it meant to be a Quaker, rather than the consent that is indicated above.
Although this notion that Friends could 'all agree' is aspirational, rather than
factual, the pamphlet writing of the period evidences considerable efforts to knit
the Quakers together as one body. Indeed, Quaker 'fellowship' in the faith is a
recurring theme of some women's writings discussed below. This chapter will
present a broad survey of the major developments occurring over the course of the
first decade, focussing on positioning women within the movement. This overview
attests to the movement's diversity – regionally, socially, and, also, ideologically
(in the sense that Quakers came to the movement from a broad range of religious
sects and churches). Detailed attention is also given to the movement's first major
crisis (James Nayler's 'sign' to Bristol), because this serves as an example of
Quakerism's troubled beginnings, and its history in relation to women.

The Quaker movement was in some respects typical of its era, in that the
position of women within it did not amount to anything like practical equality with
men. The clearest expression of a male/female divide is evidenced in the
movement's structure, with only one woman (Margaret Fell) taking an indisputably
leading role. In terms of the norms of the day, the positioning of women as
followers rather than leaders is expected, and it may be more surprising that
leadership was open to women in any sense. In fact, the roles adopted by many
women, even though outside the Quaker inner circle of leading activists, provide
evidence that women contributed significantly to the movement. The fact that a
substantial number of Quaker women took on roles as preachers, prophets, and
writers suggests that this religion should not be judged solely by the relative
absence of women in leadership positions. The prophets Priscilla Cotton and Mary

---

[1] Priscilla Cotton and Mary Cole, *To the Priests* (London, Giles Calvert, 1655), pp. 4-5.

Cole, whose sense of Quaker unity opened this chapter, for instance, showed the inclusive, and potentially spiritually egalitarian, orientation of their belief as they spoke of the group's apparent sense of collective purpose. Within this ordered society, it was relatively unusual to find a movement giving range to the controversial roles Quaker women could adopt, or professing so publicly values that would now be seen as egalitarian. Quakerism has long been represented as the religion in which women achieved their spiritual 'apogee'.[2] A survey of their contributory roles – as Quaker ministers, for instance – confirms their active presence within this movement. These women's very audacity shows that within Quakerism, something of the spiritual authority of women was being realised.

Quakerism was the fastest growing 'sect' of the 1650s: because it emerged so quickly, and in such tumultuous conditions, it is difficult to characterise it in a way that represents all its divergent elements. The movement's name derives from its members' practice of quaking in the presence of god, and it was foisted on them as a term of abuse (which may explain why quaking, as a response to a religious experience, died out as the movement became more 'respectable').[3] The collective body is also known as the 'Society of Friends', and, though this term did not come into use until much later, group members did refer to themselves and each other as 'Friends', even from the earliest days.[4] Arguably, because it was a movement (a term preferable to the more pejorative 'sect'),[5] one should not expect to find each person in full agreement as to what Quakerism represents, since movements are characteristically fairly fluid. Indeed, though it is true that by the end of the 1650s Quakerism had grown from a small band of charismatic prophets into an establishment of, perhaps, 60,000 group members, the movement in some ways remains characterisable only by its diversity.[6] Barry Reay, for instance, terms Quakerism 'a loose kind of fellowship with a coherent ideology and a developing code of ethics'.[7] Although this may not be a definitive pronouncement on group identity, it seems accurate. In a movement so diverse, so quickly assembled, and so publicly prominent, the sense of what it meant to be a Quaker was bound to be rather indeterminate. Disputes amongst the distended body of the Quaker people

---

[2] Keith Thomas, 'Women and the Civil War Sects', *Past and Present*, 13 (1958), 42-62 (p. 47).

[3] For early uses of the term see: Francis Higginson, *A Brief Relation of the Irreligion of the Northern Quakers* (London: T. R. and H. R.), sig, A3ᵛ , where Higginson observes their 'diabolical trances and raptures'; for the first use by someone apparently belonging to the society see Kate Peters, 'Quaker Pamphleteering and the Development of the Quaker Movement 1652-1656' (unpublished doctoral thesis, Cambridge University, 1996), p. 133, referring to a Mr Sikes, who spoke of his 'friends called Quakers'.

[4] Richard Vann, *The Social Development of English Quakerism* (Cambridge, Massachusetts: Harvard University Press, 1969), p. 125.

[5] See Patricia Crawford for discussion of terminology: *Women and Religion in England 1500-1720* (London and New York: Routledge, 1996), p. 131.

[6] Barry Reay, *The Quakers and the English Revolution* (London: Temple Smith, 1985), p. 27.

[7] Reay, *Quakers*, p. 9. Also see this chapter's discussion of Quaker origins.

were inevitable, and the resulting clamour over matters of identity fierce: such was the early history of the Quaker movement.

Although the contention of this book is that women played an important role in early Quakerism, it is nevertheless the case that most of the movement's leading lights were men. The movement consisted, of course, of the full body of believers, but this mass of people was led by several key figures, including George Fox, James Nayler, Richard Farnsworth, William Dewsbury, Richard Hubberthorne, Edward Burrough, George Bishop and George Fox the Younger.[8] The one female leader was Margaret Fell, a gentry woman from Lancashire, who attained a central role as an administrator of Quaker finances and charity, in addition to considerable public prominence through her pamphlet writing.[9] Fell was the most prolific woman writer.[10] Together, these leaders exerted considerable control over the formal definitions of the Quaker movement that this chapter will explore: organization and funding, for instance. My own sense, though, is that the focus on leaders provides only one angle; this book therefore deals more with the ordinary people than the movement's most directive figures. Initially, however, some sense of the standing of leading Quakers is necessary to an understanding of the kind of movement it was.

The major role-players are the people who can be shown to have actively promoted the Quaker cause over periods of time, and whose ideas and experiences have come to be associated with the movement. George Fox, an artisan from Leicestershire, was fundamental to the foundation of the Quaker movement, combining as he did the skills of a preacher, writer, and, in later Quakerism especially, administrator. This account, whilst acknowledging Fox's importance, intends to consider him alongside other figures, rather than regarding this 'first Friend' as the defining element in the movement. My brief overview will be necessarily selective, since the development was so rapid and happened on a comparatively large scale.

George Fox and a number of northern Quakers were central to the achievement of nation-wide Quakerism. They sought mass conversion. Initially, Quakers were known for taking their message into public places, such as markets, or for their mass rallies in natural amphitheatres such as orchards, fields or hilltops. The person most associated with these efforts of mass evangelisation is certainly Fox. He was responsible for the evangelising in Westmoreland to 1,000 people; he also preached in Malton to an audience of 200 for three or four days, where a great

---

[8] Reay, *Quakers*, p. 8. These men are characterised as leaders by Reay. A good overview is provided by Rosemary Moore, *The Light in their Consciences: Early Quakers in Britain 1646-1666* (Pennsylvania: The Pennsylvania State University Press, 2000), pp. 14-20; 31-34.

[9] See, for instance, Bonnelyn Young Kunze, *Margaret Fell and the Rise of Quakerism* (New York: Macmillan, 1994); Isabel Ross, Margaret Fell Mother of Quakerisn, 3rd edn (York: The Ebor Press, 1996).

[10] See Rosemary Foxton's bibliography, *'Hear the Word of the Lord': A Critical and Bibliographical Study of Quaker Women's Writing 1650-1700* (Melbourne: The Bibliographical Society of Australia and New Zealand, 1994).

number of people took to his message. Fox certainly put himself forward as a leader by acting as a key spokesman in the early days. Braithwaite's view is that 'under the influence of half-a-dozen powerful meetings and of the personal intercourse with Fox enjoyed by his hosts, and their friends, a great company was gathered in'.[11]

But James Nayler was also important, and the attention paid to him was nearly as constant as that given to Fox. Thus, in 1653, Francis Higginson derisively referred to 'the seduced followers of George Fox, James Nayler &c'.[12] Nayler probably came to his Quaker beliefs without the aid of Fox, perhaps during his time serving in the army under John Lambert, and Braithwaite observes that Nayler's account of his conversion shows that he owes nothing to Fox.[13] Initially, when the movement was in the north, Nayler and Fox's progress was in parallel. But when the movement spread into the south of England, from May 1654 onwards, Nayler clearly became something of a catalyst for the development of London Quakerism.[14] Nayler, similarly, can be seen to have been more prominent than Fox as a rhetorician. He published more than his colleague up to 1656.[15]

Other important figures worked to spread the Quaker message; many formed close alliances, travelling together on ministering campaigns, and becoming identified with particular areas. Vipont suggests that 'one of the older, experienced members of the group was sent to each main centre of population, taking with him a younger companion'.[16] Thus Edward Burrough and Francis Howgill were known for their work in London and Burrough, particularly, was known for his active role in petitioning parliament.[17] Both spokesmen also travelled more widely, ministering in Ireland, for instance. Burrough and Howgill were probably in Dublin with Elizabeth Fletcher by August 1655.[18] Howgill, who was converted (or, 'convinced') by Fox, had experience of preaching as an Independent and an Anabaptist before he joined the movement.[19]

John Camm and John Audland are identified principally with ministering work in the southwest. They were described as 'instrumental in the hand of the Almighty God of our gatherings', in the account of Bristol Quakerism formulated by Charles Marshall in 1689.[20] On one occasion, Audland and Camm's partnership was described in a trope not uncommonly used to allude to homosexual experience.

---

[11] Braithwaite, *BQ*, p. 84; p. 76; p. 86. See H. Larry Ingle, *First Among Friends: George Fox and the Creation of Quakerism* (New York and Oxford: OUP, 1994).

[12] Higginson, *A Brief Relation*, sig. A2ᵛ.

[13] Braithwaite, *BQ*, pp.61-62.

[14] Braithwaite, *BQ*, pp. 241-278.

[15] Peters, 'Quaker Pamphleteering', p. 27. Nayler single: 35; composite: 20; Fox single: 33; composite: 16.

[16] Elfrida Vipont, *George Fox and the Valiant Sixty* (London: Hamish Hamilton, 1975), pp. 64-65.

[17] Reay, *Quakers*, p. 8.

[18] Braithwaite, *BQ*, pp. 212-214; pp. 221-222.

[19] Braithwaite, *BQ*, p. 87.

[20] Charles Marshall, 'The Memory of the Righteous Revived', in *EQW*, pp. 78-82 (pp. 78-79).

They were said to be 'knit together as David and Jonathan, by the bond of unspeakable love'.[21] Other partnerships included Thomas Salthouse and Miles Halhead, who worked mainly in Devonshire, and Richard Hubberthorne and George Whitehead, who concentrated their attention on Norwich.[22]

William Dewsbury is a figure whose prominence in the Quaker movement lasted into the 1660s, though he spent much of this period in prison.[23] In the 1650s he had a clear role beyond that of writer and preacher, in establishing some of the organisational structures of the movement.[24]

Other figures such as Thomas Aldam and Richard Farnsworth clearly demonstrated their ability in polemic. Aldam was responsible for the publication of some of the earliest texts. And Farnsworth, in a letter to Margaret Fell, advised her to circulate texts 'to frends abroad [...] to be red in their meetings'. Farnsworth was the most prolific writer in 1653.[25] Margaret Fell's role has already been discussed.

Many other figures might be counted amongst the first people of importance. John Gilpin, for example, describes his conversion by Christopher Atkinson (who was later expelled from the movement for adultery).[26] John Killam was a significant northern figure of some wealth;[27] Anthony Pearson, a JP who was converted whilst on the bench at Appleby, acted in Durham to raise the profile of Friends;[28] James Parnell was the first Quaker martyr.[29] Other people were significant in their localities: Edward Pyot in Bristol,[30] Loveday Hambly in Cornwall,[31] Simon Dring and Ellis Hookes in London; there are many others.[32] Fell states of Westmoreland that an 'abundance of brave ministers came out there aways [sic]; as *John Camm, John Audland, Francis Howgil, Edward Burrough, Miles Halhead,* and *John Blackling,* with divers others'; in Lancashire, '*Robert Widders, Richard Hubberthorne,* and *John Lawson,* with many others,* were

---

[21] Cited in Leo Damrosch, *The Sorrows of the Quaker Jesus: James Nayler and the Crackdown on the Free Spirit* (Cambridge, Massachusetts and London: Harvard University Press, 1996), p. 124.

[22] Vipont, *George Fox*, pp. 69-70.

[23] Braithwaite, *SPQ*, pp. 221-222; pp. 449-452.

[24] See below, pp. 64-65.

[25] Kate Peters, 'Patterns of Quaker Authorship 1652-56', *Prose Studies*, 17:3 (1994), 6-24 (p. 15; p. 11; p. 14).

[26] John Gilpin, *The Quakers Shaken* (London: Simon Waterson, 1653), p. 2. For account of Atkinson's adultery, see Ingle, p. 127.

[27] Braithwaite, *BQ*, p. 331.

[28] See, for example, Anthony Pearson, *To the Parliament of the Commonwealth* (no pl.: no pub., 1653).

[29] James Parnell, *The Lambs Defence Against Lyes* (London: Giles Calvert, 1656); Braithwaite, *BQ*, pp. 188-193.

[30] Edward Pyot, (et al.), *The West Answering to the North* (London: Giles Calvert, 1657).

[31] L. V. Hodgkin, *A Quaker Saint of Cornwall: Loveday Hambly and her Guests* (London: Longmans, 1927).

[32] Braithwaite, *BQ*, pp. 488-489; p. 157; p. 376.

convinced.[33] Fell fails to remember the actions of women (she was writing in 1694).

Many of the accounts of early Quakerism characterise the people who made the first forays into the south of England.[34] But until recently there has been relative silence on the topic of women's role within Quakerism. Women certainly, however, contributed to the movement's growth, just as men did – by ministering, in public, even in the face of opposition. For instance, Elizabeth Fletcher and Elizabeth Leavens were the first people to take the Quaker message to Oxford;[35] Mary Fisher and Elizabeth Williams set the scene in Cambridge.[36] Anne Audland (whose trial for blasphemy will be discussed in chapter 2) is recorded as preaching to 300 people in the south;[37] William Crouch's description of London Quakerism shows that Isabel Buttery and another woman were the first Quakers in London (where they seem to have distributed pamphlets by Fox).[38] These proselytising women were publicly committed to Quakerism, and they are relatively prominent figures in Quaker history because of their preaching and travelling. Yet other areas of women's contribution are also apparent, less evangelical and more supportive though these roles are.[39]

One of the accounts of Quaker imprisonment, *The West Answering to the North*, for example, contains details of many Quaker evangelists in the Cornwall area.[40] The women include Margaret Killam (p. 93) and Barbara Patison (pp. 168-169), Priscilla Cotton (p. 93) and Mary Cole (p. 93), Anne Blacklyn (p. 46, p. 49, p. 117), Hester Biddle (p. 85) and Widow Hambly (p. 46). Also, some sense of women's supportive role can be discerned from this text: they visited prisoners and brought them provisions. Thus two women visiting the prisoners were called whores (pp.43-4); the jailer imprisoned a 'maid' of the town arbitrarily (p. 45); two unnamed London women provided food for the prisoners (p. 45); Susanna Kemp was accused of forcing an entry into the prison (pp. 63-67); Jane Ingram died shortly after being released from prison (p. 84). Other prisoners included Margaret Bestbridge (p. 93), Katherine Martingdale (p. 93), Ann Downer (later Whitehead) and Grace Burgis (p. 120). Many of the texts on imprisonment incidentally include such details of women's activities.

---

[33] Margaret Fell, 'The Testimony of Margaret Fox Concerning her Late Husband', in *HPS*, pp. 234-243 (p. 238).
[34] See, for example, Norman Penney, *First Publishers of Truth* (London: Headly Brothers, 1907).
[35] Richard Hubberthorne, *A True Testimony of the Zeal of Oxford-Professors* (London: Giles Calvert, 1654).
[36] Richard Hubberthorne, *The Immediate Call to the Ministry of the Gospel* (London: Giles Calvert, 1654).
[37] Ralph Farmer, *Sathan Inthron'd* [sic] (London: Edward Thomas, 1657), p. 44.
[38] William Crouch, 'Postuma Christiana' in *EQW*, pp. 83-90 (p. 84).
[39] In 1972, Clare Cross warned against focussing only on radical sectaries and called for more attention to 'sober protestant matrons'; '"He-goats before the Flocks": A Note on the Part Played by Women in the Founding of Some Civil War Churches', *Studies in Church History*, 8 (1972), 195-202 (p. 195).
[40] Pyot (et al.), *The West* (all subsequent references will be given in parenthesis).

In general, however, it is correct to say that male figures dominated this period of Quakerism. Initially a charismatic movement based around intransigent ministers who spread the cause, Quakerism's early energy was derived from its efforts to convert the many. It seems clear that though ordinary women took an active role in the development of Quakerism, their involvement did not, largely, position them as leaders.

The Conversion Process

It has been observed that Quaker writers display a 'capacity for collective selfhood', since, even as they wrote about their own conversion, 'the boundaries of individual selfhood could be blurred'.[41] Because Quaker women were so fully maintaining activist roles (as preachers, prophets, prisoners, and petitioners), their typical approach, in print, was to show that they perceived themselves to be connected to the movement. Conversion narratives, perhaps the most direct way in to women's opinions, do not speak of the marginality that might be expected, especially given the male-dominated hierarchy that has already been sketched. On the contrary, women's depictions of their 'convincement' indicate that they constructed themselves as integrated into their new faith's value system.

The initial sense in which women's writing connects itself to the wider Quaker body is through the metaphorical images they employ of Quaker 'fellowship' – to use a deceptively masculinised term. Phyllis Mack observes that 'Quakers saw the community as a practical basis of organization, a source of emotional sustenance, and a kind of spiritual template – a pattern of sanctified, egalitarian social behaviour that would serve as a model for outsiders', and their imagery certainly seems to confirm this.[42] Much writing, for instance, depicts the idea that ministers planted the seed of faith in others. The trope of the Quakers as the seed of god shows their righteous purpose. Hester Biddle, for example, imagines god 'arising up my own seed which hath been so long under *Pharaoh* the taskmaster,' in an image that shows the collective struggle against oppression.[43] For Dorothy White, too, 'God is advancing his chosen Seed' to the throne of David, bringing god to the people as 'the Glory of all Nations'.[44] Collectivity creates the notion that, through shared struggle and faith, the Quakers could bring 'glory' to the world. (More of these metaphors will be discussed in chapter four). Clearly, these are not only positive images of the society, but also of the female ministry. In *A Lamentation* (1660), Dorothy White addressed herself to the 'inhabitants of this nation', and elsewhere she evidences broader aspirations when predicting that 'Truth and

---

[41] Elspeth Graham, 'Women's Writing and the Self', in *Women and Literature in Britain 1500-1700*, ed. by Helen Wilcox (Cambridge: CUP, 1996), pp. 209-233 (pp. 214-215).

[42] Mack, *Visionary Women*, p. 157.

[43] Hester Biddle, *Woe to Thee City of Oxford* (no pl.: no pub, [1655]), broadside.

[44] Dorothy White, *An Epistle of Love* (London: Robert Wilson, 1661), p. 4; p. 1. Dorothy White, *A Lamentation Unto this Nation* (London: Robert Wilson, 1660), p. 5; p. 1.

Righteousness shall overspread the Earth'.[45] In both instances, White speaks in a way that is ministerial and prophetic, reflecting the early, activist, roles of women within this religious group.

Their connection to the movement might express something of the early-modern approach to identity, moreover, which has been termed, by Paula McDowell, 'collective and essentially unsexed'.[46] A woman writing within a religious movement has a formal connection to others that nurtures collectivist thought, rather than a sense of discrete, personal identity merely. This is evidently the case, since personal testimonies are regularly used to signal group membership. Paula McDowell confirms the importance of the sectarian network when characterising the Quaker writer, commenting, for instance, that 'even their most personal autobiographical writings may be understood as having been "collaboratively" produced, in that they followed highly formulaic patterns shared by the entire community'.[47] McDowell is building, here, on her perception of early-modern selfhood, which is thrown into relief in autobiographical writings. Rather than writing expressing something akin to individualist subjectivity, McDowell observes that social identities frequently emerge through women's narratives. Domestic, familial, religious and economic relations each bear on the writer's representation of 'self'.[48] As a consequence, McDowell asserts that 'for Quakers [...] the "ideology of absolute self" would have been absolute anathema'.[49] McDowell's assessment indirectly explains why women might explore their connection to the Quaker movement in print; they customarily positioned themselves in relation to a 'network of social dependencies' when writing.[50]

In part, literary convention explains why the collectivist approach best fits Quaker narratives: by conforming to relatively well-established patterns, the writer invokes notions that would be accepted by many as signs of piety. Conventional, rather than unique, descriptions of the processes leading to convincement reduce the controversiality of 'evidence', backing up the individual's claims of godliness. Owen Watkins observes that the religious writer would consequently judge whether experiences had been 'the same for him [sic] as they had been for other believers'.[51] Prospective group members gained nothing by departing from established norms – and critical accounts that berate the lack of sophistication in

---

[45] Dorothy White, *Unto all Gods Host in England* (no pl.: no pr, no. d. [1660]), pp. 6-7.
[46] Paula McDowell, *The Women of Grub Street: Press, Politics, and Gender in the London Literary Marketplace 1678-1730* (Oxford: Clarendon Press, 1998), p. 197.
[47] McDowell, *Women of Grub Street*, p. 181.
[48] McDowell, *Women of Grub Street*, p. 185.
[49] McDowell, *Women of Grub Street*, p. 191.
[50] McDowell, *Women of Grub Street*, p. 181.
[51] Owen Watkins, *The Puritan Experience* (London: Routledge and Kegan Paul, 1972), p. 144. See Watkins for an account of conventions within conversion narratives; also see John Stackniewski, *The Persecutory Imagination: English Puritanism and the Literature of Religious Despair* (Oxford: Clarendon Press, 1991), *passim*; Geoffrey Galt Harpham, 'Conversion and the Language of Authobiography', in *Studies in Autobiography*, ed. by James Olney (New York and Oxford: OUP, 1988), pp. 42-50.

conversion narratives miss such a point.[52] Paradoxically, the autobiography of conversion is so influenced by convention that, rather than being directly 'personal', it is arguably concerned mainly to reduce the possible differences between the writer's position and others'. After all, such narratives were used to assess 'fitness for admission' to a religious movement or sect.[53]

The highly formulaic writing of conversion narratives might, then, reveal more about convention than identity. Since self does not exist pre-textually, its construction according to generic tradition directs attention, principally, to the narrative's conformity (or otherwise) to literary models. Overwhelmingly, it is the convention that is articulated, and individuals provide only their own slant on pre-established norms. Most frequently, Quaker writers chart a familiar story of progress from alienation to salvation, through doubt and original insecurity to conviction of unity with god and the 'sect'. This, at least, is the standard Quaker pattern, and it pre-exists each individual utterance to such an extent that the same basic paradigms can be identified in all of the published Quaker autobiographies I have seen. Conventionality is, in fact, useful when attempting to identify group norms, as here.

Men's conversion narratives, although not the main subject of this analysis, represent pre-Quaker experiences from the point-of-view adopted once the writer has become a Friend. Most interesting for our purpose of exploring the strain of predictability in these texts, is their description of how they overcame past 'sins', such as the associatively manly vices of drinking, fighting, gaming and whoring.[54] Many, but by no means all, male writers show that Quakerism was the catalyst to changes in behaviour. Stephen Crisp, for example, confesses to 'gaming';[55] Edward Burrough to a delight in money (he likens himself to a 'son of the Bond woman', of Galatians 4:23);[56] and Francis Howgill, though representing himself as an earnest child, admits to liking 'sports and pastimes', which, critiqued from the Quaker perspective, are dismissed as 'vanity'.[57] Although something might be derived of the individual voice, constructed in response to precise experiences, the writer's representation of himself is part of a typology, also. Personal advancement, overthrowing unregenerate impulses, is being attested to as the writer confesses his pre-Quaker debauchery. As a developmental narrative, the conversion text virtually requires that a contrast between regenerate and unregenerate states should be established. Something of the aim to present a linear

---

[52] See Mary Anne Schofield, '"Women's Speaking Justified": The Feminine Quaker Voice, 1662-1797', *Tulsa Studies in Women's Literature*, 6:1 (1987), 61-77.

[53] Elaine Hobby, '"Come to Live a Preaching Life": Female Community in Seventeenth-Century Radical Sects', in *Female Communities 1600-1800: Literary Visions and Cultural Realities*, ed. Rebecca D'Monté and Nicole Pohl (Basingstoke: Macmillan, 2000), pp. 76-92 (pp. 80-81).

[54] These aspects of masculinity are identified by Lyndal Roper, *Oedipus and the Devil: Witchcraft, Sexuality and Religion in Early Modern Europe* (London and New York: Routledge, 1994), pp. 107-124.

[55] Stephen Crisp, 'A Journal of the Life of Steven Crisp', in *EQW*, pp. 197-208 (p. 201).

[56] Burrough, *A Warning from the Lord* (London: Giles Calvert, 1654), p. 34, p. 33.

[57] Francis Howgill, 'The Inheritance of Jacob', in *EQW*, pp. 167-179, (p. 169).

account is evident even when there is apparently less to confess to. For instance, James Nayler explains that the voice of god came to him directly for the first time whilst he was standing at the plough: 'I did exceedingly rejoice', he writes, 'I had heard the voice of God which I had professed from a Child, but had never known him'.[58] Here, Nayler registers the need to demonstrate that his understanding has advanced from childhood. Theological values speak through the conversion narrative, therefore, in Nayler's need to contrast pre- and post-Quaker understandings.

The conventions for women's convincement narratives anticipate the complexities of writing about individual experience within collectively generated paradigms. Quaker faith is not merely externally validated; it is founded on experience felt within the believer. Ironically, to speak of an 'inward' understanding of god is to find ostensibly personal language to witness to collectively-held values. 'The Kingdom of God is within', William Dewsbury remarks, in a comment indicating that central staff of Quaker belief: that each person individually witnesses god inside their being.[59] There was, actually, mutual reinforcement of the idea that god's presence was internalised (see chapter four), and this 'radical privileging of the spirit' has also been discerned in other sectarians' pamphlets: the belief in interiority was obviously quite diversely held.[60] Quaker women's published conversion narratives are centrally about the individual's relationship to god – as are men's – and though it seems paradoxical to argue that apprehension of this kind is both collective and individual, simultaneously, this apparent contradiction is nevertheless worked out in Friends' texts.

Quaker women's conversion narratives are usually brief endeavours; when they are not speaking of their god, these writers commonly anticipate states of union with others. Something of this intention is registered in their self-conscious reflections on the process of writing. 'This is my testimony friends, which I must bear amongst you' declares Hester Biddle, before describing her conversion.[61] Another Quaker first addresses '*the seed of God in you all*', before speaking of her spiritual desolation when 'convincd' of 'sin'.[62] In both cases, the life account that promptly follows is made available to the readership for their encouragement. This proffering of the individual life story for the instruction of others might confirm

---

[58] 'The Examination of James Nayler upon the Indictment of Blasphemy', in George Fox, *Sauls Errand to Damascus*, p. 30.
[59] William Dewsbury, 'True Prophecy of the Mighty Day of the Lord', in *EQW*, pp. 93-102 (p. 95).
[60] Thomas N. Corns, 'Radical Pamphleteering', in *The Cambridge Companion to Writing of the English Revolution*, ed. by N. H. Keeble (Cambridge: CUP, 2001), pp. 71-86 (p. 77). Corns focuses on Levellers, Diggers, Ranters and Quakers.
[61] Hester Biddle, *A Warning from the Lord* (London: Robert Wilson, 1660), p. 7.
[62] Sarah Blackborrow, *A Visit to the Spirit* (London: Thomas Simmonds, 1658), p. 5; in *HPS*, p. 49.

Rosemary Foxton's sense that Quaker women recognised the 'spiritual usefulness' of their texts: conversion narratives exemplify this characteristic element.[63] The utility of printed conversion narratives to the wider body of believers is also a convention expressed in other sectarian works.[64] The Baptist/Fifth Monarchist Anna Trapnel's life narrative, for instance, is deemed 'much price and use to the Lords people' by writers prefacing this account of the 'dealings of God [...] in, and after her conversion'.[65] John Turner, husband to Jane, proffers his wife's text so that the readership will be put 'in mind of that which they are so prone to forget, namely to various workings of God in their poor hearts'.[66] Furthermore, one of the several preface writers to Mary Cary's prophetical work directly spells out the 'usefulness' of her text, as he sees it, explaining the 'new and singular' contribution made by her work on the millennium.[67] The text will make clearer 'those precious promises which concern the time to come'.[68] Each instance makes evident the public 'owning' by others of a narrative, indicating how women are launched from a particular religious platform; and each is fairly representative of the way 1650s sectarians might justify the publication of texts by women.

The Quaker woman's conversion narrative both establishes the purposive function of making accounts of spiritual progress available to readers, and the communitarian element of faith. Hester Biddle's *A Warning from the Lord* is a key example here:

This is my testimony friends, which I must bear amongst you, for the true light, against all that doth oppose it, who hath been a citizen with you in this bloody City, and hath been feeding with you upon the husks with the Swine, and alienated from God, and a stranger to his life as you are at this day, whilst I was one with you in your Religion and Worship, my soul was hungry and was even black with thirst, I had almost fallen in your streets for want of the Bread of Life, no peace nor rest amongst you could I find, yet mornings and evenings, and at noonday I sought the Lord, but could not find him, because I was not in his way, neither did I hearken to the Light, neither could any of your chief Priests tell me where it was, they knew not; the light which is pure condemned me, and no peace with the Lord could I find amongst your dead worships, and earthly performances; but at length the Lord, who is rich in mercy, he looked down from his holy habitation, and he saw there was no help amongst men, nor no refreshment to be received from their Ministry, but my soul was dying and fainting away, with a numberless number besides me, by reason of our sins and transgressions, then the Lord sent in the fullness of time his servants into this city, FH [Francis

---

[63] Foxton, *'Hear the Word of the Lord'*, p. 12.

[64] See, for instance, Carola Scott-Luckens, 'Propaganda or Marks of Grace? The Impact of the Reported Ordeals of Sarah Wight in Revolutionary London, 1647-52', *Women's Writing*, 9:2 (2002), 215-232 (pp. 224-225).

[65] John Proud and Caleb Ingold, in Anna Trapnel, *A Legacy for Saints* (London: T. Brewster, 1654), sig. A2^r; subtitle.

[66] John Turner, 'Dedicatory', in Jane Turner, *Choice Experiences* (London: H. Hils [sic], 1653), sig. A2^r.

[67] Christopher Feake, in Mary Cary, *The Little Horns Doom* (London: printed for the Author, 1651), sig. B3^r; sig. B3^v.

[68] Feake, in Cary, *The Little*, sig. B3^r.

Howgill] and EB [Edward Burrough], who spoke the word of Eternall life, whereby my weary soul was refreshed, and the dead heard, and lived. [69]

Rather than straightforwardly depicting her conversion, Biddle explores wider cultural issues by addressing people in her locale (London). She equates Londoners' degenerate behaviour with her own, pre-Quaker, irreligiosity. Hence, the first example of a writer's collapsing of discrete, personal identity is found in Biddle's way of offering herself as a metaphor for London's spiritual impoverishment. She was, pre-Quaker, 'fainting away' along with a 'numberless number' of Londoners. Explicitly, Biddle is showing that personal salvation is the answer to social disintegration; if the city followed her example, it would be free from its manifold 'sins and transgressions'.

Biddle is already extracting a meaning that has public utility, but there is further evidence of her text's collectivist orientation. She inversely works that trope found in the preface to Trapnel, Turner and Cary's works when she praises the Quakers who brought about her conversion. Rather than others 'owning' the conversion writer's narrative (through a preface), 'collective' approval is indicated by Biddle's reference to those Quaker leaders towards whom she feels most connection. Francis Howgill and Edward Burrough, she explains 'spoke of Eternal Life', bringing her to Quakerism. Hence, Biddle underscores her own legitimacy as a spokesperson for Quakerism by signalling how influential its leading ministers have been. She consequently realises that even as she is speaking personally, her conversion positions her within a religious community. This story of self is also an account of Quaker practice.

The contingencies of selfhood are manifest in Sarah Blackborrow's *A Visit to the Spirit* (1658), which is an account of relational identity. As Biddle wrote of her connection to Quakers, so does Blackborrow – but even more connectedly. In *A Visit,* conversion is instantaneous – a taking inside of precepts being 'spoken of' by ministers. What is most instructive for our purpose of exploring intersections between the self and the community is the breaking down, here, of ontological categories that are supposedly distinct. The rhetoric fractures the false distinction between self and others (I /them), through its reflection on conversion:

> I never witnessed a separation between the light and the darknesse, nor never so much as heard that such a thing was to be, for when it was spoke to me by the Servants of the living God, who declared unto me the way to life, & spake of God's witnesse and its workings in the Creature, the same in me witnessed to them, and in that I knew that their testimony and declaration was of, in, and by the life and power of God. [70]

Very often, in radical thought, the 'them' of discourse is oppositional to the 'we';[71] Blackborrow's 'the same in me witnessed to them' is different, however, in the

---

[69] Biddle, *A Warning*, pp. 7-8.
[70] Blackborrow, *A Visit*, p. 6 [misn. 9]; in *HPS*, p. 49.
[71] See Thomas N. Corns, *Uncloistered Virtue: English Political Literature, 1640-1660* (Oxford: Clarendon Press, 1992), pp. 13-16, pp. 161-164. Corns explains how 'them' used pejoratively (of enemies) allows positive associations to accrue around the 'we'.

closeness of the 'I' to 'them'. This is evident both rhetorically – this passage oscillates between one and the other – and ideologically: she was already a Quaker without knowing it. This language recognises that self is to be understood in relation to community, and that community emerges within the individuals themselves: both are mutually contingent, not opposing, elements. Something of the socially produced religious identity emerges, here, through Blackborrow's internal validation of the Quaker way. Conversion narratives hence manifest the connections between 'individual life and overarching pattern', through which Quaker identity, as it was understood by individuals, emerges.[72]

The pattern changes in later Quakerism, and prefaces such as that by Samuel Jennings, writing in 1681, show that the life-writing of this period was defended in terms showing that god, not the individual, should be venerated. Jennings accepts:

> [Some] will be ready to grudge and take offence of this our Innocent and justifiable practice, to preserve the remembrance of the faithfulness of those, who have faithfully finished their course [. . .] let such know, that it was once not only allowed, but commanded of God, to write the Dead Blessed, that die in the Lord, as well as to esteem them so [. . .] that they may glorify God of their Fathers, and after their example walk in his way, in which the Lord, who gathered us into it, preserve us to the time of our death, that the worthies of the Lord, are gone before us, we may receive the Crown of Life.[73]

More autobiographical and biographical narratives will be considered in chapter five, as well as the historical context in which these, quite different, notions of selfhood occur.

Commenting on Friends' practice, Christopher Hill makes clear the collectivist focus of Quakerism: '[their] "sense of meeting" carried over into the modern world something of the desire for unanimity which meant so much to the medieval communities'.[74] Whether or not it was the format of meetings that produced it, Quaker conversion narratives actively construct a sense of community through print. Their works were distilling a more coherent image of Quakerism than seems possible, however, when the religious and social backgrounds of Friends is considered.

Religious Heterogeneity

Quakers were 'made up of the distributed people', one writer of the 1660s observed; this is absolutely the case when their religious backgrounds are

---

[72] McKeon's view of autobiography; Michael McKeon, *The Origins of the English Novel 1600-1740* (Baltimore and London: The Johns Hopkins University Press, 1987), p. 95.

[73] Samuel Jenings, in *The Works of the Long-Mournfull [sic] and Sorely-Distressed Isaac Pennington*, by George Fox (et al.) (London: Benjamin Clark, 1681), sig. A4ᵛ. Original in italics.

[74] Christopher Hill, *Society and Puritanism in Pre-Revolutionary England* (London: Panther; Manchester: The Philips Press, 1969), p. 478.

considered.[75] Drawn to the movement from other churches and more nebulous 'seeking' backgrounds, these converts had varied theological orientations. One possible effect of such heterogeneity might be that described by Nigel Smith: 'it is not at all clear that early Friends understood each other even to the degree experienced by other sects'.[76] In the first instance, Smith's contention seems to be borne out be the diversity within the movement. Although the Quakers were pooled largely from the more radical sects or churches, the 'body' that emerged was a collective of people with different religious pasts, different political persuasions. After briefly sketching the religious character of early Quakerism, its social diversity will be considered. By drawing on the work of recent historians, a sense can be gained of the heterogeneity of the Quaker movement.

Quakers approached a number of groups trying to win supporters; their relative success meant that a host of people from diverse backgrounds came under the umbrella of the Quaker movement, and this would have implications for the sort of society that was created. They found converts in the Baptist churches and the Independents: this is clear. But they also appealed to sects that are more difficult to define: the sorts of groups that flourished during the revolutionary decades, before quickly disappearing. Amongst these nebulous groupings of individuals are Mooreans (or Manifestarians), whom James Nayler and Richard Farnsworth approached, and also Levellers, Ranters and Seekers.[77] Of these rather indistinct groups, only the Levellers made efforts to define their programme in any detail to the reading public: they used print to construct their own political identities. Of the others, the Ranters especially, much of their reputation is hearsay, though writers such as Clarkson, Coppe and Salmon claim to embrace Ranterism. Some of these schismatics seem to have been drawn to the Quaker movement when their own rather loose and short-lived religious groups died out.

In early Quaker historiography, Friends are equated with seekers.[78] Broadly speaking, seeking was a state of mind where the believer passively waited on god in the hope for union. The young Mary Penington, for instance, explained how she 'wearied in seeking and not finding', and before Quaker conversion 'entertained every sort of notion that arose in that day'.[79] Rather than seekers constituting a gathered church, as was once thought, seeking was probably a state of mind. McGregor encourages prudence by defining seeking more as 'a personification of a point of religious debate than as a movement'.[80] The seeking condition, though,

---

[75] Thomas Underhill, *Hell Broke Loose* (London: Simon Miller, 1660), p. 40.

[76] Nigel Smith, *Perfection Proclaimed: Language and Literature in English Radical Religion 1640-1660* (Oxford: The Clarendon Press, 1989), p. 63.

[77] Braithwaite, *BQ*, p. 198.

[78] Braithwaite, *BQ*, p. 129; p. 198; J. F. McGregor, 'Seekers and Ranters', in *Radical Religion in the English Revolution*, ed. by Barry Reay and J. F. McGregor (repr. Oxford: OUP, 1986), pp. 121-139 (p. 123).

[79] Mary Penington, 'Some Account of Circumstances in the Life of Mary Pennington', in *HPS*, pp. 210-232 (p. 220, p. 216).

[80] J. F. McGregor, 'Seekers and Ranters', in *Radical Religion in the English Revolution*, ed. by Barry Reay and J. F. McGregor (repr. Oxford: OUP, 1986), pp. 121-139 (p. 123).

perhaps disposed religionists to look inside themselves for spiritual guidance, thereby predisposing some of them later to turn to the Quakers' god within.[81]

Baptists were a major source of converts to Quakerism, as the religious background of some Friends indicates, and as the polemical exchanges between the two groups also signify. A number of ex-Baptists joined the ranks of the Quakers, including Elizabeth Hooton, William Ames, William Bailey, Solomon Eccles and Rebecca Travers. [82] Interaction between Quakers and Baptists could be formally negotiated: there are records of instances when Baptists invited Quakers to speak.[83] Yet it was also more sporadic: Anne Blacklyn, who accused John Bunyan of using 'conjuration and witchcraft', interrupted the Bedford meeting in 1657.[84] Such heckling of ministers was common Quaker practice.

Independents encouraged a high level of lay participation in each congregation; they were voluntarists, and like the Baptists, they yielded significant converts to Quakerism. Independents, who separated the affairs of church from the state, had a bad reputation in some quarters. Thomas Edwards disliked the Independent way, terming it the 'mother' of all errors.[85] Stating that they should 'keep the communion with the church', Thomas averred that Independents should 'submit to the Discipline and orders, and speake not against what is established by common consent nor practise to the scandal and contempt of the magistrate and church'.[86] Their very varied beliefs had a 'composite character' and Independents played a central role in secular politics during the civil wars and the commonwealth period. [87] This may explain Edwards's fears, because he seemingly finds the Independents a disruptive social and political element. A number of known Independents joined the Quaker movement. They included Thomas Aldam, John Audland, John Camm, James Nayler, Thomas Stordy and John Wilkinson.[88]

These groups began to contribute to the Quaker movement, and they came from established churches with various set codes. Since the Baptists and

---

[81] Margaret Fell was possibly a seeker; Isabel Ross, *Margaret Fell: Mother of Quakerism*, 3rd edn (York: The Ebor Press, 1996), p. 7.

[82] Vann, *Social Development*, p. 25; also see Margaret Spufford, *Contrasting Communities: English Villagers in the Sixteenth and Seventeenth Centuries* (Cambridge: CUP, 1974), p. 285.

[83] Braithwaite, *BQ*, p. 45; p. 142; see Underwood, *Primitivism, passim*. Braithwaite, *BQ*, pp. 284-285; Underwood, ibid.

[84] John Bunyan, *A Vindication of the Book Called Some Gospel Truths* (Newport: Matthias Cowley, 1657), p. 33 [misn. 23].

[85] Thomas Edwards, *Gangraena* (London: Ralph Smith, 1646), p. 125.

[86] Ethyn Williams, 'Women Preachers in the English Civil War', *Journal of Modern History*, 1 (1929), 561-569 (p. 567). Katherine Chidley replied to Edwards; see Antonia Fraser, *The Weaker Vessel* (London: Weidenfeld & Nicholson, 1984), p. 247; Patricia Higgins, 'The Reactions of Women, with Special Reference to Women Petitioners', in *Politics, Religion and the English Civil War*, ed. by Brian Manning (London: Edward Arnold, 1973), pp. 179-222 (p. 218).

[87] R. Tudur Jones, *Congregationalism in England 1662-1962* (London: Independent Press, 1962), p. 25.

[88] Vann, *Social Development*, p. 24.

Independents had pre-established notions of religion, these converts brought their own priorities to the Quaker collective. Sometimes, to the consternation of other Friends, individuals tried to incorporate the strictures of the former religion into patterns of Quaker worship. Martha Simmonds, for example, was criticised for interrupting Quaker meetings when she sang psalms, read from the Bible, and also attempted to perform the sacrament of the Lord's Supper. These are practices that, Patricia Crawford observes, 'would not have been out of place in the Anglican, Presbyterian or Independent churches'.[89] Though the charges against Simmonds were more serious, as we will presently see, her demonstration shows that when Quakers brought people of differing religious backgrounds together, conflict could ensue.

Other groups courted by the Quakers were less formal, perhaps only consisting of a very fluid membership and perhaps possessing such a loosely defined code of ideas that they cannot be said to have had an ideology. The Ranters are one such entity. J. C. Davis's *Fear, Myth and History* (1986) temporarily made it inappropriate to speak of the Ranters, except as a nexus of seventeenth-century anxiety over 'disorderly' behaviour.[90] George Fox did not think of Ranters so esoterically – he refers often in his *Journal* to meetings with men he calls Ranters.[91] Neither do later respondents to Davis's contentions, who, although now more likely to write cautiously of the Ranter 'milieu', generally reject Davis's findings.[92] Although the Ranters were 'lacking the consistency of a group', there were individuals who associated themselves with this broadly held position, and there were Quaker meetings with such people.[93] Bunyan observed that Quakers, Ranters and Familists were connected in the same manner as a wolf to a dog.[94] Similarly, anti-Quaker critics maintained that 'their principles are but the principles of the old ranters', and stated that the Quaker way *'leads to Ranting'*.[95] Contemporaries saw a connection between the two enthusiastic elements.

Establishing the fellowship between Levellers and Quakers is equally tentative, despite evidence of key individuals moving between these groups. An anti-Quaker believed that Friends sought the 'levelling [of] all conditions, witnessed likewise Magistrate, People, Husband, Wife, Parents, Children, Master,

---

[89] Crawford, *Women*, p. 179.

[90] J. C. Davis, *Fear, Myth and History: The Ranters and the Historians* (Cambridge, London and New York: CUP, 1986).

[91] For sources showing Quaker and Ranter interaction, see: George Fox, *The Journal*, ed. by Nigel Smith (London and elsewhere: Penguin, 1998), p. 45; p. 151; Laurence Clarkson, 'The Lost Sheep Found', in *A Collection of Ranter Writings from the Seventeenth Century* (London: Junction Books, 1983), pp. 176-186 (p. 185); see also Nigel Smith, *Perfection Proclaimed: Language and Literature in English Radical Religion 1640-1660* (Oxford: Clarendon Press, 1989), pp. 68-69; Smith (ed.), *A Collection of Ranter Writings*, p. 17.

[92] Christopher Hill, 'The Lost Ranters? A critique of J. C. Davis', *History Workshop Journal*, 24 (1987), 134-140.

[93] Davis, *Fear, Myth*, p. 75.

[94] Bunyan, *A Vindication*, p. 56.

[95] Thomas Collier, *A Looking Glasse for the Quakers* (London: Thomas Brewster, 1657), p. 6; Francis Higginson, *A Brief Relation*, sig. A2ᵛ.

Servant, all alike, no difference in the Quaker religion'.[96] But, as is the case with the Ranters and the Quakers, the sense of 'Leveller' identity was imposed at least in part from outside and emerged only slowly. Levellers did not fully enter the public consciousness until the late 1640s, when the links between the New Model Army and the religious radicals came to the fore at Putney (1647); and the movement had pretty much died out by the mid 1650s.[97] What is certain is that one of their leading members, John Lilburne, joined the Quakers in the final years of his life.[98] But, despite this, Reay observes that there is no substantial overlap between the Levellers and the Quakers.[99]

In summary, the Quaker movement seems in all probability to have been composed of heterogeneous individuals whose different religious backgrounds created diverse Quaker identities. To some extent, Quaker is an umbrella term during this period. Further diversity is evident, moreover, in their social character.

The Social Make-Up of Early Quakerism

Who were the people responsible for the growth of Quakerism during the 1650s? Since group membership is significant, it is important to discuss the social origins of these gathered masses. Most of this section will inevitably deal with male figures since most studies concentrate on men's social origins. There is also a problem with terminology since the word 'class' cannot be easily applied. Peter Laslett argues that the term can only be used in relation to the gentry in seventeenth-century England; they formed the only group with a concerted set of values. He defines class as 'a number of people banded together in the exercise of collective power, political and economic'.[100] Since class, in Marxist terms, requires people to unite in recognition of a shared economic condition, Laslett suggests that the word 'status' is less problematic. A status group 'is the number of people enjoying or enduring the same social status'.[101]

The terms contemporaries used to describe the social strata were often specific rather than conglomerate. Gregory King's 1690 analysis, for example, was very precise when describing the gentry, but became less clear as he moved down the social scale. King principally ranks different occupations in relation to each other: unlike modern notions of class which unite people across different occupations in

---

[96] Collier, *A Looking Glasse*, p. 12.
[97] A. S. P. Woodhouse, *Puritanism and Liberty*, 2nd edn (repr. London: J. M. Dent, 1974), pp. 78-79; H. N. Brailsford, *The Levellers and the English Revolution*, 2nd edn (Nottingham: Spokesman, 1983).
[98] *Biographical Dictionary of British Radicals in the Seventeenth Century*, ed. by Richard L. Greaves and Robert Zaller, 3 vols (Brighton: The Harvester Press, 1983), II, 186-188 (p. 186).
[99] Reay, *Quakers*, p. 20.
[100] Peter Laslett, *The World We Have Lost Further Explored*, 3rd edn (Cambridge: CUP, 1983), pp. 22-23.
[101] Laslett, *World*, p. 22-23.

their relations to the means of production, King's basic structure is like a ladder of descending status. Towards the bottom of the list, King's highly stratified model breaks down as he represents as one large category 'labouring people; servants; cottagers; paupers, common soldiers and vagrants'.[102] The interests of aristocratic demographers, therefore, made the 'common people' (as Sharpe terms them) difficult to distinguish.[103]

This is similarly the case with women. A woman's identity was tied up with her husband's and she shared his social status. In 1565, Thomas Smith observed that:

> The wife is so much in the power of her husband, that not onely her goods by marriage are straight made her husbandes, and she looseth all her administration which she had of them, but also [...] our daughters so soone as they be married loose the surname of their father.[104]

Women's status is therefore connected to that of either her father or her husband. Women's legal rights might also be described in metaphorical terms. The 1632 *The Lawes Resolutions of Women's Rights* represents the woman's loss of identity on marriage by using an analogy of water. 'When a small brook or little river incorporateth with Rhodanus [Rhone], Humber or Thames, the poor rivulet looseth her name'.[105] This image of women's subjection shows that women's identity was legally that of the femme covert. Though Amy Erickson's brilliant study of women's economic positions, *Women and Property*, has done much to clarify the legal position of women, macro-economic studies of the social origin of Quaker women have not yet been attempted.[106]

That is not to say that no studies have been completed. Alice Clark's study of the *Working Life of Stuart Women in the Seventeenth Century* gives access to some information about a number of Quaker women, for instance indicating that male imprisonment might result in a greater economic role for women. John Adams was notified, whilst travelling in Holland and Germany, that 'thy wife that used to be at the helm of thy business, is dead'; Thomas Chalkey aimed to 'settle my wife in some little Business' before setting out on a ministering campaign; Samuel Bownan aimed to 'assist my Wife in her Business as well as I could'; similarly, the pedlar Joan Dant died with £9,000 assets.[107] The father of Mary Batt left the management of his affairs to his daughter, 'I being absent, a Prisoner, for my

---

[102] Keith Wrightson, *English Society 1580-1680* (London: Hutchinson, 1982), pp. 19-20.
[103] J. A. Sharpe, *Early Modern England: A Social History 1550-1760* (London and Baltimore: Edward Arnold, 1987), pp. 198-224.
[104] Sir Thomas Smith, *De Republica Anglorum* (York: The Scolar Press, 1970), pp. 102-103. (I am grateful to Dr. Gillian Spraggs for drawing this passage to my attention).
[105] Cited in Elaine Hobby, *Virtue of Necessity: Women's Writing 1649-88* (London: Virago, 1988), p. 4.
[106] Amy Erickson, *Women and Property in Early Modern England* (London and New York: Routledge, 1993).
[107] Alice Clark, *Working Life of Women in the Seventeenth Century* (London and Boston: Routledge and Kegan Paul, 1982; first published 1919), pp.153-154; pp. 198-199; p. 33.

Testimony against Tythes'.[108] Similarly, James Wall's wife tried to continue trading in his absence, but the Mayor of Evesham forbade her from standing in the market place.[109]

Phyllis Mack's work provides some further background on the regional origins of Quaker women, in the course of which she indicates that the social character of northern Quakerism differed from that in the south. According to Mack, 'almost all northern women whose backgrounds are known were either wives or servants in farming families'.[110] By contrast, 'almost every women from an artisan, trading, or publishing family was from the South'.[111] Mack used the Quaker Dictionary of Biography (at Friends' House, London), and this could provide data for future, more quantitative studies of Quaker women. At present, however, most of the known information relates to the men.

Studies of Quaker social origins confirm that the diversity of the movement applies also to matters of status; however, it is also fairly clear that this group attracted large numbers of the 'middling sort'. Small-scale artisans and rural smallholders swelled the Quaker numbers. The problem with assessing social status within so large a movement is that no comprehensive picture has been established, and regional studies predominate.[112] Most show that there were exceptions to the overall sense of the Quakers' 'middling' status that is provisionally accepted as the general norm.

Few studies support the idea that Quakers were drawn from relatively prosperous sectors of the community, but, certainly, there were some 'substantial' figures.[113] Some rural Quakers, for instance, were yeomen with considerable acreage to their names; however, a great many more were husbandmen – they were predominant, Barry Reay contends.[114] Tradespeople, likewise, might be relatively affluent, though again the small-scale traders and shop-keepers were more prominent. Barry Reay, for example, lists amongst the common occupations those

---

[108] Clark, *Working Life*, p. 45.

[109] Humphrey Smith, *Something Laid Open of the Cruel Persecution [...] Evesham* (London: no pr., 1656), p. 5.

[110] Phyllis Mack, *Visionary Women: Ecstatic Prophecy in Seventeenth-Century England* (Berkeley, Los Angeles, London: University of California Press, 1994), pp. 413-424.

[111] Mack, pp. 145-146.

[112] See Craig Horle, *The Quakers and the English Legal System 1660-1688* (Philadelphia: University of Pennsylvania Press, 1988), p. xv. Horle suggests building a more comprehensive picture of the Quaker demographic. Richard T. Vann, 'Quakerism and the Social Structure in the Interregnum', *Past and Present*, 43 (1969), 71-91 (p. 78); Alan Cole, 'The Social Origins of the Early Friends', *JFHS*, 48 (1957), 97-118; Reay, *Quakers*, pp. 21; Bill Stevenson, 'The Social and Economic Status of Post-Restoration Dissenters, 1660-1725', in *The World of Rural Dissenters 1520-1725*, ed. by Margaret Spufford (Cambridge: CUP, 1995), pp. 332-359 (p. 354).

[113] Richard T. Vann, 'Quakerism and the Social Structure in the Interregnum', *Past and Present*, 43 (1969), 71-91 (p. 78). Vann's early study over-estimates the number of well-to-do Quakers, as he himself accepts (p. 88).

[114] Reay, *Quakers*, p. 21.

of 'blacksmiths, shoemakers, tailors, butchers, weavers and carpenters'.[115] For Reay, the 'middling sort' figured prominently within the Quaker ranks.

Bill Stevenson's recent work both confirms and complicates some of the earlier findings. Stevenson argues that the Quaker membership were predominantly of the 'lower' to 'middling' sort, and he puts a figure on it: '54% of the total was made up of husbandmen, labourers and craftsmen'.[116] His study is regionally based in four southern counties, so perhaps he understandably characterises Quakerism as a rural agrarian movement; but the benefit of such localised studies is that they also make evident the social heterogeneity within areas. Stevenson has found, for instance, that gentrified Quakers in Huntingdon constituted 2.3% of the total.[117] By contrast, he also argues that the number of labourers was significant; and his research has turned up a Quaker shepherd.[118] Like Margaret Spufford, whose work he builds on and with whom he collaborated, these findings seem to indicate that there was considerable local diversity. For Spufford, an important reason for this is that non-conformity tended to run in families; the socio-economic factor might have been less significant than the genealogical.[119]

The social status of people is hard to determine, but the most probable view is that Quakers were drawn from the middling sectors of society. Though many social historians note that terminology is particularly difficult to establish when it comes to social status, the restrictions apparent when working in a period before censuses do not invalidate these findings but, rather, merely indicate their provisionality.

One thing that has been viewed as fairly indisputable is that women were an important sector of the Quaker membership. Though their social status is certainly difficult to ascertain, their presence in the movement cannot be disguised. Reay notes that they accounted for 34 per cent of the people imprisoned for interrupting ministers in the 1650s.[120] Similarly, women were well represented in the colonial missions. Forty five percent of the people who went to America were women – though the number in total was not substantial and can in fact be separated out into a number of key missions.[121]

---

[115] Reay, *Quakers*, pp. 21-22.

[116] Bill Stevenson, 'The Social and Economic Status of Post-Restoration Dissenters, 1660-1725', in *The World of Rural Dissenters 1520-1725*, ed. by Margaret Spufford (Cambridge: CUP, 1995), pp. 332-359 (p. 354).

[117] Stevenson, 'Social', p. 340.

[118] Stevenson, 'Social', p. 354; See also Spufford's comments on this in *The World of the Rural Dissenters*, p. 9.

[119] Spufford, *Contrasting*, pp. 288-289.

[120] Reay, *Quakers*, p. 26.

[121] Reay, *Quakers*, p. 26. For American missions see, for example, David S. Lovejoy, *Religious Enthusiasm in the New World: Heresy to Revolution* (Cambridge, Massachusetts and London: Harvard University Press, 1985); See also Hugh Barbour, 'Quaker Prophetesses and Mothers in Israel', in *Seeking the Light: Essays in Quaker History in Honour of Edwin B. Bronner*, ed. by William Frost and John M. Moore (Wallingford and Haverford: Pendle Hill, 1986), pp. 41-60. Barbour cites Dunn, who notes that 26 out of 59 preachers in America (1656-1663) were women (p. 57, n. 13).

The notion that women were well represented within the movement is also confirmed from a number of other sources, both Quaker and non-Quaker. Indeed, Fox's first convert was probably Elizabeth Hooton, a woman of nearly fifty who seems to have been a teacher in the Baptist movement in Skegby before she joined Fox, in about 1647.[122] Hooton also wrote for publication, so leaving a trace of her ideas; other women's historical reputations are defined merely by hostile sources.[123] One example is the Worcester Quaker, Susanna Pearson (Pierson), who tried to raise from the dead the body of fellow Quaker William Pool.[124] To the writer of an edgy anti-sectarian pamphlet, Pearson's activities represented the errors of assigning women a role in spiritual matters; he comments on the 'arrogancy of [...] Quakers in general and the shame and sorrow [...] of Mistress Pierson in particular'.[125] Quite aside from her attempts to work miracles, Pearson was also a preacher, and when reading between the lines of the hostile pamphlet, it is clear that women were evangelising in this area. The writer asserts that 'some women of note' made their 'utmost Indeavours to seduce others'.[126] This language represents the actions of women evangelists, even as it tries to denounce their ministry.

There are common ways of writing about women in religious sects that show a misogynistic slant; writers might concentrate on outspoken women because they defied the norms of the day: female silence, passivity and obedience. For twenty-first-century readers the records have the positive benefit of making women more visible. Patricia Crawford has observed that female presence in the sectarian churches could lead outsiders to doubt their seriousness.[127] More sensitive still to the apprehensions of misogynistic scoffers are Dorothy Ludlow's remarks that women preachers could have 'antagonized more people than they convinced'.[128] Something of this axiomatic concern about women's influence is evidenced in the context of the movement's first major internal crisis. Misogynistic attitudes to women were also held by Friends, as Quaker Martha Simmonds found out during the Nayler crisis.

---

[122] Mabel Richmond Brailsford, *Quaker Women 1650-1690* (London: Duckworth, 1915), pp. 16-41; Christine Trevett, *Women and Quakerism in the Seventeenth Century* (York: William Sessions, 1995), pp. 16-22.

[123] Elizabeth Hooton (et. al), *False Prophets* (n. pl.: n. pr., 1652); Hooton (et al.), *A Short Relation Concerning [...] William Simpson* (n. pl:, n. pr., 1671); Hooton (et al.), *To the King* (n. pl.: n. pr., [1670]).

[124] Anon., *A Sad Caveat to all Quakers* (London: W. Gilbertson, 1657).

[125] Anon., *A Sad Caveat*, p. 16.

[126] Anon, *A Sad Caveat*, pp. 10-11.

[127] Crawford, *Women*, p. 25.

[128] Dorothy Ludlow, 'Shaking Patriarchy's Foundations: Sectarian Women in England 1641-1700', in *Triumph Over Silence: Women in Protestant History*, ed. by Richard L. Greaves (Westport and London: Greenwood Press, 1985), pp. 93-123 (p. 103).

The Leadership Battle

The prominence of Fox and Nayler within the Quaker movement can be seen in the now infamous events that occurred in 1656. Nayler, in an enactment of Christ's entry into Jerusalem, rode into Bristol on horseback, preceded by a party singing 'Holy, holy, holy, Lord God of Sabaoth'.[129] The furore provoked by such actions subsequently led to a highly publicised trial for blasphemy, a conviction, and to a falling out between the two former leaders of the movement – Fox and Nayler. The Nayler trial has long fascinated historians who, unsurprisingly given the contentiousness of Nayler's actions, have elaborated upon the different possible meanings and effects within the Quaker movement. For instance, Knox takes the approach that leadership struggles were a central factor in the Nayler events, arguing that Nayler was not seeking to make himself equal to Christ, but equal to Fox.[130] At the same time, Nayler seems to have been acting, perhaps unconsciously, to provide the Quaker movement with a martyr.[131]

Equally important to our picture of early Quakerism is the sense that can be derived of the Quakers' attitudes to the women involved in the episode. The historically dominant approach in Quaker historiography has been to regard them as 'hysterical' or turbulent.[132] The centrality of the Quaker Martha Simmonds to the Nayler events has, in particular, provoked much discussion. A supporter of Nayler, Simmonds had close connections to the London printing market (through her husband and her brother), taking Nayler's side when the relationship between him and Fox became one of bitterness. Many male-stream critics seem to cast Martha Simmonds almost as a seventeenth-century Eve; by contrast, other scholars point out the anti-feminism of the case, and of the approaches of later critics. Martha Simmonds, particularly, has increasingly been viewed not as a subversive figure, but as a woman who tried to take on a leadership role. Patricia Crawford notes that 'Martha Simmonds was, for a brief period, one of the leaders of the Quaker movement'.[133] Kate Peters similarly notes that she published as many texts as Margaret Fell before 1656.[134]

The events must be described firstly in as direct a manner as is possible; the textual sources, though, are mainly written by those critical of Nayler, and these depictions are unreliable. The circumstances indicate that what may have been at issue was that a leadership battle began in London, where Nayler was attracting a large number of followers. Edward Burrough and Francis Howgill had set themselves up in the city in 1655, but Nayler's followers acted to challenge the

---

[129] Braithwaite, *BQ*, p. 252.
[130] Cited in Damrosch, *Sorrows*, p. 139.
[131] Both Braithwaite, *BQ*, p. 253 and Damrosch, *Sorrows*, p. 175 argue this.
[132] For negative reactions to Simmonds see: Braithwaite, *BQ*, p. 244; Damrosch, *Sorrows*, p. 121; Kenneth Carroll, 'Martha Simmonds, a Quaker Enigma', *JFHS*, 53:1 (1972), 31-52 (p. 33).
[133] Crawford, *Women*, p. 176.
[134] Kate Peters, 'Quaker Pamphleteering' (Table 1.1; p. 27).

authority of these other ministers.[135] The event that catapulted Martha Simmonds into the consciousness of these leading Quakers occurred in mid-1656: she interrupted Burrough and Howgill whilst they were speaking.[136] Quakers were quite practiced in the art of interrupting ministers, but usually, of course, it was non-Quaker churchmen who were the recipients of the verbal challenge (see chapter two). It was quite different when Martha refused to listen to other Friends, and her action was viewed as unacceptable: she was silenced. George Whitehead later observed that 'a few forward, conceited, imaginary women, especially one Martha Simmonds and some others, under the pretence of divine motions, grew somewhat turbulent'.[137]

The follow up to this event perhaps shows that women's roles were not autonomous and that they required the support of male figures. Once challenged, Martha Simmonds sought redress from Nayler: an action that was viewed as an attempt to 'draw a judgment from him against them [Burrough and Howgill]'.[138] But, initially at least, Nayler did not intervene on her behalf. When Nayler subsequently fell ill (a circumstance which has been interpreted as revealing extreme mental anxiety at the foregoing events), Martha nursed him and thereby secured his later support.[139]

Central figures in the movement tried to separate Simmonds and Nayler by sending the recreant Nayler to Fox in Launceston prison. But Simmonds's role in trying to secure a more prominent role for Nayler led her to visit Fox herself, where she delivered a clear message of her intent. Describing their confrontation, Fox relates his side of the story; Simmonds allegedly told Fox that his 'heart was rotten, and shee said, she denied that which was Head in me'.[140] By denying Fox's headship (or leadership), Simmonds might be seen to have been issuing a challenge, though alternatively the source might be corrupted in order to emphasise Martha's obstreperousness. Equally, the letter might be a warning to Nayler of the rashness of opposing Fox's leadership. Symbolically, the issue of the 'headship' of the Quaker movement was confronted when Fox and Nayler finally met. In an attempted reconciliation that was pregnant with symbolic meaning, Nayler offered Fox an apple – which he declined to take – and Fox offered Nayler his foot to kiss.[141] By refusing to genuflect, if this is what Fox required of Nayler during this exchange, he spurned reconciliation.

The anti-Quaker writing of the period focuses on the leadership battle as a principal explanation for the events that had unfolded in Bristol. 'Here thou shalt see', one writer said, 'two chief leaders and their followers, at daggers drawing one against another'.[142] 'The sect is dangerous', a parliamentarian wrote during the

---

[135] Braithwaite, *BQ*, p. 241.

[136] Crawford, *Women*, p. 174.

[137] Damrosch, *Sorrows*, p. 117.

[138] Cited in Damrosch, *Sorrows*, p. 117.

[139] Kenneth Carroll, 'Martha Simmonds', p. 43.

[140] Cited in Carroll, 'Martha Simmonds', p. 42; p. 43.

[141] Damrosch, *Sorrows*, pp. 141-142; pp. 143-144.

[142] Farmer, *Sathan*, epistle sig. A3^v-A4^r; he also repeats this idea p. 35.

crisis, stating that all the eyes of the nation were now on the Quakers.[143] Accordingly, Fox did not stand by Nayler during the trial and indeed denounced his actions as misguided.[144] Some critics suggest that Fox sought to impose his own pattern on the movement even more forcibly from this time onwards. Fox, for example, began to publish tracts in greater number.[145] He also tried to ensure that people sympathetic to him were established in principal places of responsibility; thus, Hubberthorne and Parker were chosen for London, and furthermore, the close friend of Nayler and great publicist, Richard Farnsworth, seems to have lost prominence at this time.[146] Nayler's fall, then, might be seen to consolidate Fox's supremacy.

A sharpened sense of gender can also arguably be dated to this time. Women figure very prominently in the written accounts of these events, but since most of these texts are hostile to the Quakers, they must be read with some caution. Amongst the key factors in the anti-Quaker propaganda is the misogynistic contention that women's presence in religious movements leads, necessarily, to sexual licentiousness. Thus Nayler is made to defend himself against the charge of sexual immorality by swearing 'I abhor filthiness', and to state that he remained faithful to his wife.[147] Similarly, insults against women had a sexual explicitness, as the critical reaction to Simmonds shows: she was accused as a 'Witch, a Sorcerer, and a Whore'.[148] However, though this equation of Simmonds with a sorcerer seemingly gives her power, the opposite contention, that Nayler's power was inordinate, was also made. Nayler was said to have resembled Christ, and hostile critics believed that Nayler used this sexual and religious magnetism to mislead 'simple clowns and silly women'.[149] What might seem most evident to readers are not the real significances of the Nayler case, but the unlimited profusion of interpretations.

It is important to remember that there were also men involved in this case: Martha Simmonds's husband's response is most significant, in that it evidences fear of female leadership. Having participated in the messianic addresses to Nayler (terming him the '*King of Israel*', and Son of the most high'), Thomas Simmonds

---

[143] Crawford, *Women*, p. 168; p. 166.

[144] Ingle, *First*, p. 146; p. 149.

[145] Moore, 'The Faith', p. 185.

[146] Moore, 'The Faith', pp. 193-195.

[147] Cited in Damrosch, *Sorrows*, p. 126. Other allegations against Nayler include that he fathered an illegitimate child, and that he termed Martha Simmonds his spouse (Farmer, p. 30; p. 8).

[148] Farmer, *Sathan*, p. 9; on swearing, see Deborah Cameron, *Feminism and Linguistic Theory*, 2nd edn (Basingstoke: The Macmillan Press, 1992), pp. 105-110 and Elspeth Graham, '"Lewd, Profane Swaggerers" and Charismatic Preachers: John Bunyan and George Fox', in *Sacred and Profane: Secular and Devotional Interplay in Early Modern British Literature*, ed. by Helen Wilcox, Richard Todd and Alasdair MacDonald (Amsterdam: V U University Press, 1996), pp. 307-318 (pp. 309-311).

[149] Farmer, *Sathan*, p. 27. Simmonds was also accused of having Nayler 'in bondage' (Farmer, p. 24).

contradictorily maintained Martha was 'chief leader'.[150] Simmonds responded to what he called the 'earthly dark principle' in his wife, seemingly to equate female leadership with corruption.

As Crawford observes, 'gender was central to the incident, but the female perspective has been largely distorted'.[151] Woman here becomes a signifier of contradictions: Martha Simmonds was the ringleader (according to Thomas Simmonds), a 'sorcerer' and a 'whore' (Ralph Farmer maintained); she was one of the 'conceited imaginary women' who threatened the stability of the movement, George Whitehead believed; she was a scapegoat, we might say. The Nayler case is complex for the number of questions it raises about, for instance, the problem of leadership, the significance of signs and wonders, the Quaker sense of martyrdom – but Crawford is surely right, also, that gender was 'central'. The case does not provide closure, but opens up more issues.

The Nayler events had a major effect on the perception of the Quaker movement: most anti-Quaker pamphlets of this period drew attention to the Nayler episode and, for a brief time at least, the publication of Quaker pamphlets declined.[152] The question of discipline had to be addressed more fully from this time on. Equally, as Quaker attention turned to the international stage, funding became a central issue. I will now consider some of the attempts to formalise Quaker organisational issues: the acceleration of these processes can arguably be linked to Nayler's fall.

Discipline, Funding and the Overseas Ministry

There are significant differences between historians in relation to the perceived character of early Quaker discipline and organisation. Some argue that, though there was discipline, it was fairly fluid and not absolute. Braithwaite states that 'the subordinate, and almost accidental place of these meetings in the life of the Quaker community', means that 'they did not assume any control over the ministers who exercised spiritual leadership in the Church. They did not attempt to exercise authority'.[153] Since Braithwaite's perspective favours the view that the Quakers were an evangelised body of charismatic prophets, this attitude to organisation is perhaps unsurprising. Caroline Leachman's thesis, though bearing this in mind, tends, conversely, to the idea that formality was well established by the end of the decade. She insists that 'there are strong indications that the Quaker movement was already beginning to develop a central organization at London in the late 1650s'.[154] Discipline particularly seems to have been informally imposed in

---

[150] Farmer, *Sathan*, p.13; p. 21.

[151] Crawford, *Women*, p. 172.

[152] Moore, 'The Faith', p. 177; p. 187.

[153] Braithwaite, *BQ*, p. 339.

[154] Caroline Leachman, 'From an "Unruly Sect" to a Society of "Strict Unity": the Development of Quakerism in England c. 1650-1689' (unpublished doctoral thesis, University College London, 1997), p. 73.

the period. But the discourses of discipline also connect to other areas where judgement is revealed: that of the funding and withholding of money from Friends.

Discipline

The development of disciplinary and organisational procedures certainly modifies any sense that Quakerism's central tenet gives inner authority. The notion that the inner light guides individuals seemingly indicates that external disciplinary and organisational structures are invalid. However, the events around Nayler, as we have seen, strain the notion that Quakers ultimately were empowered to behave in whatever way they saw fit. Certainly, there is evidence that attempts were made to formulate disciplinary and other practices. Ingle suggests that Fox began to be concerned with issues of discipline early, and by the end of March 1654 had 'reconciled a revolutionary principle' with 'institutional structure'.[155] Ingle's belief that the two perspectives can meaningfully be reconciled is interesting given the oppositional nature of formality and spirituality.

It might, however, be the case that the language of disciplinary epistles seeks to obscure the potential conflicts. Probably the first dated statement that established policy was from a meeting at Balby (1656). Governance was provided for people who 'walk[ed] disorderly' in addition to providing guidance for the provision of charity, the registration of marriages, and truthful trade practice, as well as other moral issues such as advice to wives and children.[156] William Dewsbury was important in the processes leading up to this formalised policy. He was also involved in a meeting in East Riding (1652), and Farnsworth, similarly, organised affairs for West Riding. A written account appeared later (1653-1654), which both Dewsbury and Fox signed. This established regular timetables for meetings for worship, and set out structures of administration; disciplinary roles were given to particular friends.[157] Other important meetings occurred at Horsham (May 1659), and Skipton (June 1658), with another general meeting at Skipton (October 1659).[158]

These texts are very precariously balanced in their rhetorical manoeuvres. The notion of discipline is obviously repressive and, clearly, it emerges out of the perceived threat of disorderliness. But the Quaker notion of inner guidance seems to complicate the process of regulation in complex ways. Thus, Fox said that people speaking 'beyond their measure' were to be chastised in 'love and wisdom that is pure and gentle from above'.[159] This seems to assert that there is a need for discipline, whilst trying to claim that the goal is to not impose on others. In his choice of language, Fox puts himself at one level of remove from the disciplining principle by arguing that judgement is 'from above'. Clearly, however, the Nayler/Simmonds debate indicates that Fox had a tendency to invoke godly

---

[155] Ingle, *First*, p. 105; see, also, p. 285.
[156] Braithwaite, *BQ*, pp. 311-313.
[157] Leachman, 'From and "Unruly Sect"', pp. 122-123.
[158] Braithwaite, *BQ*, p. 314; p. 325; p. 331.
[159] Braithwaite, *BQ*, p. 310.

authority and write in the third person when he might, in fact, have been referring to his own disciplinary practices.

Arguably, epistles on discipline attempt to sustain an impossible contradiction between the right of the sect to impose discipline, and the right of individuals to express their inner spirit. The tentative formulation of disciplinary procedures in an early letter, for instance, might indicate that the writers anticipate a counter-response. One letter signed by Dewsbury and Farnsworth sets out structures, 'that all in order may be kept in obedience':

> The elders and brethren sendeth unto the brethren in the North these necessary things following; to which, if in the light you wait, to be kept in obedience, you shall do well. [. . .] Dearly beloved friends, these things we do not lay upon you as a rule or form to walk by, but that all with the measure of light which is pure and holy may be guided, and so in the light walking and abiding these may be fulfilled in the Spirit, – not from the letter, for the letter killeth, but the Spirit giveth life.[160]

A contradiction between 'obedience' and liberty is evident where formality is referred to: 'we do not lay upon you as a rule or form', the writers observe, knowing that 'the letter killeth, but the Spirit giveth life'.[161] This might suggest that the conflict between inner judgement and emergent Quaker 'rules' that, for instance, the Nayler events revealed, was anticipated relatively early on.

Fundraising

Disciplinary structures can be connected to fundraising since the power of either giving or withholding money could enable judgements to be made against those people who required the funding. Christopher Hill's view is useful: he notes that church charity succeeded in ensuring the voluntary submission of members to group codes and norms 'through the exclusion from the sacraments and poor relief'.[162] His idea is therefore indicative of possible connections between finance and discipline. The figure of Margaret Fell links both of these administrative and formalising tendencies in early Quakerism. From her home at Swarthmore Hall, Fell dispensed money and judgements, and created a central role for herself as a supporter of Fox.[163] In such roles, as Rosemary Moore observes, Fell was involved in disciplinary procedures up to 1657.[164]

Fell also had a central role administering charity, and if a judgement of worthiness was to be made, this gave significant power to the provider. Bonnelyn Young Kunze implies that Margaret Fell set up distinctions between worthy and

---

[160] Braithwaite, *BQ*, p. 311.

[161] Cited in Braithwaite, *BQ*, pp 310-311.

[162] Christopher Hill, *Society and Puritanism in Pre-Revolutionary England* (London: Panther; Manchester: The Philips Press, 1969), p. 480.

[163] For instance, Fell took Fox's side when she criticised Nayler for refusing the guidance of 'him to whom all nations shall bow', i.e., Fox. Braithwaite, *BQ*, p. 249.

[164] See Rosemary Moore, 'The Faith', p. 192. Post-1657, '[Fell] was still a force in the movement, but less influential than previously'.

unworthy recipients of charity. This is evident in Margaret Fell's power over the Swarthmore meeting in which philanthropic activities were carefully monitored. Kunze argues that Fell believed that the poor had to be penitential and, indeed, one woman was once denied charity because of her ingratitude; when Anne Birkett was given money to pay her rent, for example, she was accused of having a 'cross and peevish spirit'.[165] Fell was, herself, a very successful businesswoman, as Kunze's study has made evident. Her ownership of several local businesses and her running of a major estate, firstly as the wife of Judge Fell then, from 1658 onwards, single-handedly, is an indication of her aptitude.[166]

Money could thus bring the power of discrimination to its providers. The power of either giving or withholding money could enable judgements to be made against people who required the funding. Their activities could be directed. In the 1650s, for instance, Fell was able to dictate to Thomas Holmes and Elizabeth (Leavens) Holmes. When Elizabeth was expecting a child, Fell was critical that the charge would fall to the Quaker movement. Thomas Holmes wrote back with the news that Elizabeth had found work 'and is not chargable [sic] [...] neither she nor hir child must perish'.[167] The couple had already received gifts from the fund (Elizabeth's clothing £1.3s; Thomas's clothing 10s 6d plus 13s) and they subsequently gave up the child.[168] This seems to set a standard that discourages dependency on the movement and encourages labour.

Initially, voluntary contributions were called for from within the membership of the northern meetings in order to raise money. In 1654, Fell sent out a letter urging all people to 'administer freely according to their abilities' to the Quaker expansion 'that there may be some money in a stock for disbursing [...] either to Friends that go forth in the service or to prisoners' necessity'.[169] Fell was seemingly aware of the importance of this task, as were others. The Quaker JP, Anthony Pearson, also worked to raise money in the south of England. In what represents a clear sense of the division of labour, one 1657 letter shows that Fell was made responsible for the northern parts and Pearson for the south.[170] Braithwaite notes that probably £270 was raised between June 1654 and September 1657.[171] Ingle cites a document that suggests that the figure was much larger (£450 by the end of 1656) and he also suggests that the financial wranglings caused some disquiet.[172]

One example must suffice of how these monies were dispensed: the missions to America could not have been mounted without the aid of the fund, which in late 1656 had had to expand to take in voluntary contributions from the entire Quaker

---

[165] Kunze, *Margaret Fell*, p. 92.
[166] Kunze, *Margaret Fell*, pp. 101-128.
[167] Brailsford, *Quaker*, pp. 152-153; p. 149.
[168] Brailsford, *Quaker*, p. 153.
[169] Braithwaite, *BQ*, p. 135. The Kendal fund dates from June 1654 (Braithwaite, *BQ*, pp. 317-318).
[170] Leachman, 'From an "Unruly Sect"', pp. 170-173.
[171] Braithwaite, *BQ*, p. 135.
[172] Ingle, *First*, p. 125; pp. 156-157.

body north and south.[173] Servants such as Mary Fisher, and Dorothy and Jane Waugh travelled widely: Mary Fisher, with her companion Anne Austin, was the first Quaker to travel to America.[174] Fisher also travelled extensively in the Mediterranean with a number of other Friends, eventually speaking to the Sultan of Turkey.[175] Dorothy Waugh also voyaged to Boston and travelled around the Salem area and Barbados.[176] Dorothy and Jane had been servants in the house of John Camm.[177] Some of these women were the recipients of Quaker charity: Ann Austin's passage back from Barbados was paid (£8.6s) and part of Mary Fisher's passage (£2.4s.6d), and some of Ann Austin's clothes were paid for (£3.1s).[178]

Women's ministering activities could be funded by the movement; and as the case of the Holmeses makes clear, the recipients of charity would sometimes be beholden to the fund holders. Financing and discipline might have been interlinked, but in some instances the movement actively supported the female preacher. The corporate structures do not reveal a consistent pattern at work.

A Quaker Community?

During the Quakers' first decade, the Quaker movement itself was a heterogeneous body; yet evidence that organizational structures were being established suggests some attempts to construct a corporate sense of Quakerism. This indicates that the nascent Quaker body was rapidly establishing itself through practical measures designed to consolidate its growing presence. The heterogeneous character of the movement is clear from its membership's varied geographical, social, and religious backgrounds. These two factors (heterogeneity and organizational structure) are contingent. The movement, particularly its leaders, had to unite this diverse body of people. My aim, in the three following chapters focussing on 1650s Quakerism, is to address the community's sense of collective experience. I will contend that this was produced in texts that actively construct collective and personal Quaker identities. In this approach to the Quaker movement, I follow those historians and literary critics who resist attempts to define religious movements as monolithic entities. The Quaker movement clearly had a remarkably turbulent first decade. But I will show that the Quaker writers sought to develop unity between co-religionists, as they actively created collective identities.

What we have got, therefore, is a charismatic movement based, initially, round peripatetic ministry who acted as prophets and claimed a sort of Apostleship: this shows great diversity. But, conversely, it was a movement that, even from its earliest days, dealt with problems in the expression of the inner leading by

---

[173] Leachman, 'From an "Unruly Sect"', pp. 71-73.
[174] Braithwaite, *BQ*, p. 402.
[175] Brailsford, *Quaker*, pp.114-132.
[176] Humphrey Norton, (et. al.), *New Englands Ensigne* (no pl.: no pub., [1659]), p. 7; p. 15 ; p. 57; p. 69.
[177] Braithwaite, *BQ*, p. 93.
[178] Brailsford, *Quaker*, p. 112.

imposing discipline. There were male authorities who had been involved with these changes, many of whom had learnt the value of good leadership and strong order. And, incidentally, this would not be the end for the Quakers: in the early 1660s, Perrot would challenge the leadership with his own sense of the Ranterish inner light.[179] It seems clear that though ordinary women took an active role in the development of Quakerism, their involvement did not, largely, position them as leaders. Where an exception to this existed, in the case of Margaret Fell, her status as a gentry woman seems significant: though this perhaps enabled her to speak on behalf of the Quaker movement, other women, as we have begun to see, also felt empowered by the Quaker message.

---

[179] Braithwaite, *SPQ*, pp. 229-250.

Chapter 2

Prisoners

A passage in Sarah Blackborrow's *Herein is Held Forth the Gift* (1659) represents one woman's perspective on the punitive treatment of Quakers during the commonwealth period. *Herein* seeks to evoke Quaker 'suffering' at the hands of the state's officers, and Blackborrow's confrontational reaction to persecution is fairly typical of Friends' responses.[1] Blackborrow addresses people who have the power to suppress Quakers:

> Be ye warned [...] how you seek by your power or Authority to hinder the Testimony by suppressing the meetings of the Lords people, his Sons and Daughters [...] the blood of souls shall cry vengeance upon that in all men which you Priests who preach for money and prepare war if you have it not, the blood of the innocent ones who have dyed in stinking holes and dungeons (thrown in there by you because they could not deny Gods witness in them, to pay you money) that blood cryeth loud *vengeance, vengeance:* And also that blood which hath been shed by cruel whippings for no other things but declaring Christ the light in all men, with the blood of souls which cryes loud in the ears of the Lord, who will render vengeance in the day when he makes inquisition for blood upon you who are found in such practices.[2]

Specifically, this text is a warning of the judgement that is to come if authority figures do not mend their ways and cease punishing Quakers. Blackborrow's text is an uncompromising response to the persecution that Quakers suffered during the 1650s. The writing of these narratives is revealing as to the collective approaches to Quaker public testimony and discourse. They are an important source of community writing and women's writing.

Some texts are like a Chinese box, with one narrative inside another, and another: this is one of the most common ways that Quakerism preserved anti-persecution messages, and these give presence, but also context, to individual suffering. Much of this chapter will be concerned with the construction of these Chinese box (multiply-authored) texts because the formal and ideological issues

---

[1] Mabel Brailsford says that a fundamental aim was to 'lay accounts before the Judges [... and] the Protector in the hope that the guilt of persecution might be brought home to its authors': *Quaker Women 1650-1690* (London: Duckworth, 1915), p. 64. See also Rosemary Moore, *The Light in their Consciences: Early Quakers in Britain 1646-1666* (Philadelphia: The Pennslyvania State University Press, 2000), pp. 180-192; John R. Knott, *Discourses of Martyrdom in English Literature 1563-1694* (Cambridge: CUP, 1993), *passim;* Braithwaite, *BQ*, pp. 434-467.

[2] Sarah Blackborrow, *Herein* (London: Thomas Simmonds, 1659), p. 8.

that they represent, particularly in relation to gender, are of specific interest when considering how Quakers constructed their public identity in print. Multiply-authored texts reinforce the idea that suffering is a mass experience. Indeed, imprisonment or public punishment (such as whipping or stocking) was the fate of many Quakers during the 1650s (probably about 2,000 people); there is clearly unity and solidarity between Friends – as Sarah Blackborrow's bombastic comments make clear.[3] However, the analysis that follows will reveal ideological inconsistencies within the writing that are suggestive of gender differences within the movement. Women's writing and suffering is usually only a small part of any sufferings pamphlet, meaning that their voices, and actions, are given context by values operating within the wider discourse. Some of these values implicitly register anxiety about women's position.

Sufferings narratives are defined by their extended focus on the persecution, trial, and imprisonment of Quakers. Their subject matter typically represents the impact of the justice system's labelling of Quaker behaviour as criminal, and such texts are notable for their concentration on punitive responses to Friends' actions. This sub-genre of Quaker writing is a relatively recognisable one; David Runyan identifies two areas of interest: 'sufferings' narratives, and 'toleration tract[s], usually combined with [an] appeal for the sufferers'. He calculates that these produce a total of 98 published texts during the 1650s.[4] As an identifiable corpus of material, and a significant percentage of Friends' total published writing for the period, sufferings narratives are key to understanding the representation of early Quakerism.[5] By the end of the first decade, for instance, George Fox's letters were urging Quakers to document instances of persecution for present and future use.[6] Eventually, this archival material became the source for Joseph Besse's two-volume collection of evidence.[7]

The 'sufferings' material is both extensive and detailed. John Knott and Craig Horle separately confirm the extraordinary range ('no fact was too insignificant to note')[8] and the 'tremendous breadth of religious criminality'[9]; consequently,

[3] Braithwaite, *BQ*, p. 451.
[4] David Runyan, 'Appendix', in Hugh Barbour, and Arthur O. Roberts (eds), *EQW*, pp. 657-659; statistics relate to the period 1650-1659. Other statistical sources: Luella M. Wright, *The Literary Life of the Early Friends 1650-1725* (New York: Columbia University Press, 1932), p. 92; Knott, *Discourses of Martyrdom*, p. 218; Craig Horle, *Quakers and the English Legal System1660-1688* (Philadelphia: University of Pennsylvania Press, 1988), p. 164; Rosemary Foxton, *'Hear the Word of the Lord': A Critical and Bibliographical Study of Quaker Women's Writing 1650-1700* (Melbourne: The Bibliographical Society of Australia and New Zealand, 1994), pp. 20-24; Foxton defines different types of sufferings writings.
[5] The focus of this chapter is 1650s sufferings narratives, which therefore excludes, for instance, Katherine Evans and Sarah Cheevers' *This is a Short Relation* (London: Robert Wilson, 1662), repr. *HPS*, pp. 171-209.
[6] William Braithwaite, *BQ*, p. 316. Fox was writing in 1657.
[7] Joseph Besse, *A Collection of the Sufferings of the People Called Quakers*, 2 vols (London: Luke Hinde, 1753).
[8] Knott, *Discourses*, p. 219.

women's sufferings are prominent in the discourses which foreground the range and extent of Quaker criminality. Piecemeal evidence emerges in the texts, although the persecution of women has never been properly quantified. A survey of their crimes would likely indicate Quaker women's commitments to righteous law-breaking, as offences are commonly linked to the public testimony of faith. Preaching in public, and in other ministers' congregations, travelling around the country, and refusing to swear oaths might be criminal behaviour according to the lawmakers, though for Quakers such actions were staple features of their worship. The ubiquity of suffering is summed up in Knott's observation that 'persecution was [. . .] central to Quaker experience in seventeenth-century England'.[10] Moreover, the result of supporting the movement through other means, seemingly non-confrontational, might be persecution. There is evidence of women being punished for taking food to prisoners, for instance, and for doing nothing more than attending meetings.[11] My sense of the material leads me to believe that the most commonly perpetrated female crime was preaching in public, which can be supported by Barry Reay's calculation that women were involved in 34 per cent of all cases in which a Quaker interrupted a minister.[12] Such an observation might also be backed up with reference to the recurrent documentation of this crime in texts representing the sufferings of Friends *en masse*.[13] This material seems to confirm that when women were taken into custody it was regularly the result of preaching to a resistant crowd.

Men's religious criminality, though not the main subject of study in this chapter, was arguably more diverse than women's. The range of these offences overlaps with those mentioned in relation to women, but further encompasses 'male' crimes that potentially undermined social cohesion within a community. For instance, they were subject, where women were not, to being imprisoned for refusing hat honour (the convention of doffing the hat to so-called social superiors); were more likely to pay the price for not swearing oaths; and, as the economic heads of their households, men figure almost exclusively amongst those convicts detained for that major benchmark of Quaker testimony, refusing to pay

---

[9] Horle, *Quakers*, p. 273.

[10] Knott, *Discourses*, p. 5.

[11] Edward Pyot (et al.), *The West Answering to the North* (London: Giles Calvert, 1657), p. 45; Francis Gawler, *A Record of Some Persecutions Inflicted [. . .] in South-Wales and Pembrookshire* (London: Thomas Simmonds, 1659), p. 15.

[12] Barry Reay, *The Quakers and the English Revolution* (London: Maurice Temple Smith, 1985), p. 26.

[13] For instance, Joseph Besse's *[. . .] Sufferings* (London: Luke Hinde, 1753), vol. I, for Oxford documents 11 persecution cases involving women (1654-1660, inclusive); of these, 9 were for preaching/speaking in public. Equally, for London (1655-1660 inclusive), 13 of the 14 cases were brought about after the woman testified in public. The final conviction, for attending a Quaker meeting, shows another source of conflict between women and the state (p. 363; see also p. 366). Besse does not name all of those arrested for attending meetings because the numbers are too large.

tithes.[14] Legally, both men and women preachers were punishable under a range of different ordinances, some designed specifically to combat Quaker activities, others surviving from the statutes of earlier periods, thereby creating a sense of opposition between Friends and the state. Oliver Cromwell's efforts to restrict Quaker action resulted in a proclamation to prevent 'Quakers, Ranters and others' from interrupting church services, which had been restricted, earlier, in a Marian statute that was re-invoked.[15] Laws to restrict vagrancy from the Elizabethan period might also curtail the Quaker minister's freedom of movement.[16]

Both men and women were liable to be punished for preaching Quaker ideals in public places, but their experiences are not fully comparable. As historians of criminality have convincingly argued, bare statistics contribute little to the understanding of crime as 'human interaction'; yet quantitative studies have often justified the exclusion of women from specific consideration.[17] Quaker women preachers might have been convicted in fewer numbers than men, but, as Hilary Hinds observes, 'silence (particularly for a Quaker, and particularly for a woman) was a mark of godliness'.[18] Deviance from a cultural norm (here female silence) must also be considered if the study of crime is to make sense of offences, and question the presumption that the numbers speak for themselves.

Women's testimony was a particular locus of concern given the culture's prohibitive attitudes to their public speaking. One contemporary response, though not directed at Quaker proselytisers, seems to offer a summation of the central arguments employed to silence the 'weaker' vessel.[19] The New Englander Anne Hutchinson, an antinomian proselytiser, was warned: 'you have stept out of your place, you have rather bine a Husband than a wife, and a preacher than a Hearer: and a Magistrate than a subject'.[20] Hence, women who addressed controversial religious topics might be reminded that women should self-censoringly accept subordination in the church hierarchy, where the elder, father, and husband were assigned roles giving them immediate authority over the meeting and the family. This expectation that a woman subdue even the promptings of her own conscience to the will of the preacher, father, or husband was spiritually problematic. The New England 'puritans' fled old England precisely for the reason that they desired religious liberty and self-rule. Yet, the impulse to defend the hierarchy remained:

---

[14] Besse's *Sufferings*, Oxford and London (1654/5-1660, inclusive) confirms the range of men's religious criminality, for instance. For women's stance on the tithe, see chapter 3.

[15] Braithwaite, *BQ*, p. 444; see also pp. 180-181; Horle, *Quakers*, p. 48.

[16] Braithwaite, *BQ*, pp. 444-445; For Quaker opposition to 'Queen Maryes Acts' see, for instance, George Bishop (et al.), *The Cry of Blood* (London: Giles Calvert, 1656), p. 125.

[17] Numerical comparisons often 'justify' focussing largely on men. Jenny Kermode and Garthine Walker (eds), *Women, Crime and the Courts in Early Modern England* (Chapel Hill and London: The University of North Carolina Press, 1994), p. 4.

[18] Hilary Hinds, *God's Englishwomen: Seventeenth-century Radical Sectarian Writing and Feminist Criticism* (Manchester and New York: Manchester University Press, 1996), p. 57.

[19] The phrase 'weaker vessel' is in 1 Peter 3:7.

[20] Schrager-Lang, Amy, *Prophetic Woman: Anne Hutchinson and the Problem of Dissent in the Literature of New England* (Berkeley, Los Angeles and London: University of California Press, 1987), p. 41.

an ordered society prohibited such power-seeking behaviour by marking out women's subordination as their 'proper' role.

Such orderly mandates are, of course, traceable to precepts in the bible (and most obviously to the Apostle Paul's attitudes to women). The various biblical passages maintaining that it is indiscreet and insubordinate for women to assume authority in the church are evidence of the oppositional stance taken by women when they preached in public. The gravitas of the apostle Paul's instruction 'let your women keepe silence in the churches', is combined with a masculinist analysis of women's domestic subordination: 'if they want to learn anything, let them ask their husbands at home' (1 Cor. 14:34-35). Similar observations are made in comparable passages about church order in Ephesians 5:22-23, which 'place man as the intermediary between Christ and woman', and the concern about women 'usurping authority' voiced in 1 Timothy 2:12.[21] Here, in these pages of the New Testament, the apostle states that when women speak in public, they bring shame and dishonour on the church and this, accordingly, usurps the natural authority of both pastor and husband. Patriarchal leadership is enshrined in seminal passages relating to church order, constructing a role for women that was silent, passive, and obedient.

The Quakers' opponents used the apostle Paul's injunctions to chastise women preachers, attempting to shame them into silence. In *The Quakers Unmasked* (1655), for instance, William Prynne quotes 1 Corinthians 14:34 (rendering it in capitals for extra emphasis) when describing how, 'to the great Scandal of Religion', women go 'beyond the modesty of their sex' when preaching.[22] Joshua Miller's *Anti Christ in Man the Quakers Idol* (1655) similarly draws on biblical precepts to add force to his argument:

> What monstrous Doctrine is this? to suffer women to be Preachers by way of authority, condemned as against nature, Isaiah 3.12, 1 Cor. 14.34, 35, 1 Tim 2.12, 14 [...] with us some women will be rulers over, and directors of mens consciences; for so amongst the Quakers women commonly teach as well as men.[23]

These biblical injunctions, then, served to cement the idea that women's preaching was immodest and unnatural, an offence against the ordered hierarchy. Prynne and Miller were not alone in quoting Paul in order to berate women, or to slander Quaker objectives.[24]

---

[21] See Catherine M. Wilcox, *Theology and Women's Ministry in Seventeenth-Century English Quakerism: Handmaids of the Lord* (New York: The Edwin Mellen Press, 1995), p. 213; pp. 206-210. Though Wilcox notes that certain passages 'restrict women's ministry, or speak of female subordination', she is less insistent about their patriarchalism than I have been (p. 193).

[22] William Prynne, *The Quakers Unmasked* (London: Edward Thomas, 1655), 2nd edn, pp. 18-19.

[23] Joshua Miller, *Anti Christ in Man the Quakers Idol* (London: J Macock for L. Lloyd, 1655), p. 27.

[24] See *The Quacking [sic] Mountebank* (London: E.B., 1655), p. 19 [E.840 (4)]; Ralph Hall, *Quakers Principles Quaking* (London: R.I., 1656), sig. A3r. For earlier anti-feminism, see *A*

Brutal opposition to women's public testimony shows that the antagonism they provoked was not merely of a verbal nature: preaching women risked assault. In numerous cases, the travelling Quaker, preaching either in state churches, or in public places, encountered aggression from the resident community. According to Barry Reay, public testimony provoked 'xenophobia, class hatred, ignorance and superstition'.[25] When violent conflict broke out against prophesying women, misogyny was a contributory factor. Rebecca Travers, for instance, was told she was 'a mad woman', when she interrupted a church service. This response to her preaching had been coupled with violence, as she explains: '[the] people fell on me as so many devouring wolfes, railing, tearing, thrusting, hailing and pushing me down several times'.[26] Travers's action of speaking in a church was a double affront to religious norms: Quakers were forbidden by law to practise this heckling behaviour, and women, St Paul instructed, should 'learn in silence with all subjection' (1 Tim. 2:11). The attack on Travers raises the possibility that when cultural and legal structures colluded in silencing women preachers, they increased the threat of violence against them.

What is often termed 'mob' violence suggests a link between female preaching and collective antagonism, but the motives of those who attacked women are often obscure. In two texts particularly focussed on conflict, the savage practices of Quaker opponents are exposed. Both *The Cry of Blood* (1656) and *A Record of Some Persecutions* (1659) repeatedly focus on bloodshed, and these predominantly male-authored texts make evident the antagonism directed specifically against women. George Bishop's (et al.) *The Cry of Blood* reveals that Elizabeth Marshall was '*violently* assaulted' – beaten with staves and cudgels – that Sarah Goldsmith was forced to take refuge from a 'violent' crowd, and that Temperance Hignell was 'struck down'.[27] Hignell died three days after being released from prison, the crowd having inflicted '*many blows, beat*[ing] her so in the *face, that her eyes were swelled*, and *blood came from her*'.[28] Francis Gawler's *A Record of Some Persecutions* refers to the striking of the preacher Elizabeth Richard with a bible, to Alice Burkat being 'haled forth and abused' (she was pricked with a pin in her arm, beaten with stones, as well as having her clothes torn from her), and to two women being 'haled, and beaten, and drawn up a pair of stairs, and there set in stocks' (the women were Mary Richard and Mary Moss).[29] In each case, outrage at the violent

---

Spirit Moving in the Women Preachers (London: Henry Shepheard, 1646) [E.324 (10)]; Thomas Edwards (et al.), *Gangraena* (London: Ralph Smith, 1646), pp. 84-89.
[25] Barry Reay, 'Popular Hostility towards Quakers in Mid Seventeenth Century England', *Social History*, 5 (1980), 387-407, p. 407.
[26] Rebecca Travers, *For those that Meet to Worship* (London: n. pr., 1659), p. 3.
[27] George Bishop (et al.), *The Cry of Blood* (London: Giles Calvert, 1656), p. 19, p. 99, p. 114. See also Gawler, *A Record of Some Persecutions*.
[28] Bishop, *The Cry*, p. 114. Hignell's account is, then, posthumous publication; for information on this kind of authorial role, see Margaret Ezell, 'The Posthumous Publication of Women's Manuscripts and the History of Authorship', in *Women's Writing and the Circulation of Ideas: Manuscript Publication in England, 1550-1800*, ed. by George L. Justice and Nathan Tinker (Cambridge: CUP, 2002), pp. 121-136.
[29]Gawler, *A Record of Some Persecutions*, p. 7, p. 8, p. 15, p. 21.

abuse is evident in the notably shocked tone of the texts; in each case, the women had either preached in church, or spoken to a minister. Yet there is little sense that the crowd who beat these women preachers had any theological reasons for attacking opinionated women; they appear, instead, merely to have the base objective of silencing them by any means.[30]

To see how patriarchalism informed the responses to prophetesses, cultural norms on speaking can be examined. That women were instructed in subordination (to the church, to their husbands) is evident in the texts that have been examined already. That their conversation could be monitored with a sense of what was or was not proper discourse for women also emerges in the literature of the period. Richard Braithwaite's *The English Gentlewoman* (1631), for instance, says that women should talk only about 'household affairs', and not 'controversies of the Church'.[31] The notion that women and men had different priorities (homely and civic, respectively) underpins this simplification of Braithwaite's. He assumes that domestic issues, rather than matters of state, are properly women's only concern. This central theme resonates in the charges against religious women who sought to make an impact on the wider community.

Three cases indicate that the authorities' responses to women were to label their actions as a specifically female form of intransigence. Preaching women were criticised for stepping out of their place in the gender hierarchy, reminded of their proper duties, then rebuked if it was seen that they were not behaving in the manner expected of an obedient wife. For instance, Sarah Tims, who was taken before a court after addressing a priest, was informed of her proper duties by the judge: '*sweeping the house and washing the dishes was the first point of law to her*'.[32] Another authority figure suggested that the most fitting punishment for a female activist was the cucking stool – the instrument of humiliation designed to silence uppity wives who had a scolding tongue.[33] The account of Margaret Killam's trial for speaking to a minister makes other patriarchal notions apparent. Killam, who was a northern Quaker, was arrested in Plymouth after challenging a minister on religious issues. Her sentencing at trial shows patriarchy in action: 'when they were not able to lay any breach of the law to their charge, they thought to have blemished her with being from her husband'.[34]

---

[30] Quaker texts might have been selective so as to convey the brutishness of their opponents, rather than the theological reasons for opposing women's speaking.

[31] Richard Braithwaite, *The English Gentlewoman* (1631), pp. 89-90, cited in Debra L. Parish, 'The Power of Female Pietism: Women as Spiritual Authorities and Religious Role Models in Seventeenth-Century England', *The Journal of Religious History*, 17:1 (1992), 33-46 (p. 33).

[32] Anne Audland (et al.), *The Saints Testimony* (London: Giles Calvert, 1655), p. 8. Tims was imprisoned for 6 months, see Besse, [. . .] *Sufferings*, vol. 1, p. 564.

[33] F[rancis] H[owgill], *Cains Bloudy Race* (London: Thomas Simmonds, 1657), reprinted in F. Sanders, 'The Quakers in Chester under the Protectorate', *Journal of the Chester and North Wales Archaeological Society*, 14 (1908), 29-84 (p. 49).

[34] Edward Pyot (et al.), *The West Answering to the North* (London: Giles Calvert, 1657), p. 164.

These narratives give an indication of precisely the extent to which women were believed to have transgressed against the natural order, and imply a link between patriarchal values and the kinds of punishment women preachers were given. Sufferings narratives are a particularly rich source of information on the persecutory treatment of women by Quaker opponents, and because these texts reveal the level of hostility, they are relevant for establishing the obstacles women faced when taking a public role in Quakerism.

The Defence of Women's Ministry

It seems significant that when the first defences of women's preaching were set down on paper, it was often as a response to persecution – the attempted silencing of the word. Against this insistence that the proper role for women was subordinate and domestic, the sufferings narratives maintain women's spiritual authority. Perhaps women felt a common oppression, as Elaine Hobby argues: 'building in part on their experiences of shared imprisonment, [women] developed an intellectual community that can sometimes be glimpsed through their published works'.[35] Hence, in a number of texts dating from the early 1650s, the task of defending women's public role is squarely faced. Two sufferings narratives give evidence of women's justification of the right to preach – *The Saints Testimony* (1655), and *A Record of Some Persecutions* (1659).[36] Moreover, Elizabeth Fletcher, who was attacked and whipped in Oxford after preaching, defended women's godly authority when ministering in Ireland.[37] Priscilla Cotton and Mary Cole's *To The Priests* (1655) is an extended response to Pauline doctrines directing women to silence, covering in more detail issues referred to by other Quaker women writers.[38] In addition, writers such as George Fox, Margaret Fell, and Richard Farnsworth, all leaders of the movement, added to the defence of women's preaching.[39]

---

[35] Elaine Hobby, '"Come to Live a Preaching Life": Female Community in Seventeenth-Century Radical Sects', in *Female Communities 1600-1800: Literary Visions and Cultural Realities*, ed. by Rebecca D'Monté and Nichole Pohl (Houndsmills, Basingstoke: MacMillan, 2000), pp. 76-92 (p. 87).

[36] Audland, *The Saints Testimony*, pp. 14-16; Gawler, *A Record of Some Persecutions*, p. 21.

[37] Richard Hubberthorne, *A True Testimony* (London: Giles Calvert, 1654), pp. 1-4; John Rutty, *A History of the Rise and Progress of the People Called Quakers in Ireland* (Dublin: L. Jackson, 1751), p. 93.

[38] Priscilla Cotton and Mary Cole, *To the Priests* (London: Giles Calvert, 1655); Sarah Blackborrow , *The Just and Equall Ballance* [sic] (London: M.W. [Mary Westwood], 1660), pp. 13-14. See Phyllis Mack, *Visionary Women: Ecstatic Prophecy in Seventeenth-Century England* (Berkeley, Los Angeles and London: University of California Press, 1994), p. 176.

[39] See Wilcox, *Theology*; Elaine Hobby, 'Handmaids of the Lord and Mothers in Israel: Early Vindications of Quaker Women's Prophecy', *Prose Studies*, 17:3 (1994), 88-98; Kate Peters, 'Quaker Pamphleteering and the Development of the Quaker Movement 1652-1656' (unpublished doctoral thesis, Cambridge University, 1996), pp. 174-211. George Fox, *The Woman Learning in Silence* (London: Thomas Simmonds, 1656); Margaret Fell, *Women's*

What is most interesting, when considering the possible link between defending women's preaching and an emerging understanding of persecution, is that arguments for liberty were a reaction to suppression. That women could and should preach in the spirit, despite meeting with resistance and persecution from the outside world; that women would be scorned and the validity of their message questioned – these probabilities only increased their determination, and hence produced writing defending women's preaching. Their insistence was greater, the more perniciously others attempted to restrict their rights.

Women's speaking was not problematic in itself, only that which was instructional, or perceived to be so. Some opponents doubted that a woman could possess the requisite skills to interpret the scripture for others, in public; and this is the position characterised by one heresiographer, Thomas Edwards.[40] Indeed, his *Gangraena* mocks a woman's scriptural exegesis before an attentive audience, with the pointed observation 'she laboured to Analyse the Chapter as well she could'; clearly, the heresiographer believed the woman's gifts to be nothing if not limited.[41] But even though preaching might provoke the greatest outrage, women spoke in churches in a range of ways beyond those discussed in standard anti-sectarian sources such as *Gangraena*. The reaction to women who neither sought to preach, nor to directly oppose the Pauline insistence on 'silence', reveals that discussion of church affairs might also be seen to be beyond their compass. For instance, the Baptist minister Lewis Stuckley told one of the women in his congregation that she could only speak 'by a Brother', meaning that she could not give voice to her opinions personally.[42] In both the heresiographer's labelling of women's preaching as 'error', and the Baptist minister's deliberate attempt to silence outspoken women, an established belief is being asserted: that women's discussion of religion should be unobtrusive. To satisfy social expectations, the pious woman should know her place. Those women whom Bunyan praised in his spiritual autobiography as 'far beyond my reach' arguably fell into the 'better' category: if a woman was happy to sit on a doorstep in the sun talking about 'the

---

Speaking Justified (1666), in *A Sincere and Constant Love: An Introduction to the Work of Margaret Fell*, ed. by Terry S. Wallace (Richmond, Indiana: Friends United Press, 1992), pp. 63-78; Francis Howgill, *One of Antichrists Volunteers Defeated* (London: Thomas Simmonds, 1660), p. 20; Richard Farnworth, *A Woman Forbidden to Speak* (London: Giles Calvert, 1654).

[40] Thomas Edwards, *Gangraena* (London: Ralph Smith, 1646), p. 30. Error 124, reporting the 'heretical' beliefs of the sectarians, shows they maintain: 'That 'tis lawfull for women to preach, and why should they not, having gifts as well as men? And some of them do actually preach, having great resort to them'. Edwards also mocks other women (pp. 84-88).

[41] Thomas Edwards, *Gangraena*, p. 85.

[42] Susanna Parr, *Susannas Apologie against the Elders* (n. pl.: n. pr., 1659), p. 78. See *Her Own Life: Autobiographical Writings by Seventeenth-Century Englishwomen*, ed. by Elspeth Graham (et al.) (London and New York: Routledge, 1992), pp. 101-116; Karen L. Edwards, 'Susannas Apologie and the Politics of Privity', *Literature and History*, 6:1 (1997), pp. 1-16; Edwards complexifies the notion of public/private I am using here. See also Patricia Crawford, *Women and Religion in England 1500-1720* (London and New York: Routledge, 1993), especially pp. 140-159.

things of God' in conversation, her piety was exemplary, and might even be a guide to men.[43] Any other pretensions to authority typically provoked a hostile response

Because society mainly attempted to restrict women's religious experiences, Quaker women encountered great resistance. Indeed, women debated the finer points of theology when asserting that both the Old Testament and the gospels established clear precedents for women involving themselves fully in the church. Many directly confronted Pauline passages, but their broader aims, as writers, included detailing women's extensive involvement in early Judaism and Christianity.[44] Their interaction with non-Quaker antagonists, and the repeated questioning of women's authority, produced the need to formulate the earliest defences of public speaking. For instance, the northern Quaker Elizabeth Fletcher was forced to answer the 'cavils' of an Irish antagonist when preaching in Youghal. To the standard objections against women's speaking, Fletcher responded by drawing on Joel 2:28 and Acts 2:17-18, where prophesying is explicitly referred to as a female activity: 'the Lord pouring forth of his Spirit upon sons and daughters according to the prophet *Joel*'.[45] Hence, the oppositional audience had succeeded in rallying Fletcher to a defence of women's prophecy. In another case, a male-authored account of the run in between Quaker Elizabeth Holmes and non-Quaker Adam Hawkins not only gives a sense of the arguments used, but also interprets the debate's outcome as unquestionably favourable to women. Holmes apparently 'cleared with him [Hawkins]. As it is plain according to the Scripture, How Priscilla was Paul's fellow-helper; and that one had four daughters which did declare the word of truth is permitted to speak in male and female'.[46] This shows Holmes negotiating in scholarly fashion using biblical exemplars – and the writer certainly interprets this event as a victory for Elizabeth. He cannot help but point to her rhetorical triumph, observing that 'Priest Hawkins could little object'. The author explains that the priest confessed 'he did believe that Elizabeth Holmes was a woman that did convert many souls to God, and it was the truth she spake', though Hawkins had begun with the Pauline insistence that women should keep silent in church.[47]

More subtle, perhaps, in these women's words, is evidence that even in their refutations, the defence of women's preaching contains trace adherence to the

---

[43] John Bunyan, *Grace Abounding to the Chief of Sinners and The Pilgrim's Progress from This World to that which is to Come*, ed. by Roger Sharrock (London: OU Press, 1966), p. 16.

[44] See Jacqueline Pearson, 'Women Reading, Reading Women' on earlier 'revisionist' accounts of the bible, in *Women and Literature in Britain, 1500-1700*, ed. by Helen Wilcox (Cambridge: CUP, 1996), pp. 80-99 (pp. 94-95).

[45] John Rutty, *A History of the Rise and Progress of the People Called Quakers in Ireland*, p. 93. When Fletcher tired of the dispute, two other Quakers (James Sicklemore and Edward Laundry) 'took up the arguments on her behalf'.

[46] Gawler, *A Record of Some Persecutions*, p. 21.

[47] Gawler, *A Record of Some Persecutions*, p. 21. See Richard C. Allen, *The Society of Friends in Wales: The Case of Monmouthshire c. 1654-1836* (unpublished doctoral thesis, University of Wales, Aberystwyth, 1999), especially pp. 228-233.

apostle Paul's commands: his language of silence and subjection is not fully purged from their accounts. According to scripture, the religious prophet could be either male or female, but according to St. Paul, a stable gender hierarchy could only be maintained if women refrained from 'teaching' (Tim 2:12). One early defence of Quaker activism by Margaret Vivers responds to these precepts:

> [And] Paul he commended Phebe (sic) in his Epistle to the Romans [. . .] and in the same Epistle he saluted Priscilla, and also gave thanks with the Churches for her labour [. . .] So was there women guided by the Spirit of the Lord, that were the Lords Prophetesses [. . .] Miriam, Arons Sister, was a Prophetess, and spake forth the praise of God [. . .] And Deborah a Prophetess by the Spirit of the Lord [. . .] and in the dayes of Josiah King in Israel, there was one Huldah a Prophetess [. . .] And in Nehemiahs time, so there was in the Apostles time a man in Cesaria had four daughters that were virgins did prophesie [. . .] And at the coming of Christ [. . .] there was one woman, a widow, of above fourscore years of age, that had no outward husband at home to ask, who was a preacher [. . .] And Tryphena, and Tryphosa, and Persis (three godly women) did labour much in the Lord.[48]

According to Vivers, the preacher's actions were justified because being a widow she 'had no outward husband at home to ask'. Of course, this argument does not fully oppose Paul's doctrines; rather, it sidesteps them by alluding to the restrictions women were facing even as it creates a sense of women's prophetic role.

Traces of the apostle Paul's arguments can also be found in the Quakers' refutation of another biblical precept, that 'the head of every man is Christ, the head of woman is man' (1 Cor. 11:3). This was another significant biblical passage, and one that had to be negotiated. It was contested by two women who were imprisoned for their beliefs. Priscilla Cotton and Mary Cole were charged after interrupting George Hughes's church service, then committed to Exeter jail.[49] Their dual-authored *To The Priests* (1655) is perhaps the most extensive early defence of women's preaching, and it has attracted much scholarly comment, being a playful, involved, refutation of biblical passages that consigned women to silence.[50] It responds to the 'priests' who silenced their message by challenging the literal reading of crucial Pauline comments. Cotton and Cole confront the idea that a woman must accept both her husband and Christ as her 'head', or else be seen to be ignoring these spiritual intermediaries, dishonouring authority. The women reverse the traditional Pauline doctrine by conceptualising femininity in

---

[48] Audland (et al.), *The Saints Testimony*, pp. 15-16.

[49] Priscilla Cotton and Mary Cole, *To the Priests* (London: Giles Calvert, 1655), p. 8; Edward Pyot (et al.), *The West Answering to the North*, p. 169.

[50] Margaret Fell's *Women's Speaking Justified* (1666) is often wrongly cited as the first full overview of this issue. See Elaine Hobby, 'Handmaids of the Lord and Mothers in Israel: Early Vindications of Quaker Women's Prophecy', *Prose Studies*, 17:3 (1994), pp. 88-98; Hilary Hinds, *God's Englishwomen*, pp. 180-208. Christine Trevett, *Women and Quakerism in the Seventeenth Century* (York: The Ebor Press, 1991, repr. 1995), p. 49.

unexpected ways; as Elaine Hobby explains, 'the women forbidden to speak in the churches are not themselves, but university-educated ministers'.[51]

Their challenge takes the form of an ironic, deliberate, re-reading of key biblical passages invoking women's subordination to godly men. Drawing on Quaker ideas of spiritual equality, they assert 'we are all one both male and female in Christ Jesus', before overturning fixed gender categories and subverting Pauline doctrines.[52] Their argument is involved, irreverent:

> The Scriptures saith, that a woman may not prophesie with her head uncovered, lest she dishonour her head: now though wouldst know the meaning of that Head, let the Scripture answer, *1 Cor.11.3*, *The head of every man is Christ*. Man in his best estate is altogether vanity, weakness, a lye. If therefore any speak in the Church, whether man or woman, and nothing appear in it but the wisdom of man [...] Christ the head is then dishonoured.[53]

Cotton and Cole are arguing that 'whether man or woman', the godly must make Christ their guide; yet, they suggest that this question of dishonouring the 'head' does not bear on biological sex. Having begun to destabilise the idea that term 'woman' relates merely to the female sex, the authors clinch their argument by asserting that weakness or dishonour to the godhead is forbidden to speak, and this characteristic is not gender-specific. 'Now the woman or weakness, that is man [...] that must be covered', they argue.[54] Hence, they equate the priests with women's weakness, and themselves with Christly headship. The elaborateness of the argument is evidence, perhaps, of just how difficult it was for women to justify their authoritative role.

These women seem to be attempting to divorce spirituality from physicality, claiming the message should be attended to rather than the person delivering it. Growing out of the experience of oppression, and responding to an unequal social order, these defences see the contest as being between the godly and the ungodly. The right to speak is thus disputable only in spiritual terms; prophecy and preaching are god-inspired activities, lifting the spirit out of the profane female body, which means, in turn, that biological sex does not prevent women from experiencing union with god. At the same time, there is a problem with accusing enemies with possessing 'feminine' weakness. Such an argument retains categories of gender difference, thereby assigning them continued significance. Masculine characteristics remain preferable to those associated with women. The woman in communion with god might have a soul 'equal' to man's at least in theory; yet she would remain, physically, a symbol of bodily infirmity by virtue of the limitations of her own argument. According to at least one critic currently working on

---

[51] Hobby, 'Handmaids of the Lord', p. 93.
[52] Cotton and Cole, *To the Priests*, p. 6.
[53] Cotton and Cole, *To the Priests*, p. 7. Reprinted in Hinds, *God's Englishwomen*, pp. 222-226.
[54] Cotton and Cole, *To the Priests*, p. 7. An earlier example of this same rhetorical position can be found in the anti-Quaker text by Francis Higginson, *A Brief Relation of the Northern Quakers* (London: T.R. and H.R., [1653]), pp. 3-4.

seventeenth-century spirituality, the discourses maintaining women's bodily inferiority remained largely 'unchallenged and unquestioned', despite the emphasis of religious women on their exemplary piety.[55] Their bodies remained sites of infirmity, even if their souls were apparently free.

There is evidence that women experienced hostility from within their own religious community, and not only from anti-sectarians. Margaret Fell, for instance, received a letter from William Caton in which he observed that 'although to some they are all one, both male and female [...] thou knows as well as I, it is not soe with everyone'.[56] The letter reveals divisions amongst the early Quakers, and may be evidence of the persistent belief that women were unequal in the body, even despite the notional idea that women possessed equal souls. The notion that women were the 'weaker' vessel can be seen in Quaker denials that male and female preachers 'are all one'. This cultural distinction between spiritual equality and feminine corporeality is therefore useful to bear in mind.

Who speaks?

Women's voices were contained by another structure no less important than the cultural and legal methods of silencing them: narrative form. Although the great majority of Quaker texts do no more than suggest the judgement that is implicit – that the speaking woman is a source of cultural anxiety – women's voices are, nevertheless, contained by the narrative structure that seems, at first glance, to give them voice. The question 'who speaks' is an important one to attend to from a narratorial point of view, just as speaking was a major issue for seventeenth-century women. In Quaker texts on suffering, a common formal approach finds the woman's experience being described secondhand, after the event, by an author (or authors) whose task is to profile the sufferings of Quakers within a particular locality.[57] Formal issues are hence fundamentally important in sufferings narratives, and narratologist Gérard Genette's formalisation of how different voices

---

[55] Hinds, *God's Englishwomen*, p. 50. For Aristotelian versions of women's weakness, see Nancy Tuana, *The Less Noble Sex* (Bloomington: Indiana University Press, 1993).

[56] Cited in Rosemary Moore, 'The Faith of the First Quakers' (unpublished doctoral thesis, University of Birmingham, 1993), p. 206. Caton is paraphrasing Gal. 3:27 in his notion that Quakers are 'all one' in Christ. Kate Peters makes the further claim that even the publication of arguments justifying women's preaching was circumscribed, since men controlled the debate: 'Quaker Pamphleteering and the Development of the Quaker Movement 1652-1656' (unpublished doctoral thesis, Cambridge University, 1996), pp. 210-211. Of the 300 or so Quaker texts published 1652-1656, only four look at the issue of women's speaking in any depth (Peters, p. 182).

[57] The two texts explored here are of this variety, Anne Audland (et al.), *The Saints Testimony* (London: Giles Calvert, 1655) dealing with Banbury, George Bishop (et al.), *The Cry of Blood* (1656) dealing with Bristol. This is one of the commonest forms of sufferings narratives.

relate to one another within a text is an especially pertinent place to start.[58] We know that in texts 'a point of view is chosen, whether "real" historical facts are concerned or fictitious events', hence the author's (or authors') method for conveying a woman's experiences will affect the way she 'speaks' in a text.[59]

In both Quaker writing and narrative theory, multi-vocality is a particular point of interest. Although many of the narratological models have been developed with the novel in mind, being designed to describe the interplay between the narrator and fictional characters, these theories offer a starting-point for analysis of historical documents. Genette's argument is that descending levels of influence structure a text, and some of the narrative levels he identifies relate to non-fictional texts fairly straightforwardly.[60] The text (or *syuzhet*) of a sufferings pamphlet will commonly have at least two narrative levels, and the basic way of describing the narration of these two levels is a) extradiegetic b) intradiegetic; Genette terms the former the first level, whilst the latter is the second level of discourse.[61] The first (extradiegetic) is the voice closest to the reader, so this would usually equate to the author of a sufferings narrative; the second (intradiegetic) is any figure who becomes a subordinate 'narrator' because their speech, writing, or non-verbal activity is reported by the extradiegetic 'narrator' (here, the Quaker narrator).[62] Because the subordinate 'narrator' cannot directly address the reader, whilst the extradiegetic narrator can, the first voice is by definition at a higher level in the text. Hence, Genette's theory determines hierarchical relations within the different narrative levels of a text.

It is, though, possible to contend, as theorists interested in heteroglossia sometimes do, that multi-vocality is more egalitarian than this. Again, theoretical models are principally literary, though not exclusively so.[63] Best known is Mikhail

---

[58] Gérard Genette, *Narrative Discourse, and Narrative Discourse Revisited* (Oxford: Blackwell, 1980), pp. 212-262. My thanks to Bill Overton for his comments on the use of narrative theory.

[59] Mieke Bal, *Narratology: Introduction to the Theory of Narrative*, trans. by Christine Van Bohemmen (Toronto and London: University of Toronto Press, 1985), p. 111.

[60] For instance, it is useful to determine whether the narrator/author of a Quaker text takes part in the action that is being described, as an active participant, or whether (s)he is absent from events. Genette uses the term *homodiegetic* for the former, *heterodiegetic* for the latter (pp. 244-245). Homodiegetic/heterodiegetic status relates to the *story* rather than the *text*. The story (*fabula*) is a chronological list of the events (the skeletal features, if you like, that can be discerned by reading with attention to time/place of events), whereas the text (*syuzhet*) is what we read (usually discontinuous, a reconfiguring of events).

[61] 'Extradiegetic' refers to an external narrator; 'intradiegetic' to an internal narrator (Genette, *Narrative*, p. 228).

[62] Genette, *Narrative*, p. 230; embedded oral stories, letters, or even visual artefacts (Genette gives the example of a tapestry) may contribute to the effect of the overall text, and supply intradiegetic narration.

[63] See Marion Gibson, *Reading Witchcraft: Stories of Early English Witches* (London and New York: Routledge, 1999). One of the questions Gibson addresses is how 'close' the account is to the event (the witchcraft trial, for instance), p. 5. She also asks who determines the witch's story – the witch or other people (p. 71).

Bakhtin's description of language that is 'double-voiced and double-accented [...]' double-languaged', and his contention that this is a democratic (and also, possibly, demotic) form of writing.[64] Whether polyvocal multiplicity properly defines non-literary texts any more accurately than Genettian 'hierarchies', narrative theory's interest in 'voice' provides an established vocabulary and approach for defining formally complex texts. However, narrative theory's focus is not sufficient on its own to explain textual intricacies. Without attention to cultural issues, the meaning of decisions about form remain opaque; equally, without accepting that readers may read *against* the text, subverting the formal codes, an overly deterministic approach to form may result.

A case in point is the collectively written *The Saints Testimony* (1655), which explores and defends women's speaking, as we have seen. This sufferings narrative charts Quaker oppression in Banbury, dealing with the trial of a northern Friend, Anne Audland, in particular detail. As Christine Trevett writes of the life of the indomitable Audland, 'here had been a woman who was once threatened with death by burning and who had been imprisoned for her troublesomeness in frog-infested sewer rooms'.[65] The possibly unruly aspect of women's public, ministerial, role was clearly an issue for the Oxfordshire authorities, since Audland was tried first for blasphemy before being convicted of the less serious charge of misdemeanours. In narrative terms, the section in *The Saints Testimony* dealing with Audland's trial is a report of a speech act; at key stages, the narrators indicate that they are summarising, or condensing, the argument between those present (defendant, judge and jury). This text, then, tests the contention that the extradiegetic narrators are at a higher level in the narrative than the speakers, that a woman's voice might be mediated, and the writing of women's sufferings might be fitted into a male agenda.

We know that Audland's trial for blasphemy shows she was a vocal, combative, and socially unconventional figure, and that her culture variously attempted to restrict the actions of such women – but what does the text emphasise? The narrative focus of the trial scene is the interaction between defendant, jury, and judge, and though there is no direct speech quoted (in the passage we will examine), the authors of *The Saints Testimony* act as recorders of events.[66] They show Anne Audland under examination:

There in the court an indictment was read against her, charging her with blasphemy, & on they did proceed to tryal, called a Jury and brought in their witnesses, which differed one from another, and was in confusion, though they pretended to bear witness to one and the same thing, but falsely was the [sic] accused, & therefore did declare against, and deny in the presence of the living God, those things charged upon her: so he that sat as Judge in the court spoke to the Jury, that all which was proved could not be found, or would not prove blasphemy, & words to them to that purpose; so they

---

[64] Mikhail Bakhtin, *The Bakhtin Reader*, ed. by Pam Morris (London and New York: Edward Arnold, 1994), p. 117.
[65] Christine Trevett, *Women and Quakerism in the Seventeenth Century* (repr. York: William Sessions, 1995), p. 71.
[66] Direct speech is usually signified by italicising the words of an oral 'narrator'.

went aside to consider of it. & being together, whereby by Law ought to have bin kept alone, til [sic] they were agreed upon their verdict, and being together could not find the bil, for some of the jury said why should we find this bil, seeing we have not the evidence to prove it? Or words to that purpose, & so threw it by[;] one of them that sate on the Bench that same day, & is called *Magistrate* came into the Jury, when they were together, to corrupt and instigate the[m], as some of the Jury hath confessed, which was contrary to the known Law of the Nation in such cases provided, & contrary to truth and equity, which [is a] greater crime and breech of the Law, than those things which many of the servants of Jesus are imprisoned for.[67]

Multi-vocality is a feature of this passage, and it may be that the most appropriate model for this kind of discourse is one taken from Bakhtin's heteroglossia. The jury's voices are arguably the most distinct ('why should we find this bill [...]?'), though the passage also gives a flavour of the Judge's words ('that all which was proved could not be found [...]'). However, when it comes to Audland's own defence, the narrators report the speech act, and little sense is given of her actual defence: '[she] therefore did declare against, and deny in the presence of the living God, those things charged upon her'.[68] It is not possible, from this, to get a feel for her language, her actual defence, or its tenor. In this respect, Genettian awareness of the controlling influence of the extradiegetic narrator seems significant: the author(s) simply do not here allow Audland to speak.

This mediated account is more surprising when compared to other trial scenes in the Quaker corpus, showing alternative possibilities available to some male speakers; critics note, for instance, that the seminal issue in the court scene can be to record the witty response of the defendant to the judge. Neil Keeble examines showcase trials to indicate that the drama of the courtroom pits the verbal skills of the judge against those of the defendant.[69] Trials might be represented through a 'set of features [. . . which hold much] in common with theatrical drama', as was the case with William Dewsbury's encounter with the Northampton authorities.[70] In Genette's terms, the effect of Dewsbury's speech would be closer to mimesis than diegesis:

> *J.A.* But in that you are found wandering in the countrey you break the Law [...].
> *W.D.* If there be any such Law, read it to us, and if there be such a Law in thy Conscience, thou knows it is contrary to the Scripture, for the Apostles and Ministers of Christ went to and fro in the Countrey, preaching the Word of Eternall Life, and there were added to the Church dayly such as should be saved,

---

[67] Audland (et al.), pp. 2-3.
[68] See Shlomith Rimmon-Kenan, *Narrative Fiction: Contemporary Poetics* (London and New York: Routledge, 1996), pp. 108-110. Rimmon-Kenan offers an overview of the terminology used to describe speech. Audland's is indirect content paraphrase (or indirect discourse), where 'A paraphrase of the content of a speech event, ignoring the style or form of the "original" utterance [is given]' (p. 109).
[69] N. H. Keeble, *The Literary Culture of Non-Conformity in Later Seventeenth-Century England* (Leicester: Leicester University Press, 1987), pp. 52-55. See also Braithwaite, *SPQ*, pp. 70-74.
[70] Bauman, p. 104.

and the number of the Saints and Brethren was dayly increased, and the Law that is in force in this Nation, doth allow all that profess Faith in Jesus Christ, to have free liberty to walk in the Faith, which is according to the Scripture.
J.A. Thou hast an eloquent tongue and thou art proud of it.[71]

Anne Audland's relative passivity in *The Saints Testimony* is therefore important, and when her treatment is compared to men's, the mediating voices might be seen to limit women's public activity.

First-person accounts are bound to differ from secondhand accounts in tone and ideology, of course, and the most pertinent comparison is to Audland's self-penned 'A Warning from the Spirit of the Lord', which appears in another section of the same pamphlet concerning the Banbury trials. Both her 'voice' and her opinions are important. Her tone in 'A Warning' might best be described as bombastic, since she seems to wish to turn the world 'upside down'. Addressing the authorities, for instance, she invokes god's judgement against them: 'better had it been for you that a Millstone had been hanged about your necks, and you drowned in the depth of the sea, than to have offended the Little ones of Christ' (Matthew 18:6; Mark 9:42; Luke 17:2).[72] These are harsh, hierarchy-challenging, words indeed. Her language, furthermore, condemns the authorities in the threatening comment 'the Lord will sit as Judge against the Judges'.[73] This phrase invokes a common Quaker trope noted by John Knott, involving looking forward to 'the final judgement at which God would remedy all earthly justice'.[74] This presentation of authority-challenging ideas makes the ideological position of the text as a whole all the more contradictory. Opening, possibly male-authored sections of *The Saints Testimony* clear Audland from the charges of blasphemy she faced. Yet this section's silencing of her voice means that the writers fail to give presence to vocal women.[75] However, when Audland speaks directly, rather than through external writers, her godly questioning of the social order is assertively radical. The fact that *The Saints Testimony* configures her voice twice – once directly, once indirectly – of course indicates that women 'speak' in different ways in these sufferings narratives, and that a feature of collectively authored writing will be its inconsistency.

If it is always implicit that the vexed question of women's speaking is being considered, a case-by-case approach to Quaker writing is to be recommended since collectively authored narratives are not universally opposed to outspoken female sufferers. Some texts seem to privilege the speaker's words, meaning that even when women are being described, rather than writing in their own voice, their speech may have impact. A case in point is *The Cry of Blood* (1656); this text not only details a number of serious assaults on women, listing their sufferings

---

[71] William Dewsbury, *A True Testimony of [...] Northampton* (London: Giles Calvert, 1655), pp. 4-5. J. A. was judge Edward Atkins.

[72] Audland (et al.), *The Saints Testimony*, p. 12.

[73] Audland (et al.), *The Saints Testimony*, p. 33.

[74] Knott, *Discourses*, p. 223.

[75] For the collective authorship of *The Saints Testimony*, see below.

alongside the men's, but it also contains embedded texts from two women. As in *The Saints Testimony*, the women both speak for themselves and are spoken about or for, appearing as authors as well as subjects. An unknown narrator (or narrators) describes a common situation in Bristol: a Quaker being taken before the mayor and called to account. The text portrays Elizabeth Marshall, the Quaker, responding indignantly to charges of illegality:

> The Mayor demanded of her, why she went to disturbe the Minister and the Peace? *She answered, she was no disturber of the Peace.* He replyed, she was in that she had caused tumults in the streets (*whereas the tumults were made on her*) she only replyed, *wo be to me if I obey not the Word of the Lord.*[76]

Even if this is somehow a stronger voice than Audland's (it is in direct speech), the authentic female testimony is only heard in women's own compositions.[77] Marshall, for instance, explains her reason for writing: '*For Jerusalem's sake, I must not be silent*'.[78] Because speaking in public was the most likely female crime, assessing the presence (or otherwise) given to the woman's own voice in a text (whether direct or indirect) is essential in order to build up a picture of Quaker gender assumptions.

Although Quaker narratives on suffering written by men represent women being persecuted by unforgiving authorities, implicitly if not always explicitly supporting women's public role in Quakerism, their speech patterns have to be assessed carefully before it is assumed that women are being given voice. Most appropriate, I believe, is an assessment of the presence given to the speaker: although absence is absolute, presence occurs by degrees – as we have seen. No matter how carefully the male-authored text appears to directly quote the woman's words, I would not claim that even the 'fullest' of narratives are authentic, simply because the male writer has the power of definition and characterisation.[79] To this extent, the quoting of Marshall is no more 'authentic' than the quoting of Audland, although she is markedly more present in direct speech where the report of a speech act (*The Saints Testimony*) fails to give the woman's communication a register, a voice.

Contextual information on the Quaker approach to indirect speech further complicates the issue, however, since Friends seem to have been acutely aware of the problems of misquoting. Ironically, the clearest evidence about the Quaker attitude to indirect speech emerges in texts where this is a contentious issue. If only when objecting to their misrepresentation by non-Quaker antagonists, Friends were sensitive to the problem. For instance, Anne Audland herself became a victim of

---

[76] Bishop (et al.), *The Cry of Blood*, p. 20.

[77] Direct speech 'creates the illusion of pure mimesis, although it is always stylised in one way or another', Rimmon-Kenan, *Narrative Fiction*, p. 110.

[78] Bishop (et al.), *The Cry of Blood*, p. 50.

[79] By contrast, Ellen Macek describes women's voices as authentic in her discussion of 'embedded' women's narratives; 'The Emergence of a Feminine Spirituality in *The Book of Martyrs*', *Sixteenth Century Journal*, 19:1 (1988), 63-80.

misrepresentation in a non-Quaker text by Ralph Farmer, where she was depicted preaching on salvation (to 200-300 people), telling the gathered people that those who believed Christ died for their salvation were 'deceived'.[80] George Bishop, by contrast, insisteded she did not speak these words.[81] 'Controversy' literature, in other words, might have taught Quakers to be attentive to how they reported speech, and their aim might even have been to produce an impression of mimesis. The framing of the woman's story through the author's assumptions about her public role, is, hence, crucial context for understanding women's suffering and speaking in Quaker narratives.

Though it is generally the case that Friends' accounts are 'the same basic story of constancy under persecution', analysis of textual detail reveals that narrators take account of the sufferer's gender.[82] A narratorial position becomes clear when writers maintain the inhumanity of those persecuting Friends: the crowds who attack an itinerant preacher, the mayor who abuses his power, the court and penal system's weighty punishments – each is subject to comment. Underlying a good many narrative depictions is a sympathising tendency to regard women's stories as particularly shocking: it seems their perceived weakness qualifies them for extra consideration. John Knott has noted, for instance, that the Quaker martyrologist Joseph Besse details 'numerous abuses of the poor and vulnerable', so alerting readers to the apparent frailty of such subjects.[83] Indeed, Besse's clipped observation that authorities in London imprisoned Friends 'regarding neither Age nor sex', reveals the writer's predisposition when it comes to the suffering of women, the elderly, or the very young.[84] Such protective thinking also occurs in Besse's source texts, and is not, therefore, a sentimentalist, eighteenth-century invention. For instance, the experiences in New England taught Quakers about the harshness of the authorities, whom they described whipping 'weak' Nicholas Phelps, and arresting a woman with a young child.[85] Such details are recognisably aimed at hardening the reader against the authorities, and provoking sympathy for Friends.

Narrators' protectiveness comes into effect when 'the weaker sex' is subject to cruelty, registering a paternalistic impulse in sufferings narratives. Cases of what might be termed sexual harassment evoke narratorial sympathy and indignation. For instance, Evesham's mayor is termed 'uncivil' in a text depicting two women's punishment. Set with their legs rather than their arms in the stocks 'a yeard' [sic] one from another', and with a block thrust between their legs, it was insinuated that the punishment was a substitute for the sexual pleasure the women supposedly

---

[80] Ralph Farmer, *Sathan Inthron'd* (London: Edward Thomas, 1657), p. 44.

[81] George Bishop, *The Throne of Truth* (London: Giles Calvert, 1657), p. 26.

[82] Knott, *Discourses*, pp. 224-225.

[83] John R. Knott, 'Joseph Besse and the Quaker Culture of Suffering', *Prose Studies*, 17:3 (1994), 126-141 (p. 131).

[84] Besse, *Sufferings*, vol. 1, p. 386.

[85] Humphrey Norton (et al.), *New Englands Ensigne* (London: Giles Calvert, 1659), p. 15, p. 81. See also Mabel Brailsford, *Quaker Women 1650-1690* (London: Duckworth, 1915), pp. 73-74, describing a Quaker woman giving birth in prison.

sought: 'the mayor […] said they should not have them between their legs which they should [would?] have'.[86] One is reminded here of the accuracy of the observation that 'in contemporary literature and woodcuts, the picture of life in the separatist churches and the sects was of sexual licentiousness'.[87] These women, and others, were abused because of the reputation for sexual as well as religious liberty; in Cambridge, preaching women were termed 'whores' before the order was given that they be whipped 'till the Blood ran down their bodies'.[88] The conflation of sexual insult and legal violence increases the dehumanising effect of punishment, but the abuse also registers a cultural commonplace: that women were the more libidinous sex. Their 'naturally' lusty bodies become symbols to be interpreted, fetishized, by the authorities, and (arguably) by the Quaker authors.

Elsewhere in the Quaker corpus, an 'innocent woman, tenderly bred, and of a considerable estate', receives narratorial sympathy because of the 'inhuman cruelty' she suffered.[89] The woman, who had refused to go to prison at her captors' requests, was forced to ride horseback after being fastened with a rope. Given the Quakers' refusal to acknowledge hierarchy, seen most clearly in their rejection of honorific titles (they refused 'polite' terms of address to so-called social superiors, and would not doff their hats), such attention to the particular suffering of a gentle Quaker is noteworthy. In this recognition of status, social tiers are created despite the Quaker policy of denying inequality.

The significance of such paternalistic sympathy for female sufferers is that, arguably, it is the body that here 'speaks' of persecution and, consequently, visceral depictions may erase the woman's voice. More than gender is at stake, however, given the 'ideal of patient suffering' that Knott convincingly identifies as a Quaker norm.[90] One clear example of 'patient', but feminized, suffering is the case of Elizabeth Leavens (Holmes) and Elizabeth Fletcher, both of whom were flogged in Oxford.[91] It is their bodies, not their voices that 'speak'. In order to show the choices made by the narrator Richard Hubberthorne, it is first necessary to establish the common way of portraying whippings.

Quakers did not, in general, strive to avoid corporeality and viscerality in their descriptions. Rebecca Travers's text gruesomely describing how James Naylor was whipped until no part of his body was left unscathed is one sickening example. She

---

[86] Humphrey Smith, *Something Further Laid Open […] Evesham* (London: n. pr, 1655), p. 6. The women were Margaret Newby and Elizabeth Courten. The experiences of Elizabeth Fletcher and Elizabeth Holmes show that this was not an isolated case. During a debate with scholars, the men: 'proffered to put their hands under the womens aprons, and asked whether the spirit was not there?' In Jeremiah Haward (et al.), *Here Followeth a True Relation […] in Oxford* (n. pl.: n. pr., n. d.), p. 3.

[87] Patricia Crawford, *Women and Religion in England 1500-1720* (London and New York: Routledge, 1996), p. 140. See Laura Gowing, 'Gender and the Language of Insult in Early Modern London', *History Workshop*, 35 (1993), 1-21.

[88] Besse, vol. 1, pp. 84-85, cited in Brailsford, *Quaker Women*, p. 100. Brailsford states that this was the first case of Quakers being flogged.

[89] Pyot (et al.), *The West*, p. 163. The sufferer was Margaret Killam.

[90] Knott, 'Joseph Besse', *Prose Studies*, 17:3 (1994), 126-141 (p. 136).

[91] In the text, Leavens is referred to as Heavens.

remains focussed on the persecuted body: 'there was not a space bigger than the breadth of a man's nail free from stripes and blood from his shoulder to his waste'.[92] The American experience, too, brought numerous examples of corporeal suffering. In John Norton, the colonial government had an exponent of force: 'Magistrates may and ought to put forth their coercive power in matters of Religion'.[93] Thus the Quakers' bodily suffering literally figures the blood-thirstiness of New England's rulers:

> [Robert Hodgeshone was] stripped [...] to the waste, and [they] hung him by the hands, and tyed a great logg to his feet, that he could not turn his body, and set a strong Negor with rods, who laid many stripes upon him both backward and forward, where with he cut his flesh very much, and drew much blood upon him.[94]

The physicality of Hodgeshone's punishment registers powerfully against the punitive actions of the state (however, the authorities' forcing of a 'negor' here to inflict the punishment goes uncommented on in this account of oppression). Nevertheless, Hodgeshone's physical endurance becomes a statement of faith.

Richard Hubberthorne's depiction of the whipping of Elizabeth Fletcher and Elizabeth Leavens is different: the usual corporeality is avoided. It has been argued that 'to be intensely embodied is the equivalent of being unrepresented and [...] is almost always the condition of those without power', but these women's experience may confirm that to be 'disembodied', too, is to be disempowered.[95] The women, in the passage to be quoted below, are almost entirely erased from view – by eschewing physical description, the Quaker writer may be imitating earlier martyrological accounts of women's suffering.[96] But in a passage showing that authorial discretion is at work, Richard Hubberthorne describes the punishment:

> [It] was agreed upon that they should be soundly whipped, and that for the present, because of the tumult, be put in a cage. And the next morning, their wills was performed, though with much unwillingness in the executioner. Many other particulars might be mentioned of their sufferings, afflictions and patience, under reproachings,

---

[92] William C. Bittle, *James Nayler 1618-1660: The Quaker Indicted by Parliament* (York: William Sessions, 1986), p. 135.

[93] John Norton, *The Heart of New England Rent* (London: J. H. for John Allen, 1660), p. 82. See Carla Gardina Pestana, *Quakers and Baptists in Colonial Massachusetts* (Cambridge and New York: CUP, 1991); for a good introduction, see Michele Lise Tarter, 'Quaking in the Light', in *Centre of Wonders: The Body in Early America*, ed. by Janet Moore Mindman and Michelle Lise Tarter (Ithaca and London: Cornell University Press, 2001), pp. 145-162, for information on women's suffering.

[94] Norton (et al.), *New England's Ensigne*, p. 17 (misn. 14).

[95] Elaine Scarry, *The Body in Pain: The Making and Un-Making of the World* (New York and Oxford: OUP, 1985), p. 207.

[96] See Frances Dolan, '"Gentlemen, I have One More Thing to Say": Women on the Scaffolds in England, 1563-1680', *Modern Philology*, 92:2 (1994), 157-178. Dolan notes the 'elision' of Anne Askew's bodily death in *Acts and Monuments* (p. 161).

revilings, slanders and false accusations cast upon them, which is the portion of the righteous in the world.[97]

In addition to the obscuring of the women's bodies, the identity of the sufferers is also withheld until the close of the account, even despite the text repeating the Mayor of Oxford's demand to know the women's names. (Though Leavens had been active amongst a group of writers protesting against unfair imprisonment elsewhere, she does not even have signatory status in Hubberthorne's text).[98] Functioning as symbolic rather than individualised sufferers, 'speaking' through a persecuted body that is also erased, these women's powerlessness is doubly registered in the narrative.

Exploring the significance of Leavens's and Fletcher's limited presence returns us to the need to supplement observations about narrative form with cultural analysis. The passage's attitudes to gender are problematic because, of course, the text is silent on the specific meanings of female bodiliness.[99] It can be noted in comparable cases that whether erased or present bodies seem, at one level, to excite the male narrator's interest. Hubberthorne's anxiety when depicting female bodies can be contrasted to the approach taken in *New England's Ensigne*. The following account seems to be structured around the idea of male, narratorial, outrage at the treatment the New England authorities meted out to Quakers Anne Austin and Mary Fisher.

> Accusing them for witches [. . .] they took upon them to appoint women to search them [. . .] which inhumanely was in the manner following: stript them stark naked, not missing head nor feet, searching betwixt their toes, and amongst their hair, tearing and abusing their bodies more than modesty can mention, in so much that Anne, who was a married woman and had born 5 children said, That she had not suffered so much in the birth of them all, as she had done under their barbarous and cruel hands.[100]

The text foregrounds female corporeality, therefore evoking sympathy for the sufferers; even here, though, some details are omitted for the sake of 'modesty'. Although *New England's Ensign* seems more engaged with the women's suffering, it relates to women no less complexly than Hubberthorne's text. What each work seems to show is that whether through corporeal absence or presence, Quaker writing betrays a cultural understanding that we would now term 'essentialist'. Ultimately, the woman's reported experience of suffering is determined by her culture's approach to maternity, nakedness, and supposed physical weakness. This

---

[97] Richard Hubberthorne, *A True Testimony of the Zeal of the Oxford Professors* (London: Giles Calvert, 1654), p. 3. The Mayor of Oxford protested that the punishment had been too harsh, but was ignored.

[98] Hubberthorne, *A True*, p. 2. See Leavens [sigy], in Christopher Atkinson (et al.), *The Standard of the Lord Lifted Up* (London: Giles Calvert, 1653).

[99] Phyllis Mack elaborates more of the contradictions within Hubberthorne's *A True* in *Visionary Women*, p. 177.

[100] Norton, *New England's*, p. 7.

rhetoric of suffering divides the soul from the body, therefore, in a way that inscribes women's *difference* from men.

Implicit in these narratives that seem to defend women's presence in the public sphere against the prejudices of non-Quaker adversaries, then, is a subtle re-stating of gender categories. The suggestion I'm making is that women are depicted as suffering in different ways from men: the gendered realisation of suffering is expressed most clearly through essentialist depictions of the ('unequal') body. Those narratives that focus on the female sufferer's body often minimise their right to speak in the text, suggesting that women are more likely to be perceived as innocent when they are mute. Largely because their main crime, speaking in public, was in itself problematic within this culture, the main anxiety is textually represented as a problem with voice. There is certainly difference in the quality of the characterisation of the woman who speaks directly, the voice that is paraphrased, and the sufferer who is silenced because she is embodied. The same woman may, of course, speak in different ways in a text, combining direct speech, paraphrase, and bodiliness.[101] Yet these questions surrounding women's speaking continue to open up the internal contradictions and cultural contexts that can be explored through analysis of a text's form.

Masculine Form

The visibility of women within the corpus of Quaker martyrology is generally a result of their suffering, rather than their writing. Their victimisation is relatively common, but women's narratives of self-expression are contained within texts that usually underline male importance in this area of Quaker experience. Gender distinctions are apparent even in the formal dynamics of these texts: sufferings narratives are elaborate in their construction, and the result is that a woman's writing usually appears in a text where hers is not the only voice. Often, the writer responsible for the majority of the text (the main author), and the author(s) most numerically prominent, will be male. Hence, women's 'sufferings' testimonies are commonly juxtaposed to, prefaced by, or collaboratively produced with men: their writing is rarely autonomous. Although we might point to the apparent inclusiveness of Quaker texts, asserting that Quakerism produced more women writers than any other sect, this offers less comfort when it is remembered that women's speaking and writing remains an unusual activity, and one to be both framed and interpreted by men.

The thesis that sufferings narratives encode male priority on the basis of their greater formal and authorial presence, however, reads against the texts' commonly stated ideological argument: that Quakers suffer together as one, eschewing gender distinctions. The community's interest in presenting suffering as a unifying, collective, experience, as against a purely indivisualising encounter with unjust authorities, makes persecutionary narratives a source of information about Quaker

---

[101] These examples of close reading are not meant to explain the whole text from which they have been selected, but merely begin to explore some significant narratorial techniques.

ideals, as well as personal tragedies. The 'communal nature of resistance' that Knott identifies as a feature of sixteenth-century martyrology might have informed the Quaker response; Quaker writing, like the earlier *Acts and Monuments* (1563) collectivises suffering.[102] Such an ideological linking of self to a community in search of a common cause clearly shores up resistance to recalcitrant states' refusal to grant religious toleration.[103] Yet, it is a simplification to read statements on unity as giving voice to a 'fact' of Quaker experience. Quakers might state they would 'lay down their lives for one another', invoking the idea that the extended body of believers will be united.[104] Knowing what we know about Friends' offers to, for instance, change places with the incarcerated, this is no empty promise.[105] However, the shared nature of suffering contrasts with the impressions of gendered suffering that we have observed so far.

Narratorial sleights of hand are the clearest examples of writers expressing anxiety over the female role, which, consequently, fractures the community of suffering along gender lines. Quakers claimed to suffer 'as being members of the same body', yet looking behind this rhetoric at the texts' formal dynamics, it becomes clear that though there might be a parity in suffering, the writing and publishing process was selective.[106] For instance, a text that depicts women sufferers alongside men, yet contains no single handed writing by women known to be literate, conveys a different perspective on suffering from a text that, by contrast, includes testimonies by both genders. Moreover, explicit comments on the unity of Quakers in suffering that later turn out to represent *men's* collective experience also reveal much about the authors' attitudes. Collaborative texts that worked according to principles of cooperation are particularly interesting as a source of evidence of patriarchalism because they are unexpectedly masculinist. Collective texts are created, often, as if their arrangement of several voices can express the feelings of the entire group; sometimes it is even stated that a text speaks on behalf of 'all' Friends.[107] Attentiveness to gender, however, complicates this ideology of inclusiveness.

The presence of a literate woman in a multiply-authored text suggests that her experience could be described first-hand; when it is not, because there is no female writing, the text itself may give clues about the main author's attitudes. A woman might succeed in writing on suffering yet be silenced by the text, and selectivity might lead to the exclusion of women.[108] Perhaps a preacher's self-authored words

---

[102] Knott, *Discourses*, p. 84.

[103] Braithwaite, *BQ*, pp. 434-467; Barbour, *The Quakers in Puritan England* (New Haven and London: Yale University Press, 1964), pp. 207-233. Religious toleration, both critics argue, was the Quakers' main objective.

[104] Dorothea Gotherson, *To all that are Unregenerated* (London: n. pr., 1661), p. 92.

[105] Braithwaite, *BQ*, p. 455.

[106] Wastfield (et al.), *A True Account*, sig A3r.

[107] For instance, Amos Stoddard (et al.) indicate that they are representative figures by stating they write 'in the name of themselves and the rest'. *Something Written in Answer to a Lying Scandalous Book* (n. pl., n. pr., n. d.), p. 8. Thomason's date is July 1655.

[108] I suspect that detailed comparison of manuscript sources to published works would reveal that multiply-authored texts are selective.

would flout the established norm – that women speak through a (male) author who records events to his own agenda. Some cases effectively take the same approach to both men and women, however. For instance, Edward Pyot and William Salt (*The West Answering to the North*, 1657) write with a clear intention of cataloguing the oppression of many Friends, declaring they shall 'witness against all unrighteousness and ungodliness'.[109] In this text the authors speak on behalf of men who were identifiably leaders within the early Quaker movement, making this text's descriptive approach a textual commonplace, and not a specific attempt to silence women.[110] Arguably, here, the schema focuses on the communal nature of resistance, and as such, women are made very much a part of the culture of mass suffering that Pyot and Salt seek to convey.

On the other hand, writing is more problematical when tampering has occurred within a female author's work, especially when this text is otherwise solely by men to the exclusion of literate women. Humphrey Norton's (et al.) *New England's Ensigne* (1659) serves as an example. This is a decidedly shambolic text 'written at sea, by us whom the wicked in scorn calls Quakers', and despite the numerous female victims in New England, the text underplays female authorship.[111] In the first instance, one of the sufferers, Dorothy Waugh, is known to be literate, though it is not possible to ascertain if she wrote a personal testimony only for it to be excluded.[112] More problematically, however, one passage presents itself as if it is by a woman, yet narratorial interference seems clear. Katherine Scott's narrative does not present a clear authorial presence: the account speaks both from the 'I' and 'she' of discourse, moving between the subjective and the third-person, and this grammatical shift makes it a problematical example of women's writing. For instance, the 'personal' testimony reads that Scott was 'returned [...] back to the prison from whence she was brought'.[113] The narration of the text is therefore largely limited to masculine viewpoints, despite the collective structure, and it largely excludes the possibility that women's writing might be part of the picture. In an instance such as this, women's experiences might be moulded to fit a male agenda.

Still other texts give voice to a masculinist perspective, and though, again, there is no explicit evidence to suggest that male writers have been favoured over female writers, the agenda shows how suffering has been gendered. For instance, a masculine viewpoint is sometimes conveyed even despite the fact that women were sharers in the experience of persecution. This is clearly the case in Robert Watsfield's (et al.) text recounting Quaker annoyance at being accused of raising weapons against the state. They declare that 'a necessity is laid upon us to put forward this following relation in order to clear and acquit the innocent from the

---

[109] Pyot (et al.), *The West*, p. 51. Other references are in parenthesis.
[110] Sufferers included: James Nayler (85), Hester Biddle (85), Anne Downer (later Whitehead) (120), Margaret Killam, Barbara Patison, Priscilla Cotton, Mary Cole (157-172), and Mary Howgill (107). See a fuller account of this text, below, p. 16.
[111] Norton (et al.), *New England's*, title page.
[112] For Dorothy Waugh see, Norton (et al.), *New England's*, p. 7, p. 15, p. 56, pp. 69-70.
[113] Norton (et. al.), *New England's*, p. 98.

slanders'.[114] Twelve Quakers testify to the fact that they deny the charge of plotting, and one letter to the Judge and Justices is signed by nine people.[115] However, all of the signatories are men, despite the presence of 'friends in the truth, both men and women'.[116] Though notions that the Quakers suffer as 'the same body' are advanced, and though the writers criticise magistrates for showing 'respect of persons', they mark out the gender of suffering by comparing one female sufferer, Elizabeth Tucker, to the widow sent to the unjust judge (Luke 18. 1-8).[117] Here, there is a tension between the abstract, collective conceptualisation of suffering, and its gendered realisation. A clearer example of this phenomenon is Edward Burrough's *Declaration of the Present Sufferings* (1659). One hundred and sixty four signatories, all male, testify that Friends desire changes to a legal system that has criminalized them.[118] No women speak, even as signatories, to the governing party.

Arguably, moreover, the writers of Wastfield's (et al.) *A True Testimony* are constructing a particularly masculine conception of the Quaker movement when, in order to repudiate the charges of raising weapons, they state that 'most of us; who own and witness the Truth [. . .] have constantly adhered to, and conscientiously engaged for the commonwealths interest'.[119] The evocation of soldierly dissatisfaction with the commonwealth is, in fact, a fairly common trope. Edward Pyot, likewise, notes his disillusionment at the fact that the commonwealth has not brought about what they fought for during the 1640s –'Liberty of Conscience'–[120] and Edward Burrough, in another text, complains that for nothing men 'hazarded all in the time of war for the good of the Commonwealth'.[121] In each of these arguments, Friends' loyalty to the new government is invoked to show that their suffering is unjust. The exalted role of commonwealthsmen, though politic when approaching puritan authorities, is also associatively masculine.

More speculatively, it also seems likely that men had a principal role in the overseeing of some texts, and that this may have had an impact on women. The circumstances under which two texts were produced serve as examples of the connection between writing or compiling a tract, and activities in the 'public' sphere. Judicial hearings in Somerset and Banbury produced texts written by enraged eyewitnesses, angered by the law's intolerance. The opening of *The Saints Testimony,* by anonymous eyewitnesses gathered from 'Bristol, Glocestershire

---

[114] Wastfield (et al.), *A True Testimony*, sig. A3^r.
[115] Wastfield (et al.), *A True Testimony*, p. 16. See also p. 48 (misnumbered; it actually precedes p. 64 and follows p. 35); pp. 71-73.
[116] Wastfield (et al.), *A True Testimony*, p. 8.
[117] Wastfield (et al.), *A True Testimony*, sig. A3^r; p. 74, p. 77.
[118] Edward Burrough, *A Declaration of the Present Sufferings* (London: Thomas Simmonds, 1659). Burrough is the only writer named in addition to the signatories.
[119] Wastfield (et al.), *A True Testimony*, p. 40; see also p. 43.
[120] Edward Pyot (et al.), *The West*, p. 22. It reads: '*is not Liberty of Conscience a Natural Right [...] For Liberty of Conscience hath all the blood been spilt, and the miseries of the late Wars undergone?*'
[121] Edward Burrough, *The Woefull Cry* (London: Giles Calvert, n. d.), p. 34. [Thomason's date is 1657].

[sic], Barkshire [sic], and other parts of the Nation', suggests to me that the writing of a post-trial report was a male endeavour.[122] Wastfield's *A True Testimony,* also, was a heat-of-the moment protest, recorded immediately after legal proceedings had finished.[123] It seems probable that men would have been present at formal proceedings in greater numbers than women, and that texts compiled after trials should be read for evidence of male 'overseeing'.

The sufferings text was a tract requiring careful thought as to its construction, and it is perhaps unsurprising that reflections on how this process occurred again often come from men. George Bishop (et al.) comment on the importance of bringing reports together in a composite text aimed at pricking the authorities' conscience: 'we drew up together, and set in order before them, much of what had been done, and shewed how contrary it was to the Law of God'.[124] The aim of Francis Gawler's *A Record of Some Persecutions [. . .] in South Wales* was likewise the cataloguing of regional events, and his reflections on the writing process are not dissimilar to Bishop's comments on multiple authorship. Though Gawler's is a detailed work of single-handed authorship written from prison, the action of going into print is shown to be a mutually desired action. Publication, Gawler states, is 'not a thing that we have done hastily, but have long waited in it [. . .] we thought it good so to do good for evil'.[125] The suffering of Quakers within a particular region hence produced texts that were carefully compiled, and their rationale was based on the need to record mass Quaker experience. The authorial decisions that informed these texts' productions, however, often testify to men's primary involvement.

Quaker practice also commonly signals a collaborative element to the writing process by presenting the signatures of persons agreeing with the sentiments of a particular statement, or text. Four main texts written in the 1650s present women as signatories. In *False Prophets* (1652), three men and three women sign a text protesting against tithes, and written whilst the Quakers were incarcerated inside York Castle.[126] *The Standard of the Lord* (1653) has five male signatories, and 11 female;[127] another anti-persecution text, *A Discovery* (1659), presents 11 male signatories and one female.[128] Burrough's *A Declaration* (1660) has single-authored passages written by Mary Dyer; yet it also appends signatures by six men and one woman to different statements of collective protest.[129] In fact, texts where a number of signatures represent the interests of various persons are far more

---

[122] Audland (et al.), *The Saints Testimony,* p. 1.

[123] Wastfield (et al.), *A True Testimony,* p. 61.

[124] Bishop (et al.), *The Cry of Blood,* sig. A4ᵛ.

[125] Gawler, *A Record of Some Persecutions,* p. 4.

[126] Thomas Aldam (et al.), *False Prophets and False Preachers* (n. pl.: n. pr., 1652).

[127] Christopher Atkinson (et al.) , *The Standard of the Lord* (London: Giles Calvert, 1653).

[128] Edward Sammon (et al.), *A Discovery of the Education of the Schollars (sic) of Cambridge* (London: Giles Calvert, 1659).

[129] Edward Burrough (et al.), *A Declaration of the Sad and Great Persecution [...] in New-England* (London: Robert Wilson, [1660]).

The CRY of BLOOD. 3

AND

Herod, Pontius Pilate, and the *Jewes* reconciled, and in confpi-
racy with the *Dragon,* to devour the *Manchild.*

BEING

A *Declaration* of the Lord arifing in thofe people, of the *City*
of BRISTOL,who are fcornfully called *Quakers,* and of the mani-
fold *Sufferings,* and *Perfecutions* fuftain'd by them from the *Priefts, Rulers, Profeffors*
and *rude multitude,* contrary to *Law, Liberty, Juftice, Government,* the *righteous ends*
of the *Wars,* and the *Scriptures* of *Truth.*

TOGETHER

With a true Account of the material Paffages in fubftance between the *Rulers* and them at their feveral *Examinations,* and *Commitments,* and at two general *Seffions* of the Publick *Peace* : And of the *Tumults,* and in.
furrections, with other neceffary *Obfervations,* and *Occurrences.*

Gathered up, written in a *Roll,* and delivered to *John Gunning*
late Mayor of that *City* (being the *fruits* of his Year) for the
private *Admonition,* and *Conviction* of *himfelf,* and *Brethren* concern'd,
and named therein: with a *Letter,* declaring the *end,* and *reafon* of what
is fo done, (of which a Copy followes in the enfuing pages) Subfcribed by

<table>
<tr><td rowspan="2">*Geo: Bifhop,*</td><td>*Thomas Goldney,*</td><td>*Edw: Pyott,*</td></tr>
<tr><td>*Henry Roe,*</td><td>*Dennis Hollifter.*</td></tr>
</table>

And now after five moneths fpace of time Publifhed, for the *Reafons*
hereafter expreffed.

*And they cryed with a loud voyce, faying, How long, O Lord, holy, and true, doft thou not
judge, and avenge our blood, on them that dwell on the earth ?* Rev. 6. 10.
*And fhall not God avenge his own Elect, which cry day and night unto him, though he bear
long with them ? I tell you, that he will avenge them fpeedily ; nevertheleffe, when the Son
of man cometh, fhall he find faith on the earth ?* Luke 18. 7, 8.
*And the fame day Pilate and Herod were made friends together, for before they were at Em-
nity among themfelves.* Luke 23. 12.
For of a truth againft thy holy child Jefus, (whom thou haft anointed) *both Herod and Pontius Pilate, with the Gentiles, and the people of Ifrael were gathered together,* Acts 4. 27.
*And the Dragon flood before the woman, which was ready to be delivered to devour her child
as foon as it was born: and fhe brought forth a man child, who was to rule all Nations with
a rod of Iron, and her child was caught up to God, and to his Throne ; and the Dragon was
wroth with the woman, and went to make war with the remnant of her feed, which keep
the Commandements of God, and have the teftimony of Jefus Chrift,* Rev. 12. 4, 17.
And the Devil fhall caft fome of you into Prifon, Rev. 2. 10.

London, Printed for *Giles Calvert,* at the *Black-fpread-Eagle* at the Weft-End
23 *July,* of Pauls, 1656.

Illustration 2.1   George Bishop (et al.), *The Cry of Blood* (1656)

common than this scant list implies: the focus here is only texts where women are signatories as well as men.

When examined further, the collaborative aspect of writing represented in multiply-signed texts on Quaker sufferings encode individualism in the midst of collectivism, and masculinity in the midst of gender neutrality. Multiply-authored texts encode many voices by using the 'we' of discourse; but the collective position may dissolve when examined closely for signs of single-handed writing, of which the clearest indication is the switch from 'we' to 'I'. Christopher Atkinson (et al.'s) text, for instance, is multiply-signed. However, it switches between individualism and collectivism, being simultaneously 'Written from the Spirit of the Lord, which is the word of the Lord, by *one* who suffers in bonds for the truths sake', and by

> Wee [who] for the witnessing of the Truth, are kept in Prison by corrupt Magistrates who live in the World, and turn the Grace of God into Wantoness and refuse to do justice.[130]

It is impossible to identify the authorial 'one who suffers', here, from the collectively authored position the text adopts. Theoretically, it may be one of the eleven female signatories. Another text, *A Discovery of the Education of the Schollars [sic] of Cambridge* (1659), is signed by eleven men and one woman (Mary Godfrey). This also takes on the collective 'we'. However, for one brief passage, the account also represents John Pearce as a narrator when giving account of his persecution: 'I told him I spake the Truth'.[131] Some voices can be singled out in multiply-authored texts, showing how a specific author (often male) might have been more active than the rest.[132]

An alternative way of approaching Quaker prose style is to identify verbal patterns that seem to encode multi-vocality particularly strongly; there appears to be a register, shared by men and women, for speaking collectively. The style that I recognise as characteristically collectivist emerges when rhetoric is 'heightened' by the inclusion of rhetorical questions. A collectivist style can be identified in individuals' works as well as multiply-authored texts, in exclusively male collaborative writing and in texts that men and women wrote together. The collaborative style can be found in one of the earliest known Quaker texts, *False Prophets* (1652). Signed by both men and women, and written from prison as a

---

[130] Atkinson (et al.), *The Standard of the Lord*, p. 30; p. 27. My italics.

[131] Edward Sammon (et al.), *A Discovery of the Education of the Schollars [sic] of Cambridge* (London: Giles Calvert, 1659), p. 9. John Bolton (et al.) also wrote in a way that specifically replaced personalised authority with collective loyalty. The authors term themselves the 'children of light', and write of various contributors' activities, but this text also includes a brief authorial address. John Bolton (et al.), *A Declaration from the Children of Light* (London: Giles Calvert, 1655), p. 4.

[132] See Steven Roberts, 'The Quakers in Evesham 1655-1660: A Study in Religion, Politics and Culture', *Midland History*, 16 (1991), 63-85 (p. 69), for evidence that the act of signing a text was enough to provoke the authorities to arrest all the Quaker contributors.

protest against the system of funding that supported the state church (the tithe), the writing demands that the priests explain themselves:

> He that saith he is in Christ ought to walk as he walked; did he ever preach for Money, or did he ever give forth Command for his to take Hire? How dare any of you Hierlings say you are sent of Christ? did he say one thing and do another? was he not what he spoke in all things? were not his ministers examples for others to walk by, and exhorted others to minde their conversation?[133]

This seems to harness the power of the collective voice: the rhetorical questions exhort, accuse and cajole the reader in a few short sentences.[134] Yet, just as individualism has been found amongst collectivism (the 'I' in rhetoric written from the 'we' of discourse), so, too, can this multi-vocality be found in single authored texts, including a resonant passage by George Fox in George Benson's *The Cry of the Oppressed* (1656), beginning 'Was there ever such merchandize made of any people since the world began as these false teachers have done in our age before mentioned? Was there ever such oppression'.[135] Collectivist rhetoric might as often be written by a single author as by a group of writers seeking to convey shared ideals; the important matter, from the point of view of women's place in the Quaker collective, is that this rhetorical style is not by any means an exclusively male technique – as we have seen in the *False Prophets*.

Despite the positive advantages to women of being part of a community formulated on collectivist principles, it seems likely that sufferings narratives multiply the number of men in authorial and decision-making roles. Little or no evidence as to women's involvement in the careful work of compilation so far exists, and hence it seems likely that men took primary responsibility for the construction of texts. It is important to bear such a background in mind when considering women's authorship of sufferings narratives, since a female testimony may be overwhelmed by the wider Quaker corpus of suffering where men's authorial role was the greater.

---

[133] Aldam (et al.), 'False Prophets', in *EQW*, pp. 361-362 (p. 362).

[134] See also John Bolton (et al.), *A Declaration*, p. 6, who addresses the 'workers of iniquity' in a series of rhetorical questions to the imagined respondent. It reads, in part: 'do you live sumptuously and in pleasures in your life time? Did not he go into torment who lived so? Is not he an example to you all'. The comments pile up in this highly vocalised manner.

[135] Fox writes: 'Was there ever such merchandize made of any people since the world began as these false teachers have done in our age before mentioned? Was there ever such oppression and such heavy burdens laid upon any people since the world began as these false priests and teachers have done in our age that the Reader may find before mentioned?'; George Fox, 'Was there ever such Merchandize made of People' [first line], in Gervase Benson, *Cry of the Oppressed* (London: Giles Calvert, 1656), p. 38.

Women's Writing

When it comes to assessing the 'voice' in Quaker women's writing, it should be noted that rather than their texts seeking to register their autonomy, women aim to speak for god.[136] Mary Dyer, who was hanged in New England for Quaker activities, maintains, for instance, that she has a message from god that the earthly authorities must attend to, which was specifically that they should 'Repeal all such Laws, that the Truth and Servants of the Lord may have free passage among you'.[137] Rather than women's single-handed writing escaping fully the masculine paradigms that were evidently at work in male-authored accounts of female suffering, the godly text attributes to god the most forceful words of condemnation. For instance, Dyer explains 'The Lord will overthrow both your Law and you, by his Righteous Judgements and Plagues poured justly upon you'.[138] Another writer, Sarah Blackborrow, whose message of 'vengeance' opened this chapter, maintains that the voice in her text is attributable to god, explaining that she declares what she has 'seen and known, heard and felt' in the godly power, and confessing 'if I bore witness of it my self, it were not true; but my witness stands in him'.[139] The most acceptable way for a woman to write is in the voice of god, and through the pre-determined stories in the bible (Dyer, for instance, represents herself as the biblical Esther, in her account).[140] Together, these features indicate that the woman ostensibly writes within male structures of discourse.

Quaker women could, however, directly recognise patriarchalism when it was translated into punishments specifically aimed at silencing them, and the result is that male authority is challenged in some texts. The Quaker Dorothy Waugh's confinement to a scold's bridle is one such instance; though she was not the only Friend to be treated in this way by the legal authorities, she was the only person to write an account.[141] Her account is relatively short, and can be quoted at length:

> Upon the 7th day about the time called *Michaelmas* in the yeare of the world's account 1655. I was moved of the Lord to goe into the market of *Carlile*, to speake against all deceit and ungodly practices, and the Mayor's Officer came and violently haled me off the Crosse, and put me in prison, not having any thing to lay to my Charge, and presently the Mayor came up where I was, and asked me from whence I came; and I said out of Egypt where thou lodgest; But after these words, he was so violent and full of passion he scarce asked me any more Questions, but called to one of his followers to

---

[136] See chapter four, where this paradigm is discussed.

[137] Mary Dyer, 'Here Followeth the Copy of a Letter', in Burrough (et al.), *A Declaration*, p. 25.

[138] Dyer, 'Here Followeth', in Burrough (et al.), *A Declaration*, p. 27.

[139] Sarah Blackborrow, *A Visit from the Spirit in Prison* (London: Thomas Simmonds, 1658), p. 9 (misn. 7); see *HPS*, p. 52.

[140] Dyer, 'Here Followeth', in Burrough (et al.), *A Declaration*, p. 26. See the Book of Esther for her confrontation with Ahasueras.

[141] John Davenport had a key placed over his mouth, see Norton, *New England*, p. 50; Jane Holmes and Anne Robinson were put in a bridle, see Christine Trevett, *Women and Quakerism in the Seventeenth Century* (York: The Ebor Press, 1995), pp. 25-28.

bring the bridle, as he called it, to put upon me, and was to be on three houres, and that which they called so was like a steel cap [...] they tare my Clothes to put on their bridle as they called it, which was a stone weight of Iron by the relation of their own Generation, & three barrs of Iron to come over my face, and a peece of it was put in my mouth, which was so unreasonable big a thing for that place as cannot well be related, [...] and the mayor said he would make me an Example to all that should ever come in that name. And the people to see me so violently abused were broken into teares, but he cryed out to them and said, for foolish pity, one may spoil a whole Cittie. [...] and after a while the Mayor came up againe and caused it to be put on againe, and sent me out of the cittie with it on, and gave me very vile and unsavoury words, which were not fit to proceed out of any mans mouth, and charged the Officer to whip me out of the town, from Constable to Constable, to send me, till I came to my owne home, when as they had not anything to lay to my Charge. D. W.[142]

Waugh does not bite her tongue when challenging her confinement to the scold's bridle.

The punishment of the scold seeks to forcibly restrain women's speaking, when the cultural systems that actively encouraged women to self-censor had failed.[143] Scolding women were either constrained in a bridle, or cucked on a ducking stool, until 'the party beg[an] to show all external signes imaginable of humiliation and amendment'.[144] The bridling or cucking of the scold therefore enacts patriarchal control of language at a literal level. The authorities involved in such cases seem to justify the silencing of the scold by depicting her speech as inherently malicious; she is typically accused of 'railing', 'cussed' or 'unruly' words. However, in 'A Relation', Dorothy Waugh maintains that the mayor conforms to the established norms that identify the scold, and this textual manoeuvre is evidence of the sophistication of her writing, since it shows her re-directing the charges against her to others. For instance, Waugh states that the law's officer speaks language that is 'vile and unsavoury' – precisely the terms used often to characterise the scold (p. 30). The mayor is, moreover, enunciating language 'not fit to proceed out of any man's mouth' (p. 30). Waugh shows that the characteristics of the scold are human, rather than female, and establishes codes

---

[142] Dorothy Waugh, 'A Relation Concerning Dorothy Waugh's Cruell Usage by the Mayor of Carlile', in James Parnell, *The Lambs Defence Against Lyes* (London: Giles Calvert, 1655), pp. 29-30. Cited in full in Hinds, *Gods Englishwomen*, pp. 227-228.

[143] See Natalie Zemon Davis, *Society and Culture in Early Modern France* (London: Duckworth, 1975), pp. 124-151; Martin Ingram, 'Ridings, Rough Music and the "Reform of Popular Culture" in Early Modern England', *Past and Present*, 105 (1984), 79-113; Martin Ingram, '"Scolding Women Cucked or Washed": A Crisis in Gender Relations in Early Modern England', in *Women, Crime*, ed. by Kermode, pp. 48-80; William Shakespeare, *The Taming of the Shrew*, ed. by Frances E. Dolan (Boston and New York: Bedford Books of St Martin's Press, 1996); D. E. Underdown, 'The Taming of the Scold: The Enforcement of Patriarchal Authority in Early Modern England', in *Order and Disorder in Early Modern England*, ed. by Anthony Fletcher and John Stevenson (Cambridge: CUP, 1985), pp. 116-136.

[144] Cited in Linda E. Boose, 'Scolding Brides and Bridling Scolds: Taming the Woman's Unruly Member', *Shakespeare Quarterly*, 42:2 (1991), pp. 179-213 (p. 207).

for acceptable speech that men should conform to. In this way, her text refuses to capitulate to patriarchal methods of describing women's language. Another Quaker woman, Sarah Blackborrow, presents an opposite case when she directly addresses her enemies '[you] do want a bridle for your tongues'.[145] Blackborrow's remark shows some acceptance of ideologies that seek to silence loose tongues, even though she would use the bridle against others. Waugh is different because she would have people mind their own language, rather than be subjected to the punishment she has experienced.

More than this, though, Waugh's 'A Relation' seeks to challenge the language as well as their power of the law's officials. For instance, she actively destabilises the terminology they apply as the first step to undermining their legitimacy as magistrates. She notes, therefore, the mayor's call to place her in the 'bridle as he called it' (repeating her focus on the 'bridle as they called it', and the 'relation of their own generation') (p. 30). What is being suggested in this destabilization of language is that Waugh refuses others' labels. Her defiant rejection of the legal structure and its officers is most pointed when she turns to matters of power and control, though. She terms the mayor an 'Egyptian', invoking generally the stock of anti-Egyptian comments in the bible to support her implied meaning: that the law's officer is tyrannical. The apt use of biblical parallel to diminish Quaker enemies is a common practice in the corpus, moreover. Elizabeth Hooton's address to the mayor of Derby, for instance, referred him to the story of Dives (Luke 16:19-31), when suggesting 'woe be to the crown of pride [...] mind these things, for they are very near to you'.[146] Biblically derivative slurs were a common feature of the Quakers' rhetorical armoury. These Quakers put the scripture to their own advantage to challenge earthly authority.

Because Waugh's text disputes on so many levels the terms and effects of her punishment, she represents the outrage that a woman might publicly express in print. 'A Relation' is a demonstrably subtle and assertive example of godly writing. What seems clear is that women such as Waugh might subvert patriarchal norms (and language) through their own forceful denunciations of those in power.

Non-Quakers, however, maintain the comparison between speaking and scolding that godly writers refused. Joshua Miller, in *Anti Christ in Man the Quakers Idol* (1655), fuses biblical and contemporary references when condemning Quaker speech acts. He observes:

> I think they [Quakers] cannot bridle their tongues *James 1:26.* Such words as these I have had from them, thou Priest, deceiver, False prophet, hireling, thou preachest nothing but lies blind guide; with such a bed-role of junctives, that the Oyster women of Billingsgate would blush to name.[147]

---

[145] Sarah Blackborrow, *The Just and Equall Balance* (London: M. W. [Mary Westwood], 1660), p. 10.

[146] Elizabeth Hooton, SM Mss 2:43, 1651; in *EQW*, pp. 381-382 (p. 382).

[147] Joshua Miller, *Anti Christ in Man the Quakers Idol* (London: Thomas Brewster, 1657), p. 1.

By this account, Quaker speakers are no better than the market sellers at Billingsgate, such traders being known for their expletive-ridden language.[148] Quakers might also be compared explicitly to 'scolds',[149] and their utterances deemed 'more fit for Billingsgate than the press'.[150] The assertion that Billingsgate women would 'blush' to speak as Quakers did implies that, contrary to their contemporary reputation, oyster-sellers at least have a modicum of modesty. Once again, this pointed comparison draws attention to the hostile climate for women's public speaking.

Though Waugh's account is a distillation of the conflicts faced by women prophets, the complexities do not stop there, as so often in multiply-written texts. We have to consider the effectiveness of Waugh's protestation of innocence. 'A Relation' leads one to believe that the spectacle of the scold had been erased from the text: and in some senses of the word, it has. However, within the text more generally the figure of the scold is very much present, showing the continuing charge of scolding being to applied to women.

Waugh's text is wedded to an account of the suffering of the first Quaker martyr, James Parnell, at the hands of a cursing woman, who acts as a vocal reminder of the cultural associations between scolding and femininity. The spectacle of the disorderly female is not in fact banished from this text, but is central to it. Parnell was one of 21 Quakers to die in prison during the period.[151] Though responsibility for this was debatably his – the official verdict was self-starvation – the text shows that he suffered great indignities in prison.[152] The person figured as most responsible was the jailer's wife who subjected Parnell to both physical and verbal abuse. Preventing his friends from bringing him food, she termed them 'whores and Rogues, witches and Bastards and the Devils Dishwashers'.[153] The text clearly figures her as a cursing, disorderly woman; Parnell observes that, when lambasting him, she was driven to 'calling me witch, and Rogue, shake and rake-hell, & the like'.[154] At a textual level, the general proscriptions against cursing women continue to operate; perhaps Parnell is emasculated by such an exchange, and the text enacts its revenge.[155]

Since the narratives of imprisonment are always a dialogue between the persecutor and the persecuted that represent the ideas of both, traditional morality

---

[148] See the fictional depiction, specifically the characterisation of Ursula, in Ben Jonson's *Bartholomew Fair*, ed. by Michael James, *Three Comedies* (London: Penguin, 1985).

[149] For another example of such a comparison see Braithwaite, *BQ*, p. 284, citing Baxter.

[150] Thomas Collier, *A Looking-Glasse for the Quakers* (London: Thomas Brewster, 1657), p. 1.

[151] Braithwaite, *BQ*, 465.

[152] Anon, *A True and Lamentable Relation of the Most Desperate Death of James Parnel [sic], Quaker, who Wilfully Starved Himselfe in the Prison of Colchester* (London: T.C for William Gilbertson, 1656), pp. 1-6.

[153] Parnell, *The Lambs Defence*, p. 9.

[154] Parnell, *The Lambs Defence*, pp. 10-11.

[155] James C. W. Truman argues that protestant martyrs are 'gendered' as female even though most were male. I would not press the argument this far in relation to Parnell. See 'John Foxe and the Desires of Reformation Martyrology', *ELH*, 70:1 (2003), 35-66.

and gender prescriptions continue to feature in the texts. This means that writers (such as Waugh) might use print to enter into contestations of power, including challenges to punishments aimed specifically at silencing women, and yet, ironically, the texts also give voice to misogynistic ideas. These multiply-authored texts might, therefore, be especially likely to exhibit ideological dissonance, owing to the range of voices and opinions conveyed within them.

Analysis of sufferings narratives reveals that the woman's position was tenuous within oppositional discourse, due to the prevalent anxieties surrounding women's public speaking. The collectively authored sufferings narrative routinely presents the spectacle of the woman preaching in public being restrained by the legal authorities and either imprisoned, whipped, or, on occasion, punished as a scold. In the majority of cases, men write on behalf of the women who have effectively been silenced by the legal system. The mediated account of women's suffering might reinforce the legal system's attempts to force women's silence by limiting her presence in the text. Arguably, the doubly public aspect of combining single-handed women's writing with an account of their preaching might explain the reluctance to allow women to speak for themselves, in print. Awareness of the silencing and embodying of women in Quaker texts reveals that the community of sufferers was represented as fractured and 'gendered'.

In these sufferings narratives, collectively arrived at, shared, depictions of the godly's malign treatment by the hostile world reveal an ideal of communal suffering that seems to be operating. The collectivity of suffering might not ring true when considering how textual representation of women both silences and embodies them. Yet collectivity could be the means through which women's unity was finally asserted. The case of Sarah Goldsmith makes this clear. In 1655, she wore sackcloth and ashes through the streets of Bristol, '*in obedience to the light in her Conscience*' – god's calling.[156] When Goldsmith was taken before the Mayor, and accused of being 'mad', other Friends spoke to her defence. It is here that the kind of idea advanced by Dorothea Gotherson, in a different text, becomes valid: '[Quakers] were a people who could lay down their lives for another'.[157] First Margaret Wood, then Anne Gannecliffe, jumped to Goldsmith's defence, and for this they were sent to prison. The narrative uses the situation to assert the women's innocence:

> And thus was her friend *Margaret Wood*, who was only with her, in her usual habit, and *Anne Gannycliffe*, who seeing the *tumult* about her, came from her occasions, out of love, to see she had no injury, sent to *Bridewell* together.[158]

Quakers used conventionalised rhetoric when describing suffering, as is the case here. It is customary for the criminalized figure (or author) to assert Friends' innocence, whilst stressing the unjustness of imprisonment, throughout the process

---

[156] Bishop (et al.), *The Cry of Blood*, p. 100.
[157] Dorothea Gotherson, *To all that are Unregenerated* (London: n. pr., 1661), p. 92.
[158] Bishop (et al.), *The Cry of Blood*, p. 102.

of trial and persecution. In common parlance, Quaker texts show that the 'innocent' are 'persecuted', the 'seed' is 'slain' and that publication of sufferings will 'acquit the innocent from slanders and false reports'.[159] In the case of Goldsmith, Wood, and Gannycliffe, the other convention underpinning martyrological narratives emerges. This is the belief that the community experience as one body the punishments meted out by earthly justices. Women such as Gannycliffe, Goldsmith and Wood acted 'out of love' to each other. Female unity emerges conclusively as a factor, here. If they didn't fully have unity with the fractured, gendered community of sufferers, they at least could find it between themselves.

---

[159] See Audland (et al.), 'the innocent are persecuted and sent to prison', in *The Saints*, p. 32 (misn. 34); Mary Howgill, *A Remarkable Letter* (London: n. pr., 1657) states that 'the seed of God is slain by you' (p. 5); Wastfield (et al.), *A True Account*, sig A3^r.

Chapter 3

Petitioners

In the examination of the Quaker sufferings so far, little emphasis has been placed on a major aspect of the Quaker experience: the tithe protest. When Quakers proclaimed their prophetic messages in churches and market places, sometimes suffering imprisonment as a result of their actions, they attacked the state ministry verbally. As we have seen, Quaker writing registers the confrontations between Friends and orthodox churchmen, and Sarah Blackborrow, for instance, addressed herself to 'ye Priests which are found in this desperate wickedness'.[1] For Quakers such as Blackborrow, the act of testifying to the Quaker faith meant challenging the preconceptions of others both at a personal level and through their writing. But Friends also challenged the state ministry in another more material way: Quakers believed that the state ministry should be self-funded, and should not be supported through a national tax that, regardless of the tax-payer's religious affiliation, went to maintain the established church. Since the Quakers did not worship in these Anglican congregations, they believed that they had the right to withhold their taxes: non-payment of the tithe tax was a both principle and a practice.

The anti-tithe debate, its implications and its discursive features, will be examined in relation to one text in particular: the petition that Quaker women presented to parliament in their bid to abolish the tithe. The text, *These Several Papers* (1659), offers a snap shot of women's involvement in the political process.[2] A petition, *These Several Papers* is signed by some 7,750 women from varied geographical regions.[3] A two-page preface by London Quaker, Mary Forster, opens

---

[1] Sarah Blackborrow, *The Just and Equall Balance [sic]* (London: M. W. [Mary Westwood], 1660), p. 3.

[2] See *HPS*, pp. 58-128.

[3] Mary Forster, *These Several Papers* (London: Mary Westwood, 1659). All subsequent references will be given in parenthesis. The title page declares the text to be signed by 'above seven thousand' Quakers; my count puts it at approximately 7,750, though there may be some repetition within and between lists (see Appendix One). For identification of some of the women and, therefore, some proof that the list reflects Quaker membership (rather than the general population), see pp. 88-89 below. The distribution is as follows: 'We who are the seed of woman': 154; Lancashire: 482; Northumberland: 163; Cumberland: 438; Cheshire: 449; Yorkshire: 743; Durham: 170; Northamptonshire: 102; Nottingham: 87; Lincolnshire: 180; 'Essex, Norfolk, Suffolk, Cambridge, and Huntington': 574 (sub-categories Essex: 49; Cambridgeshire and Ely: 62; Parts of Huntingdon: 52); 'Berkshire, Hampshire and Wiltshire': 753; Somerset: 259; Oxford: 112; Buckingham: 274 (sub-category, Warwickshire: 388); Gloucestershire: 232; London and Southwark: 725; 'To the Parliament' (pp. 58-60): 236; 'To the Parliament' (pp. 60-62): 256; 'Wales and Hereford': 243; 'To the Parliament' (pp. 65-68): 232; Dorset: 229 (sub-category, Hertfordshire: 109).

with an address to the parliament outlining the objections to the tithe that she assumes to be shared by herself and the rest. Elsewhere, other women's views are given voice, as separate addresses from particular regions expanding the anti-tithe sentiments in Mary Forster's preface (illustrations 3.1 – 3.4 show the petition's typical format). Women's involvement in the dispute is evidenced throughout, since the text was printed for Mary Westwood, who was responsible for bringing some 51 other Quaker texts to print.[4] Her texts were usually radical, even in Quaker terms, yet none was as substantial a work as this. Through the publication of *These Several Papers*, Quaker women took part in a debate that had important political implications, being an issue of state: they also commented on a topic that was central to Friends' collective identity.

These Several Papers is a published document testifying to the involvement of women both within the Quaker movement, and in the political process. Female Quakers were prepared to demonstrate their mass strength, and the work therefore indicates that they wanted to harness the power of the collective voice in order to challenge dominant groups. The signatories of *These Several Papers* range themselves against tithe-taking priests and secular tithe takers, by denying their right to subtract funds from people who did not worship within the state church. This action challenges the political and economic precedence of powerful groups, as we shall see.

Yet, *These Several Papers* is a demonstration of collective power that is compromised by a number of extraneous factors. The first is that the text itself was not petitionary in the strictest sense: *These Several Papers* was published despite the fact that the outcome of the tithe debate had already been arrived at.[5] The subject of church maintenance had been decided by Parliament (without altering the tithe tax), on 27 June.[6] During the events of spring to summer 1659, when the tithe once more became a subject of dispute in the newly installed Rump parliament, Quakers had pushed for a favourable repeal of the tithe tax. Another Quaker petition against tithes, for instance, was presented to the parliament on the day of the debate and it was said to have been subscribed to by above fifteen thousand people (although none of the signatories are listed in the published document).[7] Quakers were a significant lobbying body, but the women did not have this impact.

Nevertheless, *These Several Papers* demonstrates that women could create roles for themselves in the public sphere. Even despite the fact that the tithe issue

---

[4] Maureen Bell, 'Mary Westwood: Quaker Publisher', *Publishing History*, 23 (1988), 5-66 (p. 5; pp. 46-50). Westwood seems to have been 'primarily an agent for arranging publication' (p. 45).
[5] The petition was apparently presented to parliament on the 20th July 1659 (title page).
[6] For a good overview, see Austin Woolrych, 'Historical Introduction (1659-1660)', in *Complete Prose Works of John Milton*, ed. by Robert W. Ayers, 8 vols (rev. edn, New Haven and London: Yale University Press, 1980), VII, pp. 77-95 (p. 81).
[7] Woolrych, 'Historical Introduction', p. 81. The Quakers' other petition is *A Copie of a Paper Presented to the Parliament: And read the 27th of the fourth moneth, 1659* (London: A. W. for Giles Calvert, 1659) [Thomason E 988 (24)].

had already been resolved, the women commit themselves to public action; their arguments indicate that anti-tithe feeling had widespread support, and that abolition was of sufficient interest to fuel the protests of a massive number of women. Their political commitment takes varied forms. I will argue that their economic concerns as Quaker women are significant testimony to the shared nature of the tithe protest.

The publishing of *These Several Papers* shows how far Quaker organisation had advanced by the end of the movement's first decade; the petition, signed by 'above seven thousand' women, offers extensive insight into women's anti-tithe protest. It contains a preface and collective addresses 'to the parliament', in addition to 29 regionally specific protests from named cities and counties. Responding to the depiction of widespread anti-tithe feeling in *These Several Papers*, one recent critic referred to the document as 'an immense feat of organization'.[8] Top marks must go to the person who set the type, whose efforts are immense. Even though the unknown printer occasionally runs out of type-face – common letters like 'm' are not always capitalised at the beginning of women's names – signatures are meticulously reproduced.[9] This must have been an extremely laborious process, but these efforts allow readers to see the local distinctions important to early Quakers. Later readers can immediately perceive the distinctions between Lancashire and London (for instance), and that national protest develops out of regional support. The petition also supplies the names of Quaker women for whom local identity is not the issue: women of unspecified regions directly address the parliament in four different mini-petitions. These printing decisions show that anti-tithe belief is widespread and give a number of levels of meaning to Friends' activism.

Most current studies of early-modern mass activism have to credit the assertions of the petitioning body, since the level of support is not explicit. Few documents published, either by Quakers or non-Quakers, list the names of any but the principal actors. This absence creates problems for twentieth-century empirically minded scholars. For instance, the historian Keith Lindley notes that most petitions 'boasted signatures (and marks), in their thousands, and sometimes in their tens of thousands', but he is suspicious of the non-factual element, referring to the 'apparent' number of signatures, rather than taking the petitioners'

---

[8] Rosemary Moore, 'The Faith of the First Quakers' (unpublished doctoral thesis, University of Birmingham, 1993), p. 247.
[9] For evidence of the shortage of typeface see, for instance, pp. 26-27. For information on the labour involved in compiling texts see Ronald B. McKerrow, *An Introduction to Bibliography for Literary Studies*, 2nd edn (Oxford: The Clarendon Press, 1927), pp. 6-24. Bell, 'Mary Westwood', notes that in all probability Westwood's texts were set 'by an apprentice', though this remains 'only speculation' (p. 45).

accounts at face value.[10] True, there is often a gap between what the petitioners say they represent, and what they actually do represent. One collective petition by Leveller women, for instance, is said to represent 'many thousands' of people, but only four names are given on their petition.[11] In addition to these empirical problems, the petitions often invite scepticism, partly because they evidently engage in self-aggrandisement. Petitioners in Chester and Dorset declare that they have the support of the many: the writers of *The Humble Petition of the Freeholders, and the rest of the Inhabitants within the County of Chester* claim that the petition was generated through the unlikely collaboration of 'freeholders [...] and the rest'.[12] The writers of *The Declaration of the County of Dorset* similarly assert that they have the assent of 10,000 of the county, but this obscures its more limited Royalist position.[13] Historians are surely right to hesitate before viewing such documents as solid evidence of mass support.

Surviving evidence reveals, however, that efforts to collect signatures, and to organise support, were considerable. Lindley, the same historian who recognised the understandable tendency to exaggerate mass support, also asserts that 'petitions were read out and explained to potential signatories'; and he further shows that petitioning advanced collective identity.[14] To refer, again, to the Leveller women's protests for confirmation of the dutiful efforts to collect signatures, we can see that women were involved in the process; key figures were chosen from 'every Ward and Division to receive the same [the signatures]'.[15] Since surviving evidence seems to show that the Levellers were able to raise thousands of signatures in only

<hr>

[10] Keith Lindley, 'London and Popular Freedom in the 1640s', in *Freedom and the English Revolution: Essays in History and Literature*, ed. by R. C. Richardson and G. M. Ridden (Manchester: MUP, 1986), pp. 111-150 (p. 121).

[11] *The Womens Petition [...] The Humble Petition of Many Thousands of the Poor Enslaved, Oppressed and Distressed Men and Women in the Land* (n. pl.: n. pr., [1652]). The final remarks declare that 'this Petition was presented on Monday the 27th of October, 1652, by K. Frese, D. Trinhale, E. Bassfield, E. Cole. [B.L. 669.f.16 (26)].

[12] *The Humble Petition of Freeholders*, in *The Revolt of the Provinces: Conservatives and Radicals in the English Civil War 1630-1650*, ed. by J. S. Morrill (London: Allen and Unwin, 1976), pp. 150-152. The petitioners address topics such as the tithe, property law suits, the use of oaths, the day of court appearances, the lack of school masters in the county, and the 'excessive fines' levelled by the gentry on their tenants.

[13] *The Declaration of the County of Dorset, 15 June 1648*, in *The Revolt of the Provinces*, pp. 207-208. The petitioners demand: the re-instatement of the King, the calling of a religious assembly, legal reform, and the return of their pre-civil war political privilege, including the return of monies and estates taken from them.

[14] Lindley, 'London', pp. 125-126. Also see Anthony Fletcher, *The Outbreak of the English Civil War* (London: Edward Arnold, 1981), p. 123; chapter 6; p. 301; p. 307; Christopher Hill, *The World Turned Upside Down* (Harmondsworth, Middlesex: Penguin, 1975), p. 22; p. 30; p. 63.

[15] *To the Supream Authority of this Nation [. . .] The humble Petition of Divers Wel-Affected [sic] Women* (London: n. pr., 1649), p. 8. [B.L. E551 (14)].

a few short days, their appeal to the people in the southern counties, particularly London, demonstrates considerable organizational ability.[16]

Evidence of the Quakers' petitioning methods survive principally in anecdotal evidence. The general anti-tithe petition, *A Copie of a Paper*, was said to have been gathered by Quakers who, on horseback, traversed the country to collect the hands of fifteen thousand anti-tithers.[17] Quakers no doubt targeted regions in which Quaker activity was well developed. In many counties, for instance, the Quaker meetings seem to have achieved a degree of order by 1659; they had begun holding regular countywide talks to co-ordinate matters such as discipline and finance. Given the degree of organizational development, it is tempting to speculate that Quaker structures of organization were quite advanced. If the women's petition is anything to go by, local groups could unite within and between counties and, furthermore, organizational competence is evident in the establishment of the women's meetings, which had begun to emerge by the end of the decade.[18] However, the women's petition, *These Several Papers*, is sometimes said to have been the inspiration of George Fox, who is believed to have called the women to the task. In an undated letter, Fox appealed to the women who had been 'witnesses ag^t Tythes' to 'send their names with speed to London'.[19] Though we should not discount this evidence of male agency (and we will look at the language of Fox's letter in more detail later), this call to action presupposes that the infrastructure was in place to facilitate the petition's creation. We will see that, on the contrary, considerable innovation is evident in the presentation of the petition, which is significant for our sense of the local involvement of women, above and beyond the Quaker leader's instigation.

The printer's decision to preserve a set of different identities, personal (Mary Forster), regional, and non-specific, creates a diverse text with a number of different formats. Regional identities are sometimes independent, and in some cases specific. Independence, perhaps the most favoured approach, is where a single county contributes; this is the means adopted by 11 of the 29 named locations.[20] Another common form of address is for the people of different counties to act as a kind of conglomerate. Here, signatories stand as Quakers *per se*, rather than stipulating their independence. The 753 women of 'Berkshire, Hampshire, and Wiltshire', for instance, collaborate on their portion of the petition (pp. 38-44); similarly, the women of 'London and Southwark' unite in one address (pp. 53-58), as do the petitioners of 'Part of Wales and Herefordshire' (pp. 62-65). By contrast, there is one instance where the women of five different areas sign a collective

---

[16] H. N. Brailsford, *The Levellers and the English Revolution*, ed. by Christopher Hill, 2nd edn (Nottingham: Spokesman, 1983), p. 296; pp. 312-313; pp. 317-318; p. 347; pp. 486-487; pp. 573-575; p. 616.

[17] Barry Reay, *The Quakers and the English Revolution* (London: Temple Smith, 1985), p. 83.

[18] William Braithwaite, *SPQ*, pp. 269-289 (p. 272).

[19] George Fox, 'For all Women Friends' [First Line], Swarthmore MSS: SM ii. 96.

[20] Lancashire, Northumberland, Cumberland, Cheshire, Yorkshire, Durham, Nottingham, Lincolnshire, Somerset, Oxford, Gloucestershire.

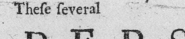

Thefe feveral

PAPERS

Was fent to the

PARLIAMENT

The twentieth day of the fifth Moneth, 1659. Being
above feven thoufand of the Names of the

HAND-MAIDS

AND

DAUGHTERS

OF THE

LORD,

And fuch as feels the oppreffion of Tithes, in the
names of many more of the faid HANDMAIDS
and DAUGHTERS of the LORD, who wit-
nefs againft the oppreffion of Tithes and
other things as followeth.

LONDON,

Printed for *Mary Weftwood,* and are to be fold at
the *Black-fpread Eagle* at the Weft end
of Pauls, 1659.

Illustration 3.1   Mary Forster, *These Several Papers* (1659), p. 31

(32)

Anne Fricknal	Anne Langford	Eliz. Brandrith	Anne Crofts
Susanna Reynold	Sarah Clay	Mary Fields	Jane Anclife
Eliz. Clay	Sarah Brandrith	Martha Grace	Anne Crofts
Margret Whitworth	Eliz. Brandrith	Anne Brandrith	Elizabeth Rogers
Mary Clay	Mary Blackeborn	Alice Woodhead	Anne Noden

LINCOLN SHIRE

We whose names are subscribed, do hereby declare that we are very sensible Tithes are a great oppression set up in the time of Popery; and we desire the removal of them.

Anne Leverton	Anne Sharp	Dorothy Foster	Bridget White
A. Frotheringham	Ruth Pannel	Eliz. Gathorn	Mary Rosse
Eliz. mason	Eliz. Harpham	Dorothy Pickaver	Alice Winsor
Eliz. Woolley	Eliz. Fletcher	Thomasin Norton	Ellenor Gibson
Susanna Holland	Martha Teff	Eliz. Hobson	Mary Parker
Jane Preston	Eliz. Jasnil	Anne Haldenby	Kath. Pid
Eliz. Brinckle	Jane Harrison	Susanna Parret	Anne Pid
Mary Greswel	Anne Hird	Mary Scot	Eliz. Bainton
Mary Pheasant	Eliz. Smith	Grace Scot	Eliz. Pid
Martha Wright	Anne Winch	Anne Garton	Mary Crosby
Anne Recket	Eliz. Smith, junior	Alice Beck	Eliz. Gaskin
Anne Northern	Mary Smith	Margret mayston	Anna Whiteworth
Sence Northern	Susanna Cussons	Eliz. marshal	Susan Smith
Sarah Mosse	Mary maple	Eliz. Lee	Anne Parker
Eliz. Harrison	Mary Cussons	Mary Berrier	Eliz. West
Ursula Hooton	Ellen Smith	Anne milner	Anne Bagaley
Ursula Burroughs	Katharine makaril	Cassandra Chapman	Mary Trueblood
Eliz. Northern	Anne Thornton	Ellin Gilliot	Eliz. Parker
Mary Garland	Didolis Carie	Frances Hobson	Anne Crosby
Anne Pheasant	Mary Oliver	Rachel Beck	Susanna Billidge
Eliz. Rogers	Anne Beck	Mary Chandler	Eliz. Hutchinson
Anne Freestone	Alice Sharp	Anne Sherman	Jane Sanders
Prudens Fisher	Anne Foster	Eliz. Robinson	Anne Berrier
Sarah Thompson	Ester Hart	Eliz. Waterford	Mary Thistleton
Jane Wilkinson	Mary Foster	Eliz. Higham	Margret Dounham
Mary Hudson	Anne Cook	Margret Darlinton	Hollen marshall
Jane Lightfoot	Eliz. Barnard	Mary Turner	Mary Chanler
Ellen Brumby	Anne Spain	Alice Tate	Jone Westwood
Anne Gaunt	Katherine Pickaver	Mary Trevis	Anne Shoreman
Anne Pheasant	Hannah Seaton	Susanna Torksey	Grace Robinson
Mary Northern	Mary Packins	Isabel Drury	Anne Stoker
Eliz. Williamson	Ellen Foster	Anna Brown	Bridget Turington
Eliz. Jackson	Anne Hobson	Sarah Otter	Sarah Claffon
Ellen Gaunt	Dorcas mell	Eliz. Clark	Sarah Kirk
		Mary White	

Eliz.

Illustration 3.2   Mary Forster, *These Several Papers* (1659), p. 32

(33.)

Elizabeth Waterfal	Elizabeth Davie	Anne Thornton	Mary Lumkin
Anne Waterfal	Anne manby	Jane Hempsted	Anne Bellamy
Elizabeth Haigham	Anne Havey	Anne Hempsted	Anne Rofe
Ellen Wilfon	Jane Phillips	Mary Hempsted	Anne Haris
Margret Smith	Elizabeth mathews	Dorothy Armstrong	Rebecka Day
Mary Wilfon	Anne morris	Elizabeth Wilkinfon	Mary Gibfon
Frances Seagrave	Anne makepeace	Sarah Fotherby	Anne Fifher
Rebecka Thornton	Eliz. Boot	Katheren makaril	Anne Johnfon
Mary Sowter	Katheren Swayer	Alice Streaton	Eliz. Wray
Dorothy Rawbuck	Sufanna Whitman	Anne Stelworth	Anne Thomlinfon
Eliz. Kirk	Margaret Afhley	Mary Blackney	

ESSEX, NORFOLK, SUFFOLK, CAMBRIDG, and HUNTINGTON.

To the Parliament of England, *&c.*

Now friends, you being firſt choſen by the Nation as a Parliament for to do the Nation the right, and to take off the Nations oppreſſions; are not you to ſearch out the oppreſſion? and are not people to lay their oppreſſions before you, without petitioning you to do them juſtice? and is not petitioning often for exalting ſuch that will not do juſtice without flattering petitions, and then have but thanks, and ſeldom the thing done? and has not flattering petitions and addreſſes exalted ſuch as God hath overthrown, that hath not done juſtice, nor will not do juſtice to the juſt, when oppreſſions and grievances have been laid before them? the cry hath been, It hath not been a petition, it hath not been an addreſs, becauſe it hath not been in the Worlds method and form; therefore the oppreſſed ſhall not have juſtice done to them, which ought according to juſtice and equity, when the thing is made known unto you in the ſimplicity and innocency, without flattering petitions and addreſſes, you ought to do them juſtice, (for that end are you of the Nation choſen) if the grievance to you be made known, elſe the grievance will lie upon you; if you do approve your power and not abuſe it, you will remove the grievances off you and the Nation, which if you do not, God will overturn you by it; and if you will ſet up a miniſtry, and own a miniſtry, let them be ſuch as will keep the Goſpel of our Lord Jeſus Chriſt, the ſecond Prieſthood, without charge; for here are our Names who are the witneſſes of Chriſt Jeſus, that he hath diſannulled the Commandment that gave Tithes, and hath ended the Prieſthood that took them, and we are witneſſes for Chriſt Jeſus againſt this Popiſh Anti-Chriſtian Miniſtry that

E   takes

Illustration 3.3 Mary Forster, *These Several Papers* (1659), p. 33

(34.)

takes them,who are of the Popes tribe,got up since the Apostles, with
their law and commands for Tithes(out of the power of God)which
must be ended and disanulled by the power of God , which are not
of the tribe of *Aaron*, nor of the tribe of *Christ* , for neither Christ
nor the Apostles after they had disanulled the commandment of
God , never set up a command in the World after that was disanulled, for to give the tenths to a minister ; for the first command was
only to the Jewes that gave Tithes,which Christ the everlasting Priest
denied,whom we confess ended,in whom ye live, who is our life; and
this is our Testimony given in to you,our faith stands in that power
that bringeth down the mountains , and exalteth the valleys, and
layeth them down with the valleys which are grown to be mountains; & thus dothGod overturn by his power & arm all transgressors.

REbecca Havens	Hester Potter	Anne Taylcot	Christian Burch
Mary Till	Margret Bray	Mary Danks	Martha Went
Joan Johnson	Elizabeth Sanders	Mary Grant	Eliz. Gilman
Mary Catchpool	Elizabeth Selly	Sarah Grant	Tomasin Warner
Mary Clark	Susan Belsher	Anne Langly	Eliz. Hospit
Mary Relph	Katheren Lamb	Jene Desborrow	Grace Dersly
Judith Tomblin	Margret Gray	Anne Stamage	Judith Shortland
Dorothy Crisp	Sarah Osburn	Mary Renolds	Mary Allen
Anna Cook	Sarah Luke	Mary Renolds	Mary Cream
Elizabeth Crisp	Mary Middleton	Susan Pateradg	Frances Cakebread
Anne Humphery	Johannah Lamb	Sarah Hatcher	Elizabeth Simmons
Alice Parnel	Elizabeth Rice	Anne Keyes	Margret Lenlee
Elizabeth Garlea	Abigael Ludkin	Hester Haward	Mary Rolph
Mary Turner	Elizabeth Gibson	Hester Haward	Dennis miller
Hannah Ham	Ellen Midleton	Eliz. Till	Ellin Hoy
Mary Love	Mary Hadly	Jane Banks	Jone Barker
Mary Lucas	Mary Llyod	Margret Banks	Jane Cakebroad
Rebecca Lucas	Mary Ansel	Ellen Palmer	Susan Spark
Elizabeth Lucas	Elizabeth Langly	Mary Wandewel	Margret Web
Lydia Chittum	Anne Wethered	Grace marson	Cordala Symonds
Lydia Read	Mary Steddal	Rebecca Hodson	Margret Ludgater
Mary Williams elder	Margret Ball	Margret Christmas	Martha Bawrel
Mary Williams	Sarah Chandler elder	Mary Dagnet	Martha Harp
Mary Gibson	Sarah Chandler	Anne Cookwith	Anne Green
Sarah Lonskin	Elizabeth Green	Bridget Ball	Tasse Hulback
Mary Cook	Alice condel	Anne Clark	Mary michel
Elizabeth Rolph	Susan Crumplin	Anne Clark	Susan Halls
Sarah Banning	Grace Reynolds	Sarah Clark	Eliz. Tober
Elizabeth Godwood	Alice Gorlyn	Mary Stampford	Sarah Burch
Sarah Reynolds	Susan Cockeril	Mary Stampford	Unes Lynly
Susan Swan	Emlin Wyer	Mary Boocher	Joan Symonds
Mary Reeve	Mary Bliant	Eliz. Westrop	Sarah White
Elizabeth Overel	Mary Petfeild	Eliz. mascal	Susan Upsheard
			Faith

Illustration 3.4 Mary Forster, *These Several Papers* (1659), p. 34

statement, but preserve a sense of their regional distinctiveness. There are 574 names in one section, that part of the petition devoted to the women of 'Essex, Norfolk, Suffolk, Cambridge and Huntington', but they subdivide into Essex (49 names), Cambridgeshire and Ely (62 names), and 'parts of Huntington' (52 names), which consequently shows regional consciousness within this broad group (pp. 33-38). Likewise, the petition from Buckingham also sub-divides to represent protesters from Warwickshire (274 names and 388 names, respectively), and the petition from Dorsetshire also includes Quaker contributions from Hertfordshire (229 names and 109 names, respectively) (pp. 47-51; pp. 68-72).[21]

Genuine local interest, and a high level of local involvement, is therefore demonstrated in the petition. The women of Northampton convey only a brief, indistinct, explanation of their support for the anti-tithe protest; but their choice of format indicates that the regional interest is more specific. Declaring that 'these are the names of the women, who are witnesses against the oppression of tithes, taken at *Northampton*', they subsequently reveal that 'these are the names of Friends in *Wellingborough* and thereabouts' (pp. 30-31). Similarly, the list of women from Cambridgeshire and Ely begins with the names of the widows of the meeting (p. 37). Their decision to order the signatures is idiosyncratic, though it is not the only anomaly in *These Several Papers*. Lancashire petitioners, for example, have one list of 39 names that breaks with the established formula. Most of the 482 women are listed conventionally enough, with a Christian name followed by a surname, but the rogue list does not give the full name – only the initialised given name (p. 11). This suggests that women, at least in one meetinghouse, had not seen the rest of the petition and adopted an independent structure as a result.

The printer's efforts mean that the anti-tithe protest was closely identified with the demands of local activists. The depiction of Quaker support is extensive, given the efforts to reproduce the signatures, regional differences, and local priorities. This attention to detail means that the identification of Quaker actors is possible, though these identifications are also somewhat tenuous. The lists often yield up the names of women who we know were associated with particular regions. The list of London petitioners, for example, is a particularly rich source for identifying well known activists. The names of southern Quaker women, such as Sarah Blackborrow, Martha Simmonds, Susanna Bateman, and Margaret Greenaway, are particularly prominent due to their publishing activities (pp. 55-58). But local knowledge can take identification further. Sarah Tims, listed in the Buckinghamshire section (p. 49), could be the woman who told a priest to 'fear the Lord' – her bombast resulted in imprisonment.[22] Another woman, Anne Norris, who vocalised anti-clerical feeling, and gained some notoriety when interrupting a priest in Over, Cambridgeshire, is listed amongst the widows of this county.[23] For contemporaries, of course, identification would have been far easier, though I

---

[21] See 'Appendix' for a list of the names reproduced in 'We who are the Seed of the Woman' and the Lancashire section.
[22] Anne Audland (et. al), *The Saints Testimony* (London: Giles Calvert, 1655), p. 8.
[23] Margaret Spufford, *Contrasting Communities: English Villagers in the Sixteenth and Seventeenth Centuries* (London: CUP, 1974), p. 283.

could also amplify my own identifications further.[24] However, the critic should resist an approach that gives too much credence to the identification of individuals: the name of a 'Grace Barwick' occurs both in the Lancashire and the Yorkshire petition (p. 9, p. 28).

We cannot be sure whether the regional differences, discussed above, are there by design, or are errors or accidents arising during the compilation of the text; it is difficult to know how much to read into these idiosyncrasies. However, uniformity in structure might have indicated a desire to bring the different petitions into line, whereas the variations offer a sense that genuine aspects of local interest have been preserved by the printer. Regional variety is created in the text in the absence of uniformity; specific identities and concerns emerge through the varied approaches to county, nation and people. Though we cannot be sure that the text faithfully renders the signatories' efforts, one thing is certain: the signal effort by Mary Westwood to publish the names of Quaker women petitioners is remarkable. The women signatories become individuals in a way that is extremely unusual in petitions: they are distinct, not homogenised, and Quaker support is therefore explicit, not implicit. The impression, reading the text, awed one critic into observing that 'the sense of communal energy and solidarity of these women, mobilised up and down the nation, is explosive'.[25]

Radical Approaches to the Tithe Issue

If we examine the tithe issue nationally, moving beyond the rhetoric of the women's petition, we can see contradictory factors operating; this was, paradoxically, a campaign that was simultaneously both popular and divisive. The explosive potential soon becomes clear. In 1659, the campaign for the abolition of the tithe was, according to one historian, 'probably the greatest pressure for a single reform'.[26] The most outspoken anti-tithe arguments were probably coming from sectarians, with Quakers and Independents participating in the debate alongside godly men such as John Osborne and John Milton.[27] Rejection of the tithe-tax by demanding sectarians, of many persuasions, was not the only note to

---

[24] Jane Holme (p. 9), Elizabeth Milner (p. 9), Mary Fisher (p. 13), Priscilla Eccleston (p. 55) Dorcas Erbery (p. 57), Dorothea Gotherson (p. 59). See Phyllis Mack, *Visionary Women: Ecstatic Prophecy in Seventeenth-Century England* (Berkeley, Los Angeles and London: University of California Press, 1994), Appendix Two.

[25] Stevie Davies, *Unbridled Spirits: Women and the English Revolution 1640-1660* (London: The Women's Press, 1998), p. 92.

[26] Ronald Hutton, *The Restoration: The Political and Religious History of England and Wales 1658-1667* (Oxford: Clarendon Press, 1985), p. 47.

[27] See Woolrych, 'Historical Introduction', pp. 77-95 (for Osborne see p. 81); John Osborne, *An Indictment Against Tithes* (London: Livewel Chapman, 1659) [E989 (28)]; John Milton, 'Considerations Touching the Likliest Means to Remove Heirlings' (London: T.N. for L. Chapman, 1659), in *Complete Prose Works of John Milton*, ed. by Robert W. Ayers, VII, pp. 273-321.

be sounded in the debates of 1659 however: both pro-tithers and anti-sectarians made their fears known, by discussing the social implications of abolition. Some supporters of the state-funded ministry, for instance, published their texts to coincide directly with parliament's discussions.[28] Indeed, the tithe issue provoked such heated debate that it became, in the words of the Scottish Commander and instigator of the return of Charles Stuart, General Monck, that 'issue of blood'.[29] In the end, of course, the argument was won through bloody-mindedness: Monck's regiments imposed military rule, thereby curtailing the debate.

The various spokespeople in the debate often tried to present their argument as though they voiced the opinions of the majority. Sectarian writers, as though oblivious to their minority position, often deployed rhetoric implying that the hatred of the tithe was universal. They suggest a general antipathy to the tithe, believing that people begrudged paying the tax not because they were tight-fisted, but because their consciences could not permit it. The Quaker Anthony Pearson, himself a JP, commented on the frequency of tax evasion by noting that 'scarce the tenth person in England payeth the tithe'.[30] Pearson showed the righteous principle that underpinned non-payment; he argued that 'the greatest part of the people of England deny tithes to be due by God's law'.[31] Supposedly, the godly would take any parliament to their heart that succeeded in abolishing the hated tax. John Lilburne said as much in his address to the parliament on 26 February, 1649. With Machiavellian insight, the Leveller leader attempted to persuade MPs that abolishing the tithes, if not entirely to their own taste, would certainly be in their interest. It would 'so fasten you in the affections of the people and of the honest soldiers, as you should not fear any opposite power whatsoever', he claimed.[32] Where Lilburne wrote of 'affections', the Quaker Richard Hubberthorne wrote of 'love'. Speculating that the end of the tithe was near, he suggested that abolition would 'beget Love in the Nation'; the hearts of the English populace were (naively) shown to belong to the sectarians; only through abolition could parliament gain the people's love.[33] Unlikely confirmation of the popularity of the tithe issue also appears in *Gangraena*, Thomas Edwards's anti-sectarian polemic. Making Henry Denne the object of his scorn, Edwards observes that Denne 'preacheth much against Tithes, whereby he draws the people after him'.[34] The implication of these passages certainly seems to be that anti-tithe protest had popular support, particularly amongst the godly.

---

[28] See my discussion of William Prynne, p. 94 below.
[29] Margaret James, 'The Political Importance of the Tithes Controversy in the English Revolution 1640-60', *History*, June (1941), 1-18 (p. 1).
[30] Anthony Pearson, *The Great Case of Tithes Truly Stated* (London: Edward Couchman, 1835), p. 19. The text was first published in 1657.
[31] Pearson, p. 19.
[32] Brailsford, p. 470.
[33] Richard Hubberthorne, *The Real Cause of the Nations Bondage* (London: Thomas Simmonds, 1659), p. 4.
[34] Thomas Edwards, *Gangraena* (London: Ralph Smith, 1646), p. 76.

The popular appeal of the anti-tithe protest to radical sectarians has long been established by historians. Barry Reay, who found that Quakers earned the respect of dissenters by their 'opposition to tithes', shows that early converts often had a background in anti-tithe activity.[35] According to Reay, the Quakers' firm stance on the tithe was part of their appeal: Quakerism secured the surest footholds in places where belligerence, and the refusal to pay, were already an established tradition. Reay expands B. G. Blackwood's work on the Lancashire dissenting tradition, widening the focus out to Somerset, Kent, Essex, Suffolk, and some parts of northern England. In Somerset, for instance, ringleaders who co-ordinated the resistance to tithe, which included non-payment, went on to become committed Quakers. On the basis of this, and other evidence, Reay asserts that 'many Quakers had a background in anti-tithe activity'.[36] John Bray, similarly, who traced the history of rural dissent in Kendal back to the Pilgrimage of Grace, suggested that early Quakerism established itself in the regions, and amongst the people, for whom agrarian resistance was already coupled to religious dissent.[37] Concern over the tithe pre-dated the Quakers, going at least as far back as the Reformation, so that, according to one historian, anti-tithe protest during the civil wars only intensified an 'already latent controversy'.[38] The tithe was a controversial tax, even before the Quakers took up the cause.

The review of state funding promised by the Rump parliament, in 1659, therefore re-ignited hopes that the change of government would also bring a radical change of direction. The Rump promised a review of this radical sectarian issue, and in June alone received pro-abolitionist petitions from Kent, Bedfordshire and Herefordshire, as well as others that are no longer extant from Somerset, Devon, Dorset, Wiltshire and Hampshire.[39] The Quaker petition, *A Copie of a Paper*, finally brought the issue to a head. The Rump brought their debate forward to coincide with the presentation of this petition, on June 27, but they voted against making immediate changes.[40] The radical hopes of annulment were temporarily dislodged, but the subject did not go away; printing presses churned out anti-tithe propaganda, including Milton's *Considerations* and the Quaker women's *These Several Papers*, well into July and August.[41]

---

[35] Barry Reay, 'Quaker Opposition to Tithes 1652-1660', *Past and Present*, 86 (1980), 98-120.

[36] Reay, 'Quaker Opposition', p. 100.

[37] John Breay, *Light in the Dales: The Agrarian Background to the Rise of Political and Religious Dissent in the Northern Dales in the 16ᵗʰ and 17ᵗʰ Centuries*, 3 vols. (Norwich: The Canterbury Press, 1996), (vol. II and III combined), II, chapter seven, pp. 49-54, and *passim*.

[38] James, 'The Political Importance', p. 4; also see Susan Brigden, 'Tithe Controversy in Reformation London', *Journal of Ecclesiastical History*, 32:3 (1981), 285-301.

[39] Woolrych, 'Historical Introduction', p. 75.

[40] Woolrych, 'Historical Introduction', pp. 75-76.

[41] For instance, John Osborne's *An Indictment Against Tithes*, July 18; *A Few Proposals Offered to the Parliament*, August 20; John Milton, *Considerations*, August. Thomason's dates.

The Rump's failure to satisfy radical hopes, seemingly in defiance of popular interest, is one possible context for the publication of the women's petition, *These Several Papers*; another is the general belief that the Rump was sympathetic to sectarian causes. Confidence in the new parliament was, of course, highest in the early months, and only began to wane after the Rump's fragile alliance with the army compromised its power. The Rump appealed to disenchanted sectors of the populace, those whose revolutionary principles had been disappointed during Cromwell's rule, and who believed that the Rump represented a return to the radicalism of the late 1640s and, possibly, the 'good old cause'. When the Rump had returned to parliament (on May 7), ending the instability of Richard Cromwell's brief regime, radicals wrote optimistically of their hopes for change.[42] It was a 'time of general scribbling': as ever, political upheaval increased the publication of polemic.[43] It was also, however, a time for action. Quakers offered to take up arms; numerous men joined the county militias, perhaps re-affirming their stance as commonwealthsmen.[44] By October, the Quaker Edward Burrough was declaring that 'we look for a New Earth, as well as a New Heaven'.[45]

The Quaker women petitioners pressurised the Rump parliament to enact reforms, perhaps reflecting the hopes, as well as the despairs, of radicals at this time. *These Several Papers* is a complex response to the process of parliamentary reform. The Essex women petitioners, for instance, press for further reforms by making the Rump answerable for its actions. They try to force parliament to end 'oppressions', but their only recourse is persuasion. Arguing that the Parliament must serve the people, they address the Rumpers as equals, in seemingly defiant rhetoric:

> Now friends, you being the first chosen by the Nation as a Parliament for to do the Nation the right, and to take off the Nations oppressions; are you not to search out the oppression? (p. 33)

But their optimism is short-lived; they are aware that parliaments often respond better to flattery than to honesty and, furthermore, simply reject petitions that they do not agree with. The women resent the fact that 'the world' requires greater formality and honorific titles:

> And has not flattering petitions and addresses exalted such a thing as God hath overthrown, that hath not done justice, nor will not do justice to the just, when oppressions and grievances have been laid before them? The cry hath been, it hath not been an address, because it hath not been in the Worlds method and form; and therefore the oppressed shall not have justice done to them. (p. 33)

---

[42] Woolrych, 'Historical Introduction', p. 24, pp. 67-69, p. 71.
[43] Hutton, *The Restoration*, p. 47.
[44] Barry Reay, 'The Quakers, 1659, and the Restoration of the Monarchy', *History*, 63 (1978), 193-213 (pp. 200-203); Hutton, *The Restoration*, p. 53, p. 57, p. 61.
[45] Reay, 'The Quakers, 1659', p. 194.

Though the Quakers' colloquialisms suggest that they speak as equals (they address the parliament as 'friends') the rhetorical postures are compromised by real power inequalities. Parliament has the authority to reject advice; people can only try to persuade them to accept ideas of popular sovereignty. The Welsh petitioners, aware of the Rump's failure to respond to popular demands, remind the parliament that its continuance is dependent on the people's support: 'Friends, you have thrown your selves away out of the affections of the sober people [...] and the well-wishers of the choicest of the Nation' (p. 62). Though the Quaker women seem to believe in the supposed dependence of parliament on the support of 'the people', they also recognise the failure of parliament to respond to it.

The abstract notion of people power is a useful, if inflated, idea that achieved the currency of popular truism, and dated back at least as far as the civil wars. Parliamentarians were seen as public servants, as the republican MP Sir Arthur Haselrig so self-effacingly put it, in 1659: 'we cannot set up any power equal to the people'.[46] He clearly remembered to pay lip service to past revolutionary theories, where these ideas were powerfully advanced. Henry Parker's 1642 text about constitutional issues, *Observations*, for instance, was arguably one of the most influential of such civil war tracts. In it, he asserted that 'power is but secondary and derivative in princes, the fountaine and efficient cause is the people'.[47] It is possible that ideas like these fuelled the support for parliament, and that Charles I, conversely, failed to tap into this language of mutuality, consequently losing the war on ideological, as well as military, lines.[48] It is also possible that ordinary people believed the rhetoric of popular sovereignty, becoming aware of their power as citizens. Finding themselves newly empowered, they may, possibly, have developed a new sense of their public duties. As Megan Matchinske observes: 'State subjects, instead of seeing themselves as beholden to a ruling body outside and above, embodied in the king, symbolically become the state (via parliament)'.[49]

Quaker women advance the idea that the people are sovereign despite, and perhaps even because of, the Rump's deafness to their pleas. Quakers appeal to the Rump for recognition of their public rights, by representing themselves as a body of 'sober' petitioners (p. 62). The women of Wales, using this term to reproach parliament, show that the failure to abolish the tithe offends moderate people. Rhetorically competent as this is, 'sobriety' is not always the first term that comes to mind when describing early Friends. Indeed, Margaret Fell used the term 'sober minded people' to describe Quakers who interrupted Church of England ministers,

---

[46] Woolrych, 'Historical Introduction', p. 17.

[47] Henry Parker, 'Observations', in *Tracts on Liberty in the Puritan Revolution 1638-1647*, 3 vols, ed. by William Haller (repr. New York: Octagon, 1979), II facsimiles, part I, pp. 165-213 (p.168) ; also see Nigel Smith, *Literature and Revolution in England 1640-1660* (New Haven and London: Yale University Press, 1994), pp. 98-101.

[48] Elizabeth Skerpan, *The Rhetoric of Politics in the English Revolution 1642-1660* (Missouri: University of Missouri Press, 1992), p. 114.

[49] Megan Matchinske, *Writing, Gender and State in Early Modern England: Identity Formation and the Female Subject* (Cambridge: CUP, 1998), p. 131.

and Martha Simmonds, hardly the most demure of characters, defined the Quakers as a people who 'hath sobriety'.[50] Though the Quaker women petitioners grafted the term 'sober' into their petition, a critical readership might not take to their terminology.

Quakers also figured mass activism by deploying terms used, more commonly, by other sects; most problematic is the appearance of the term the 'elect', since the theory of election has little place in Quaker theology. According to one contemporary of the Quakers, the elect represented 'a certain select number of particular men (commonly called the Elect, invisible true church of Christ)'.[51] This representation of worship is endogamous, since membership is exclusively defined, it being the preserve of only those people who knew that they were saved. Elect status was the subject of speculative commentary, and sometimes anguished concern, in the seventeenth century.[52] But it is relatively uncommon in Quaker texts since in general they believed that salvation was universal, the inner light creating a new beginning for people. As the petitioners of Somerset proclaimed, Quaker belief brought people out from sin, 'being in the Light of Christ entered into a new Covenant' (p. 44). However, the Cheshire petitioners and the Berkshire petitioners (independently) quote Acts 3.21 when they assert that Quakers 'witness our Redemption out of the earth, and Election before the World began' (p. 20, p. 39). Since 'election' typically describes an unchangeable state, which makes key the believer's patient endurance, salvation is not an active choice. The rather static determinism of this theology is quite different from Quaker expression, which is generally more fluid. George Fox's sense was that the religion was about opening the spirit; his ideas may even be the antithesis of Calvinist predestination theory.[53] The women petitioners' echo of Calvinism is therefore theologically unexpected.

Other subsidiary meanings, and associative usages of the term 'the elect' suggest, however, its applicability for descriptions of the kinds of mass activism in which the women were participating. Activists with a sense of their own election were able to fuse the personal with the political; their purpose was to establish the

---

[50]Fell tells 'sober minded people' to come out from under the ministry of men 'made by the will of men'. Margaret Fell (et. al), *A Paper Concerning Such as are Made Ministers by the Will of Man* (London: M.W. [Mary Westwood], 1659), p. 1; Martha Simmonds states that the inner light 'will teach thee to be sober minded, and upright in all thy dealings', in *A Lamentation for the Lost Sheep of Israel* (London: Giles Calvert, 1656), p. 5.

[51] A. S. P. Woodhouse, *Puritanism and Liberty; Being the Army Debates 1647-9 from the Clarke Manuscripts with Supplementary Documents*, 2nd edn. (London, Chicago, Dent: University of Chicago Press, 1974), p. 232.

[52] John Bunyan, *Grace Abounding to the Chief of Sinners and The Pilgrim's Progress from this World to that which is to Come*, ed. by Roger Sharrock (London, New York, Toronto: OUP, 1966); also see John Stachniewski, *The Persecutory Imagination: English Protestantism and the Literature of Religious Despair* (Oxford: Clarendon Press, 1991).

[53] Braithwaite, *BQ*, p. 33. Fox believed that 'Christ, who hath the key, and opened the door of light and life unto me [...] He it was that opened to me, when I was shut up, and had not hope, nor faith'. Also see J. William Frost, 'The Dry Bones of Quaker Theology', *Church History*, 39 (1970), 503-523; Geoffrey Nuttall, *The Holy Spirit in Puritan Faith and Experience*, 2nd edn (Chicago and London: The University of Chicago Press, 1992).

'rule of the saints'. Though this is a nebulous and widely used term, and though 'saintly rule' resulted in sectarian movements as diverse as Independency, Baptism and Fifth Monarchism, there is no specific need to etymologise the term since its usefulness seems, actually, to be its openness to interpretation.[54]

Mary Forster, the writer of the preface to *These Several Papers*, prepares her readership for direct action, and this appears to be the principle function of her address. She writes with millenarian tenor when urging Quakers to stand firm in their anti-tithe beliefs, knowing that their god will 'conquer' all opposition; and she encourages them with the phrase 'let us testifie our Saint-ship to the World'.[55] A further belief, the idea that the godly shall have the dominion, emerges in a personal story and historically ambiguous reference:

> Now I live, yet not I, but Christ liveth in me, and the life that I now live is by the faith of the Son of God, *which faith overcometh the world, through which faith the Saints and faithful of old* subdued Kingdoms, wrought righteousnesse.[56]

Forster doesn't need to be historically specific in her reference to '*old* subdued Kingdoms', because it is a trope; by connecting personal salvation to public action, Forster points the way for committed citizens to behave. Believing that political action is necessary in the godly, and arguing that Christ has returned in spirit, Forster asserts that '*surely the Lord is risen, he is risen indeed and hath appeared unto many*'.[57] Her millenarian language figures the imminent arrival of the 'rule of the Saints'. This concept, then, is not exclusively a theological one, though saintship and election might be terms that are theologically over-determined, but a political concept that figures mass-activism.

These Several Papers is an enactment of collective protest against the tithe-tax intending to bring about its abolition, but this approach opposes the signatories to people who had a fixed interest in retaining the state funded ministry. Tithe-taking ministers, of course, believed that the tithe was necessary, but so too did numerous others whose interest in the tithe was equally partisan. The tithe was a major source of revenue not only for the church, but also for many gentry. The rich could buy the rights to exact the tithe, and they could thereby install their preferred minister – to whom they paid a stipend – whilst also impropriating the tithe from their lands. This for them had a double benefit: the preferment of ministers allowed some gentry control of the church, and the revenue from the tithe became another form

---

[54] Bernard Capp, *The Fifth Monarchy Men: A Study in Seventeenth-Century English Millenarianism* (London: Faber, 1972); William Lamont, *Godly Rule: Politics and Religion 1603-60* (London: Macmillan, 1969); A. H. Woolrych, 'The Good Old Cause and the Fall of the Protectorate', *Cambridge Historical Journal*, 13:2 (1957), 133-161. Woolrych quotes John Rogers, *The Plain Case of the Commonweal*, in which he describes the rule of the saints: 'their People, Deputies and Representatives shall be in Power, and rule for their Interests, in the Cause and concernments of them and of the whole People that adhere to the cause, and go on with them joyntly for a Godly Common-wealth' (pp. 141-142).

[55] Mary Forster, 'To the Reader' л ᵛ.

[56] Forster, 'To the Reader', л ʳ.

[57] Forster, 'To the Reader', л ᵛ.

of property right.[58] These factors made the tithe a politically sensitive issue, during the Rump's short parliament. The historian Austin Woolrych refers to the probable factors that influenced the Rump's decision to continue the tithe:

> The Rump nursed few illusions about the very narrow range of public support that it enjoyed, and it knew that the upholders of the established parochial ministry carried more political and social weight than the voluntaryists. It would have been rash indeed to alienate the lay patrons of the livings and the owners of impropriate tithes – not to mention the great majority of the beneficed clergy, with all the influence that they wielded in the pulpit.[59]

The anti-tithers were therefore challenging the rights of people who not only had a financial interest in the retention of the tithe, but also had considerable political influence. Though the radicals tried to argue that the anti-tithe was a popular grievance, others hostile to the abolitionist movement could dispute the people's right to turn the public debate against their betters. William Prynne, the appearance of whose pro-tithe pamphlet coincided precisely with the Rump's debate, cut the sectarians down to size. The Rump, he argues, should not listen to 'poor mechanical persons, of such mean inconsiderable fortunes, estates, condition (without any *Titheable lands, livings, estates*)', and he further contends that the propertyless stand against the *'Nobility, Gentry, Farmers, Citizens, Freemen of the Whole Nation'*.[60] This pamphlet puts the anti-tithe movement in a very ominous light, conflating the abolition movement with revolt. 'Mean' people of lower status, he insinuates, oppose the social hierarchy by contesting the gentry's financial, and political, privilege.

The tithe tax benefited both church and gentry, but because its calculation was complex, it benefited people in different ways. The tithe was levied on three main forms of income: personal, predial and mixed. Predial tithes constituted arable produce, such as fruits and grain, and also extended to livestock, fish, and fowl. The tithe collector was entitled to ten percent of these goods. Other products such as milk, cheese, and wool were classed as 'mixed' tithes, and were deductible at a similar rate. These tithes could be calculated with relative ease: the yield was visible to all the population. The tax on personal possessions caused the collector of tithes more difficulty; being levied on wealth accrued in non-manual occupations, it could be avoided more easily since the profits were more invisible. In the cases where the church owned the rights to take tithes, further complication existed in the division of 'great' and 'small' tithes between rector and vicar. Great tithes – hay, corn and wood, most usually – were taken by the rector, though antagonistic exchanges between rector and vicar over rights were not uncommon. The vicar's rights to small tithes generally extended to predial, mixed, and personal

---

[58] Christopher Hill, *Economic Problems of the Church, from Archbishop Whitgift to the Long Parliament* (Oxford: Clarendon Press, 1968), pp. 63-73; pp. 138-144.
[59] Woolrych, 'Historical Introduction', p. 76.
[60] William Prynne, *Ten Considerable Quaeries Concerning Tithes* (London: Edward Thomas, 1659), pp. 1-2.

income. The collection of the tithe, then, was complex in itself even before we consider the different interests of church and gentry.[61]

Though the tithe was perceived as a tax to maintain the church, it also acted to maintain landed property owners, perhaps to the detriment of churchmen. The gentry seem to have approached the tithe as just another kind of property; income from the tithe was similar to the income from tenants' rents and fines. This means that the beneficiary of the tithe might also be the tithe-payer's landlord; approximately a third of the livings were in lay hands.[62] One example of the many instances in which this was the case must suffice. Sir John Brampton's mother bought a lease of impropriated tithes for £20 a year, and then sub-let the land for £120 whilst also collecting rent worth £30: a profitable enterprise, then, that had little to do with financing the public ministry.[63] Indeed, the gentry's financial power could be seen as contributing to the impoverishment of the church; though some churchmen could live relatively prosperously, others felt the necessity to take on the ministry of several parishes (this is known as 'pluracy') or, even, to have other jobs, in order to boost their income.[64] Indeed, the interests of the gentry could be seen to predominate over the interests of the church; this was certainly the view of Sir Thomas Wilson. His observations on declining church finances are sympathetic towards the clergy: 'their wings are well clipped of late by Coutiers and noblemen', he writes, 'some are quite cut away, both feather, flesh and bone'.[65]

Quakers hit at an already impoverished ministry: in addition to challenging the tithe, Friends also contested the minister's rights to exact other forms of income such as fines and collections. Quakers objected to the payment of varied fees that supplemented the minister's income, taking an approach that was potentially very damaging to the church. The Quaker Thomas Ellwood believed that the anti-tithe protest could bring about the Church's destruction: 'stop the Oyl, the lamp goes out … with-hold Tythes, the Priest gives over'.[66] Anti-clericalism brought about other combative measures, as the women's address 'To the Parliament' reveals. Disputing the clergy's rights to take fees, they complain that ministers exact

> Tythes, Easter reckonings, Gleab-lands, mortuaries, ten groats a grave, 10 or 20 shilling a sermon over the dead, church women for money, sprinkle infants for money, and are made ministers of men, and by men. (p. 66)

Quakers further advocated the avoidance of the fees that benefited individuals, such as Clerk's fees, Communion rates, and fines for non-attendance, as well as the monies raised when a church was in need of repair (p. 54, pp. 65-66). The church's recourse to the law – instigating the fining and imprisonment of Quakers – was

---

[61] Hill, *Economic Problems*, pp. 77-84; p. 103.

[62] Hill, *Economic Problems*, p. 144.

[63] Hill, *Economic Problems*, p. 117.

[64] Hill, *Economic Problems*, pp. 224-241; pp. 216-219.

[65] Sir Thomas Wilson, *The State of England, Camden Miscellany*, xvi. 22-23; Hill, *Economic Problems*, p.1.

[66] Reay, 'Quaker Opposition', p. 108. Ellipsis in original.

bitterly opposed. Women petitioners declare of the clergy that their motivations are 'covetous'; 'this is to save themselves' the Quakers observe, 'and not so much that they care for their Ministry' (pp. 53-54). Quakers opposed the established church through anti-tithe protest, issuing a challenge to the ministers who profited from them, and to the courts that imprisoned them; their approach to the principle was enacted through radical measures.

The tithe was a controversial issue in the seventeenth century, but it has also generated a number of opposing responses since then; scholarly opinion is divided as to the impact of the protest, and also its social effects. The case for radicalism has been advanced by scholars such as Christopher Hill and Brian Manning. Hill shows that anti-tithers could use their protest as a cover for a wider social programme, one that could lead to a re-assessment of diverse issues such as land rights, property, and social inequality.[67] Brian Manning maintains that 'the question of tithes was potentially the most revolutionary issue of the English civil war', arguing that 'it could unite the economic grievances of the mass of small farmers with the religious programme of the separatists'.[68] However, the tithe resists easy interpretation, and because it was at the apex of radical concern, there was considerable variation in the range of responses. The terms of the debates can juxtapose both conservative and radical ideas. Laura Brace therefore encourages scholars to recognise the complexity of the debates:

> The creation of the Commonwealth involved debates about the legitimacy of state interference with private property for taxation, and the formation of a common treasury. Tithes reflected all these concerns and demonstrate the restrictions of trying to produce exhaustive definitions of property that do not account for disputes and imprecisions.[69]

Whatever present-day interpreters make of the issue, however, it is the case that radicals referred frequently to the oppression of tithes. This was a point of common concern across the radical political spectrum, but beyond a shared belief in abolition there are many variations. Gerrard Winstanley's approach perhaps best illustrates the tendency to radical imprecision, since his writing sets up widespread connections. He declares that:

> There shall be no tyrant kings, lords of manors, tithing priests, oppressing lawyers, exacting landlords, nor any such like pricking briar in all this holy mountain of the

---

[67] Hill, *World*, p. 26; p. 63; p. 99. p. 102; p. 140-141.
[68] Brian Manning, *The English People and the English Revolution 1640-1649* (London: Heinemann, 1976), p. 292.
[69] Laura Brace, *The Idea of Property in Seventeenth-Century England: Tithes and the Individual* (Manchester and New York: Manchester UP, 1998), p. 88. For another literary approach to the land, see *Enclosure Acts: Sexuality, Property and Culture in Early Modern England*, ed. by Richard Burt and John Michael Archer (Ithaca and London: Cornell University Press, 1994).

Lord God our righteousness and peace; for the righteous law shall be the rule for every one, and the judge of all men's actions.[70]

Moving from the specific 'tyrant Kings' out to 'all men', Winstanley declares his resistance to varied institutions, named and un-named, that are a thorn in the flesh of the righteous. John Milton, similarly, opened out his discussion of the tithe into constitutional theory; he argued that the commonwealth could only succeed if the church was 'set free from the monopolie of hierlings'.[71] Milton's arguments were framed through his perceptions of the godly commonwealth, whereas the Levellers sought to reform many aspects of state, including the tithe. Usually, the Levellers' response to this issue was brief; they made the abolition of tithes one of their many objectives in petitions that also dealt with wide-ranging concepts such as the franchise, the Norman Yoke, and state censorship.[72]

If the radical import of the tithe issue was its applicability to disputes in the wider political arena, the conservative elements of the arguments concern the radicals' perceived rights to profit from their own enterprise. The radicals can be characterized as an industrious people, whose concerns to live moderately, soberly, and within their own means, create a conscientious approach to production. The clergy are criticised because they do not earn the respect of the sectarians, and their desire for the tithe runs counter to the work ethic because the clergy themselves take money from the sectarians whilst providing no service. Clearly, this approach differs widely from the one favoured by Hill and Manning. Nicholas Morgan suggests that sectarian radicalism has been over-stated:

> In as much as Quakers did present important economic and social objections to tithes, these arguments for the most part reflected fundamental support for the social order rather than opposition to it.[73]

Morgan's ideas remind us that the opposition to the tithe-tax did not automatically represent a desire to subvert the social order; the anti-tithe movement might indeed maintain it. However, the 'imprecisions' in the argument (to use Brace's term) might finally obscure their intentions – radical or conservative.

---

[70] Gerrard Winstanley, 'The Law of Freedom in a Platform, or True Magistracy Restored' (1651), in *Gerrard Winstanley, The Law of Freedom and other Writings*, ed. by Christopher Hill (Harmondsworth, Middlesex: Penguin, 1973), pp. 273-389 (p. 313).

[71] John Milton, 'Considerations', in *Complete Prose Works of John Milton*, ed. by Robert W. Ayers, VII, pp. 273-321, (pp. 275-276).

[72] Lilburne (et. al), 'An Agreement of the People' [10 December 1648], in Woodhouse, *Puritanism and Liberty*, p. 365; Anon [Levellers], 'The Humble Petition' [1648], in *The Leveller Tracts 1647-1653*, ed. by William Haller and Godfrey Davies (Gloucester, Massachusetts: Peter Smith, 1964), pp. 147-155 (p. 153); Brailsford, *The Levellers*, p. 136; pp. 190-191; p. 329; p. 352; p. 380; pp. 389-391; p. 445; p. 447; p. 470; pp. 529-530; p. 559; p. 628; p. 645; p. 648.

[73] Nicholas Morgan, *Lancashire Quakers and the Establishment 1760-1830* (Halifax, England: Ryburn Publishing, 1993), p. 172.

The women's petition against tithes, *These Several Papers*, manifests the contradiction between radicalism and conservatism, perhaps explaining the possible responses, so different in emphasis, between scholars such as Hill, Manning and Morgan. In *These Several Papers*, radical opposition to the clergy is evident, and the disestablishment of the state church intended, but so too, as we shall see, were impropriators appeased.

Radical arguments in *These Several Papers* are generated in response to clerical tithe taking. The ministers' financial plight receives little sympathy, since the Quakers were voluntarists, in common with numerous other sectarians. The state beneficed clergy, they argue, could not support themselves if it were not for the compulsory tax. Quakers think that the compulsory element is revealing; people 'have not so much love to their Minister as to maintain them themselves', and they therefore advise the people to 'give them what you will give of your own Freely' (p. 53, p. 63). The practice of voluntary payments operated well in non-Anglican churches, where commitment was a choice: groups such as Baptists and Independents organised their finance through voluntary funds, rather than coercion.[74] But the religious commitment of the Anglican masses was less dependable; indeed, they are sometimes believed to have been an ungodly lot.[75] Voluntarism was less of an option for the Church of England, because it was a catchall for the many and did not operate at the small, congregational level. Radicals such as Quakers had little sympathy, then, for the Church of England since Friends raised their own funds themselves. Voluntarism is a no compromise position; it offers no sympathy to the beneficed clergy. However, the sectarians' other enemies, the impropriators, elicit a more cautious response. Considerable pains are taken to defuse the issue of impropriation.

The arguments recommend that the landed gentry receive compensation for their financial investment in tithes. In every case, the writers of *These Several Papers* propose to pay back money to the owners of impropriated tithes. Gentry 'investment' is to be returned, the lands are to be bought back, and wealthy laymen are thereby to be recompensed from the 'common' wealth. One of the addresses 'to the Parliament' brings together the range of fiscal proposals referred to in less detail elsewhere in the petition. Their proposals entail selling

> All the Gleab-lands, and Abbey Lands, and Monasteries, and Nunneries, and Kings rents, and his houses, and the bells to pay the Impropriators, who have bought their Tythes of Kings, let their rents and parks be sold to pay them again, and let the Earth be restored again to its place, and they that have bought them of Colledges [sic], let the Gleab-lands be sold to pay them, and so let the Earth be redeemed. (p. 59)

---

[74] On Baptists, see Brace, p. 32; on Independents see R. Tudur Jones, *Congregationalism in England 1662-1962* (London: Independent Press: 1962), pp. 29-30.
[75] Patrick Collinson, *The Religion of Protestants: The Church in English Society 1559-1629* (Oxford: Clarendon Press, 1982), pp. 189-194; Keith Wrightson, *English Society 1580-1680* (London: Hutchinson, 1982), pp. 204-205; Keith Thomas, *Religion and the Decline of Magic* (repr. London and New York: Penguin, 1991) pp. 191-194.

They state that funds can be raised to cover the return of the investment: lands can be sold, in order that the impropriator does not go without. The women's approach is not atypical of Quaker appeasement, which most usually concerns itself with devising means of compensation, in recognition, seemingly, of the impropriator's political clout.[76] There is, however, one notable aberrant: George Fox calls impropriators 'robbers'.[77]

The notion of popular power is compromised by the reliance of the parliament on the gentry, whose political influence had remained a distinct feature in the state, despite the political revolution of 1649. The pro-monarchist gentry, despite having their land sequestrated for their military role in the civil wars, gradually increased their influence during the Commonwealth period. Gentry of all persuasions had power in their county constituencies, and on the national level, though their influence seems to have fluctuated. As MPs in Westminster, taking their places in a Commons that was only notionally different from earlier parliaments, they had national status; as JPs, they had local status. The social composition of these two important institutions changed only slightly, during the Commonwealth period.[78] The failure of the anti-tithe movement is arguably as good a mark as any of the continued influence of the impropriating gentry.[79]

The anti-tithe dispute was therefore conducted within complex historical and discursive paradigms. Radical rhetoric can be found alongside other, more conservative, discourses negotiating the structured nature of inequality: humble petitioners try to enact change whilst recognising that they face considerable

---

[76] Anthony Pearson, *The Great Case of Tithes*, p. 30. He states that impropriators should receive compensation 'seeing it was the state that sold them, and that the whole nation benefit from their moneys'.

[77] George Fox, *An Answer to Doctor Burgess his Book* (London: Thomas Simmonds, 1659), p. 20. He observes to Burgess that 'thou hast made all the impropriators robbers, and the Pope, and all the Chief Magistrates, and Kings that take the tenths, robbers, and the great men that takes Tythes, robbers'. Mentioned in Moore, 'The Faith', pp. 212-213.

[78] See Austin Woolrych, *Commonwealth to Protectorate* (Oxford: Clarendon Press, 1982), pp. 165-193. This chapter, dealing with 'The Quality of the House', shows that even the most plebeian parliament (supposedly), the 'Barebones', was comprised largely of men who held power prior to the revolution (pp. 169-174). See also Derek Hirst, 'Concord and Discord in Richard Cromwell's House of Commons', *English Historical Review*, 103 (1988), 339-358. Hirst argues that the parliament functioned in much the same ways as earlier parliaments, particularly through their attempts to create a sense of unity. J. S. Morrill, *Cheshire 1630-1660: County Government and Society During the English Revolution* (London: OUP, 1974), chapter 6, pp. 223-253. Morrill shows that 9 of the 30 men who served on the benches as JPs were from families who served before the revolution (p. 224). However, despite the continued influence of men of traditional social prestige, their authority was undermined during the rule of the major generals (p. 233; p. 252). Cheshire, of course, was also the site of the Royalist rising instigated by Sir George Booth.

[79] See also Kevin Sharpe, '"An Image Doting Rabble": The Failure of Republican Culture in Seventeenth-Century England', in *Refiguring Revolutions: Aesthetics and Politics from the English Revolution to the Romantic Period*, ed. by Kevin Sharpe and Steven N. Zwicker (Berkeley, Los Angeles and London: University of California Press, 1988), pp. 25-56.

opposition from the preservers of the social order. The arguments, then, are strategic.

The Tithe: A Tax on Families

What about the gender order?[80] Women petitioners take an issue of economic concern into the public sphere, seemingly into arguments beyond the compass of women's domestic experience. The tithe is an issue of state interest, because the effects of abolition would have had an impact on ministers and the rich. Protestors establish that petitioning on issues of state is within their godly remit, and their rights as sovereign people. However, women's citizenship is compromised by the fact that, as a disenfranchised sector of the population, they were of dependent status. Women petitioners sometimes were rebuked by Parliament in terms that recalled the idea that women belonged in the domestic sphere. Indeed, Parliament once admonished Leveller women for their intransigence; they 'bad them to goe home and meddle with their House-keeping'.[81] Addresses to Leveller women by patriarchally minded parliamentarians show how easily women's action could be denigrated. On the other hand, Ann Hughes has argued that 'gender roles and household relationships [...] were a fundamental part of the political identity offered to the readers of Leveller literature'; her important study prompts re-evaluation of the significance of familial relationships.[82] We will see that in Quaker writing, too, women's particularly domestic concerns could be used to their advantage.

The Quaker anti-tithe protest was represented in terms of its effects on economic prosperity; financially, the hardship of tithe suffering impacted on the family, which was the main economic unit. Hughes has shown that Leveller writings emotively depict the household under threat of disintegration, due to the absence of the male breadwinner during periods of imprisonment. Likewise, in *These Several Papers,* Quaker opposition to the tithe is shown to affect the family unit. Rural families are particularly prominent, their suffering being detailed in numerous accounts as a matter of particular comment. Agricultural workers may

---

[80] The ensuing argument is greatly influenced by Ann Hughes's work. See 'Gender politics in Leveller literature', in *Political Culture and Cultural Politics in Early Modern England: Essays Presented to David Underdown*, ed. by Susan D. Amussen and Mark A Kishlansky (Manchester: MUP, 1995), pp. 162-188.

[81] *Mercurius Pragmaticus*, 24 April – 1 May 1649, no. 52, no page number – the quotation is five pages into the newspaper [E 552 (16)]. Patricia Higgins cites a similar response in her essay on the Leveller women: 'The Reaction of Women, with Special Reference to Women Petitioners', in *Politics, Religion and the English Civil War*, ed. by Brian Manning (London: Edward Arnold, 1973), pp. 179-222 (p. 203). Also see Ellen A. McArthur, 'Women Petitioners and the Long Parliament', *English Historical Review*, 24 (1909), 698-709; Anne Marie McEntee '"The [Un]Civill-Sisterhood of Oranges and Lemons": Female Petitioners and Demonstrators, 1642-53', *Prose Studies*, 14:3 (1991), 92-111. There are no such sources for the Quaker women's protest since Commons Journals for the Rump do not exist.

[82] Hughes, 'Gender and Politics', p. 167.

have suffered severely, since the assessment of taxable goods was easiest to levy on visible produce; taxes seem to have fallen disproportionately on rural inhabitants.[83] The Quaker Anthony Pearson's complaint backs this up: he contends that, 'the rich pay little, and the poor husbandman bears the burden'.[84] Though the financial plight of the small landowner probably was particularly severe, Pearson's reference to the 'poor husbandman' releases more than an economic judgement. His sympathy reflects the wholesome nature of agricultural work, and possible emotional responses to the land. Accordingly, the rural worker's labours are shown to be impeded; consequently the tithe taker's actions disrupt agricultural life, and this impacts both on the man who provides the nation with bread,[85] and his family:

> Did but the magistrate see what havock is made in the north, what driving out of oxen out of the plow, the cows from poor and indigent children, what carting of pots and kettles, yea, and fetching the very clothes off poor people's beds, he would be ashamed of such justices.[86]

Pearson's sympathy moves out from the male breadwinner, to the most piteous and innocent sufferers – children. He shows that all suffer on behalf of the tithe protest; the goods he lists notably invoke the domestic sphere in addition to the economic.

It is perhaps unsurprising, therefore, that in *These Several Papers* the petitioners of some rural areas – Dorset, Yorkshire and the cathedral town of Durham – approach the tithe with statements that reflect very practical fiscal concerns. In their short statement, the Durham Quakers refer to the 'hard hearted tax-masters' who collect tithes, and the Dorset women agree that the priests 'serve not the Lord Jesus, but their own bellies' (p. 29, p. 68). These complaints focus on the detrimental effect of the tithe, by hitting at the beneficiaries; other writers, though, demonstrate the impact of the tithe protest on them directly. Yorkshire women document the upset in the home; indignantly, they blame the priest for disrupting domestic harmony by 'making spoil (and waste) of other goods, to the utter undoing of them and their families' (p. 25). Surely, the family is here mentioned in order to invoke sympathy, much as the suffering of children operates piteously in Pearson's account, and the weakness of women invokes pathos in prison narratives.[87]

Rural women represent financial hardship by announcing its direct impact upon family coffers. The Gloucester Quakers' detailed response, like Pearson's, gives the financial suffering a particularly rural colouring, with its itemisation of the appropriation of horses, oxen, and plough gear:

---

[83] Hill, *Economic Problems*, pp. 84-92, pp. 106-108.

[84] Pearson, *The Great Case of Tithes*, p. 35.

[85] For a similarly romanticised idea of the land see *A Copie of a Paper*, where the tithe is said to be the means by which 'the poor are oppressed who are labouring in the ground and tilling the earth for bread, the staffe and stay of the Nation' (p. 5).

[86] Pearson, *The Great Case of Tithes*, p. 25.

[87] For the pathos in the representation of women's physical weakness see chapter 2.

> How do you who are the heads of the Nation expect we should pay your taxes, when you suffer the Priests to take away our goods [...] If the Priest come and pretend 151 [pounds] Tythes they will take a hundred pounds [...] and drive away our horses and our oxen, and plough geer, and take ten times as much as the value [...] judge in yourselves, and how in this case we are like to pay your taxes. (pp. 51-52)

This is subtly more engaged than the protests from Yorkshire, Dorset and Durham. Unlike the Yorkshire petitioners, who complain of the spoil made to 'their' families, the Gloucestershire women write directly of hardship falling on 'us' and 'ours'. More intriguingly still, the women mischievously represent themselves as taxable citizens. The feminised 'we' of discourse draws parliament's attention to the difficulties they experience as taxpayers, which is possibly a veiled attempt to defend the withholding of parliamentary taxes. They use the opposition between ecclesiastical taxation and state taxation to drive a wedge between Commons and clergy.

The consideration of the effects of taxation on the family is more extensive than the tithe issue; paying taxes was compulsory, but the women believe that more is at stake – loyalty. The London women, like those of Gloucester, write as though the tax falls to their charge, thereby creating a rhetorically authoritative position from which to discuss their strained allegiance to parliament:

> How do you who are the heads of the Nation expect that we should pay taxes when the Priests takes our Friends goods, and plunders them whom he doth no work for? and some of our friends who have been for the Parliament ever since the beginning of the late Wars, have suffered more by these Priests, then by the Plundering Cavaliers. (p. 54)

Financially speaking, the Quakers are arguing that they are worse off during the Commonwealth than were in the civil wars, because parliament's support of ecclesiastical taxation is more crippling. The comparison is significant. Cavaliers' plunder of local hospitality during the war was particularly infamous, so the conflation of parliament with monarchy reflects badly on the new government.[88] Though the women criticise the parliament, they use this comparison pointedly: it reminds the Westminster MPs that many Quakers were formerly commonwealthsmen. The matter of taking sides is merely alluded to here, whereas greater detail is given to it in the Dorset petition. They emotively argue that parliament is 'worse than the Ecclesiastical Courts [...] and yet profess Liberty of Conscience' (p. 68). Again, the conflation of two different interest groups demonstrably undermines the righteous position of commonwealth MPs. Clergy and Parliament are opposed in this account, but the Berkshire women show them working in tandem. They observe that 'The Priests that sues our Friends in the Courts for Tithes, said, They could not pay the Protector his Tenths, who took the Tenth of the Tenths, and that was their excuse' (p. 38). A portion of 'our Friends'' tithe money was entailed to Cromwell during his Protectorate, and the tithe

---

[88] I. Roy, 'England Turned Germany: The Aftermath of the Civil War in its European Context', *Transactions of the Royal Historical Society*, 28 (1978), 172-244.

collector used this argument to justify his charge. The women's loyalty to successive parliaments is implicitly established in *These Several Papers*, thereby creating a sense of their perception of the duties of public citizens. Hughes has shown that Levellers adopted a similar approach.

The women might, of course, be stretching a point, against a possible commonsense reading of this as rhetorical prose: at the level of state economics, they were not the main taxpayers.[89] We must therefore note that it is possible to register the terms of the tithe debate as masculine, unlike the inclusive comments discussed earlier. The Quaker Anthony Pearson, for instance, showed the law's effects by using masculine pronouns, contradicting his sense that suffering is a family affair: 'the law requires every man to set out the tenth and so makes him a voluntary agent in that, against which his conscience testifies'.[90] Corroborating this masculinist observation is his sense that the tithe ranges 'man and man', which shows that Pearson figures the tithe issue as principally affecting patriarchs.[91] In this text, women only suffer by the tithe vicariously.

For male householders, anti-tithe protest brings their responsibilities in the domestic sphere into focus; they chose to follow their consciences when they suffer for tithes, thus potentially depriving married women of a wage earner. This dilemma is considered in the Quaker petition to parliament, 27 June, wherein the 'ruine of families' is discussed. The male Quakers show that they put their conscience first, setting out their hardships to demonstrate their public commitment:

> Some of us suffering in the body, but moneths, and yeares Imprisonments, and some till death: Others in our estates by chargable suits, synes, judgments and unreasonable distresses, to the ruine of families, and [have] been made the subjects of almost all manner of Cruelty and injustice; we have stood single and in the integrity of our hearts been preserved from worldly compliance; waiting for the good day, that the Lord would remove the hand of the oppressor.[92]

Here, the family is not defended against 'ruine' as in other accounts, but is ruined in the name of Quaker testimony. Putting the Quaker movement before the domestic unit, by relinquishing worldly goods, the male householder demonstrates his righteous task. Here again, there are parallels to the Leveller approach, as identified by Hughes.

Ideologically speaking, god is the protecting patriarch who cares for his Quaker family disrupted by the tithe protest; however, practically speaking this role was fulfilled by Quaker charity. Many Quakers claim to give up their temporal concerns, casting their care on god, when devoting themselves to the movement.

---

[89] J. V. Beckett, 'Land Tax or Excise: The Levying of Taxation in Seventeenth and Eighteenth-Century England', *English Historical Review*, 395 (1985), 285-308; Martyn Bennett, *The Civil Wars in Britain and Ireland, 1638-1651* (Oxford and Cambridge, Massachusetts: Blackwell, 1997), pp. 185-187, p. 197.

[90] Anthony Pearson, *The Great Case of Tithes*, p. 24.

[91] Pearson, *The Great Case of Tithes*, p. 36.

[92] *A Copie of a Paper*, p. 3.

Godly men and women, particularly those called to the ministry, often forsook the family in order to preach. James Nayler, for instance, confided that he rejoiced upon hearing a voice telling him to *'Get thee out from thy Kindred and from thy Fathers house'*.[93] Preachers and prisoners believed that selflessness was one of the signs of their commitment; their willingness to put god before family is represented, commonly, as a sacrifice. However, once the conjugal unit has been displaced in terms of its significance, god becomes the protecting father or husband. The writer of the preface to *These Several Papers*, Mary Forster, wrote in 1669 that people 'of low estate [...] having many depending on thee' had only to trust in god, 'and assuredly thee and thine shall be fed'.[94] A widow by this time, she indicates that god stands in place of father and husband. She also, however, knew that Quaker charity protected those in the household of faith.[95] Quaker efforts to care for their poor, formalized in the later period, are also evident in the earlier perception that unity meant compassion towards all. Richard Hubberthorne's anti-tithe tract demonstrates Quaker charity, perhaps anticipating later, more formal, kinds of care. He observes: 'if any of us have of this Worlds good, & see our Brother stand up in need, & shuts up the bowels of compassion from him, the love of God doth not dwell in us'.[96] Hubberthorne conflates the 'love of God' with the love and charity between Quaker brothers.

The metaphorical depiction of the Quakers as an extended family of worshippers is based on idealisation (both of the movement, and of the family), and thereby constructs a misleading idea of harmony. Religious belief did not always establish conjugal accord; on the contrary, it might exacerbate differences between people. Disharmony is most clearly evident in cases where religion disrupts the usual patriarchal family unit. Gender relations within the family are supposedly organised by the idea that the male is dominant; but conjugal stability was disrupted if the woman's religious beliefs differed from her husband's. In these cases, Patricia Crawford notes, loyalty to the sect displaces loyalty to the patriarch.[97] Probably the clearest, because the most combative, account of this comes from beyond the Quaker movement. Anne Wentworth, a Baptist, believed that she was required by god to 'absent myself from my earthly husband in obedience to my heavenly bride-groom'.[98] The priority of religious worship was also shared by Quakers. In one instance, disobedience to the patriarch was specifically endorsed – Jane Adams was advised to attend Quaker meetings against

---

[93] James Nayler in George Fox, *Sauls Errand to Damascus* (London: Giles Calvert, 1653), p. 30.

[94] Mary Forster, 'A Few Words of Encouragement', in *A Declaration of the Bountifull Loving Kindness of the Lord, Manifested in his Hand-Maid Mary Harris* (n.pl.: n. pr., 1669), pp. 8-11 (p. 10).

[95] On Quaker charity, see Braithwaite, *SPQ*, pp. 251-289.

[96] Hubberthorne, *The Real Cause*, p. 4.

[97] Patricia Crawford, *Women and Religion in England 1500-1720* (London and New York: Routledge, 1993), p. 150, p. 152.

[98] Anne Wentworth, 'A Vindication', in *Her Own Life*, ed. by Elspeth Graham (et al.) (repr. London and New York: Routledge, 1992), p. 187.

the wishes of her husband.[99] Other cases show the possible strain on conjugal relations. George Fox was protected from stoning by James Lancaster, but the person doing the stoning was Lancaster's wife; in another instance, Fox believed that god punished a woman who married outside the movement, and therefore without Fox's consent.[100] Because most versions of the family are idealised in Quaker writing, few examples of this kind remain as evidence of the strain placed on the family by Quaker group membership. We will examine conjugal relations more thoroughly in the final chapter.

Consideration of the economy of the family is important to our understanding of Quaker anti-tithe protest, since just as the notion of the idealized patriarchal family makes religious differences between spouses invisible, so too does the notion of the male bread-winner make women's economic role obscure. Historians show that the experience of ordinary women would make them aware of their economic role. Many women worked, albeit at lesser rates of pay than men, and in more seasonal forms of occupation, but they worked, nevertheless, in order to support the family. They were not economic dependants, save perhaps during some stages of childbearing, and indeed the rates of employment amongst women of child rearing age were high.[101] This is not because they worked only alongside their husbands (this was Alice Clark's contention); they were also in female jobs. In both contexts, there was probably gendered division of labour.[102] Arguably, women did have a direct economic interest in the tithe debate.

Poor women had a particular reason to contest the tithe. The tax, in its original form, was intended to provide support in the temporal sphere: in the biblical accounts, tithe-payments made provision not only for the priest, but also for poor families. Biblical scholars, such as John Selden, discussed the precedents for the tithe by examining the charitable angle; his 1618 text was a major influence on later writers, including the Quaker Anthony Pearson.[103] Selden tried to calculate how the tithe would have been levelled during the Levitical priesthood and the early apostolic church. Arguing that Bible sources demonstrate that provision for

---

[99] Christopher Durston, *The Family in the English Revolution* (Oxford and New York: Basil Blackwell, 1989), pp. 96-97.

[100] On the stoning of Fox, see Mabel Brailsford, *Quaker Women 1650-1690* (London: Duckworth, 1915), p. 141; on Fox's criticism of the woman see George Fox, *The Journal*, ed. by Nigel Smith (London: Penguin, 1998), p. 174; also see Patricia Crawford, *Women and Religion*, pp. 147-152.

[101] See Peter Earle, 'The Female Labour Market in London in the Late Seventeenth and Early Eighteenth Centuries', *Economic History Review*, 42:3 (1989), 328-353 (p. 338).

[102] Pamela Sharpe, 'Literally Spinsters: a New Interpretation of the Local Economy and Development in Colyton in the Seventeenth and Eighteenth Centuries', *Economic History Review*, 44:1 (1991), 46-65; Stevi Jackson, 'Towards a Historical Sociology of Housework: A Materialist Feminist Analysis', *Women's Studies International Forum*, 15:2 (1992), 153-172; Alice Clark, *Working Life of Women in the Seventeenth Century*, 2nd edn (London, Boston and Henley: Routledge and Kegan Paul, 1982), also see Amy Erickson's introduction to the 1992 edition of Clark's *Working Life* (pp. vii-xlii).

[103] John Selden, *History of Tythes* (n. pl.: n. pr., 1618); Pearson, *The Great Case of Tithes*, p. 10.

the needy was levelled once every three years, he concluded that this replaced other charges, rather than being an addition.[104] Selden therefore endorsed the charitable function of the tithe-tax; this is not an academic argument, since many people then associated clericalism with luxury and greed.[105] The vulnerable groups believed to be most needing of charity were widows, fatherless and the poor. The Quaker women reflect this aspect in their consideration of the tithe. Cheshire women, for instance, argue that 'the Law made provision for Levi and for all the strangers, fatherless and Widows, that there need not be a beggar in *Israel*' (p. 19); Gloucestershire women represent the priesthood as an ever open mouth that 'swallowes down all; (mark) the fatherless part, the widdowes [sic] part, and the strangers part, and so are worse than the Jews' (p. 51). The church's neglect of charity is represented as one explanation of the Quakers' refusal to pay.

Concern over 'the widow's part' introduces economic and ideological issues; widows were often numbered amongst the poor, but they were also one of the most autonomous sectors of the female population. The economic autonomy of widows has been depicted by some scholars. Barbara Todd argues that rates of re-marriage (which declined in the later seventeenth century) illustrate economic and cultural factors.[106] Since fewer women re-married in post-civil war Britain than earlier periods, Todd believes that the personal benefits of widowhood had improved. At any one time, only a third of the adult female population was likely to be married; this means that the status of widows is significant.[107] Amy Erickson, whose economic study devotes much attention to bereaved women, examines the transfer of property by examining wills by husbands, and by widows.[108] The conditions were, of course, very varied. Broadly speaking, however, Erickson's study gives cause to see widowhood as securing the return of property to women. The woman's 'portion' (the more common name for dowry) was usually returned to her after the death of the spouse, and her legal entitlement (to only a third of the revenue from his estate) was often exceeded.[109] This meant that, even considering the male partner's debts, women were relatively well provided for under the legal

---

[104] John Selden, *History of Tithes*, pp. 14-17.

[105] See, for instance John Milton, 'Lycidas', in John Milton, *The Complete Poems*, ed. by John Leonard (London: Penguin, 1998), pp. 41-46 (ll. 100-131). For critical accounts of this poem see, for instance, Christopher Hill, 'Lycidas', in *Milton and the English Revolution* (London: Faber and Faber, 1977), pp. 49-52; David Norbrook, *Poetry and Politics in the English Renaissance* (London: Routledge: 1984), pp. 235-285. Also see John Milton, 'Considerations', p. 319; he argues that churchmen were 'fed at the publick cost, good for nothing els [sic] but what was good for nothing, they soon grew idle: that idleness with fullness of bread begat pride and perpetual contention with thir [sic] feeders the despis'd laitie'.

[106] Barbara J. Todd, 'The Remarrying Widow: A Stereotype Reconsidered', in *Women in English Society 1500-1800*, ed. by Mary Prior (London and New York: Methuen, 1985), pp. 54-92.

[107] Amy Erickson, *Women and Property in Early Modern England* (London and New York: Routledge, 1993), p. 100.

[108] Erickson, pp. 153-222.

[109] Erickson, on 'portions' see pp. 79-97; on the return of portions see p. 162, p. 181.

entitlements established in the husband's will. Even despite this, however, bereaved women were likely to have been one of the poorest sectors of seventeenth-century society.[110]

These Several Papers reflects the Quaker concern to protect widows, probably the sector of the female population who were the most vulnerable to the tithe-tax, and this concern is reflected in sufferings tracts more widely. Widows become the head of the household, and because they were the taxable citizens, they show up in the writing of anti-tithe persecution more than do their married co-religionists.[111] Widow Ball, for instance, was imprisoned for nine weeks for her anti-tithe testimony.[112] Others' marital status cannot be identified by the texts alone.[113] However, when married women appear in the tithe sufferings, their conjugal relation might be described. In one case, a woman arrested alongside her husband was threatened with violence. Her anti-tithe stance provoked a particularly hostile response in the priest, who held a pike to her breast, and threatened to 'run her through for denying the Tithe'.[114] The author, Francis Gawler, depicts this event with particular pathos, invoking the idea of women's physical weakness; he also perhaps implicitly shows her strength since she acted as a good wife by standing alongside her husband.

Women's role in the family economy is therefore the single most significant element influencing their response to the tithe. Whether employing the idea of family membership, by implicitly indicating that their anti-tithe protest supports the domestic unit, or whether, as widows, they were directly liable, women's protest maintains the sanctity of the home from outside threat. Their position on tithe-resistance maintains the status within the family's economic unit, and it does so by attacking the fundamental claims of church and state for maintenance.

The implication is that the church and state do not care for families, and so represent the worst kind of behaviour. The family is undermined, and the beneficiaries of the tithe are represented as greedy, self-interested men. Dorset petitioners in *These Several Papers* show parliament's misplaced allegiance in

---

[110] Erickson, p. 209; Erickson contends that the median amount left from the husband's estate (which equals the residual wealth) was £33 (p. 222).

[111] Widow Milner and Widow Royle are represented in one text (Francis Howgill, *Caine's Bloudy Race*, London: Thomas Simmonds, 1657, p. 49, p. 51); widow Joan Reed, in another (Francis Gawler, *A Record of Some Persecutions [. . .] in South-Wales*, London: Thomas Simmonds, 1659, p. 20); widow Margaret Slee, widow Head, widow Backbarrow, and widow Preslman appear in another (Gervase Benson, *The Cry of the Oppressed*, London: Giles Calvert, 1656, p. 2, p. 9, p. 10, p. 11).

[112] Burrough, *A Declaration of the Present Sufferings* (London: Thomas Simmonds, 1659) p. 6.

[113] Sisly Cleaton, Ann Janney, Ellin Boulton (Howgill, *Caine's Bloudy Race*, p. 47, p. 50, p. 51), Ellin Emerson, Valantine Jonson, Alice Wilson, Annas Tarne, Janet Dickenson and Alice Woodhead (Benson, *The Cry*, p. 7, p. 18, p. 23, p. 23, pp. 23-24), Loveday Hambly (Burrough, *A Declaration*, p. 5). Hambly was probably a widow, see L. V. Hodgkin, *A Quaker Saint of Cornwall: Loveday Hambly and her Guests* (London and New York: Longmans, 1927).

[114] Francis Gawler, *A Record of Some Persecutions*, p. 20.

voting for the tithe. This satisfies the wrong economic interests; according to their account, priests 'lie begging' with their petitions at parliament's door (p. 68). Whereas the needs of the Quaker family are shown to be real, the churchmen's financial arguments are dubious. Quaker women suggest this by paralleling churchmen to Jews, thereby invoking comparison to one of the century's scapegoats.[115] Cheshire women, for instance, state that priests are 'worse even than the Jews' and once more observe that 'the Levitical priesthood took care of widows and the fatherless' (p. 21). The women's comparison works by 'othering' Jewish people, in a similar way that later comparison of priests to 'the Heathen as they make their Powoughs' inserts an 'exotic' dimension (p. 66). Such 'othering' conflates 'anti-Christian' behaviour with English churchmen, to negative effect. Possibly, this parallelism also reflects badly on the parliament that voted in the 'anti-Christian' tax.[116]

Female Subjectivity

Women whose status as public citizens arises out of their familial role address parliament, but they also consider how their gender might affect the reception of the petition. Their belief that women belong to the private sphere (that is not really private) is what generates the need to explain women's actions. Despite the fact that the women seem able to create roles for themselves in the Quaker community that stress collective identities (as mothers, as wives) their gender also, conversely, creates the need to explain their public actions. It seems 'strange' that they appear in this demonstration, as preface writer Mary Forster indicates:

> It may seem strange to some that women should appear in so publick a manner, in a matter of so great concernment as this of Tithes, and that we should also bring in our testimony even as our brethren against that Anti-christian law and oppression of Tithes, by which so many of the Servants of the Lord have suffered in filthy holes and

---

[115] For an accessible and easily available overview see Jay L. Halio, 'Introduction', in William Shakespeare, *The Merchant of Venice*, ed. by Jay L. Halio (Oxford: Clarendon Press, 1993), pp. 83. For a the seventeenth-century approach to the conversion of the Jews, see Nabil I. Matar, 'George Herbert, Henry Vaughan, and the Conversion of the Jews', *SEL*, 30:1 (1990), 79-92; Judith Gardiner, 'Margaret Fell Fox and Feminist Literary History: A "Mother in Israel" Calls to the Jews', *Prose Studies*, 17:3 (1994), 42-56.

[116] Biblical passages to support the payment of tithes are largely taken from the Old Testament; some, however, are taken as precedents of the Christian church. The main passages on the Levitical priesthood are in Numbers 18. In Hebrews 7, Abraham is said to have given Melchisadec a tenth of his goods (Hebrews 7:1). Because Melchisadec was seen as a Christ-like figure, some pro-tithers claimed justification for the tithe (Hebrews 7:21; Psalms 110:4). The sections dealing with these biblical arguments in *These Several Papers* are 'To the Parliament', pp. 1-6, 'We who are the Seed', p. 7, and Cheshire, pp. 18-21. Milton also refers to these passages in 'Considerations', p. 286. He says that 'the true Melchisadec is in us, and we in him who can pay to none greater'.

dungeons until death; But let such know, that this is the work of the Lord at this day, even by weak means to bring to pass his mighty work in the earth.[117]

Though Forster recognises that women's action is 'strange', her deference might be seen as a rhetorical manoeuvre. One recent critic, though writing in relation to the Levellers, interprets this kind of language as rhetorical strategy: it marks the women's familiarity with the petitioning process, since it employs conventional tropes knowingly.[118] In similar fashion, the Quaker Mary Forster illustrates customary deference, before listing good reasons for godly women to take action.

Female petitioners knowingly invoke particular stereotypes of women's secondary status when they defend their actions. Central to the Quaker rhetoric is the idea that their protest is auxiliary: Mary Forster sanctions her protest by claiming that it is compatible with the actions of Quaker 'brethren'. The Quaker women of Buckinghamshire, likewise, use a concept of the shared nature of Quaker protest, thus explaining the political appearance of 'a remnant of the Lords hand-maids in *Buckingham-shire*' (p. 47). They represent themselves in a manner that reveals several associatively female characteristics, and several features (now familiar to us) that invoke the discourse of Quaker unity. They argue:

Truly wee cannot, whose hearts are upright in the Lord, but joyn our testimony with our Brethren, against the unjust Oppression of Tythes; and have with one consent our Hands set, in the Power of God, to stand in the time of Tryal, witness for the Lord God against the same. (p. 47)

Acting by 'one consent', they show that Quaker unity enables them to behave both righteously and emotionally. This is a depiction of pious femininity, one made still greater by the sense that they employ their collective stance in support of a policy earlier advanced by male co-religionists.

Though deference is necessary in some contexts, godly women claim that spiritual authority makes them equal to the work of petitioning.[119] In *These Several Papers*, Mary Forster's spiritual justification comes directly from the Bible, where the 'foolish' are compelled to upbraid the ungodly 'wise' (1 Cor. 1:25-7). Quaker women also depict themselves as the brides of Christ, using the vision of the new

---

[117] Mary Forster, 'To the Reader' л ʳ. Original is in italics.

[118] Ann Marie McEntee, "'The [Un]Civill-Sisterhood', p. 106.

[119] Other than the Quaker women's petition, numerous women argued that God's will made them address parliament. Women such as Margaret Fell and Dorothy White wrote addresses specifically to lobby the groups in power during 1659: Margaret Fell, *To the General Council, and Officers of the Army* (London: Thomas Simmonds, 1659); Dorothy White, *This is to be Delivered to the Councellors* (London: Thomas Simmonds, 1659). Mary Howgill addressed Cromwell in an earlier period, informing the Protector that his position was 'most lamentable' (p. 1): *A Remarkable Letter of Mary Howgill to Oliver Cromwell* (London: n. pr., 1657). Petitioning on behalf of God, Quaker women found ways to address their betters; for the anti-tithe petitioner Grace Barwick this meant travelling to present her message 'a hundred and fifty miles in obedience to the Lord' (p. 1): *To all the Present Rulers* (n. pl.: Mary Westwood, 1659).

Jerusalem in Revelation 21:2 to invoke the idea that the bride prepares herself for her husband:

> The Saints shall have victory, the Lamb, the Bride is known again, preparing for her husbands coming out of the wilderness, and the daughters of Abraham are meeting of her. (p. 39)

Feminised language serves a dual focus, since it both figures women's godliness (as daughters and wives) and also makes the church itself a bride. At the level of metaphor the tithe issue is equated with women's godly testimony.

However, it is possible that the auxiliary status of women informed the production of *These Several Papers*. George Fox, who was perhaps the instigator of the petition, forcibly retained the idea that women's protest was supplementary. Justifying their public action through spiritual and the secular arguments, Fox's letter validates women's petitioning by signifying that he has made their protest possible:

> For all women friends to sett their hands ag^t Tythes they may freely, as they are moved, and doe not quench the spirit of the Lord in any; for the women with Truth feeles the weight as well as the men, for the seed of God in the women beares witness ag^t Tythes in the Priest and Pope the authour of them, and sufferers in Prisons and are summoned by up into Courts, soe that is good which beareth the testimony ag^t them [tithes] and is to be received, and set a top of the authors of the holders of them up. And soe if all the women in England send their hands ag^t Tythes I shall send them by women to parliamt [sic] for many women have sent up their names, and some have not, but have been stopped. Therefore that all may send their names that be free with speed to London.[120]

This is ideologically significant since it shows that male approbation for the women's petition was granted; however, it also gives an impression of male agency and male priority in the tithe issue. The publication of the petition, by a female publisher, and with 'above seven thousand names' surely, though, makes *These Several Papers* one of the most powerful demonstrations of women's public action in all seventeenth-century writing.

These Several Papers demonstrates extensive commitment to the anti-tithe protest, creating a female response to an important issue of state, against and perhaps because of common cultural beliefs that their actions were supplementary. Though these arguments are caught up in stereotypical ways of figuring women's auxiliary status, the individualised, feminine, subject position is created alongside other, more collective, identities. In contrast to the individualised subject-position created by Mary Forster's preface, the text retains a sense of the multi-vocal, collaborative aspect of petitioning. Writing as members of the Quaker family, these women put their voice to the anti-tithe debate. Married women protested against the tithe as good wives, safe in the fact that they were taking a supportive role; similarly,

---

[120] George Fox, 'For all Women Friends' [First line of Letter], The Swarthmore manuscripts SM ii. 96. (Quoted with the permission of the staff at the Library, Friends' House, London).

widows protested because their feminine weakness meant that they should be cared for, not cast out. Through such measures, arguably, Quaker women created a position from which to defend their action as public figures, thereby integrating the domestic and the spiritual into the masculinised notions of public citizenship.

Chapter 4

Prophets

> The truth is, the very substance of the Quakers religion and faith is, viz. that men may have the light so eminently within themselves, that thereby they may come to be Prophets, Christs or Saviours, and what they then speak, utter, or write, is as truly and really a declaration of the minde and word of God, as any part of the Bible is, touching that whereof it treats, even so are their writings.[1]

This view of Quaker prose and speech, though written by a hostile, but contemporary observer, touches on several matters that are noteworthy for any analysis of Friends' pamphleteering. The significance of the inner light as a metaphor for the possible union between the believer and Christ (or the holy spirit) is evidenced in this account of the theological features thought to be particularly distinctive to Quakerism. The light is the 'very substance' of Quaker theology, and it relates to an inwardly experienced connection to the godhead that the believer might profess to be manifest 'within' their being. Friends' emphasis on the spirit, which, we will see, is typical of their writing, emerges even in this anti-sectarian account of their most trenchantly held values. The anti-Quaker writer (Ephriam Pagit) recognises the 'inward' character of Quaker worship as the feature leading most to prophetical inspiration, in turn producing biblically inflected writing. This, too, marries with Friends' own accounts of their relationship, firstly, to the inner, living god, and, secondly, to the prophetic mode that allows them to speak as did biblical prophets or apostles – from a direct understanding of the godhead. Their involved explanations of prophetic inspiration will be one of the matters to consider in this chapter. Pagit's other contention, that the Quakers assigned their works a parallel importance to the bible, may be overstating the case somewhat; Friends were unlikely to state such an idea, in print.[2] However, the development within Quakerism of a episteme that valued inner authority over external sources, even the scripture, will be seen to ring true, overall, for many Friends who were writing at this time.

The Quaker approach to writing had more material aims than Pagit's overview makes evident. Alongside this focus on the inner spirit, Quakerism developed corporate strategies that effectively served to bind the community together. To pursue an explanation of women's writing, and its contexts, the corporate aspect that is of the greatest importance is print culture. Quaker norms and values when

---

[1] Ephriam Pagit, *Heresiography*, 6th edn (London: William Lee, 1661), p. 259.

[2] They were also accused, by Thomas Underhill, of valuing their works above the scripture. *Hell Broke Loose* (London: Sam Miller, 1660), pp. 17-18; p. 44.

writing for publication are becoming clear, and research is suggesting they took a focused, systematic approach to print.[3] Women writers were part of a community that placed a high value on print, which it recognised could further the Quaker cause by feeding contemporary interests in this new religious movement. Women writers' approaches to print will be assessed through their commentary on such issues as, for instance, the imagined audience projected for the texts. Maureen Bell (et al.) has quantified the Quaker contribution to print culture, and has noted that one third of the surviving texts by religious women produced (roughly) during the seventeenth century, were by Friends.[4] The Quaker woman who wrote within this community therefore was the least isolated of any female sectarian writing for publication. Indeed, the quantifiably high number of texts by Quaker women indicates that print culture was relatively open to them. Friends' attitudes to print put into practice radical notions about its importance. Prophetic writing was such an instance of women's radical relationship to print culture, and possibly as much as 36 per cent of women's writing was of this genre (a further 16 per cent seems to have been 'exhortations' to people in authority).[5] Prophetical writing works on the premise that the speaker conveys a message assumed to be from god, and this construction gives women the scope to deliver radical judgements on behalf of themselves, and the movement.

This intersection between 'self'-aims and community-aims will be the principal subject of this chapter. Women might write most extensively of their relationship to god, but writing for publication focuses the purpose beyond the mere expression of internalised religiousness. This chapter will contend that women aimed simultaneously to *write the community* whilst also depicting the inwardly understood relationship to god.

In the early stages of the Quaker movement, Friends were ambitiously pursuing a policy of active proselytising and extensive publication. They seem to have sought the widest possible audience for their word, on the basis of an optimistic belief in the power of god to work nationwide changes to the country's religious character. The word that they delivered in person, the text they distributed (sometimes in parallel to the evangelising mission), worked towards mass integration into the

---

[3] Kate Peters, 'Quaker Pamphleteering and the Development of the Quaker Movement 1652-1656' (unpublished doctoral thesis, Cambridge University, 1996). The book of Peters's work is in progress. For a brief overview see Peters, 'Patterns of Quaker Authorship 1652-1656', *Prose Studies*, 17:3 (1994), 6-24.

[4] Maureen Bell, George Parfitt and Simon Shepherd, *A Bibliographical Dictionary of English Women Writers 1580-1720* (New York: Harvester Wheatsheaf, 1990), p. 250. See, also, Patricia Crawford, 'Women's Published Writings, 1600-1700', in *Women in English Society 1500-1800*, ed. by Mary Prior (London: Methuen, 1985), pp. 211-244 (p. 213; p. 269).

[5] Hugh Barbour, 'Quaker Prophetesses and Mothers in Israel', in *Seeking the Light: Essays in Honour of Edwin B. Bronner*, ed. by J. William Frost and John M. Moore (Wallingford and Haverford: Pendle Hill Publications, and Friends' Historical Association, 1986), pp. 41-60 (p. 46).

ways of the Quaker movement.[6] Their texts figure their hopes for the future. 'The Lord will raise up to himself a pure and large people', John Audland observed;[7] 'the work of the Lord shall prosper', states Rebecca Travers.[8] If the statements by Audland and Travers are evidence of Friends' approach, their preaching up and down the country in the name of their god was charged with the expectation of success. In tandem, the Quakers produced quantities of pamphlets for distribution and sale. Ministering campaigns, controversies with non-Quakers, changes in national government and to parliamentary policy – each of these situations might bring a new rash of pamphlets to the public's attention. More often than not, Quakers wrote about their connection to their god, especially during the early years of the movement when He was calling to many of them to fulfil his will.[9] For instance, Rebecca Travers explained that an earlier confrontation between herself and churchgoers at St John Evangelist Church (London) was pre-ordained: 'I was brought thither of the living God whom I serve'.[10]

Although print was only one part of Friends' campaign during the 1650s to take their 'word' to an extended audience, it was singled out for special attention in recognition of its importance. Women's writing was produced within a community where print was materially provided for. Some women's texts would likely have been paid for from the central Kendal Fund that financed Quaker publications through Friends' contributions. Financing is an aspect of the publishing process that is of fundamental importance.[11] Yet it is at present too little understood, and it has yet to be established which specific texts were corporately funded. Knowing the corporate nature of funding introduces an element of tension to any analysis of women's writing, especially that which writes the community. And it introduces the notion that there is an organizational structure behind each writer's description of the ministry and of god. In the absence of specific studies of how women's texts were funded, a level of community involvement must be assumed. Yet until studies demonstrate that the funding structure was a decisive factor, this control cannot be assumed to be absolute.

What is instead widely recognised, especially following Kate Peters's research into the Quaker publishing community, is that Friends used print to actively create their public image. A woman writing within this community might be fully aware of the material and ideological impact of being a Quaker; her writerly role might be anticipated by the community's wider values, and her text's publication made possible with its funds. Kate Peters indicates that texts were employed as polemical tools, for instance, in being used to publicise Friends' activities to new audiences whilst, also, maintaining existing networks, to 'consolidate Quaker meetings',

---

[6] For the distribution of texts in conjunction with the ministry see Kate Peters, 'Quaker Pamphleteering'; for instance, p. 124.

[7] Braithwaite, *BQ*, p. 115.

[8] Rebecca Travers, *Of That Eternal Breath* (n. pl.: n. pr., n.d.), p. 7 (actually, page 5).

[9] I will refer to the deity as 'he' because this is the Quakers' approach.

[10] Rebecca Travers, *For those that Meet to Worship* (London: n. pr., 1659), p. 3.

[11] See, though, Peters, 'Quaker Pamphleteering', 86, pp. 92-96, p. 101, p. 297.

within the movement.[12] In one instance, the London printer and bookseller Giles Calvert was approached by Christopher Atkinson, who purchased £3.10s worth of pamphlets in advance of an evangelising mission to Norwich.[13] Peters uncovers the public utility of print for Friends, which implicitly gives context to women's writing of the period, most notably confirming that there will be patterns of shared emphasis on the usage of print. Friends targeted audiences, using print to spread their message faster, and wider, than was possible in person.[14] Throughout the country, Friends dispersed their religio-political tracts to allies and enemies alike. Their texts recognise the use of print as a shaper of public opinion.

The readership addressed by women in their pamphlets indicates their awareness of the extended usage of print, and implicitly its public character. Their realisation of the readership is variously defined. Women direct their messages to those inside the movement when writing for Friends, often encouraging them to maintain their focus. Peters has noted that texts were used to supplement the personal contact between Quaker preachers and the population, and, hence, women's writing might support this.[15] Alternatively, Quaker women turn to either denunciation or appeal when writing to outsiders, such as non-Quaker ministers, or specific 'enemies'. Two examples of the Quaker norm of foregrounding the text's address to its intended audience must suffice to illustrate this common feature of women's writing. Hester Biddle's *The Trumpet of the Lord* (1662) realises the need to support Friends in times of suffering, shoring up resistance to the kinds of persecution that this book has already discussed (chapter 2). She sees fit to address 'Companions, and fellow sufferers', advising 'stand up for God's cause', and noting 'be continually prepared to die'.[16] Her instruction is evidence of Quaker fellowship being maintained through print under the most hostile of situations. Sarah Blackborrow's *A Visit to the Spirit* (1658) shows how diversely the readership for Friends' texts might be figured. She seeks to appeal to 'ministers and teachers of the people' (in her subheading), as well as 'Neighbours, Kindreds and People', to whom she writes as 'a lover of your souls, but a Witnesse against your deceits'.[17] Since many of the texts considered in this chapter make clear their audience, Biddle's and Blackborrow's techniques will be seen to be typical of the public construction of authorship. Through their references to the consumption of texts, they indicate purposive and sophisticated approaches to writing that appeals, simultaneously, to insiders and outsiders alike.

Women positioned themselves within the sect when writing for publication, which might involve referring to their allegiance, or writing on behalf of the movement; Margaret Killam [Killin] and Barbara Patison's text (see illustration 4.1) is declared to be written by persons 'scornfully' called Quakers. Common

---

[12] Peters, 'Quaker Pamphleteering', p. 56.

[13] Peters, 'Quaker Pamphleteering', p. 124.

[14] Peters, 'Quaker Pamphleteering', *passim*.

[15] Peters, 'Quaker Pamphleteering', p. 55.

[16] Hester Biddle, *The Trumpet of the Lord* (London: n. pr., 1662), p. 19.

[17] Sarah Blackborrow, *A Visit to the Spirit in Prison* (London: Thomas Simmonds, 1658), p. 7; p. 5; see *HPS*, p. 50; p. 49.

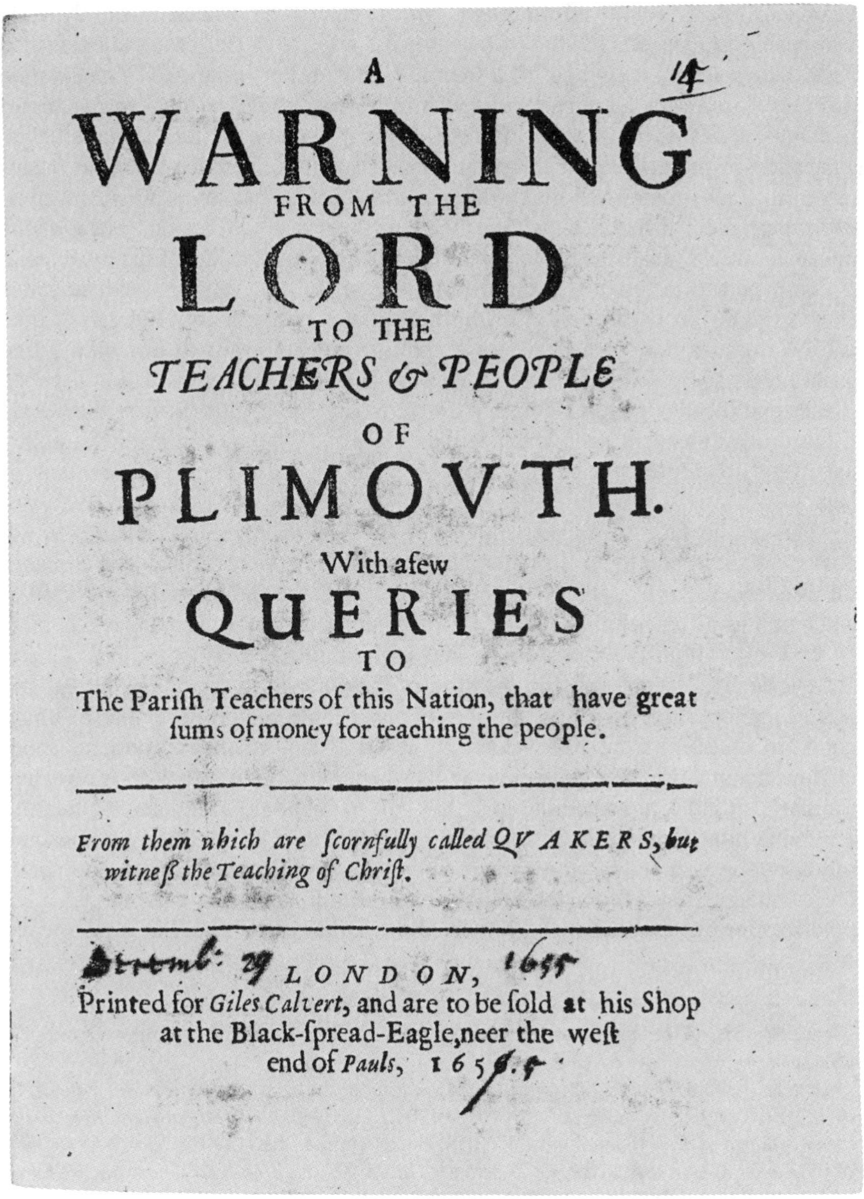

A *4*

WARNING

FROM THE

LORD

TO THE

TEACHERS & PEOPLE

OF

PLIMOVTH.

With a few

QUERIES

TO

The Parifh Teachers of this Nation, that have great
fums of money for teaching the people.

From them which are fcornfully called QVAKERS, *but
witneſſ the Teaching of Chriſt.*

Decemb: 29 LONDON, *1655*
Printed for *Giles Calvert*, and are to be fold at his Shop
at the Black-fpread-Eagle, neer the weſt
end of *Pauls*, 1656.

Illustration 4.1   Margaret Killam [Killin] and Barbara Patison, *A Warning
from the Lord* (1656)

techniques were employed, through which authors indicated their dynamic relationship to Quakerism. One of the simplest ways to signal group allegiance is the textual practice of signing off a tract as a Friend. For instance, *A Lamentation* (1657) is closed with the remarks of a woman '*in scorn called a* Quaker, *but known to many by the name of* Jeane Bettris'.[18] Many women writers signalled their connection to the movement this way, though such an approach is by no means universal. Each woman can claim the name of Quaker, but, on a purely practical level, there were differences within their positions that writing on behalf of the movement might make clear. Margaret Fell, as one of the leaders of the movement, can be expected to write as such; a lesser figure will not have immediate status when speaking to or on behalf of the movement. For instance, Margaret Fell's confident assumption of her role as a spokesperson emerges in one of the first Quaker texts addressed to Charles Stuart promising some accommodation between Friends and the new government. In *A Declaration,* Fell begins 'We are the people of God called Quakers, who are hated and despised', before outlining the policy that Friends' later peace testimony drew on.[19] She speaks both *as a Quaker* and *for* them.

The public face of Quakerism begins to emerge in texts that refer to the movement's rise, and to its character, and some of these were written by Fell in her role as a leader. For Margaret Fell, the Quakers enact the Galatians notion (6:10) of the church as a 'household of faith'.[20] The 'light' (of Christ), Fell argues, is most felt by those within the 'household'. Fell is figuring the body of believers, here, metaphorically. Yet the specific message of the passage to which she refers, and which therefore underpins this allusion, is that people should never tire of doing 'good' to others sharing like values. A message that is already hopeful about religious community, then, is even more so when the implicit reference is revealed. It might also indicate something of Fell's will to shape the religious community, employing print as a tool in this process. Fell had a level of control over financing that cannot be assumed of other writers in that she administered the Kendal Fund.[21] Hence, she was in a commanding position within the print community; such authority emerges in instructions contained within her pamphlets. For instance, she

---

[18] Jeane Bettris, *A Lamentation for the Deceived People* (London: Thomas Simmonds, 1657), p. 8.

[19] Margaret Fell, *A Declaration and an Information from Us, the People Called Quakers* (1660); see Terry S. Wallace (ed.), *A Sincere and Constant Love: An Introduction to the Work of Margaret Fell* (Richmond, Indiana: Friends United Press, 1992), pp. 49-55 (p. 49). For the Quaker peace testimony see Rosemary Moore, *The Light in their Consciences: Early Quakers in Britain* (Pennsylvania: The Pennsylvania State University Press, 2000), pp. 180-183.

[20] Margaret Fell, *False Prophets, Antichrists, Deceivers* (London: Giles Calvert, 1655), p. 21.

[21] On Fell's control over funding, specifically charitable endeavours, see Bonnelyn Young Kunze, *Margaret Fell and the Rise of Quakerism* (New York: Macmillan, 1994), p. 92; pp. 101-128; Mabel Richmond Brailsford, *Quaker Women 1650-1690* (London: Duckworth, 1915), p. 149; pp. 152-153.

writes that her pamphlets should be 'read and published among thy Brethren';[22] and, on an issue particularly important to her, she could order the international distribution of her writings, as was the case in the organisation required to translate her tracts that figured the anticipated conversion of the Jews into Hebrew.[23] Fell engages with the public creation of the Quaker image in texts that *write the community*, and she has a role in both reflecting and shaping it.

Other women's self-reflective comments signal their involvement with the community, affirming the Quakers' strength and vision; the vigour of their assertions shapes the movement's image. One distinctive feature of women's interaction with Quaker print culture is, indeed, their developed use of metaphors that *write the community*. With some regularity, women's writing constructs bands of horizontal alliance between Friends, by which they implicitly attempt to create a community through print. Although no other woman than Fell could write as a leader, others contributed by punctuating their texts with metaphorical representations of the body of believers. Whether or not it is from genuine connectedness to the movement, their pamphlets take only positive images of collectivity (some from the bible) as their guide. Dorothy White and Hester Biddle both define the movement in biblical terms suggestive of the rewards of holding a communitarian belief. Dorothy White's reference to the 'General Assembly of Saints' and 'Church of the first-born' (from Hebrews 12:23) is a positive image of collectivity in that the source distinguishes between those who recognise Jesus and those who do not.[24] The fact that her message specifically designates Quakers as the recipients of the text establishes a clear sense of the collective salvation being imagined for Friends. (She states it is 'to be read in your meetings in the fear of God').[25] This allusion, added to Fell's notion of the religious 'household', indicates the bible's potential to construct positive images of collectivity which may explain their appearance in print as much as a desire to shape the community's public image. With Hester Biddle's reference to 'Fellow Citizens of that new *Jerusalem*' (Revelations, chapter 21), there is implicit connection to the vision of a 'new heaven and a new earth' (21:1) that apocalyptic writing dreamed of.[26] Biddle, White, and Fell each variously imagine the bible's promises and instructions, and for Biddle, there is a sense that the old has been swept away in this apocryphal fervour, producing a heightened sense of fellowship. She comments:

> I am ravished, I am filled with life and love towards you my Companions and Fellow Citizens of that new *Jerusalem,* which is free born, and is the Mother of all the Faithful, which is beautified with the Glory of the Lord. Glory, Righteousness and purity compasseth about the Throne of the Lord, and Equity attendeth his Throne for ever.[27]

---

[22] Margaret Fell, *For Manasseth Ben Israel* (London: Giles Calvert, 1656), p. 20.

[23] Kunze, *Margaret Fell*, pp. 213-215.

[24] Dorothy White, *Unto all God's Host in England* (n. pl.:, n. pr., n.d.), p. 5.

[25] White, *Unto all God's Host*, p. 5.

[26] Hester Biddle, 'Something in Short', in Thomas Woodrowe, *A Brief Relation of the State of Man* (London: T.W. and Thomas Simmonds, 1659), p. 33.

[27] Biddle, 'Something in Short', p. 33.

The fact that such views appear in writing destined for publication means that the positive images maintain an expected public face of unity, understanding, and optimism; and this is arguably more indicative of texts' intended utility than anything else. Clearly, there are sound reasons for publishing writers who endorse the movement's emerging ethos, and it might be the case that the corporate background that seems to cherish and develop women writers in fact restricted them. Perhaps negative images of the movement were censored. And perhaps Phyllis Mack's observation is accurate: that what 'would not immediately resonate' was suppressed, with individuals tailoring their messages to the predicted needs of the movement.[28] Each of these explanations might account for such conclusive affirmations of community spirit as they appear in women's writing. However, an alternative argument is also possible with respect to Biddle and White.

By viewing texts in relation to the publishing conditions they refer to, more can be understood about these positive images of collectivity. The two texts (quoted above) in which White and Biddle affirm their connection to Quakerism occupy an atypical position in the print community, and this is significant. In terms of their printing, these texts are unusual. What makes them interesting for our purpose of exploring the community's creation of its identity in print is the reference to the printer. It would be premature to suggest that positive images of the Quaker movement in some of these women's writings indicate a fellowship that inclusively embraces all, and to which women therefore felt a sense of spontaneous connection; however, individuals occasionally manipulated print culture, suggesting it could be used to their advantage. Hence, Biddle's text is contained in a tract brought to print by the main author, Thomas Woodrowe, who probably therefore worked with Quaker publisher Thomas Simmonds. Intriguingly, White's text has no printer identified on it.[29] White, especially, seems to work outside the standard Quaker communities.[30] Her texts were fairly likely to enter the pamphlet market without the attribution of a standard Quaker printer or publisher: men such as Giles Calvert, Thomas Simmonds, or Robert Wilson – each a key figure in Quaker publishing and printing. The emergence of female printers within this community (Mary Westwood and Elizabeth Calvert) also indicates that women were engaged in the material processes of textual production, moreover.[31] What the existence of these texts begins to suggest is that the Quaker corpus, though essentially corporate, contains anomalies; these have be borne in mind before

---

[28] Mack, *Visionary Women*, p. 161.
[29] Rosemary Moore refers to writing 'for the author', *The Light*, p. 232, 'which may indicate that they went beyond the limits of what Friends would officially acknowledge'.
[30] See bibliography at the end of this book. For the little known on Dorothy White's biography see Catie Gill, 'Dorothy White', in *The New DNB* (forthcoming).
[31] See Maureen Bell, 'Mary Westwood – Quaker Publisher', *Publishing History*, 23 (1988), 5-66; Bell, 'Women Publishers of Puritan Literature in the Mid-Seventeenth-Century: Three Case Studies' (unpublished doctoral thesis, Loughborough University, 1987); Maureen Bell, 'Elizabeth Calvert and the "Confederates"', *Publishing History*, 32 (1992), pp. 5-50; Bell, '"Her Usual Practices": The Later Career of Elizabeth Calvert, 1664-75', *Publishing History*, 35 (1994), pp. 5-64.

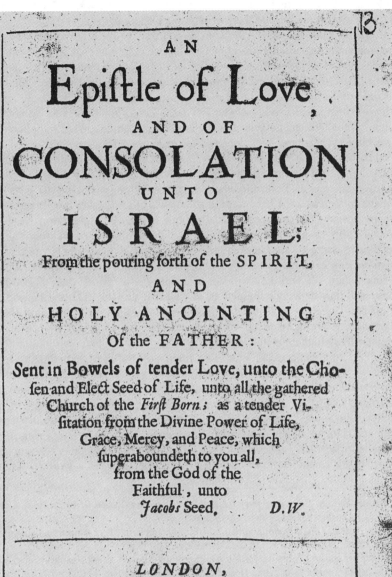

Illustration 4.2   Dorothy White, *An Epistle of Love* (1661)

assuming these women were, in effect, merely circumscribed by the publishing conditions that pre-existed their writing of a Quaker pamphlet.

A possible reason for establishing links between the individual and the movement is that such connections are a pragmatic response to the possibility of opposition – to the writing, to the movement. Women such as Fell and Biddle anticipated that their writing might be rejected, particularly by non-Quakers. Biddle writes of the 'great gulf and separation between the two seeds', referring, through comparison, to those who 'serve the Lord', and those who do not.[32] She is figuring the Quaker movement as the seed of god (an extensively applied image in the bible).[33] Margaret Fell, meanwhile 'makes a separation' between those who 'come in the flesh' and others who 'dwell in the light'.[34] Each writer anticipates that the worldly, carnal nature in people will deliberately work to undermine the godly's intentions. Ironically, the fact of the writing appealing to such a varied audience increases the need to produce images of the Quaker movement that relate their greater unity and godliness. In another text, Priscilla Cotton writes of this relationship to a readership fairly explicitly characterised as scornful, as she maintains that god orders her to print her text despite them. In conversational tone, Cotton first explains her response to god's instruction to speak his words in a 'lamentation': 'I said they will not hear nor regard'. 'God' then replied 'whether they will hear or forbear publish it, that all may see it'.[35] The assumption that the possible audience will reject Friends' messages has a significant impact on community writing. Quakers recognise that there is greater difference outside the movement than there is inside it.[36]

Even prophetic texts, which are seemingly the most individualised form of writing, might rhapsodise the relationships between co-religionists; and, here, emphasising sectarian alliance provides external authority that, in other respects, inspired writing eschews. The prophet designates speaking the word of god her only purpose; the singular relationship established is between the individual and her god. The instability of the prophet's identity has been analysed in a significant number of scholarly articles and books as a result of her tenuous position as author and vessel, caught between producing and receiving god's word.[37] Yet, for our

---

[32] Hester Biddle, *A Warning from the Lord God* (London: Robert Wilson, 1660), p. 20.

[33] See, for instance, Gen. 17:8; Rom. 9:2; John 8:33, 37.

[34] Margaret Fell, *A Testimonie of the Touchstone* (London: Thomas Simmonds, 1656), p. 20.

[35] Priscilla Cotton, 'As I was in the Prison-house' (n. pl.: n. pr., n. d.), broadside.

[36] Another image of this process is the sorting of sheep from wolves, see Ezek. 34:10-16; John 10:11-16; see its usage in Hester Biddle, 'Wo to thee City of Oxford' [first line] (n. pl.: n. pr., [1655]), broadside; also, Sarah Blackborrow, *The Just and Equall Balance* (London: M. W. [Mary Westwood], 1660), p. 3.

[37] See Mack, *Visionary Women: Ecstatic Prophecy in Seventeenth-Century England* (Berkeley: University of California Press, 1989); Hillary Hinds, *God's Englishwomen: Seventeenth-Century Radical Sectarian Writing and Feminist Criticism* (Manchester and New York: Manchester University Press, 1996); Elaine Hobby, *Virtue of Necessity: English Women's Writing 1649-88* (London: Virago, 1988) Margaret Ezell, *Writing Women's Literary History* (Baltimore and London: The Johns Hopkins University Press, 1993). See articles on prophets/religious women in the following collected volumes: *Debating Gender*

present purposes, the communitarian focus of prophecy is the most pertinent aspect to consider. The prophet's message might be addressed to her community, which is the case, for instance, in Dorothy White's *An Epistle of Love and of Consolation Unto Israel* (1661), where the Quakers are symbolically Israel. Told to *'Publish the day of the Lord God'*, White writes a poetic, biblically inflected prophecy. Her writing is free flowing when constructing relational identities: 'My soul doth swim within the Sea of love, as doth fishes in the water move'. Her ambiguous syntax, here, could either make the 'Sea of love' representative of god, or of the Quaker movement – the latter being possible because, almost immediately, she is addressing herself to 'my dear friends', assuring them that 'my love floweth freely unto you'.[38] By speaking to the movement, White is arguably using a little of the legitimacy that comes from writing *as a Quaker* to the established community of friendly readers. Rather than the relationship being exclusively to god, the prophet establishes more extended, and external, material relations through figuring the unity within the Quaker movement.

Hester Biddle maintains that Quakers 'dwell together in the unity of the Spirit'; when Biddle, White, Cotton, Fell, and many more, reflect on the movement they commonly idealise it.[39] Certainly, their works are a construction designed for public consumption, but their approach is, at the very least, a pragmatic acknowledgement of the importance of print. At best, it is an effort to shape the movement from the inside by manipulating print so that the images of the Quaker body signal its gender inclusiveness.

The Light

Female Quakers wrote and spoke from a position of connection to the godhead, and their sense of revelation was due, in large part, to the community's method of writing about the spirit's immediacy within the believer, whether they be male or female. Women could write forcibly and confidently of their personal understanding of the godhead, achieving a vigorous prose style that was rarely anything other than assertive. For instance, Jeane Bettris puts into action the notion

---

in *Early Modern England 1500-1700*, ed. by Cristina Malcolmson and Mihoko Suzuki (New York: Palgrave Macmillan, 2002); *'This Double Voice': Gendered Writing in Early Modern England*, ed. by Danielle Clarke and Elizabeth Clarke (Basingstoke: MacMillan, 2000); *Women, Writing, History 1640-1740*, ed. by Isabel Grundy and Susan Wiseman (London: B. T. Batsford, 1992); *New Feminist Discourses*, ed. by Isobel Armstrong (London and New York: Routledge, 1992); *A Companion to Early Modern Women's Writing*, ed. by Anita Pacheco (Oxford: Blackwell, 2002); *Literature and Power in the Seventeenth Century: Proceedings of the Essex Conference on the Sociology of Literature*, ed. by Frances Barker (et al.) (Colechester, University of Essex, 1991); *Pamphlet Wars: Prose in the English Revolution*, ed. by James Holstun (London: Frank Cass, 1992); *Women and Literature in Britain 1500-1700*, ed. by Helen Wilcox (Cambridge: CUP, 1996).
[38] Dorothy White, *An Epistle of Love and of Consolation* (London: Robert Wilson, 1661), pp. 8-9.
[39] Biddle, *A Warning from the Lord*, p. 9.

of speaking for god, showing the bombasticism and authority that was possible: 'I am full of power by the Spirit of the Lord and of judgement, and of might, to declare unto you your transgressions and your sins', she maintains.[40] The significance of women speaking a forcible message that conveyed their assurance, their certainty, that they acted according to god's will, is that it presents a public face of spiritual equality. 'There is neither male nor female here but they are all one in Christ Jesus', observes Margaret Fell in another image of the religious community that print culture gave voice to.[41] The writer who uses print to reflect on the Quaker movement's openness to the women therefore does so because, in the spirit, people are 'all one' (Fell's words). In print, women are regularly found explaining the word of god, as it was conveyed to them in revelation, and as it had to be communicated to the readership that was imagined for Quaker texts. Their texts foreground this spiritual relationship to god, which was expressed, most often, through ideas of interiority. The godhead was understood to communicate directly to the believer, through an inner sense of connectedness to the spirit. For the writer within this religious community, then, print culture's main purpose was served if the writer expressed the will of god. Women's access to print can be now explained in terms of their godly duty to express a religious message to their readership.

The task of speaking for god was not wholly incompatible with the idea of testifying to the community. Where movement-wide notions of the relationship between the believer and the deity were being foregrounded, even as the writer expressed her particularised response to god's presence, something of a shared value system is apparent. Each description of god is at one level a theorisation of the abstract, and each pamphlet's intention is to make the deity's presence seem tangible. As a result, shared understandings of the godhead emerge in Quaker writing. The community's commonest approach was to assert that inner comprehension of god was produced within a believer who opened her/himself up to the light of Christ. Drawing on John (12:46), Quaker references to the inner light focus on how god is a felt presence *within* the believer, owing to the Johannine promise that 'the light of the world' would enlighten everyone. Rather than the Quaker inner light being an example of solitary piety, though, the references that appear in Friends' writing have been said to bear the hallmarks of a communitarian philosophy. According to Geoffrey Nuttall, for instance, 'Friends never stood for a bare individualistic principle of the "inner light"': instead, the society has always existed to 'bear corporate witness to the principles and practices for which it stands'.[42] Through repeated references to the light, Quakerism becomes, in many respects, a religion that emphasises that even personal, one-on-one, religious experiences register something of the community's theological orientation. In so far as the inner light is said to work directly within the believer, it is an individualised experience. Yet, at the same time, reference to the inner light

---

[40] Bettris, *A Lamentation*, pp. 6-7.
[41] Margaret Fell, *An Evident Demonstration* (London: Thomas Simmonds, 1660), p. 1.
[42] Geoffrey F. Nuttall, *The Holy Spirit in Puritan Faith and Experience*, 2nd edn (Chicago and London: University of Chicago Press, 1992), p. 45.

connects the individual believer to the religious movement that she belongs to, because John's gospel was accounted so fundamental in the Quakers' published output.

In their writing, Quaker women recognise the personal and the political impact of the light as a force on their consciences; they literally take to heart the Quaker notion that Christ's light is within each believer. Though their published accounts are distinct in their focus, each conversion in the light that is described is a contribution to the community's definition of its central theological tenets. One favoured position is the idea that the light brings salvation. Writers within this publishing community commonly make reference to the same key passages. In John 8:12 and again in John 14:6 the promise of spiritual assurance, through Christ who is equated with the light, is explained; and the Quakers were implicitly developing this theme and others when they wrote on moral issues, specifically salvation.[43] There is a common sense, often repeated, of the light as a moral force, checking the tendencies of the writer's darker nature. In Quaker pamphlets, the light supplies correction. According to Margaret Killam and Barbara Patison, it shows 'sin and evill'.[44] Sarah Blackborrow confirms this application when compelling her readers to 'see all you have been and are a doing [sic], is in the ungodly nature'.[45] Each of these positions is recognition of Christianity's aim to provide a code for godly behaviour, and the light brings personal salvation into focus.

Quaker women's references to the moral reformation experienced in the Johannine light continue in other writers' works. Martha Simmonds, for instance, advises 'minde the light, and waite in it, which is given the grace of God that hath appeared to thee, there is the first step to pure redemption'.[46] Her text describes experiences that are presumably autobiographical by pointing the way for others to find salvation in the light (see Illustration 4.3). Her text therefore not only uses an established trope for salvation that would be recognised, by Quakers, as a sign of enlightenment, it also speaks to others seeking spiritual guidance. More than a merely personalised indulgence, the writers' descriptions of salvation fit with the publishing ideals, already discussed, that demonstrate the purposive approach to spreading Quaker ideas. Dorothy White, too, maintains that 'they who have waited, who have *believed* in the Light, such receive Life'.[47] Margaret Fell's working of this metaphor is slightly different, drawing on the contrast between night and day. She explains her condition before and after her convincement: 'when I went through the vale of misery, in the cloudy and dark day, when no light appeared,

---

[43] The specific issue, here, is the idea that the light is a 'natural' light within the conscience (Romans 1:18-20). This is less contentious than the other constructions of inner-light theory that this chapter will discuss, see Moore, *The Light in their Consciences*, p. 101.

[44] Margaret Killam [Killin] and Barbara Patison, *A Warning from the Lord* (London: Giles Calvert, 1656), p. 6.

[45] Blackborrow, *A Visit*, p. 7; *HPS*, p. 50.

[46] Martha Simmonds, 'When the Lord Jesus Came' (n. pl.: n. pr., n.d), broadside. Thomason's date is April 25, 1655.

[47] White, *An Epistle of Love*, pp. 4-5.

then was I following men, but darkness was over the whole earth in me'.[48] She elsewhere tells her readership 'as you love your souls, turn to the light'.[49] Resolving to accept change, these women describe the end to spiritual darkness, whilst also showing that the light was a fundamental concept in Quaker theology. Beyond the issue of salvation that was, clearly, of most concern to them, something more can be discerned about their position within Quakerism through these references to the inner light. It allowed them to experience a conceptualisation of the godhead that was simultaneously of personal and communitarian significance. Hence, believers who, individually, testify to their salvation through these references to the light ensure that their message dovetails with the community's wider accounts of godliness. The light is within the believer, but it is recognised as a marker of righteousness by the community. Since it has been asserted that in conversion narratives the 'public political debate over personal religious freedom necessitated public articulation of one's own faith/position', the task of writing can be viewed as an act of speaking to a wider religious agenda: one prompted by the community's public focus on the inner light.[50]

When these women's references to the light are examined in terms of the texts' creation, publication, and reception, the apparent inward-focus of inner light theology is modified somewhat. Quaker women can be said to *write the community,* reflecting on varied aspects of sectarian allegiance and constructing themselves, therefore, in relation to the movement. Hence, as Quaker women wrote about the light in their conversion narratives by invoking John's metaphor for salvation, they were implicitly writing as spokespeople for Friends' shared faith. Though the collectivist principle is less evident in this aspect of their writing than, for instance, in their metaphorical descriptions of the Quaker body, the references to the light stand as witness to the effectiveness (or otherwise) of the movement to establish core values – to define, in other words, what it meant to be a Quaker, through print. Sarah Blackborrow, for instance, makes clear the purpose of writing about inner salvation, when demonstrating the absolute authority of Friends' enlightened understanding. She formulates her position in print thus:

> I bring in my Testimonie (though one of the least who witness life) according the measure of life received, That is light, and doth enlighten, and gave light to me, in which I saw all things acted in me contrary to the life of Christ; and being believed in, and obeyed, it hath led me out of the Devil's kingdom, into Christ, and so to God the Father and of the Spirits; and truly, people, there is no other way to Christ.[51]

---

[48] Margaret Fell (et al.), *A Paper Concerning such as are made Ministers by the Will of Man* (London: M. W. [Mary Westwood], 1659), p. 1. 'Man' is a reference to non-Quaker ministers.

[49] Margaret Fell, *A Call unto the Seed of Israel* (London: Robert Wilson [1668]), p. 11.

[50] Linda S Coleman, 'Gender, Sect, and Circumstance: Quaker Mary Penington's Many Voices', in *Women's Life Writing: Finding a Voice Building a Community*, ed. by Linda S. Coleman (Bowling Green: Bowling Green State University Popular Press, 1997), pp. 93-107 (p. 95).

[51] Sarah Blackborrow, *Herein is Held forth the Gift* (London: Thomas Simmonds, 1659), p. 5.

In effect, Quaker theology's focus on the light working *within* each believer's conscience necessitates some personalising language in relation to the individual's coming to an understanding of god. This position does not, however, eclipse the other context in which the writer produced her text: as confirmation of the publishing community's emergent values. Blackborrow's assertion that there is 'no other way' than the Quaker 'way' to salvation shows how a pamphlet might systematically validate key concepts. Indeed, Quaker writing is interesting for the striking co-existence of communitarian and apparently personal viewpoints.

Another characteristic of the Quaker project is its radical acceptance that each individual might interpret god's will; forging a sense of direct communication, Friends' writing establishes another relational identity – not the individual to the Quaker movement, but the believer to god. The speaker shows her congruence to wider Quaker thought, and produces an authoritative writerly position through shared understandings of god (as description of conversion in the light makes clear). Yet inward experience was also significant in its own right, since the light engendered fuller understanding of god's presence within each believer. Bauman has summarised the Quaker approach thus: '[god] spoke not only *within* Quakers, but *through* them'; hence, Friends tenaciously extend their understanding of the godhead *within*.[52] The light is no longer exteriorised in this construction of the believer/god relationship, but is a speaking subject who is making his will known on more than matters of salvation. 'There is something upon me as from the Lord to write', observes Margaret Fell, announcing the theocentric theory of communication that she, and most other Quakers, upheld.[53] Friends contend that the light is a trope for Christ or the holy spirit, whose supernatural presence elevates the spoken words of the prophet to the level of revelation. This application of Johannine theology shows that Friends' descriptions of their god could be focussed intensely inwardly, which adds another level to Quaker writing. Such inwardness is a fundamental feature of Friends' community writing.

Individuals are not being merely egotistical when they describe their personal experiences; prophetic identity requires some foregrounding of the believer's experience of the light, god, or Christ. Hence, the believer's allegation of godly inspiration has relied on the earlier depiction of 'self'; stories of personal salvation announce the writer's devotion, and these catapult him or her into prophetical mode. As Nigel Smith observes: 'the prophet's self-presentation is crucial for the communication of inspired authority'.[54] The Quakers' desire to speak for god, Christ, or the light is what drives them to write themselves into their texts. Hence, even when engaging in 'self-presentation' (Smith's term), the woman writer aims to speak of something that is bigger than the individual: in this case, community

---

[52] Richard Bauman, *Let Your Words Be Few: Symbolism of Speaking and Silence among Seventeenth-Century Quakers* (repr. London: Quaker Home Service, 1988), p. 25.

[53] Margaret Fell, *An Evident Demonstration to Gods Elect* (London: Thomas Simmonds, 1660), p. 1. The message is largely to Friends.

[54] Nigel Smith, *Perfection Proclaimed: Language and Literature in English Radical Religion 1640-1660* (Oxford: Clarendon Press, 1989), p. 55.

understandings of god. Self-validating accounts of the believer's relationship to the godhead are set before the publishing and reading community with a will to reinforce the Quaker movement's understanding of the inner god. A key achievement of much Quaker writing is therefore its ability to combine self and community aims, balancing the two.

The social and shared aspects of community theory provide patterns through which the individual can understand inwardness, and language usage demonstrates this point that personal meanings are generated within the communitarian context. The Quaker approach to language usage, for instance, draws attention to the inwardness of experience, to the individual, and writing becomes an indicator of the author's receptiveness to god's speech. Quaker theorisations show that the words conveyed to the prophet are understood to be, in effect, written in their interiors – just as illumination had occurred within, writing is logocentric and internal to each person.[55] Women writers make clear the relevance to them of Quaker theories of enlightened language usage. Their expressions show that they are figuring a radical relationship to god's word, with Rebecca Travers, for instance, proclaiming the 'new Covenant written in the heart, put in the inner parts', and Margaret Fell referring to the 'ingrafted word of god'.[56] Each writer here maintains that words have an internal, corporeal reality. The inner light's prominence in early Quaker pamphlets is textual as well as theological, therefore, in that it produces a theory that explains writing as a practice of interpreting the inwardly experienced word.

The Quakers' familiarity with Johannine theology made possible this deified logos, contained in the suggestive possibility that Christ the prophet might be accounted 'the word made flesh' (John 1:14). Considering how god's will (expressed through his word) was apparently given physical form (through Jesus), leads to assumptions that spiritual authority is literally embodied.[57] Quakers might state 'Christ was the Word': flesh and language are literally interlinked.[58] Since Quakers used their own writing to construct a version of theology to account for their prophetic leanings, their speaking in the spirit, this creative reading of John's theology shows the community developing an explanation of godly speaking that was appropriate to their own times. Prophecy, they believed, was the language of god speaking within the flesh; writerly authority was established through the fusion of flesh and spirit that they perceived might occur in the light. Even though what is here personal is also collective (the shared Quaker understanding of how god's language spoke within), the act of writing is figured by tropes that construct a primary relationship between the flesh and the spirit; writing is initially justified by an inward experience.

---

[55] See Nigel Smith, 'Hidden Things Brought to Light: Enthusiasm and Quaker Discourse', *Prose Studies*, 17:3 (1994), 57-69. I use Smith's term 'substance' to refer to Christ within.
[56] Rebecca Travers, *For those that Meet to Worship* (London: n. pr., 1659), p. 32; Fell, *Testimonie of the Touchstone*, p. 12.
[57] John's gospel is language-centred, opening with 'In the beginning was the Word' (1:1).
[58] Edward Pyot (et al.), *The West Answering to the North* (London: Giles Calvert, 1657, p. 164. Thomason's date is 24 January 1656 [i.e. 1657].

in Edmonition

76

Hen the Lord Jesus came to *Jerusalem*, he beheld the City, and wept over it, with this lamentation : *Oh that thou hadst known in this thy day the things that belong to thy peace !* The same tenderneſſe is witneſſed now in them which the Lord hath enlightned. I cannot but mourn over you, to ſee how you lye wallowing in your filth, and joynt hand in hand, and ſmite with the fiſt of wickedneſſe, and yet lean upon Chriſt for ſalvation : Know you not that *many ſhall ſay in that day, Lord, Lord ?* but remember what will be your anſwer ; *Go you curſed into the lake, I know you not.* Oh that thou wouldſt but ſtand ſtill a little, and turn thy eye inward ; Sit downe a little, and conſider thy poore foul that lyes in death : What will become of thee, thou murdereſt the juſt in thee, there is a Talent to be improved in thee, how wilt thou give an accompt of it ; the Steward is now come : In the coole of the day , then *Adam* heard the voyce of God, and then he ſaw his nakedneſſe, and ſo mayeſt thou ; If thou wilt turn in thy minds to the light of Chriſt in thee, the light will diſcover to thee thy fallen ſtate, and how thou art turned out from the preſence of God, and art in the gall of bitterneſſe, and the earth is curſed for thy ſake : Now if thou wilt minde the light, and waite in it, which is the grace of God that hath appeared to thee, there is the firſt ſtep to pure redemption : And if thou take diligent heed to this light in thee, thou ſhalt finde it checking thee continually for all thy evill deeds, and it will teach thee to be ſober minded and upright in all thy dealings as in the ſight of God : and ſo thou wilt come to ſee the ſtraight gate and narrow way that leads to life ; but thou wilt ſay, Chriſt hath done all this for me, I have nothing to do but believe : but it will be ſaid unto thee, when thou thinkeſt to ſit downe with thy Lord ; *Friend; how cameſt thou hither without a wedding-garment ?* then know what thy portion will be. Faith is another thing then thou takeſt it to be ; He that hath Faith, if it be never ſo little, ſhall witneſſe Chriſts words to be true, *he ſhall remove mountains :* Now in the ſtill ſilence, in the light that ſhines in darkneſſe in thee, thou wilt come to reliſh that little grain of Faith which is held in a pure conſcience, and ſo feele the mountains remove, which preſſeth downe thy ſoule : but ye *will not come unto me that ye may have life,* ſaith Chriſt Jeſus ; It is thy will that hinders thee, for in thy will the Devill lodges. *Adam* when he diſobeyed the minde and will of God, then he entred into his own will, and ſo was turned out into the Devils Kingdome. Now Chriſt Jeſus the ſecond *Adam,* who is God manifeſt in fleſh, condemning ſinne in the fleſh, if thou live in him in thee, and believe in him in thee, then thou ſhalt witneſſe his power to the cutting down of thy will ; for thy will muſt come to death, that the will of God may be done, and ſo that Scripture comes to be fulfilled in thee, which are the words of Chriſt ; *Loe I come, in the volume of thy booke it is written of me to doe thy will O God,* which is the book of conſcience in thee, there the will of God is to be done : And as thou comeſt to love the light, and live in it, thou wilt come to ſee the righteous law of God fulfilled in thee, Death reigns in thee. Now Death reigned from *Adam* till *Moſes,* and when *Moſes* came, then was the Law given forth ; and ſo *Moſes* and the Prophets till *John :* But thou wilt ſay, *thou art not under the Law, but under Grace ?* let the light ſearch thee , and it will aske thee, how cameſt thou to be under Grace? Is not the law for cleanſing, When waſt thou cleanſed ? or where doſt thou think to be cleanſed ? Doth not Chriſt Jeſus ſay, that he is come to fulfill the Law, and that one jot nor tittle ſhall paſs unfulfilled, and wilt thou ſpeak of his words, and not believe him ? Yea, thou ſhalt know, that for that very end is there a meaſure of Chriſt given unto thee ; that if thou deny thy ſelfe, and yeeld obedience to his will, thou ſhalt witneſſe the whole Law fulfilled in thee, but it is through judgment, and through burning, for through judgement is Zion redeemed : but *hearken a little, and conſider, hear and thy ſoule ſhall live.* If thou be willing to take up the Croſſe of Chriſt , and deſpiſe the ſhame, thou ſhalt witneſſe pure peace of conſcience : and though it may ſeem hard to the world, yet there is living refreſhments : Yea, glorious is the worke of redemption, but none can ſee it but thoſe that come through it : And now the way of eternall life is laid before thee, if thou ſlight it, it ſhall lye at thy doore : and therefore take heed what thou doſt ; for when the booke of conſcience is opened, thou ſhalt witneſſe thou haſt been warned in thy life-time.

Martha Simmonds

Aprill 25 · 1655 · giue· about, by ye Quaker

Illustration 4.3   Martha Simmonds, 'When the Lord Jesus Came' (1655)

The prophet's understanding of the word of god *within* is, hence, perceived to be the first stage in the process of writing for publication; yet I would contend, with Maurice A. Creasey, that Quaker writing mediates between outward and inward focus. Creasey has argued that the Quakers' 'quasi-philosophical' model for godly experience relies on a contrast between the inward understanding of god and external, or socially learned, forms of worship.[59] I would add a communitarian element to this understanding of the duality of the Quaker pamphleteers' approach, instancing Friends' purposive understanding of how writing in the spirit advances community values. The prophet Dorothy White, for instance, shows her relationship both to the community and to her god in writing that establishes the prophet's inner certainty as arising from group principles. In *Unto All Gods Host* [1660], which is directed towards Friends, the dualistic focus on inwardness and outwardness is apparent. The prophet asserts:

> Verily the Lord God hath sent me to declare and publish, and sound forth his message unto all Israel, even to declare the day of free Love, and everlasting consolation, how blessed a thing is it for the Brethren to dwell together in the unity of love and of the holy Spirit, in the Covenant of Love and Peace, in the union of Saints in the light.[60]

Clear in its orientation as community writing, White's passage shows both how the Johannine light functions as a principle binding together the movement (in 'union'), and how writing *for* god brings her tract into existence within this publishing community. (Its message of 'consolation' may indicate that towards the end of the Quakers' first decade, Friends needed their continuing sense of purpose re-affirmed). The inward focus of another text, *This Is to be Delivered* (1659), gives some context to White's understanding of prophetic authority occurring, firstly, within the believer:

> Upon the seventh day of the third moneth 1659. the word of the Lord came to me, and it stuck close in me: And again on the eight [sic] day of the same moneth, as I was waiting upon the Lord with his people, the Word of the Lord came to me, and it stuck close in me [...] and the word of the Lord came to me, saying, write.[61]

My juxtaposition of these two passages cannot fully reconcile the twin focus of Quaker writing, because this simultaneously inward and outward element is certainly a tension that needs to be acknowledged. However, I am suggesting that Quaker inwardness is coupled to outwardness because the texts acknowledge that each message is to be received, and interpreted, by a reading community. White demonstrates this, even as she describes the moment of connecting to the god within. She is constructing herself in relation to the parameters of Quaker theology, print culture, and the specific meeting she attended. The inwardness of godly language does not mean that these are introspective pamphlets: their material

---

[59] Maurice A. Creasey, ' "Inward" and "Outward": A Study in Quaker Language', *JFHS*, supplement 30 (1961), 3-24 (p. 23).
[60] Dorothy White, *Unto All God's Host* (n. pl.: n. pr., [1660]), p. 2.
[61] Dorothy White, *This to be delivered* (London: Thomas Simmonds, 1659), p. 2.

purpose (to explain Quaker ideas, to convert others, to shore up community feeling) emerges in prophetical writing. Writing is determined by publishing imperatives, as much as inward spirituality.

Although Quaker theories do not often acknowledge it, the application of divine light theory to language usage was particularly contentious; to this effect, Quaker writing about the 'ingrafted' word must inevitably construct the community's certain belief in an experience that other contemporaries held in contempt. The inner light's application to writerly concerns was arguably as problematical as it was enabling, because in as much as the reading of John's gospel 'explained' the writing process, it likewise fuelled sceptics' critiques of Friends' theology, hardening the reception to Quaker pamphleteers' texts. Friends' doctrine took a certain amount of licence, and writing that broke down the division between god and the believer whist claiming the age of prophecy to have arrived, was subject to critique. Some opponents insinuated that the interpretation being placed on John's logocentric gospel was a misreading. Friends' logic was questioned: 'it is a grosse absurdity to say this word of the Lord was Christ', Thomas Weld (et al.) states, before continuing 'when the word of the Lord came to the Prophets, *Samuel, Isaiah, Jeremiah, &c.* it cannot be understood of the word that was made flesh, the Lord Jesus; but must necessarily signifie the mind or Message of the Lord contained in those words of Scripture Writings'.[62] This gloss shows errors understood to be within Quaker theory. Weld (et al.) contends that Friends (wilfully?) misunderstand the scripture when asserting that the word heard inwardly brought the believer to Jesus. To the same extent that membership of a religious community united co-religionists in understanding of and sympathy towards, collectively held ideas (such as the inner light), the acerbic critic exists to debunk cherished values. The exact meaning of the inner light was picked over extensively by anti-sectarian critics.[63] Yet what Weld (et al) makes apparent is that Friends' representation of inward godly experience might be subject to dispute. This discussion of interiority is, hence, constructed by external factors, such as the possible reactions of anti-sectarians. Friends seem, then, caught by the need to defend community theology in apparently personal terms.

The complex theorisation of the inner light that occurs in Friends' writing shows something more than merely personalised responses to John's promise of spiritual union; the community's pamphleteers, it has been argued, 'wrote very definitely as Quakers', and there is no other notion that better encapsulates the Quakers' theological character than this idea of the inner light.[64] Friends and enemies alike wrote about the light as the 'very substance' of the Quaker religion.[65] Those pointing to the light as the Quakers' 'main subject' might be voicing

---

[62] Thomas Weld (et al.), *The Perfect Pharise* (London: Robert Tomlins, 1654), p. 23. (Thomason's date is January 14, 1653).
[63] See Moore, *The Light*, pp. 98-111.
[64] Peters, 'Quaker Pamphleteering', p. 151.
[65] Pagit, *Herisiography*, 6th edn., p. 259.

opposition.[66] This was the case in *A Brief Relation of the Irreligion of the Northern Quakers* (1653) in which Francis Higginson showed the centrality of Johannine theology: 'their speakings [instruct others to] mind only their light within for teaching, which they tell them is sufficient to salvation'.[67] Writers might, alternatively, show that Johannine principles are so fundamentally installed as a marker of Quaker faith that believers should lay down their lives in defence of this concept. The light 'is worthy of all we have suffered', maintains the southern Friend Priscilla Cotton.[68] Each position shares the common idea that Quakerism is profoundly concerned with the inward experience of the light, recognising it as a marker of community-wide belief.

Of course, even though the light was ubiquitous in Quaker prose, it was also invoked in other writers' works: Friends did not have sole ownership of the concept. It is not my purpose, here, to explore the overlap between Friends' works and other radicals' use of the idea that each believer could be illuminated through the divine light within. This has been others' purpose when assessing radical writings in the 1650s.[69] It is clear that Quakers were drawing a line of connection between themselves and earlier puritan and radical sectarians when invoking this spiritual metaphor for the godhead's presence. Writing on inwardness occurred within the context of wider sectarian interest in immediate revelation. For instance, the Ranter Joseph Salmon writes of the 'eminent appearance of the light' in his *Heights in Depths* (1651), which leads some critics to draw connections between Ranter and Quaker writings.[70] Yet, the central point to bear in mind is that proof of extensive reference to this spiritualised 'light' outside the Quaker movement confirms, rather than confounds, the Quakers' relative success in producing an identifiable public image. They made their own a concept that had already been quite widely developed within sectarian writing. Reference to the light was one way, therefore, of capturing radical interest.

The light was also key to Friends' prophetic activity as well as their radicalised, sectarian identity. Quaker women wrote within a community that carved out a prophetic identity for its pamphleteers and activists; the inner light's relevance to inspired writers was profound, and evidence from the pamphlets indicates that its significance to women was not lost on the movement's main

---

[66] Francis Higginson, *A Brief Relation of the Irreligion of the Northern Quakers* (London: T. R. for H. R, 1653), p. 13.

[67] Higginson, *A Brief Relation*, p. 13. See Higginson in *EQW*, p. 72.

[68] Priscilla Cotton, *A Testimony of Truth to all Friends* (n. pl.: M. W. [Mary Westwood], n.d.), p. 7.

[69] See Nuttall, *The Holy Spirit*, *passim;* Smith, *Perfection Proclaimed*, especially p. 68, pp. 234-236, pp. 248-251. Thomas N. Corns, *Uncloistered Virtue* (Oxford: Clarendon Press, 1992); David Loewenstein, *Representing Revolution in Milton and his Contemporaries: Religion, Politics, and Polemics in Radical Puritanism* (Cambridge: CUP, 2001); Christopher Hill, *The World Turned Upside Down* (Harmondsworth, Middlesex: Penguin, 1975).

[70] Joseph Salmon, 'Heights in Depths', in *A Collection of Ranter Writings from the Seventeenth Century*, ed. by Nigel Smith (London: Junction Books, 1983), pp. 203-223 (p. 204). See Smith, *Perfection*, p. 68.

leader, George Fox. In *The Woman Learning in Silence* (1655), Fox indicates how inner light theory impacted on women writing or speaking within the prophetic mode. Prophetic women's messages were considered valid if they demonstrated connection to the spirit. This text maintains a position of universalism, as Fox explains: 'The light is the same in the male, & in the female which cometh from Christ, him by whom the world was made, and so Christ is one in all, and not divided'.[71] A leader such as George Fox speaks for the movement, so his contribution to the topic in print is a significant event. Fox's undifferentiating approach to enlightenment, in *The Woman Learning*, adds weight to the idea that all people are equal in the light, because it is available to everyone as a source of spiritual guidance. This statement on the side of women is further notable because it constructs a sense of unity between men and women; and, even, in its reference to 'same'ness, Fox's statement might also indicate that a movement believing in the power of the spirit to work within all people, must, inevitably, hold egalitarian views. It might be argued that when women wrote within a community, they suffered the effects of dogma: that writing which constructs the Quakers' public identity necessarily enforces a degree of conformity to the movement's central tenets. In this first instance of Fox's public support for women, however, the communitarian approach seems enabling rather than restrictive, in that it argues that women could, and should, write with the energy and vigour that results from this collective sense of godly purpose.

The prophetic mode established in Quaker texts de-essentialises the woman writer, however, and the act of writing *for* the godhead is double-edged because it conforms to masculine notions of writerly authority. Again, the notion of women's connection to the inner light is pivotal to understanding their position within this community's values (here, prophetic). In *The Woman Learning in Silence* Fox argues that to prevent a woman from speaking in the light is to 'stop' the mouth of Christ – a theory he can arrive at only by pushing his interpretations to their most extended, and contentious, conclusions. 'Who is it that dares stop Christs mouth?' he asks.[72] It is implied that Christ speaks through the woman whilst she is in the light. Fox assumes the case is closed once Christ speaks, and once the masculine model of godly authority has been asserted. The case is far from closed, however, in that the strength gained through this woman's fusion with the light brings a corresponding weakness, since her own will is sublimated to the godhead's. This ambiguous mode of empowerment attracts paradoxical analysis of its impact on women. Phyllis Mack's seminal *Visionary Women*, for instance, champions Friends' prophetic writing by noting that gender norms are extensively interrogated in women's works. Yet in Mack's comment that the Quaker writer's 'disengagement from her own social identity or "outward being" was more radical [than other sectarians']', the contradictions facing women begin to emerge.[73] Women's interaction with print culture, according to this thesis, was a profoundly

---

[71] George Fox, *The Woman Learning in Silence* (London: Thomas Simmonds, 1656), p. 5. Thomason's date is 22 March, 1655 [i.e. 1656].

[72] Fox, *The Woman Learning*, p. 5.

[73] Phyllis Mack, *Visionary Women*, p. 174.

alienating experience. It is clear that women might assert Quaker identity (which, of course, is a form of 'social identity' ignored in this comment by Mack), yet speak from a de-essentialized position – as Christ, the light, his 'substance', or god. Mack elsewhere terms this 'transcendence'.[74] If the social and collective meanings to 'inwardness' are masculinized, however momentarily, when merging with the spirit, this seems to imply that Friends cannot simultaneously write both *as Quakers* and *as women*.

One pertinent example must here suffice of the problematical implications of this focus on the loosening of 'social identity', though more will be discussed in due course. Early in the 1650s, when Quakerism was emerging in the north as a sect of growing significance, one woman's reference to her deified status had weakened the movement's reputation. The Quaker known only as Williamson's wife apparently told people 'she was the eternal Son of God'.[75] We will shortly see that such audacity is atypical when compared with other women's writerly constructions. Her audience's incredulity not only at the deification being claimed, but also the switch to a male subject position, led them to contend 'she was a woman, and therefore could not be the Son of God'.[76] The fact that this exchange was recorded in an anti-Quaker text says something about the contentiousness of the assertions being made; Francis Higginson uses this moment to fuel his exposure of Friends' 'horrid blasphemies'.[77] The implication to be drawn from this example of female enthusiasm is that the more extreme applications of inner light theory to women brought them ridicule and denunciation. The consequence of Friends' theological tenets is that women speak in a 'double' or multiple voice (in that god, Christ, the light, and the woman might appear to speak) as they attest to the action of the god channelling his words through them.[78] This is the condition of the godly generally; yet women's writing might present evidence that these expectations produce irreconcilably contradictory ways of speaking.

The utility of John's gospel to women writers is seen in its wide-ranging applications – as a theory of salvation, prophetic experience, and writerly authority. Although a great many of these applications of theory are implicitly rather than explicitly pertinent to women's situation, there is evidence of many female Quakers relating these concepts to their own condition. Writing about (and *in*) the light, produces a position of connection to the movement and its dominant metaphors for spiritual union. The effect of writing *within* an established episteme is twofold. In the first instance, women speak from an integrated and communitarian position which insists upon the rights of each believer to prophetical inspiration. Their 'social identity' *as Quakers* is produced as they write of their connection to the light. Their personal connection to the godhead, moreover, is predicated on the Quaker focus on inwardness, so yoking together

---

[74] Mack, *Visionary Women*, p. 173.

[75] Francis Higginson, *A Brief Relation of the Irreligion of the Northern Quakers* (London: T.R. for H.R, 1653), p. 3. See Higginson in *EQW*, pp. 63-78.

[76] Higginson, *A Brief Relation*, pp. 3-4.

[77] Higginson, *A Brief Relation*, p. 3.

[78] See *'This Double Voice'*, ed. by Clarke and Clarke, *passim*.

'self' and community aims. A singular focus on the 'masculinized' subject position of prophet explains the perceived transgressiveness of women such as Williamson's wife. However, the prophetic writer's usual practice is to speak of her sense of *fusion* with the godhead, and this merging is not quite the same thing as 'transcendence'. The practice of writing within this episteme allows women to exploit the potentials of this theology, to speak of a further relational identity – the believer's connection to god – and this produces mutable subject positions. As they shaped the prophetical mode, women also contributed to collective, public definitions of godly inspiration.

Self-Presentation

Women's explanations of how and why they wrote for publication best indicates their relationship both to their community, and to their gender. For our present purpose of exploring women's relationship to print, comments establishing the godly woman's writerly purpose advance our sense of Quakerism's appeal. London Quaker Rebecca Travers's work provides between-the-lines reflection on what it meant to write with an oblique awareness of gendered identity, showing the particular dilemmas usually faced by women writing for publication. In *Of that Eternal Breath* (n. d.), the writer's comments are indicative of the 'anxiety of authorship' that Hilary Hinds identifies as a feature of women's pamphlets of the period: 'writers frequently voice misgivings and reluctance' about their writerly position '[by] suggesting [...] that their own part in the production of the text is minimal, non-existent, or simply irrelevant'.[79] Travers, in like manner, defends the practice of speaking and writing thus:

> The Lord is my Witness whom I serve in the spirit, that I have not envy or hatred or wrath towards any man, Teacher, or Hearer, but in the meek spirit and fear of the Living God, have spoke and writ in good will unto all being thereto called of him who warns all.[80]

Being careful of appearing to speak from a personal agenda, she writes of her subservience to god; Travers's 'anxiety' also emerges in her use of the word 'meek' to represent herself. Although we should be careful of reading too much into a single word, the evidence from the period suggesting 'contradictions between femininity and authority' might seem to be invoked by this 'meek' approach.[81] Travers attempts to neutralise her act of speaking to 'man, Teacher and Hearer', by reminding her readership that she is a humble subject of the god she serves. So rarely does prophetic writing of the 1650s show a Quaker woman's awareness of the unconventionality of speaking for god, in his voice, and with his

---

[79] Hinds, *God's Englishwomen*, p. 88.
[80] Rebecca Travers, *Of that Eternal Breath* (n. pl.: n. pr., n. d), p. 4.
[81] Hinds, *God's Englishwomen*, p. 93.

authority, that more has to be made of these textual moments than is, perhaps, entirely justifiable.

Some other examples, though, expose a defensive element to the writing. The two writers considered below show that they are conscious that others have the power to silence them. Hester Biddle and Susanna Bateman recognise that they face prejudice, and they indicate that their messages might meet resistance. To write, they have to overcome the expectation that they should be modest, and they have to counter patriarchal society's scepticism that god could speak through women. Hester Biddle shows the earthly dilemmas facing the female prophet. Her anxieties seem to emerge when her god speaks about his intentions: 'I will not be quiet [...] I will not be silent, but I will roar and thunder', Biddle/god state.[82] The language alludes to conditions that seem to be entirely social: the particular pressures on the woman writing authoritatively within a culture that silenced unlicensed speech. Susanna Bateman's phraseology is, likewise, revealing. When writing about Jesus's saving grace she maintains 'a witness for it I am', averring '[I] dare not keep silence'.[83] What these references betray are anxieties of a material nature: the risk of writing as the amanuensis of god, the effects of social marginalisation, the audacity of writing, though a woman.

Although we can trace godly uncertainty in these women's writings, such doubts are not commonly voiced by Quaker prophets. As Hilary Hinds observes, pre-Restoration Quaker texts usually 'preclude the apologies or justifications for writing and publishing that customarily accompany the work of other women writers in the radical sects'.[84] The reason that female meekness is not a common theme in Quaker writings is that women Friends could maintain that they had direct access to the spirit of prophecy. Fox shows this when stating that men and women have equal aptitude: 'every one receiving the Light which comes from Christ, shall receive the spirit of prophecy, whether male or female'.[85] Inner-light theology, specifically, produces potentially egalitarian prophetical models.

In Rebecca Travers' *Of that Eternal Breath*, the practice of writing within a community focused on spiritual equality is evident in her comments on prophecy. She writes, again, of her motivations:

> Hereof you are warned by me who am a witness of the new Covenant in the heart, written in the inner parts, taught of God, knowing the pouring forth of his spirit upon the sons and daughters [echoing Joel 2:28; Acts 2:17], & in it prophesie of the things that shall shortly come to pass; as I have freely received, so I give forth.[86]

She is here combining the notion of 'inwardness' that comes from Johannine theology with biblical explanations of prophetic outpouring (from Joel and Acts).

---

[82] Hester Biddle, *The Trumpet of the Lord* (London: n. pr., 1662), p. 14.
[83] Susanna Bateman 'I matter not how I appear to Man' [first line] (n. pl.: n. pr., [1656]), p. 6. Thomason's date is 10 May 1657.
[84] Hinds, *God's Englishwomen*, p. 149.
[85] Fox, *The Woman Learning*, p. 6.
[86] Travers, *Of that Eternal*, p. 8.

This approach enables her to justify prophecy in 'daughters' who have a direct, inner connection to god. In addition to the feminized prophetical role, Travers comprehends something of her own power. She creates an authorial 'I' in the text, when explaining why she ventures into print 'freely'. The Quaker focus on inwardness, then, foregrounds the woman's spiritual state, and she will sometimes write directly of her own experience. And this fusion with the godhead often produces something other than an awareness of female meekness, even when writing directly as an authorial 'I'. The Quaker woman worked within an episteme that was potentially empowering. Beyond the abstract theory of prophetic experience, the practice of writing further shows how women established a godly 'voice'.

Prophecy

The construction of the prophetic voice in Quaker writing foregrounds the believer's relationship with their god: 'the Lord hath spoken, and therefore I will speak, for God hath unloosed my tongue, to speak to the promise of his name', so affirms prophet Dorothy White in her *Epistle of Love*, 1661.[87] White explains her entry into print by foregrounding her understanding of the spirit's impact, which is to 'unloosen' her tongue to speak god's praise. Many different circumstances account for women's entry into print as prophets writing a godly message. The specific experience of the light as a felt presence is one possible occurrence. Prophets might describe god, Christ, or the light working within them. Others draw on different models taken from the bible and establish Old Testament and apostolic precedents for prophecy. Some women's sense of a prophetic heritage will be considered here by way of establishing their approach to inspiration. The texts show how women exploited the potentials of speaking for the godhead, or in His voice. They were creating roles for themselves as prophets within their religious community, and their society. Some of the women who apparently 'masculinize' the practice of prophesying will be analysed here. Several appear to acquire prophetic status by imitating male, biblical prophets. Yet the concluding part of this chapter will show how women were manipulating the possibilities available to them when speaking in the prophetic voice. Women were writing within a genre that was relatively open to personal interpretation, and their works begin to express the multiple potentials of this mode.

Some Quaker women admit to drawing their inspiration from male biblical role models, referring to the old testament patriarchs and new testament apostles who serve as their guide. Even when the precedents are male, the prophet may still be exploiting the egalitarian possibilities of the Quaker faith. According to Margaret Killam and Barbara Patison, for instance, Christ, Ezekiel, Jeremiah, Isaiah, and Micah show the godly how to behave, since each 'cried against false teachers'.[88] Barbara Patison had interrupted a 'false teacher' (Thomas Martin, of

---

[87] Dorothy White, *An Epistle of Love* (London: Robert Wilson, 1661), p. 2.
[88] Killam [Killin] and Patison, *A Warning from the Lord*, p. 6.

Plymouth), and this very act makes her subservience to patriarchy seem untenable.[89] Masculine role models provide justification for some very unfeminine behaviour. This role of prophet as antagonist to the establishment is imagined more clearly in Priscilla Cotton and Mary Cole's *To the Priests* (1655) – both of these writers were imprisoned contemporaneously with Killam and Patison.[90] *To the Priests* maintains that Quaker prophets rightly disturb the public peace, because biblical characters (namely, Amos, Christ, and Stephen) did so. They argue: 'true Prophets were troublers of Israel'.[91] Something of the confrontational aspect of the prophet's role is given voice in each of these texts, indicating how anti-establishment aims were justified. Prophetic warnings or admonitions, here written to the 'priests' and people of Plymouth and Essex, show the Quaker intention to shake up local communities by delivering a bombastic godly message.[92] These writers negotiate entry into the public sphere by adapting the male prophetic role to their own needs.

The prophet's public role is not only presented in masculine terms, however, and other biblical definitions of the inspired state cut across the patriarchal norms. Margaret Fell's pamphlets from the 1650s commonly indicate her concern to establish the significance of prophecy. In several different texts, she actively works towards a definition. Her approach in *A Testimonie* (1656), for instance, is to assert that prophets are to follow in the paths of the apostles, referring to Peter 'and those that draws to the light'.[93] She states that 'prophecie came not in the old time by the will of man, but the holy men of God spoke as they were moved of the holy Ghost'.[94] Though her language seems exclusive ('holy men'), her sense that the spirit speaks directly to the believer is, in the context of Quaker thought, inclusive. Community values show that prophecy is available to all people who are 'moved' by god, regardless of gender. In *An Evident Demonstration* (1660), Fell attempts to firmly establish the difference between 'true' and 'false' prophets, and she indicates that godly interpreters are known for their sensitivity to dreams. She explains that 'When God called *Moses, and Aaron* and *Miriam,* he said, […] If there be a Prophet among you, I the Lord will make my self known unto him in a vision & speak unto him in a dream' (Numbers 12:6).[95] Fell subtly confirms women's prophetical legacy through mention of Miriam. The authorities being drawn on, here, represent a female prophetic tradition that can justify women's activities.

By exploiting the prophetic conventions, and by speaking in the voice of god as did the chosen men and women in the bible, women create a role for themselves

---

[89] Pyot (et al.), *The West*, p. 168. The same text shows that Margaret Killam was arrested for speaking to the Mayor of Plymouth (p. 168).
[90] Pyot (et al.), *The West*, p. 169. Again, the women were imprisoned for preaching.
[91] Priscilla Cotton and Mary Cole, *To the Priests* (London: Giles Calvert, 1655), p. 2. This text is discussed in Chapter 2.
[92] See Hinds, *God's Englishwomen*, p. 11 for a definition of prophetic admonition.
[93] Margaret Fell, *A Testimonie of the Touchstone* (London: Thomas Simmonds, 1656), p. 19.
[94] Fell, *A Testimonie*, p. 19.
[95] Margaret Fell, *An Evident Demonstration* (London: Thomas Simmonds, 1660), p. 2.

within the Quaker community. As Patricia Crawford has observed, 'women's authority as prophets was enormous. [...] In uttering prophecy, some women transcended weakness and experienced great power'.[96] Women such as Cotton and Cole defy male authority when interrupting churchmen, showing contempt for earthly patriarchs. Their certainty about prophetic inspiration makes possible their assertions of godly authority. Mary Cole, for instance, tersely defended the practice of prophesising when being asked to explain her action of preaching in public. Cole explained that 'she wish't that all the Lord's people were Prophets, and that his spirit was poured out on all' in response to a magistrate questioning her outpouring: her statement reveals the extensiveness of the community's prophetic aspirations.[97] Cole is speaking for the Quaker body, here, in sure knowledge that it endorses her perception of mass-inspiration. Implicitly, of course, she is indicating that this community embraces female prophets.

The prophet's prose style shows how these community values were further developed in practice, and reveals more about the Quaker approach to inspiration. If the Quakers can be said to share an approach in common, it is only that at the broad level of a generalization most prophets constructed biblically inflected prose. Some 'revitalize prophetic scriptural language, metaphors and myths' through their use of quotation.[98] Others' language is a more loosely-worked scriptural patchwork of references that builds through juxtaposing different sections of the bible. Their writings are more or less derivative, because the Quakers had a logocentric approach to language, and the bible was the most immediate source for god's word. Rosemary Foxton maintains that 'whatever their subject-matter' Quaker women's writing 'in general' assumed itself to be 'divinely rather than personally determined'.[99] Quaker prose style also represents the writer's attitudes to the divinising force of the deity, therefore. God, Christ, or the light might instigate the message, and each may use the prophet as a vessel. Theological assumptions about the believer's relationship to the godhead are thus revealed through attending to prose style. The final part of this chapter will examine prophecy as writerly practice and theological experiment, through analysis of three different approaches.

Killam and Patison's *A Warning from the Lord* shows that interpreting the scriptures is a key aspect of the prophetical mode. Their writing directs the inhabitants of Plymouth to a sense of their apparent wrongdoings, and they punctuate their address with comments making clear who is speaking. 'Thus saith the Lord, I have sent my Sons and Daughters from far, I have raised up Prophets amongst you, I have placed my witness in you': the writers are constructing this

---

[96] Patricia Crawford, *Women and Religion in England 1500-1720* (London and New York: Routledge, 1996), p. 112.

[97] Mary Cole, in Pyot (et al.), *The West*, p. 170. Thomason's date is 24 January 1656 [i.e. 1657]; Cole's trial, at which this statement was made, was in August 1656.

[98] David Loewenstein, 'The War of the Lamb: George Fox and the Apocalyptic Discourse of Revolutionary Quakerism', in *Prose Studies*, 17:3 (1994), pp. 25-41 (p. 38).

[99] Rosemary Foxton, *'Hear the Word of the Lord': A Critical and Bibliographical Study of Quaker Women's Writing 1650-1700* (Melbourne: The Bibliographical Society of Australia and New Zealand, 1994), p. 13.

part of the message as though they are quoting or paraphrasing god.[100] In the space of 23 printed lines, they repeat the phrase 'thus saith the Lord' seven times, as they establish the godly tenor of this address, building up a sense of their god's presence.[101] When 'god' is said to become the voice speaking in the text, the substance of the address echoes selected passages from the bible that remind the ungodly of their disobedience:

> Howle ye Rich men, for the misery that is coming upon you, for the rust of your Silver and Gold shall eat you thorow [sic] as a Canker, and shal rise up in judgement against you [James 5:1-3].
> Howle ye proud Priests, for the misery that is coming upon you, for ye shall run to and fro, as drunken men, and none shall be to pitie you [echoing Joel 1:13]. Wo to you that have fed your selves with the fat, and cloathed your selves with the wool [echoing Ezek. 32: 2-3], and the people perish for want of knowledge; ye run and I never sent you, saith the Lord, therefore ye shall not profit the people at all [echoing Jeremiah 23:21-22]: If ye had stood in my counsel, I wil spread dung on your faces [Mal. 2:3]; yea I have cast dung on your faces already.[102]

These writers are constructing biblically infused prose, and it might be argued that the scripture is here shown to speak – even in this passage where the 'I' of the text relates to god rather than the authors, the repetition of 'saith the Lord' indicates something of the writers' efforts to attribute the source. In this passage, the writers Margaret Killam and Barbara Patison seem to assume that their aim is to represent multiple voices – their own, the godhead's – that remain, in crucial respects, distinct. God is seen as having a 'separate identity' from the prophets, who rely, mainly on biblical quotation to construct their godly message at this point.[103] God is a more or less externalised force, here, and the practice of writing prophetically is, largely, scriptural exegesis. For these women, the source of god's 'word' is principally textual, here.

Another prophet, Hester Biddle, uses her work to express a recurring concern with 'voice', as she registers her response to the powerful authority of the deity within. Her works begin to indicate the quality of the believer-god relationship that is more direct than that imagined by Killam and Patison. In several texts dating from the mid-1650s to 1662, Biddle makes reference to the voice of god, defining its character. In *The Trumpet of the Lord* (1662), the prophet maintains that god speaks in a language all can understand (rather than in Hebrew), as she outlines her approach. Biddle makes allusion to Joel 2:28 (repeated in Acts 2:17) in order to justify the prophetic role:

---

[100] Killam [Killin] and Patison, *A Warning*, p. 1.

[101] I am counting from the first example (quoted) to 'he will plead with you by sword and by fire' (p. 2).

[102] Killam [Killin] and Patison, *A Warning*, p. 2. My thanks to Elaine Hobby for sharing her notes on this text with me.

[103] See Smith, *Perfection Proclaimed*, p. 62: 'whilst God the speaking subject is in the prophet, he has a separate identity, giving the impression that he is outside and around the prophet'; see also Smith, p. 26, for the 'puritan' practice of 'expounding of the Scriptures'.

*He would pour out his Spirit upon Sons and Daughters, and they should Prophesie;
and they shall all be taught of me* [...] So the Lord doth not speak unto us in an
unknown Tongue, but in our own Language do we hear him perfectly.[104]

Biddle's response to god is oral, here, as to a speaking voice. Her earlier *Wo to
thee City of Oxford* [1655] explains the circumstances in which the deity speaks to
the pious subject. 'God', through Biddle, instructs the readership to 'mind what I
shall say, and where I do speak be still, and low, and wait in silence; and then you
shall hear a voice'.[105] The voice of god is externalised no longer, here, as the Elaine
Hobby's observations on Biddle's text makes clear: '[she is] using the word "I" to
stand both for herself and her God [...] merging his will with hers and naming her
enemies with his'.[106] Biddle therefore presents herself as the present focus of god's
message, and she is making her prophecy speak of this inwardly felt spirituality.

In fact, the deified voice speaking in *Wo to thee City of Oxford* is not constant,
and Biddle's text moves between complete union with the deity, and a more
restrained depiction of god as an external force. She is enacting a process of
moving from understanding of self, to comprehension of the self that is fused with
god. Prefatory phrases such as 'saith Christ Jesus' sporadically appear in this text,
in observance of the fact that the voice in the text is not unmediated (yet also
revealing the Christopresentist focus of early Quaker writing). Some portions of
the text also show the movement between god in the third person, and god in the
first person. This occurs even within the space of a couple of lines of printed text:
'God exalteth the poor in spirit, but the rich *he* sendeth empty away; it is the
humble and lowly mind trembles at *my* Word, that *I* teach'.[107] The precarious
movement between 'he' and 'I' signals the fluidity of this text's construction, and
this elision between self and believer reveals the tensions within a text that
professes to speak in god's voice, rather than responding to his (outer, exteriorised)
command. These are productive tensions in that they produce multivocality, even
within a single text. Biddle has variously created different voices for god, showing
that the writer might be directly fused with god (as in *Wo to thee*), or that the act of
responding to the speaking voice positions the writer as a kind of translator (as is
apparent at some stages in *The Trumpet*). These different positions mean that there
is considerable openness to the construction of Quaker works, as well as
considerable movement within them, and force to the writing.

Some of Margaret Fell's texts more fully realise the divinising force of the
deity within, as god and she speak as one. Margaret Fell's texts show how Quaker
women negotiate a prophetic role whilst writing within godly paradigms, and her

---

[104] Hester Biddle, *The Trumpet of the Lord* (London: n. pr., 1662), p. 11; see *HPS*, p. 133.
[105] Hester Biddle, *Wo to thee City of Oxford* [n. title, first line], (n. pl.: n. pr., n. d.),
broadsheet. Thomason's date is 24 May 1655.
[106] Elaine Hobby, '"O Oxford Thou Art Full of Filth": The Prophetical Writings of Hester
Biddle, 1629[?]-1696', in *Feminist Criticism: Theory and Practice*, ed. by Susan Sellers
(Hemel Hempsted: Harvester Wheatsheaf, 1991), pp. 157-169 (p. 162).
[107] Biddle, *Wo to thee City of Oxford*, broadside. My italics.

works further advance our sense of what this inspired state might have meant to women. Fell's writing often indicates her interest in the prophetic persona, which she maintained was an important aspect in texts published into the Restoration period: for instance, *Women's Speaking Justified* (1666), which has been read as a defence of prophecy,[108] and *The Daughter of Sion Awakened* (1677), are examples.[109] During the 1650s, Fell's interest was particularly manifest in the eschatological tenor of texts addressing Jewish readers: here, the expectation that in the 'last days' the Jews would be converted is given voice by Fell. A subtle and convincing reading of Fell's Jewish texts by Achsah Guibbory confirms the radicalism of the Quaker's interpretation of the prophetic role. According to Guibbory, in the four texts addressing the Jewish question, Margaret Fell created for herself a 'prophetic, messianic identity'.[110] Fell was, Guibbory maintains, 'presenting herself in her pamphlets to the Jews as their Messiah'.[111] Quoting from Fell's *A Loving Salutation* (1656), Guibbory demonstrates how this prophetic role was realised in print: 'God … said unto *Moses*, … I will raise them up a prophet, from among their brethren, like unto thee, and will put my words in his mouth, he shall speake unto them all that I command him'.[112] The significant factor in this passage (which is a direct quotation from Deuteronomy, 18:15) is contained in the word 'prophet', which is read in the Christian tradition as a person predicting the coming of Christ. However, what Fell subsequently does is to introduce an indeterminate second reference to 'the prophet' that seems to speak more directly of her self-elected role as the Jews' converter. She explains: 'now is the prophet speaking to you in the Spirit, which is light, which is in the midst of thee'; of this statement, Guibbory observes: 'the "prophet speaking," of course, is Margaret Fell, in whom Moses and Christ have merged'.[113] The creation of a prophetic identity that goes so far as imagining a Christly role is worked through in Margaret Fell's early writings. It is evidence of the leader's uncompromising support for the notion that the light brought Christ's presence inside the believer in a fully realised sense: the work here maintains that Fell had merged with the deity.

How far a *literal* reading of Fell's alienation from her social identity can be maintained is, of course, subject to debate. The language of inspiration and

---

[108] Marilyn Serraino Luecke, '"God hath made no difference such as men would": Margaret Fell and the Politics of Women's Speech', *Bunyan Studies*, 7 (1997), pp. 73-95.

[109] *The Morning Meeting's Book of Records.* Quotations are taken from the transcript, and are given with the permission of the Librarian. 'A book of MFs entituled the daughter of Zion awakened & c Read and severall heads in it being objected against, John Burnyeat and Jasper Batt to write to MF & give the perticuler reasons why friends object against it, and cannot print it, as it is, without it being Altered or Corrected', I. Trans. 15, 23rd 5th (July) 1677. See also Mack, *Visionary Women*, pp. 367-371.

[110] Achsah Guibbory, 'Conversation, Conversion, Messianic Redemption: Margaret Fell, Menasseh ben Israel, and the Jews', in *Literary Circles and Cultural Communities in Renaissance England*, ed. by Claude J. Summers and Ted-Larry Pebworth (Columbia and London: University of Missouri Press, 2000), pp. 210-234 (p. 229).

[111] Guibbory, 'Conversation', p. 230.

[112] *A Loving Salutation*, p. 21, cited in Guibbory, 'Conversation', p. 29.

[113] *A Loving Salutation*, p. 21, cited in Guibbory, 'Conversation', p. 29.

apparent masculine subjectivity in Fell's constructions defies literal interpretation. Fell's act of speaking from the de-essentialised position of the Christly 'prophet' is a moment of uncertainty: has transformation occurred from profane to sacred, woman to man? The mode of writing practised by the Quaker prophet opens up potential meanings that are radical when there is apparently a temporary sense of disconnection from gendered identity. Yet Fell, particularly, uses a writerly technique that is perhaps intentionally free flowing. At one level, these comments are evidence, primarily, of Quaker prose stylists' movement between literal and metaphorical language.[114] The shift into biblical register is a hightened, figurative mode of writing, producing a sense that messianic positions are not necessarily to be interpreted literally. Thus, her theology is all the more tenuous, especially in respect to the most contentious aspect of her prophecy – the believer's adoption of a Christly role. After all, the Quakers' way of figuring the relationship between the believer and god (the light) is metaphorical. This is the language of transformation and possibility: it resists fixity by allegorising the believer's relationship to god, Christ, or the light.

The prophetic writer characteristically insists that the spirit working within the believer determines the content of the message. The act of speaking *for* god provides the writer and activist with self-assurance, and the mortal, female writer gains authority in 'the spirit' that she does not automatically have when speaking, as it were, for herself. Whilst the Quakers making up this community endorsed these radical definitions of the spirit, the prophetical mode allowed women to triumph over social disadvantage. The Quaker Anne Gargill's promise that 'the wisdom of God [shall be] revealed to the simple' is typical of Friends' social egalitarianism.[115] Such hierarchy-challenging comments emerge in the context of an episteme where each person, regardless of status or gender, could speak from a position of power. As these writers demonstrate, the Quaker woman prophet could speak of the injustices perceived to be most divisive within her society (Killam and Patison's critique of 'rich men' is an example). That the prophet spoke in a multiple voice when conveying a bombastic message to others evidences the openness of this godly position to radical thinkers. Women's writing cannot justify its own assertive position, except through the voice of god. The contradictions of this position are enabling in so far as they produce texts resonant both of power and authority, yet it is not difficult to read between the lines of their defiance. The socially disadvantaged had little option other than to write in the voice of a 'higher' power than their own.

I will conclude my survey of 1650s Quakerism with some comments on the community's changing attitudes to divine inspiration. Of the reasons put forward to explain women's public speaking or writing as members of the Quaker community, the openness of the 'spirit' to all believers was surely one of the most important. Potentially a divinising force, according to early Quakers, the light explained how the believer could experience unity with Christ, or his substance, through the

---

[114] Jackson I Cope, 'Seventeenth-Century Quaker Style', *PMLA*, 71 (1956), 725-754.
[115] Anne Gargill [Gargell], *A Warning to all the World* (London: Giles Calvert, 1656), p. 1.

flesh's interaction with the spirit. The theological emphasis justified prophetical inspiration. The focus began to change after Friends faced serious charges of blasphemy, and Quakers changed their tone as they became more sensitive to external criticisms of their prophetical mode. Three women writers particularly attest to the shifting sense of the prophet's relationship to god. Sarah Blackborrow, Rebecca Travers, and Dorothy White provide insight into the community's changing values. These writers instance a subtle re-appraisal of Johannine doctrine by focussing on 1:7 rather than 1:9, which points to distinctions between the believer and Christ. Dorothy White, for instance, differentiates between god and his messenger when writing in 1659 that '[John] said that he was not that light, but was said to bear witness of that light'.[116] In this formulation, 'de-divinisation' of the light is evident.[117] Blackborrow and Travers also repeat the idea of 'witnessing' to the light rather than becoming one with Christ's substance. In *Herein is Held forth the Gift* (1659), Blackborrow explains: '[John] said he was not that light', before citing the rest of John 1:7 ('he came to bear witness of that light').[118] Travers shows the longer-term impact when writing for publication in the late 1660s. She asserts: 'the Light only shews that in us, is not of us'.[119] This reappraisal points to separation from the godhead, since the believer no longer expects fusion with the light. With the exteriorisation of god, the inner certainty of prophetic authority was bound to become less secure.

These changes within Quaker prophetic writing are somewhat concealed by the revolutionary tenor of texts produced by the movement's prophets. The Quaker response to changes within society towards the end of the commonwealth period, in particular, seem to have brought renewed impulse to respond to contemporary and contentious issues, forcing the pace of political change (see chapter 3). The parliamentary overturnings that were occurring in 1659-1660 seem to have been interpreted providentially. Dorothy White's version of events in the same text where she 'witnessed' to the light shows the charged expectations:

> Although many are saying, there are a people risen up now that go about to turne the world upside down, if we let them go on; But I tell you it is not the people, but it is the power of God, for he is come to turne the World upside down[.] That that, which hath ruled over may be brought down under, and that which hath been of low degree, may be raised up by the power of God, to rule and have the dominion.[120]

Written in May 1659, during the final stages of the commonwealth period, White's vision of a world turned upside down is expressive of the sort of radical sentiment that was being shouted from many quarters during the revolutionary decades. Quite

---

[116] Dorothy White, *A Diligent Search* (n. pl.: n. pr., [1659]), p. 2.
[117] See Richard Bailey on the de-divinising of the inner light: *New Light on George Fox and Early Quakerism: The Making and Unmaking of God* (San Francisco: Mellen Research University Press, 1992), p. 222.
[118] Blackborrow, *Herein is Held forth*, p. 5.
[119] Travers, *A Testimony for God's Everlasting Truth* (n. pl.: n. pr., 1669), p. 25; in *HPS*, p. 335.
[120] White, *A Diligent Search*, p. 4.

apart from the movement's re-estimation of the light's meanings, some prophecies evidence the renewed vigour that is to be found in White's pamphlet. In Sarah Blackborrow's *The Just and Equall Balance* (1660), too, prophetical belief is still evident in radical assertions that seem undiminished by her changing approach to the light. She predicts that '[god] will overturn, overturn', paraphrasing Ezekiel 21.27, before writing with millenarian expectation that 'the great ones of the earth, must bow down before our God and Saviour', asserting '*He whom we have waited for is come*'.[121]

What emerges, then, is not a straightforward teleology: charismatic early Quaker belief in the inner light as a divinising force did not immediately give way to less radical ideas. Instead, the fact that the Quakers were a religio-political movement instances its varied religious and social concerns; and these construct a series of radical options for the writer. In this respect, print culture evidences the changing nature of Quakerism, rather than a static, rigorously narrow, agenda. Whilst emphasis was placed on the 'spirit', writers could shape this fluid identity. Witnessing to the collectively held, egalitarian belief in universal prophecy produced texts in which speaking from the spirit granted the writer license to assert radical, unsubmissive, and reformist values. When core beliefs changed, and the light's meanings were modified, the Quaker writer's sense of purpose became far less sure. In the long-term, the Quaker movement lost much of its radicalism as it retreated from its expectation that believers could be fused with the light of Christ.

Prophecy was a type of writing that could be used to establish women's collective experience of god's workings within the movement, and within themselves. The prophet's divided position neatly encapsulates the latent tensions within the Quaker approach: its concentrated focus on the inwardness of experience and the (equally weighty) concern to establish collective identity; its sense of equality in the spirit, yet its understanding that women's authority often comes about through their submission to the godhead. Here, Quaker prophetic writing's ability to maintain contradictory positions is manifest. Quakers were cumulatively shaping their prophetic role as they wrote, producing speculative, and sometimes contrasting, accounts of godly inspiration. The plurality of Quaker approaches is further evidence that the community was not narrowly enforcing a single understanding of prophecy. This is important because it suggests that community writing was potentially enabling, since it opened up spaces for the woman writer to occupy through its fluid and changeable notions of prophetical inspiration. The lack of fixity to this key genre is arguably a key reason why so many women wrote in this mode.

---

[121] Blackborrow, *The Just and Equall Balance*, p. 4.

Chapter 5

Domestic Identities in Post-Restoration Quaker Writing

The changing character of Quaker writing can be discerned in the types of works published in the post-Restoration period, after the high point of religio-political radicalism of the 1650s had passed. The 1680s, which is the key decade under analysis in this chapter, saw declining numbers of proclamatory (or, prophetical) tracts being printed, and this was no longer the dominant genre through which to express Quaker belief. According to David Runyan, who notes that the printing of proclamations was 'highest' in the early decade, this waining of prophecy indicates that for later Quakers, 'the appeal for total change of life and will became less hopeful'.[1] Sufferings narratives, too, almost halved in number, when the 1650s is compared to the 1680s.[2] Instead of the genres that were predominant in the early period, the memorial became key. As the Quakers began to respond to the changes that occurred in post-Restoration England, they sought to commemorate people who died in the Quaker faith, and 106 texts of this nature were published during the 1680s (Runyan shows). The memorial (or, deathbed testimony) is the central genre under consideration in this chapter; yet it also explores some other texts that were important in giving women a collective voice. Tracts written by women within the separate women's meeting are also considered, as is the work of one prophet, Joan Whitrow.

Deathbed testimonies are an attempt both to remember the life and to record the death of a Quaker subject. In these accounts, the deceased's relation to his/her family is given extended consideration, and the domestic unit is represented as the structure that to a great extent defines the deceased. Like most of the other texts that have been examined in this book, the deathbed testimony was created within pre-established generic conventions, and these norms will be assessed in this analysis of post-Restoration Quaker identities. The domestic role represents perhaps the most frequently memorialised subject position for adult women.

The demise of a Friend has an explicit social relevance; for many testimonial writers, a Quaker death was a loss to the movement. Comments from witnesses

---

[1] David Runyan, 'Appendix: Types of Quaker Writings by Year – 1650-1699', in *EQW*, p. 574. Runyan found that between 1680 and 1690 (inclusive), 45 proclamatory texts were published; in the period 1650-1660, the figure was 334.

[2] Runyan, 'Appendix'; between 1650 and 1660, 96 sufferings texts were published; between 1680 and 1690, 45.

show that the death of an individual created a gap: the community experienced an absence, since the deceased's role, great or small, contributed to the maintenance of group identity. Death raises issues about the continuance of the community, and writers consider these deaths in a wider sense as the movement's loss. The Quaker John Samble addressed such anxieties in his testimony to Ann Whitehead, published in 1686, averring that surviving Quakers had to increase their own commitment in order to fill the vacuum:

> Some are concerned in the consideration of how many dear and honest friends are lately taken from us, we had need be girt up in mind and Spirit, that we fall not short of the work of our day.[3]

The deathbed testimonies, seen as a way of preserving the heritage of the Quaker movement through commemoration of its dead, offer insights into the collective attitudes of later Friends. When seen in relation to other texts – from the women's meetings – the character of later Quakerism begins to be sketched. The separation of women's tasks from men's tasks, we will see, seems to be reflected in deathbed testimonies in which the domestic sphere resonates as the proper domain of women. The texts give voice to 'the many': the recording of testimonies to a deceased Friend meant that collective writing continued to figure greatly within the Quaker corpus, but community consciousness was shaped around notions of gendered difference.

Hundreds of Quaker texts memorialise death; the conventional deathbed testimony is a record of selected events, leading to the person's final hours, that takes the form of collectively written testimonial.[4] Deathbed testimonies exonerate the dying person, aiming to convey the individual's godliness by indicating his/her commitment, even in the final hours of life, to the godly maker. A 'good' death is indicated, in the accounts of witnesses to the death scene, by pious acceptance of the inevitability of death.[5] Dying well – that is, freely relinquishing earthly hopes – was important not only for the individual, whose awareness of the immanency of god's judgement results in individualised responses to salvation, but also to the observers, and scribes, who point to the significance of the death. A good death, conventionally, is the reward for the commitment to a godly Quaker life. The lived experiences of the recently deceased are therefore a model for the surviving members of the community. An account of the death of one pious individual gives

---

[3] George Whitehead (et al.), *Piety Promoted, Manifested by Several Testimonies Concerning that Servant of the Lord Ann Whitehead* (n. pl.: n. pr., 1686), p. 71.
[4] See Rosemary Foxton, *'Hear the Word of the Lord': A Critical and Bibliographical Study of Quaker Women's Writing* (Melbourne: The Bibliographical Society of Australia and New Zealand, 1994), *passim*.
[5] See *Death, Ritual, and Bereavement*, ed. by Ralph Houlbrooke (London and New York: Routledge, 1989); David Cressy, *Birth, Marriage, and Death: Ritual, Religion and the Life-Cycle in Tudor and Stuart England* (Oxford and New York: OUP, 1997), pp. 379-475; Nancy Lee Beaty, *The Craft of Dying: A Study in the Literary Tradition of the Ars Moriendi in England* (New Haven and London: Yale University Press, 1970).

access to the thoughts of many others, whose involvement with the deceased might be either intimate or relatively distant, but whose observations set the standards for a multi-vocal biography. The dying Quaker's life is viewed from a variety of perspectives, creating a cumulative picture of the deceased, and also a brief sense of the subjectivity of the testimony writer. The relationships between 'self' and society are paradigmatically conveyed, therefore, in intimate accounts of death.

Memorials to leaders, particularly those in which the deceased's works are reprinted, clearly indicate that in celebrating the person's achievements, his/her exemplary commitment is mourned. Figures such as George Fox and Margaret Fell, both pivotal figures in the Quaker community, of course receive stellar praise: William Penn beheld in George Fox 'the marks of God's finger and hand visibly', and Margaret Fell's centrality led to commemoration of her as a 'Mother in Israel'.[6] Other leaders from the 1650s, dying early, often due to the harshness of persecution, effectively reduced the number of experienced ministers in the Quaker ranks, and the loss of figures such as Burrough, Farnsworth, and others, was mourned.[7] Through the collectively authored memorials, the writers preserve the heritage of the Quaker movement (as illustration 5.1 shows).

Death is a community event in its seventeenth-century manifestation, where suffering on the deathbed was a shared experience bringing witnesses together: for Quakers, the mourners might represent the movement in microcosm. Unlike the twentieth century, in which it is common to regard death as a private moment, seventeenth-century customs favoured the communal.[8] The bedside of the sickening person was visited by many, and the roles of the healthy, aside from the act of sharing in the witness of the death, of course entailed also numerous acts of caring and ritual. Nursing did not belong only to the close family, as tending the sick was a demanding task made easier by sharing the burden.[9] Once death

---

[6] William Penn, 'Extracts from William Penn's Preface to the First Edition, 1694', in George Fox, *The Journal*, ed. by Nigel Smith (London: Penguin, 1998), p. 500; William Mead (et al.), *A Brief Collection of Remarkable Passages and Occurances Relating to the Birth [. . .] Margaret Fell* (London: Tace Sowle, 1710), sig. A2ʳ; also see George Whitehead, 'George Whitehead's Testimony', in *A Sincere and Constant Love: An Introduction to the Work of Margaret Fell*, ed. by Terry S. Wallace (Richmond, Indiana: Friends United Press, 1992), pp. 1-2.

[7] Braithwaite, *SPQ* on Burrough, p. 27; on Howgill, p. 37; on Hubberthorne, p. 25; on reprints and testimonies pp. 416-427; for testimonies see, for instance, Francis Howgill (et al.), *A Testimony Concerning the Life [. . .] of Edward Burroughs* (London: William Warwick, 1662); Josiah Cole, *The Last Testimony of [. . .] Richard Farnworth[sic]* (London: n. pr., 1667); for critical consideration of these commemorative texts see Luella M. Wright, *The Literary Life of Early Friends 1650-1725* (New York: Columbia University Press, 1932), chapters 13-21.

[8] Lucinda McCray Beier, 'The Good Death in Seventeenth-Century England', in Houlbrooke, *Death, Ritual and Bereavement*, pp. 43-61 (p. 45); Cressy, *Birth*, pp. 389-392.

[9] On Quaker nursing see, for instance, Anon., *The Ungrateful Alms-Man Rebuked* (n. pl.: n. pr, 1674), *passim*. Also see Thomas Fell (et al.), *A Short Testimony Concerning the Death and Finishing of Judith Fell* (n. pl.: [Andrew Sowle], [1682]), for a particularly physical account of illness and death.

THE
Life of Chrift
Magnified in His
MINISTER

Or, certain Teftimonies thereof, relating
to his faithful Servant,

Giles Barnardifton.

Who departed this Life the 11th day of
the 11th Moneth, 1680.

Which were given forth feverally by,

Samuel Cater,	*Samuel Waldenfeild*,
William Bennet,	*Edward Melfupp*,
John Furley,	*Jacob Baker*,
Thomas Bailes,	*Benjamin Bangs*,
Jonathan Johnfon,	*William Welch*,
John Wilsford,	*Elizabeth Gibfon*,
Thomas Burr,	*Hefter Melfupp*,
John Cornwell,	*Mary Gridle*,

And *George Whitehead.*

To be difperfed only amongft Friends and Friendly People.

Phil. 1. 20. *Chrift fhall be magnified in my Body, whether
it be by Life or by Death.*
Heb. 11. *God teftifying of his Gifts—he being dead yet fpeak-
eth—having obtained a good Report through Faith, &c.*

London, *Printed for* John Bringhurft, Stationer, *at the Sign
of the* Book *in* Grace-Church-ftreet *near* Cornhill, 1681.

Illustration 5.1   Samuel Cater (et al.), *The Life of [...] Giles Barnardiston*
(1681)

occurred, the living would sit with the body, particularly before the funeral.[10] At the symbolic level, as well as the practical, death resonated within the community; traditionally, the ringing of bells to signify the death of an individual was an element of Catholic ritual, but it continued to be observed in our period.[11] The mortality of all, not only the deceased, made death the focus of extensive consideration. For Quakers, the significance of the deathbed scene is sometimes exhaustively portrayed in texts that move beyond the nucleus of the family, to testimonies from meetings, friends, ministers and, occasionally, even strangers. Deathbed testimonies therefore juxtapose diverse parties with different relations to the deceased. One noted 'pillar of the House of God', for instance, was commemorated not only by his family, but also by both George Fox and Margaret Fell, thus clearly signifying his contribution to the movement.[12] Another notable Quaker figure, Rebecca Travers, was seemingly invited to the deathbed of people whom she barely knew, providing accounts that point the symbolic significance of the death to readers who, like her, were not personally acquainted with the deceased.[13] Deathbed testimonies capture the many different responses to bereavement, and create a sense of the many-voiced community.

Despite the multi-vocality of these deathbed testimonies, however, the texts are generically conventional, and have their base in the Ars Moriendi tradition, which in the sixteenth and seventeenth centuries fused classical and Christian concerns.[14] Ars Moriendi is the literary template for elite writers familiar with classical works, and reflected by notable seventeenth century poets such as Ben Jonson, amongst others, but the Quakers' attitudes to death are also a response to convention.[15] The template most habitually deployed, both in Quaker writing and

---

[10] Cressy, *Birth*, p.p. 427-428; for a fascinating study of the culture of dissection see Jonathan Sawday, *The Body Emblazoned: Dissection and the Human Body in Renaissance Culture* (London and New York: Routledge, 1995).

[11] Cressy, *Birth*, pp. 421-425, see also John Donne, Meditation XVII, in *The Oxford Authors John Donne*, ed. by John Carey (Oxford and New York: OUP, 1990), pp. 344-345.

[12] The phrase 'Pillar in the House of God' is used by James Pask in *The Memorial of the Just Shall not Rot [. . .] William Wilson*, by Dorothy Wilson (et al.) (London: Thomas Northcott, 1685), p. 19.

[13] Volumes to which Travers contributed include: 'A Short Testimony', in *A Collection of the Several Writings of William Bayly*, by John Crook (et al.) (n. pl.: n. pr., 1676), sigs. C^v-C2^v; 'A Testimony Concerning Alice Curwen', in *A Relation of the Labour, Travail and Suffering [. . .] Alice Curwen*, by by Anne Martindall (et al.) (n. pl.: n. pr., 1680), sigs. C4^r-C4^v; 'A Testimony Concerning our Antient [sic] and Dear Friend', in *Piety Promoted [. . .] Ann Whitehead*, by George Whitehead (et al.), pp. 28-30, 31-32; [Testimony], in Rebecca Travers (et al.), *The Work of God in a Dying Maid [. . .] Susannah Whitrow* (n. pl.: n. pr., 1677), pp. 2-7. Travers was invited as a relative outsider to the deaths of Curwen and Whitrow. For a full bibliography of Travers's testimonies, which are beyond the scope of this study, see Foxton, 'Hear the Word of the Lord', pp. 69-70.

[14] Beaty, *The Craft of Dying*, p. 2 and *passim*.

[15] Lawrence Stone cites as influential to the emergence of the spiritual autobiography the figures of Augustine, Plutarch, Seneca and Marcus Aurelius, *The Family, Sex and Marriage in England 1500-1800* (London: Weidenfeld and Nicholson, 1977), p. 12. For Ben Jonson see 'Epigram XXII: On My First Daughter', and 'Epigram XLV: On My First Son', in *The*

in Ars Moriendi more generally, is the one used to describe a godly death. In many accounts, the spiritual concerns of the sickening person are shown to transcend the physical experience of pain: the person pledges him/herself to god by enduring suffering willingly, and by looking towards a joyful, godly, end.[16] All of the Quaker texts I have examined follow this pattern – even those where an ungodly life was turned around, in the eleventh hour, by deathbed conversion.[17] Since the Quaker writing on death is essentially conventional, the act of recording the life spent in 'the truth' exists within pre-established literary boundaries.

Critics often contend that the literature on death reveals subjective, or individualised, consciousnesses; furthermore, deathbed testimonies in fact act as biographical studies and, since this makes the individual the main point of focus, questions of subjectivity emerge. Ariès' study of death is the most celebrated account of the process of individualisation through death, though in the early modern period he also conveys a sense of the collective ritualization of bereavement. He makes two important points:

> Death in bed, as we have seen, was a calming rite which solemnized the necessary passing [...]. It was an essentially collective rite.
> On the other hand, the judgement – even though it took place in great cosmic activity at the end of the world – was peculiar to each individual, and no one knew his fate until the judge had weighed the souls, heard the pleas of intercessors, and made his decision.
> Thus the iconography of the artes moriendi joins in a single scene the security of a collective rite and the anxiety of a personal interrogation.[18]

For Ariès, the collective aspects of death are residual; attitudes to death change alongside attitudes to human identity: by throwing off the sense of a communal death, the newly individualised subject can emerge. Of course, the notion that the Renaissance period gave rise to a new individualism has long been an historical

---

New Oxford Book of Seventeenth Century Verse, ed. by Alastair Fowler (Oxford and New York: OUP, 1992), p. 125; for women's poetry, see Mary Cary, 'Wretten [sic] by me [...]' on the Death of my 4th & Only Child', in *Kissing the Rod: An Anthology of 17th Century Women's Verse*, ed. by Germaine Greer (et al.) (London: Virago, 1988), pp. 156-158; for a critical view see Raymond A. Anselment, '"The Tears of Nature": Seventeenth-Century Parental Bereavement', *Modern Philology*, 91 (1993-1994), 26-53 (pp. 49-50).

[16] A central text is Jeremy Taylor, *The Rule and Exercises of Holy Dying* (London: R. Royston, 1651); see Beaty, *The Craft of Dying*, pp. 211-240.

[17] See George Whitehead (et al.), *Saul Smitten to the Ground [. . .]Matthew Hide* (n. pl.: n. pr., 1676); Rebecca Travers (et al.), *The Work of God in a Dying Maid [. . .] Susannah Whitrow*. For a contrasting sense of death, because ungodly, see Samuel Pepys, *The Diary of Samuel Pepys*, ed. by Robert Latham and William Matthews (London: George Bell, 1971), V, pp. 80-87 (11-16th March 1664). I am grateful to Dr. Gillian Spraggs for alerting me to this reference; and see Nat. Bacon, *A Relation of the Fearful Estate of Francis Spira, in the Year 1548* (London: T. Ratcliff and N. Thompson for Edward Thomas, 1672).

[18] Phillippe Ariès, *Western Attitudes toward Death: From the Middle Ages to the Present*, trans. by Patricia M. Ranum (Baltimore and London: The John Hopkins University Press, 1975), p. 37.

paradigm.[19] In line with these developments, the Quaker focus on the death (and life) of a group member seems to evidence the susceptibility of Friends to wider social and literary changes, and I will examine these literary developments in the course of this chapter.

The particular concerns of the spiritual autobiography are, though, a complex fusion of interiorised subjectivity and externalised forces. Since a providential pattern is to be perceived in the account of a godly life, several writers indicate that the act of recording is to be explicitly contained within godly paradigms. The central concern is that god is to be praised rather than the individual, as Sarah Plumley maintained, in her account of Ann Whitehead, noting that 'the Lord alone is the Author of every good thing that a People or Person doth enjoy [...] he is to have the Praise and Honour over all'.[20] Because these narratives have a spiritual tenor, the individual is represented principally in terms of his/her godly commitment.

Good Wives and Mothers

There are four principal subject positions for married women in deathbed testimonies, representing different embodiments of wifely, and motherly, duty. The subject positions available to women can be distinguished both in terms of the person's proximity to death, and to the act of writing the Ars Moriendi. Firstly, when the texts depict the dying moments of Quaker wives, the familial context is often provided by framing the narrative around the testimonies of the husband and the children. Since the woman is herself the subject of the text, her presence is central in the sense that she is the chief actor, but peripheral to the text's construction: to state the obvious, this is simply because one cannot write an account of one's own death. Testimonies by husbands and children are idealized depictions of the deceased, and the subject positions in this sort of memorialised writing often prioritise the woman's roles as wife and mother. In deathbed testimonies, the second wifely formulation is the conventional inclusion of a wife's testimony to her deceased husband, which offers her a writerly role but also spotlights a life other than the woman's own. Nevertheless, such texts can be revealing as to the paradigmatic features of self-construction, since the act of writing enables the woman to represent her relation to her husband. Where wifely compassion is demonstrated in texts to Quaker husbands, the motherly sense of loss for a loved child, shown in a number of deathbed testimonies, reveals another

---

[19] The classic study is by Joseph Burckhardt, see Tony Davies' overview in *Humanism* (London and New York: Routledge, 1997), p. 15. For other influential studies working with different formulations of self, see: Catherine Belsey, *The Subject of Tragedy: Identity and Difference in Renaissance Drama* (London: Routledge, 1985); Stephen Greenblatt, *Renaissance Self-Fashioning from More to Shakespeare* (Chicago and London: The University of Chicago, 1980).

[20] Sarah Plumley, 'A Testimony Concerning Ann Whitehead', in *Piety Promoted [. . .] Ann Whitehead*, by George Whitehead (et al.), p. 81.

aspect of women's domesticity. The family is often the nexus of these texts; therefore the subject positions for women conveyed therein commonly establish relational dynamics between husband and wife, mother and child. The portrayal of dying wives shows that, for women, the conventions of making a 'good death' enable them to direct the future behaviour of their husband, children, and others. Despite the woman's physical frailty, her depiction commonly conveys a sense of her vocality: words on the deathbed acquire a particular weight due to the imminence of death, and the woman's voice is therefore authoritative and instructive.[21] For Sarah Beck, the act of taking leave provided the forum in which she was able both to quit herself of her family, and also to instruct other gathered Friends by telling all to 'Rejoyce' (sic).[22] Though Beck's recorded words were few, the willingness of testimony writers to convey her voice shows that conventional expectations are being fulfilled; in more detailed textual accounts, the desire to convey the substance of the woman's words is more fully developed. George Whitehead, for instance, when writing of his wife, makes it his charge to 'recommend unto you some of her Living Testimonies, Expressions and Desires to Almighty God for his People, upon her dying bed'.[23] The weighty instructive role accorded his wife, Ann, indicates that women could command considerable respect: death could be an empowering experience, for women.[24]

Authoritative behaviour is also depicted in scenes in which the woman discharges her domestic responsibilities, which indicate that these deathbed testimonies conventionally record female assertiveness. Terminally ill women were expected, by the terms of the deathbed convention, to acquit themselves of their worldly care in order to prepare both themselves and their family for death.[25] Female domestic power is evident in the records of these moments, but so too is the propriety of acting this way. Worldly, familial, responsibilities intersect with spiritual piety displayed on the deathbed – as the demise of one Quaker, Jane

---

[21] Francis Bacon indicates the prevalent sense that a good death involves no loss of articulacy during the final illness: 'It is no lesse worthy to obserue, how little Alteration, in good Spirits, the Approaches of Death make; for they appeare, to be the same Men, till the last Instant', *Francis Bacon, The Essays 1625* (Yorkshire: Scolar Press, 1971), pp. 6-9 (p. 8). See also the paradoxical observations of Alice Cobb, on the deathbed of Alice Curwen, that: 'she lay making Sweet Melody to the Lord when she could not speak', in *A Relation of the Labour [. . .] Alice Curwen*, by Anne Martindall (et al.), sig. C3ᵛ.

[22] John Beck (et al.), *A Certain Relation of the Heavenly Enjoyments [. . .] Declared upon the Dying-Bed of Sarah wife of John Beck* (n. pl.: n. pr., 1680), p. 5.

[23] George Whitehead, *Piety Promoted [. . .] Ann Whitehead*, p. 7.

[24] Ralph Houlbrooke argues this in 'The Puritan Death-bed, *c.* 1560-1660', in *The Culture of English Puritanism 1560-1700*, ed. by Christopher Durston and Jacqueline Eales (Basingstoke: Macmillan, 1996), pp. 122-144 (pp. 139-140); Similarly, this position was taken by Lucinda Becker, '"The Absent Body": Representations of Dying Early Modern Women in Several Seventeenth-Century Diaries', conference paper delivered at the *Women's Study Group 1500-1825* (London, 18 April, 1998).

[25] John Evelyn's mother, for instance, instructed her family and resignedly accepted death; see Beier, 'The Good Death', in Houlbrooke, *Death*, pp. 45-46.

Whitehead, revealed. Thomas Whitehead's sense of the 'Heavenly Presence' whilst his wife was dying informs his portrait of her final hours. He observes:

> The Lord, he was good unto her to the very last, she was kept sensible, and did acknowledge that she had the Testimony of his Love, and that it would be well with her, and that she had no desire to live any longer in this World: and a little before her departure, she had no desire to have her Children with her, though they were very neer [sic] and dear unto her; but having given them a Charge to be obedient to their Father, and that they should mind the Truth, and then the Blessing of the Lord would be with them, so she desired to be retired; and the morning before her Departure, she had a sense that the time of her Departure was at hand, so she tould [sic] a Friend that she was going to her long home; and that morning she desired me to go about my occasions, though all along before she still desired Company; and I being sometime wanting, was called in again, she being now upon Departing, our dear Friend *J. Anderton* being with me, we went in unto her, and held her by the hand, and I held her up about the neck, and she manifested her sensibleness, and her Faithful Constant Love to me unto the very last, and so departed in the Love and Peace of God, as several had a Testimony of it that were there present.[26]

Jane Whitehead was thus remembered fulfilling her duties as wife, mother, and Quaker, in an account that demonstrates that a woman lays down patterns of instruction for others to make a good death.

The testimony writers endeavour to fix women within a stereotype of wifely duties: husbands commonly fulfil ideological expectations of women's familial role by portraying their wives as their helpmeets. For Thomas Curwen, the remembrance of his wife leads him to observe, in conventional terms, that '*she was given me of the Lord; who was a meet help*'.[27] Other writers are more precise when they describe the blessing of a supportive wife: conjugal understanding allows them properly to fulfil their public testimony. Thomas Brown, for instance, commended his first wife for her fortitude, particularly during his periods of imprisonment, by observing that this 'true yoke-fellow' and 'help-meet' was willing to part with him 'though I was very dear unto her as a Husband could be to a Wife'.[28] The belief that commitment to Quaker public duty is a priority, over and above familial responsibilities, is perhaps most ideologically resonant when women themselves show their acceptance of this norm. Ann Whitehead's dying words exemplify her selflessness, for instance. Her husband records that Ann said that the Lord '*blessed and prospered my Husband in his Service*,' in a reciprocal

---

[26] Thomas Whitehead, 'Here followeth her Husband's Testimony', in *A Testimony Concerning the Life and Death of Jane Whitehead*, by T.T. [Theophila Townsend] (et al.), (London: n. pr, 1676), pp. 11-15 (pp. 14-15).

[27] Thomas Curwen, 'His Testimony', in *A Relation [. . .] Alice Curwen*, by Anne Martindall (et al.), sig. Bʳ. For a theological discussion of the term 'help-meet' see Catherine M. Wilcox, *Theology and Women's Ministry in Seventeenth-Century English Quakerism: Handmaids of the Lord* (New York: The Edwin Mellen Press, 1995), p. 198.

[28] Thomas Brown, 'Some Testimonies', in *Living Testimonies Concerning [. . .] Joseph Featherstone and Sarah his Daughter*, by John Field (et al.) ([London]: Andrew Sowle, 1689), pp. 34-44 (pp. 39-40).

passage that demonstrates his own public commitment alongside his wife's humility.[29] Declaring that this gave her *'great satisfaction'*, Ann apparently further stated that she was pleased that she *'never did detain him one quarter of an hour out of the Lord's service'*.[30] A crucial subject-position for women is defined in these testimonies to conjugal harmony: one that assigns women a selfless, domestic, role.

Through their depiction of wifely domestic roles, the Quakers perhaps participate in the ideological construction of the family in terms that echoed the norms of the day; as many twentieth-century critics have observed, texts on marriage frame the representation of conjugal relationships around a concept known as the companionate marriage.[31] Of religious significance, this essentially Puritan model of conjugal harmony posits the interdependence of husband and wife, who discharge separate, but supposedly complementary, spiritual and material tasks. According to some depictions of marital companionship, spouses are harmoniously joined in their efforts to order their household along godly lines.[32] Though both husbands and wives could be an instructive presence in the lives of their children, wifely subordination was of course preferred, so the concept of companionship is an idealised one that has a gender element. Depictions of conjugal love are the norm; divorce doctrines and accounts of marital breakdown are more rare; but the quality of the writing finally indicates not the reality, but the convention.[33] That Quakers, generally speaking, chose to focus on companionship is nevertheless significant since it demonstrates the priority assigned to harmonious relations.

---

[29] George Whitehead, *Piety Promoted [. . .] Ann Whitehead*, p. 8. On the reciprocal relationship between biographers and their subject see Ira B. Nadel, 'The Biographer's Secret', in *Studies in Autobiography*, ed. by James Olney, pp. 24-31. She argues that texts are 'declarative of the life of the biographer as well as the subject' (p. 30); See also Liz Stanley, 'Feminist Auto/Biography and Feminist Epistemology', in *Out of the Margins: Women's Studies in the Nineties*, ed. by Jane Aaron and Sylvia Welby (London: Falmer, 1991), pp. 204-219. Stanley argues that 'biography cannot be treated as sealed from autobiography, for its production has many autobiographical reverberations which in turn impact on biography itself' (p. 214).

[30] George Whitehead, *Piety Promoted [. . .] Ann Whitehead*, p. 8. For a critical overview of such female selflessness see Luella M. Wright, *The Literary Life of Early Friends*, pp. 185-186.

[31] Lawrence Stone, *The Family*, pp. 102-1055, pp. 135-142, pp. 154-156, p. 158, pp. 195-202; pp. 325-404. Stone, though, argues that 'affective relations' were not always the norm.

[32] Christopher Durston, *The Family in the English Revolution* (Oxford and New York: Basil Blackwell, 1989); K. M. Davies, '"The Sacred Condition of Equality": How original were Puritan doctrines of Marriage?', *Social History*, 5 (1977), 563-580; R. Houlbrooke, *The English Family* (London: Longman, 1984); Chilton Powell, *English Domestic Relations 1487-1653* (New York: Columbia University Press, 1971); Margo Todd, 'Humanists, Puritans and the Spiritualised Household', *Church History*, 49:1 (1980), 18-34; William and Malleville Haller, 'The Puritan Art of Love', *Huntington Library Quarterly*, 5:2 (1941-1942), 235-272.

[33] On Milton's divorce doctrine, see W. Haller, 'Hail Wedded Love', *Journal of English Literary History*, 13:2 (1946), 79-97.

Though Quaker writing on wifely duty is essentially orthodox, the pattern is not entirely consistent, since in the post-Restoration period the prophetic spirit of earlier Quakerism had not entirely died out.[34] Orthodox writers idealise domesticity by depicting the woman as the helpmeet, but other factors destabilise gender norms. In Thomas Curwen's conventionalised account of his wife, for instance, notions of the supportive wife are undermined in one description of the wife's power 'over' her husband. This unusual formulation is found alongside other, more expected, figurations:

> And this I can say concerning my dear and Loving Wife, who was dear and tender over me, to serve me in anything that might do me good either for Soul or Body.[35]

'Over', in this sense, might signify Alice's concern for her husband, but its more typical usage is hierarchical, implying supremacy, even despite Thomas Curwen's attempt to depict himself as the principal actor.[36] Likewise, Thomas' description of his wife's public testimony employs masculinist models: like the bombastic women of the 1650s, Alice's testimony is part of the Old Testament prophetic tradition:

> She did follow Christ Jesus fully, who was the Captain of her Salvation, and did make war in the Righteousness with the Beast and the False Prophet.[37]

---

[34] For prophetic statements in the deathbed testimonies see 'R.T.' [Rebecca Travers], 'A Testimony', in *A Relation [. . .] Alice Curwen*, by Anne Martindall (et al.), sigs. C4^r-C4^v. Travers confesses her early anxiety about contributing to the biography of Curwen, since '*In my mind I had not much for printing it, there being not much Prophecy in it*' (sig. C4^v). For another mystical experience see Mary Penington's account of the death of her husband, Isaac, in which she declares that her spirit ascended with him at the moment of death. Mary Penington, in *The Works [. . .] Isaac Penington*, by George Fox (et al.), [A2^v]; this book has two A gatherings. This is the second of the A gatherings. See also Elizabeth Smith, in *Balm from Gilead [. . .] William Smith*, by Ellis Hookes (et al.) (n. pl.: n. pr., 1675), unpaginated. She has a vision of her husband's death, and she imagines them walking together in a light room. For Quaker controversy generated by John Pennyman's enactment of prophetic signs see: J. P., *The Following Words the Lord Required* (n. pl.: John Pennyman, 1670), also see: A. M. [Anne Mudd], *A Cry, A Cry: A Sensible Cry* (London: n. pr., 1678). See also Phyllis Mack, *Visionary Women: Ecstatic Prophecy in Seventeenth-Century England* (Berkeley, Los Angeles, London: University of California Press, 1994), p. 313; p. 315; pp. 318-319; p. 341; pp. 388-391.

[35] Thomas Curwen, 'His Testimony', in *A Relation [. . .] Alice Curwen*, by Anne Martindall (et al.), sig. B^r.

[36] For other more conventional uses of this term see Elizabeth Smith, in *Balm from Gilead [. . .] William Smith*, by Ellis Hookes (et al.), unpaginated. Elizabeth states that, as a father of six children, William 'ever bore a good testimony over them'. Dorothy Wilson states of her spouse: 'he was a dear and tender Husband over me'; 'His Wives Testimony', in Dorothy Wilson (et al.), *The Memorial of the Just [. . .] William Wilson*, sig. B^r.

[37] Thomas Curwen, 'His Testimony', in *A Relation [. . .] Alice Curwen*, by Anne Martindall (et al.), sig. B2^r. Elaine Hobby, though, argues that Curwen's memorialisation is due to the fact that she is representative of the quietistic aspects of later Quakerism. See Elaine Hobby,

Thomas Curwen's 'help-meet' was therefore represented not only in stereotypically wifely terms, but was commended also enacting her public witness. Though this particular figuration seems to have an analogue with earlier Quaker visionaries, we will see that a central public role for women in the post-Restoration period was no longer the ministry, but the women's meetings. In general, the schematic deathbed testimonies represent women's setting in principally domestic terms, and though there is the potential for them to adopt authoritative roles, their subject positions are discreetly circumscribed.

When considering women's own writings in the deathbed testimonies, the reciprocity between biographer and subject are of interest: since women's chief aim is not the depiction of her own life, but that of a husband or beloved child, relational aspects of identity emerge. In these relations, as we will see, the wifely role differs from the motherly role in terms of the writer's depiction of her own authority. Arguably, the cultural expectations of women within the domestic setting were contradictory. As wives, they were expected to occupy a role that was essentially supportive and subordinate and, as long as the husband was himself godly, the home was the husband's 'microcosmic empire'.[38] However, as mothers, their authority to command and instruct was significant. Such contradictions suggest that women's identity was fractured; it was created within sometimes contrasting cultural norms, and the competing prescriptive discourses created the possibility for expression. As the historian Natalie Zemon Davis observes, 'a patriarchal family unit could stimulate people within its borders toward self-discovery and self-presentation'.[39] What emerges, however, will not constitute a stable authorial 'I' any more than an essential identity; instead, the 'splitting' of identity and the 'indeterminacies' of identity will become apparent.[40]

Where self-assertion is most concealed, in the wives' testimonials to their husbands, the most striking contrast is between the relatively assertive authorial 'I' of discourse, and the relatively passive role the woman assigns herself. Since the

---

Virtue of Necessity: English Women's Writing 1646-1688 (London: Virago, 1988), p. 49. Alice Curwen's text has also been examined for its portrayal of race. See Moira Ferguson, 'Seventeenth-Century Quaker Women: Displacement Colonialism and Anti-Slavery Discourse', in *Culture and Society in the Stuart Restoration*, ed. by Gerald Maclean (Cambridge: CUP, 1995), pp. 221-240.

[38] Lawrence Stone, *The Family*, p. 158.

[39] Natalie Zemon Davis, 'Boundaries and the Sense of Self in Sixteenth-Century France', in *Reconsidering Individualism: Autonomy, Individuality, and the Self in Western Thought*, ed. by Thomas C. Heller (et al.) (Stanford, California: Stanford University Press, 1986), pp. 53-63 (p. 59).

[40] Neil Keeble uses the term 'splitting identity' to describe the presence of Lucy Hutchinson in her representation of the life of her parliamentarian husband. See Lucy Hutchinson, *The Memoirs of Colonel Hutchinson with a Fragment of Autobiography*, ed. by N. H. Keeble (London and Vermont: Everyman, 1995), p. xxxvi. Elspeth Graham writes of the 'indeterminacies' evident in women's life-writing: See 'Women's Writing and the Self', in *Women and Literature in Britain, 1500-1700*, ed. by Helen Wilcox (Cambridge: CUP, 1996), pp. 209-233 (p. 212).

Quakers were anxious to represent the domestic unit in harmonious terms, female assertiveness is rarely portrayed. However, the act of writing involves figuring self-representation even within passive notions of femininity; women's support of the husband's ministerial endeavours demonstrates this conflict. Dorothy Wilson's depiction of the possible 'hindrance' of domestic care, for instance, recognises contradiction whilst repressing it:

> I was never his hindrance, but was freely willing to give him up to service that the Lord had called him unto, for I have often bidden him take no care for anything he left behind, but have said perform thy journey as thou sees the Lord makes thy way.[41]

Dorothy's voice has an imperative tenor; the 'I' in the text is distinct, but this nevertheless acts to represent the wifely role as a supportive one. Mary Beth Rose terms such textual manifestations as 'the felt conflict between self-effacement and self assertion'.[42] Though the women might invert some of the typical terms used to describe marriage, implying that the husband is their 'yoke fellow', for instance, such a sense of equality is belied by the essentially supportive role they seemingly embrace.[43]

Essentially conservative ideas of the family are evident in the testimonies in which women accept the authority of their husbands to direct their behaviour from beyond the grave. Here, the woman's piety is inscribed in the text alongside her deference: this is approved behaviour, as John Whiting's account indicates. Describing his father's deathbed instructions to his mother – '*that as she had believed in the Light, so she should walk in it*' – John Whiting approvingly observes that 'accordingly she did'.[44] Where women represent their own acceptance of patriarchal authority, as in the case of Richard Samble's wife, Jane, the woman can gain credit by conveying her joyful acceptance of patriarchal instruction. Her husband's deathbed wishes were clear: '*God will be to thee a Husband, and a Father to our little Children, as thou abidest faithful to the Lord*'.[45] Though this sets the pattern for Jane Samble's period of bereavement, she also uses her testimony to foreground her personal struggles. Detailing the grieving process, Samble observes:

[41] Dorothy Wilson, 'His Wives Testimony', in Dorothy Wilson (et al.), *The Memorial of the Just [...] William Wilson*, sig. Bʳ.
[42] Mary Beth Rose, 'Gender and Genre, Women's Autobiographies in the Seventeenth Century', in *Women in the Middle Ages and Renaissance: Literary and Historical Perspectives*, ed. by Mary Beth Rose (Syracuse: Syracuse University Press, 1986), pp. 245-278, (p. 247).
[43] Sarah Featherstone, 'There hath Something Lain as a Weight', in *The Living Testimonies Concerning [. . .] Joseph Featherstone*; by John Field (et al.), p. 10. Sarah states of her husband that: 'The Lord made Instrumental in his Hand towards my Convincement; he was a true Yoke-fellow indeed'.
[44] John Whiting (et al.), *Early Piety Exemplified* (n. pl.: n. pr. [1681]), p. 2.
[45] Jane Samble, in *A Handful after the Harvest-Man [. . .] Richard Samble*, by Thomas Salthouse (et al.) (London: Andrew Sowle, 1684), sig. B3ʳ.

Oh! It was so hard a thing, to part with so good and loving a Husband, it even weighed me down, then did I cry to the Lord for strength to undergo that great Exercise; and the Lord appeared to me, and gave me strength to undergo with Patience that great Tryal [sic].[46]

Here, personal anguish generates the subjective observations, but there is also a doctrinal point: individual crises are to be overcome by accepting god's guidance. Even whilst the authorial 'I' is at its most insistent, Jane Samble accepts patriarchalism on two levels: the husband's recommendations and the patriarchal god's ability to give strength.

The sense that wifely subordination could give rise to a dependent, passive, subjectivity is evident in one Quaker text that, though unusual in its explicitness, articulates marriage in terms of self-annihilation. Mary Penington's testimony to her husband, Isaac, exists within a contradiction established for women writers attempting to depict themselves as virtuous.[47] Though writing of her husband foregrounds the authorly 'I' of discourse, and creates some assertive subject-positions, Mary represents herself as personally decrepit. Tropes of female weakness abound in this text, as Mary depicts herself as 'a poor worm, a very little one to him, compassed about with many infirmities'.[48] And though the 'worm' could turn, as the critic Hilary Hinds has shown, this image of female abjection can be redeemed only if the woman shows that her passivity equates to godliness.[49] Female selflessness, for Penington and others, can demonstrate the righteous acceptance of god, as Thomas Whitehead's account of his wife, Jane, indicates. He observed that 'though of her self she was weak and could do nothing, yet had Faith in Christ, who enabling her, could do all things that he called her unto'.[50] What is therefore significant in Mary Penington's text is her own choice of these abasing images; in deploying images of her own weakness, she falsely represents her role as supplementary – it was not, as her later account of her own life indicates – and as she herself contends in her testimony to Isaac: 'I gave up much to be a *Companion* to thee'.[51] Where the woman represents herself as little more than the

---

[46] Jane Samble, in *A Handful after the Harvest-Man*, by Thomas Salthouse (et al.), sig. B3ᵛ.

[47] See Elaine Hobby, *Virtue of Necessity: English Women's Writing 1646-1688* (London: Virago, 1988), *passim.*

[48] Mary Penington, in *The Works [. . .] Isaac Penington*, by George Fox (et al), [A2ᵛ].

[49] Hilary Hinds, *God's Englishwomen: Seventeenth-century Radical Sectarian Writing and Feminist Criticism* (Manchester and New York: Manchester University Press, 1996), pp. 94-96. Hinds is here discussing the use of the worm image in Anne Wentworth, Katherine Chidley, Anna Trapnel and Elinor Channel.

[50] Thomas Whitehead, 'Here Followeth her Husband's Testimony', in *A Testimony Concerning [. . .] Jane Whitehead*, by T. T. [Theophila Townsend] (et al.), p. 13.

[51] Mary Penington, in *The Works of [. . .] Isaac Penington*, by George Fox (et al), [A2ᵛ]. For Penington's life-writing see 'Some Account of Circumstances in the Life of Mary Penington', in *HPS*, pp. 210-232; Catherine La Couroge Blecki, 'Alice Hayes and Mary Penington: Personal Identity within the Tradition of Quaker Spiritual Autobiography', *Quaker History*, 65 (1976), 19-31.

shadow of her husband, despite evidence to the contrary, the discourses of wifely virtue seem problematically constraining.[52]

Virtuous wives, writing of the deaths of their husbands, seemingly commend their husbands' public duties whilst accepting for themselves a circumscribed domestic role; however, their representation of the motherly role is an enlargement of their authority. Since families acted as the training ground for children, the mother's role could be fundamental in the process of socialisation and this, as Catherine Belsey shows, marks a 'discursive instability'.[53] Women's appointment to the task of training children, as we will see, was enshrined in the statements from the women's meetings, which created a sense that child-care was both a public and a private duty. Similarly, in the deathbed testimonies, evidence exists of women's pivotal role. John Beck observes, for instance, that his wife Sarah's 'mouth [was] opened to pray to God in our Family' and, similarly, Thomas Curwen remarks of his wife Alice, that 'her Children and many more were convinced by her wise walking'.[54] Indeed, the duty of caring for children meant that, for Alice Curwen, the opportunity to travel abroad at god's command was taken only after her children had grown up.[55] Because the motherly role has such significance, the construction of the authorial 'I' can bring a woman out from the shadow of the husband.

The resonant depictions of the sacrifices that the mother had made for her child and, in turn, the child's sense of their emotional debts to their mother, create a venerable subject-position for women. For instance, Sarah (Featherstone) Brown, who lost her only surviving child in her seniority, displays particular distress in her account of her daughter (also called Sarah). Her only surviving child's death, from a family in which nine other children failed to outlive their parents, is much lamented:

> Oh, the consideration of my great loss of so dear a Child now in my Old Age, hath caused me sometimes to say in my heart of *David* said of *Absolom, would God I had*

---

[52] Non-Quaker woman, Lucy Hutchinson, uses the shadow image. See Lucy Hutchinson, *The Memoirs of the Life of Colonel Hutchinson with a Fragment of Autobiography*, ed. by N. H. Keeble (London and Vermont: Everyman, 1995), p. 26. See also N. H. Keeble, '"The Colonel's Shadow": Lucy Hutchinson, Women's Writing and the Civil War', in *Literature and the English Civil War*, ed. by Thomas Healy and Jonathan Sawday (Cambridge and New York: CUP, 1990), pp. 227-247. For another example of a woman writing of her husband see the non-Quaker Theodosia Alleine, in *The Life and Death of Mr Joseph Alleine*, by Richard Baxter (et al.) (n. pl.: n. pr., 1671), chapter 6.

[53] Catherine Belsey, *The Subject of Tragedy: Identity and Difference in Renaissance Drama*, p. 149.

[54] John Beck, *A Certain True Relation [. . .] of Sarah wife of John Beck*, p. 6; Thomas Curwen, 'His Testimony', in *A Relation [. . .] Alice Curwen*, by Anne Martindall (et al.), sig. Cᵛ.

[55] Alice Curwen, in *A Relation [. . .] Alice Curwen*, by Anne Martindall (et al.), pp. 2-3.

dyed for thee, O Absolom, *my Son!* [2 Sam. 18:33; 19:4] Surely I have far more cause than David had, having no more of my own to be a comfort to me.[56]

Like Jane Samble's account of her grief, personal suffering is foregrounded; but Brown's approach is self-aggrandising in comparison. Though the image of David's love for Absolom is not confined, in Quaker writing more generally, to maternal grief, the image principally requires the reader to recognise that the parental bond is emotionally charged.[57] Indeed, it initially refuses even the consolation of religion. Whatever the despair experienced, however, these depictions of motherly grief are a prologue to increased piety. The suffering mother Anne Gardner, for instance, remembered her fraught emotions, confessing that 'It was hard for me to refrain from Weeping', though she, like Sarah Brown, also eventually accepts that 'my loss is her everlasting gain'.[58] The mother's grief seems to be represented as a particular site of pathos, and her willingness to surrender her child to god, a particularly pious femininity. Indeed, as Phyllis Mack has argued, in the mother's care for her children there was a spiritual metaphor: 'the paradigm for the experience of spiritual striving and ultimate union with god was the relationship between mother and her infant child'.[59]

The representation of the parental bond is a resonant one, despite former claims by historians that affective relationships were not stimulated within the family. Though the historian Lawrence Stone has asserted that, due to the frequency of child mortality, the emotional bond between parent and child was a relatively weak one, this thesis has been challenged.[60] Parental bereavement, as Raymond A. Anselment has shown, is demonstrated by the 'palpable sorrow' at the loss of a child and, certainly, Quaker writing also displays the parent's sense of devastation.[61]

Children's remembrance of their mothers also assigns them a venerable spiritual role, one that indicates that domestic duties can be conflated with obedience to god. A notable scriptural parallel, asserted in two texts, is that between a Quaker mother and Mary of Bethany, the latter of whom chose to sit at Jesus' feet instead of serving food (Luke 10:38-42). This story is cited in Susannah Whitrow's praise of her mother, reported in a text probably by Joan Whitrow herself, when the dying child observed 'thou art *Mary*, thou art *Mary*; My Mother,

---

[56] Sarah Brown [formerly Featherstone], 'A Brief Relation', in *Living Testimonies [. . .] Joseph Featherstone*, by John Field (et al.), pp. 18-19.
[57] The other example of this trope can be found in Mary Bayly's remembrance of her husband. Mary Bayly, in *A Collection of the Several Writings of [. . .] William Bayly*, by John Crook (et al), p. 747.
[58] Anne Gardner, 'A Testimony of Anne Gardner her Mother', in *A Brief Relation of the Life and Death of Elizabeth Braythwaite*, by Anne Gardner (et al.) (n. pl.: n. pr. [1684]), pp. 3-4.
[59] Mack, p. 39.
[60] Stone, *The Family*, pp. 105-114; chapter 9.
[61] Anselment, 'The Teares of Nature', p. 27; Also see Anne Laurence, 'Godly Grief: Individual Responses to Death in Seventeenth-Century Britain', in *Death, Ritual, and Bereavement*, ed. by Ralph Houlbrooke, pp. 62-76 (pp. 67-71).

thou hast chosen that good part'.[62] In more expansive terms, Elizabeth Bols remembers her mother, Mary Watson, in a spiritually dense passage that also invokes the comparison to Mary:

> And for my own part, I have been, as it were raised from the brink of the Grave, and I am as one of the Monuments of the Lord's mercy [. . .] And when I was in my greatest calamity, the Thoughts of her from whence I came, was as Marrow to my Bones [Prov. 3:8], blessing the Lord on her behalf, That he was pleas'd to suffer me to spring from such a Root, which brought Honour to his great Name, and the desire of my Heart and Soul is, that we are her Branches, who are yet left behind, may receive the same Sap and Virtue from Christ the Root, which will be in us as a well of water springing up unto Eternal Life [John 4:14] [. . .] My dear Mother, tho' but weak of Body, yet formerly was much given to fasting on Religious Accounts, and spending much of her time in private Retirements, fervent Prayers and praising the Lord, delighting much in Meditations and like *Mary*, that Christ said, *had chosen that better part* [Luke 10:42].[63]

Since the mother's spiritual commitments could, potentially, clash with her domestic duties, the inclusion of such reifying testimonies are ideologically significant. Furthermore, it can be observed that in this formulation of female piety the mother is, like Christ, figured as the 'Root', thereby collapsing the distinctions both between male and female, sacred and profane.

To assert the woman's fundamental role in the socialisation of children might challenge the sense conveyed, in some writing, that the patriarchal father figure was the main instructor. Such was apparently the opinion of Dorothy Tickell, who represented not only patriarchal duty, but also figured the children as male. Exhortation is the 'natural' role of men, she asserts:

> Now dear Friends, receive my Mite into your Treasury; strive not so much for earthly Possessions, for your children, as to instruct them in the right way of the Lord – What Father so unnatural, but would have his children Wise? because a wise Son maketh a glad Father: So teach them to fear of the Lord, that is, the beginning of Wisdom; teach them to depart from Iniquity, that is, the good understanding, still having your eyes Sion-ward [sic]; forget her not, she is the City of our Solemnity.[64]

Though the text raises the image of feminised subjectivity in the image of the writer's 'mite' – a possible allusion to the widow's mite (Mark 12:41-44; Luke 21:1-4) – this particular figuration is deferential to patriarchal order.[65] Once more,

---

[62] [Joan Whitrow? The text is unsigned], 'These are the Dying Words of the Maid', in *The Work of God [. . .] Susannah Whitrow*, by Rebecca Travers (et al.), p. 31.

[63] Elizabeth Bols, 'A Few Words', *An Epistle by way of Testimony [. . .] Mary Moss*, by Samuel Watson (et al.) (London: Thomas Northcott, 1695), pp. 12-13.

[64] Dorothy Tickell, *Some Testimonies Concerning the Life and Death of Hugh Tickell* (London: Thomas Northcott, 1690), p. 3.

[65] For another representation of the widow's mite see Elizabeth Hinks, *The Poor Widows Mite* (n. pl. n. pr, 1671). I am grateful to Elaine Hobby for sharing her notes on this text with me.

therefore, masculine authority is naturalised through its association to good reason and judgement, and feminine self-assertion is only circuitously invoked.

The dominant subject positions for adult women – wife and mother – though paradigmatically established within the domestic sphere, nevertheless have significance in the Quaker community's construction of its self-image. Beyond the fractured identity of domesticised women, the family model is usefully employed to describe leading Quaker figures. Characterising key Quakers as the movement's parents is a way of mapping personalised subject positions onto the collective body of believers. The female role of the 'mother in Israel' was assigned both to Margaret Fell and Ann Whitehead, and the term 'nursing father' was assigned to Richard Samble and Giles Barnardiston: these representations are clearly intended to evoke a sense of the familial closeness between Quakers.[66] The idealised approach to the family, as we have seen, represents parents in separate though complementary roles, and under-represents possible conflicts of interest. In a similar manner, the Quaker movement developed its formal structures along lines of gender segregation: the principal site for female activity became the women's meetings. And the notions of femininity continued to be important in the women's own images of their public action; it is to these collectively developed identities that we will now briefly turn.

The Women's Meetings

When the Quaker family developed formal organisational structures, one of the outcomes was the annexing of women's power into separate meetings. The process of gendered separation (into relatively discrete men's and women's meetings) was not simple: it could both formalise power and entail it away from women; it could result both in a sense of separation and a feeling of mutuality between Friends. As a consequence of this complexity, the evidence amassed by historians is contradictory, with some seeing the positive aspects, and others arguing that the women's meetings lacked power.[67] Where such differences of opinion exist as to

---

[66] William Mead (et al.), *A Brief Relation of Remarkable Passages [. . .] Margaret Fox*, A2ʳ; George Whitehead (et al.), *Piety Promoted [. . .] Ann Whitehead*, p. 19; p. 51; p. 73; pp. 87-88; Thomas Salthouse (et al.), *A Handful after the Harvest-Man*, sig. Bʳ; Samuel Cater (et al.), *The Life of Christ Magnified [. . .] Giles Barnardiston* (London: John Bringhurst, 1681), p. 37; p. 42; p. 44; p. 60.

[67] Mack, *Visionary Women*, p. 349, observes that 'on balance, and in the long run, I believe that the separate women's meeting was good for women; indeed, it may be said to have been a cradle not only for modern feminism but of the movements of abolitionism, women's suffrage, and peace activism, all of which were, and are, enlivened by the presence (even predominance) of Quaker female leaders'. By contrast, Christine Trevett states that 'to the modern student of Quakerism what is most remarkable about the Women's Meetings (after the fact of their existence) is the lack of power associated with them'. See *Women and Quakerism in the Seventeenth Century* (repr. York: Ebor Press, 1995), p. 81. For other studies see Bonnelyn Young Kunze, *Margaret Fell and the Rise of Quakerism* (New York: Macmillan, 1994), chapter 7; Isabel Ross, *Margaret Fell, Mother of Quakerism*, 3rd edn

the collective expressions of women in later Quakerism, the instabilities of women's power can continue to be perceived.[68] Indeed, since the establishment of the women's meetings was one aspect productive of a deep schism within the Quaker ranks (the Wilkinson and Story separation), gender issues clearly continued to be divisive.[69] In the pages that follow, the defences written by representatives of the women's meetings will be examined; these texts were a response to the internal conflicts within the Quaker movement, and an attempt to define their power.[70] As we will see, their representations of the available subject positions indicate that, as in the deathbed testimonies, feminine role models were important.

The establishment of the women's meetings provoked controversy; therefore, when women began to write defences of their public roles, in the 1680s, their texts registered the amount of hostility directed against them. The women's meetings were championed by leading Quakers, of whom George Fox was the foremost.[71] On the other side, however, were the Westmoreland separatists, Wilkinson and Story, whose resistance to the formal innovations within the Quaker movement included a refusal to accept the authority of the separate meetings.[72] At the height of these internal divisions, two women wrote to defend the women's meetings. The text by Ann Whitehead and Mary Elson (1680) is indicative of the corporate

---

(York: William Sessions, 1996), chapter 19; Irene L. Edwards, 'The Women Friends of London', *JFHS*, 47 (1955), 12; Braithwaite, *BQ*, on the men's meetings: pp. 323-324; on women's meetings: pp. 340-342; Braithwaite, *SPQ*, on the establishment of Quaker organisation: chapter 9, on the women's meetings: chapter 10; also see George W. Edwards, 'The London Six Weeks Meeting: Some of its Work and Records over 200 Years', *JFHS*, 50: 4 (1964), 228-245. For a brief history of these meetings see also the *Extracts from the Minutes and Proceedings of the Yearly Meeting of Friends Held in London* (London: Office of the Society of Friends), in the 1857 volume see 1861, pp. 25-26; in the 1897 volume see 1900, pp. 96-97; in the 1902 volume see 1904 (sic), pp. 165-169.

[68] Baptists also established separate meetings. See Christopher Hill, *A Tinker and a Poor Man* (New York: Alfred A. Knopf, 1989), p. 78.

[69] See Braithwaite, *SPQ*, chapter 11; Mack, pp. 293-304.

[70] Other women also defended the women's meetings. For instance, Alice Curwen, in *A Relation of the Labour [. . .] Alice Curwen*, by Anne Martindall (et al.), pp. 24-26, p. 34; Joan Vokins, 'God's Mighty Power Magnified' (London: Thomas Northcott, 1691), in *Hidden in Plain Sight: Quaker Women's Writings 1650-1700*, ed. by Mary Garman (et al.), pp. 255-273 (p. 263). See also the extract in *Her Own Life: Autobiographical Writings by Seventeenth-Century Englishwomen*, ed. by Elspeth Graham (et al.), (London and New York: Routledge, 1989), pp. 211-224.

[71] Braithwaite, *SPQ*, p. 273, p. 286; Mack, *Visionary Women*, pp. 286-292. See also George Fox, *The Journal*, ed. by Nigel Smith, p. 370; p. 423; H. Larry Ingle, *First Among Friends: George Fox and the Creation of Quakerism* (New York and Oxford: OUP, 1994), pp. 250-265.

[72] See John Wilkinson (et al.), *The Memory of that Servant of God, John Story* (London: John Gain, 1683), pp. 37-38; William Rogers, *The Christian Quaker* (London: n. pr., 1680), book I pp. 63-66, book III, p. 52; book IV, pp. 37-40, p. 56; book V, pp. 1-8. For another, earlier, group that rejected the formalising impulse of post-Restoration Quakerism see William Smith (et al.), *A Real Demonstration of the True Order in the Spirit of God* (London: n. pr., 1663).

backbiting; indeed, the separatist William Rogers used his defence of Wilkinson and Story to attack the women as ciphers of the Quaker leader.[73] The women, by contrast, refer to the troubles without naming the detractors, and write only of 'a contrary Spirit that will not be Subject to Unity in wholesome Practices amongst us'.[74] And five years later the London women's meeting remembered the 'unruly spirits [who had] printed and written so many slanderous reproachful Books against us'.[75] Given these acrimonious circumstances, the representation of the work engaged with by the women in their meetings is highly charged.

The disunity meant that, wherever possible, women defended their meetings as extensions of their traditional gendered roles. A central aspect of the women's responsibilities towards the Quaker family – their role in distributing charitable donations – indicates that feminised notions are important to their own self-representations. According to one important defender of the women's meetings, Ann Whitehead, women discharge such duties in 'Christs Family':

> As the good women of Old were Helpers in the gospel, as such things as are proper to us, as visiting and Relieving the Sick, the Poor more especially, and Destitute amongst us, that they be helped.[76]

Though this present study cannot assess the actual pattern of charitable activities, several writers indicate that caring was viewed as an extension of traditional female roles, as the case of George Begardner shows. A one-time recipient of Quaker charity, Begardner was nursed by female Friends who had been instructed to attend to him 'according to their capacity, [. . .] as it had been for one of their own Family'.[77] In the sense of their available subject positions in these caring tasks, then, the texts establish feminine propriety: they are 'helpers' whose public roles extended their own compassion as family members.[78] The adoption of such images suggests that the women were complicit in processes that resulted in self-enclosure.

---

[73] William Rogers terms the women 'George Fox's party', see *The Christian Quaker*, post-script [to the introduction], p. 27. Whitehead's and Elson's tract was indeed easily passed by the Quaker Second Days Meeting, see *The Morning Meeting's Book of Records, from the 15th of the 7th month 1673, to the 6th of the 4th month 1692, inclusive* (Friends' House, London) I. 36; Trans. 33; 18. 8 (Oct.) 1680.

[74] Anne [sic] Whitehead, *An Epistle for True Love, Unity and Order* (London: Andrew Sowle, 1680), p. 4.

[75] Mary Forster (et al.), *A Living Testimony from the Power and Spirit* ([London]: n. pr., [1685]), p. 5.

[76] Anne [sic] Whitehead (et al.), *An Epistle for True Love*, p. 6.

[77] Anon, *The Ungrateful Alms-man Rebuked*, p. 4.

[78] Anne Tobin's study of Quaker charity appears to have never been completed, but see Elaine Hobby's reference to the unpublished work of Anne Tobin, in *Virtue of Necessity*, p. 48. Tobin suggests that women could use charity to support families denied by the men's meetings. See also Mack, *Visionary Women*, pp. 334-336; Trevett, pp. 120-123; Braithwaite, *BQ*, p. 341.

By contrast, however, statements from the women's meetings also cut across the notions of gendered difference by asserting that men and women were co-dependants. Thus, the London women's meeting, in one collectively produced statement, broke away from describing the tasks appropriate to women, such as tending to the sick, to show their capabilities in other areas. Accordingly, they portray themselves 'sometimes assisting the Men, our Brethren, to placing out poor Friends children to Apprentices'.[79] This is a politic observation: it undermines the gendered division of labour, whilst also deferentially accepting the primacy of men. Indeed, the texts seem to sustain contrasting notions of women's power in relation to men. Ann Whitehead and Mary Elson, two prominent members of the London women's meetings, approvingly note that men have 'pre-eminence'. However, Ann also writes, on one occasion, in a way that evades ideas of patriarchal governance.[80] Ann tells women to 'be Discrete, Chaste, Sober, keeping at Home, that the word we profess be not blasphemed'; drawing upon here Titus 2: 4-5, she makes a doctrinally secure point. Whitehead's reading of the Titus passage, though, is selective: the passage also mentions the necessary subordination of women, who it is said must be 'obedient to their owne husbands'. In Whitehead's figuration, though, this recommendation is discreetly omitted. Clearly, the women who wrote defences of their women's meetings strove both to represent their actions as essentially supportive, and therefore relatively unthreatening, and also endeavoured to show their capabilities to discharge 'male' tasks. This establishes contradictory images of mutuality and separation.[81]

The separation of tasks did, however, give women some authority over men, particularly in their roles as overseers of marriages. Since all potential husbands and wives had to submit themselves to the separate meeting before they could marry, women might be seen to have considerable power, though an assessment of these duties is beyond the scope of this study.[82] Instead, attention to their representations of power indicates that women defended their involvement in conjugal issues in gendered terms. The women of the London meeting assert that because they had greater knowledge of the circumstances in marriage, they rightly shoulder the responsibility: 'for many times we have seen, and so see more in the Young People and Widdows [sic] state and Condition, than some of the Men, because we are more amongst them'.[83] Nevertheless, despite this seemingly sound reasoning, the women's authority over marriage was much debated. Quakers in

---

[79] Mary Forster (et al.), *A Living Testimony*, (p. 5); the women also explain that 'if any thing the Men do see that is more proper for the women to do, and to look into, they do let us know of it, as Sisters of the Truth; and if any thing we see that is more proper for the Men, then for us we let them know as out Brethren in the Truth' (p. 7).

[80] Anne [sic] Whitehead, *An Epistle for True Love*, p. 6.

[81] On such mutuality, see Mack, *Visionary Women*, pp. 336-339.

[82] See Trevett, pp. 87-89, pp. 92-94, pp. 96-99, Kunze, pp. 157-158, p. 162, p. 164; Mack, pp. 337-341.

[83] Mary Forster (et al.), *A Living Testimony*, p. 4. The women of the York meeting also refer to marriage: Katherine [Catherine] Whitton (et al.), *Epistle from the Women's Yearly Meeting at York, 1688* (n. pl.: n. pr., [1688]), pp. 6-7.

Westmoreland published their opposition to the separate meetings, averring that people should 'forebear [. . .] any to lay their Intents of Marriages before them'.[84] Though the antagonists did not entirely refuse to recognise the legitimacy of the meetings – they said that they saw some reasons for centralised charitable measures in cities – the measures over marriage were clearly perceived to give women too much power.[85] In vain were the defences of the women's meetings as 'consistent with good Homewifery', which Katherine Whitton put forward, since the women's meetings were actually established in a maelstrom.[86]

The traditional values foregrounded in the defences by the women of the separate meetings are also echoed in their choice of biblical role models. The most common formulations equated directly to their gendered roles; they typically termed themselves 'daughters of Abraham', 'mothers in Israel' or 'aged women in the truth'. The daughter of Abraham (1 Pet. 3:1-6) invokes the precedent of Sarah, praised as a model of chastity and virtue for her submissive conduct towards her husband. Deborah, the original 'mother in Israel', was a warrior prophetess (Judges 5:7; 2 Samuel 20:19), though this element of her conduct is discreetly omitted from Quaker texts where the focus, instead, is on more domestic notions of nurturing. In Titus 2:4-5, 'aged' woman's role is said to involve enforcing a moral code, particularly amongst young women, and we have already seen that Ann Whitehead made use of this passage in her addresses to the women's meetings. The biblical passages chosen by the women reinforce the sense that their domestic responsibility is being mapped onto the public sphere.[87]

The 'mother in Israel' was a role assigned to venerable women in the Quaker community, and it invokes domestic notions of the caring, nurturing, role of women. This role prioritised domestic activities and, furthermore, ensured that male power was protected, as Phyllis Mack observes: 'all of her activities [the Mother in Israel] could be regarded as private and apolitical, done from motives of love and charity rather than from the desire for power over formal authority'.[88] The deathbed testimony commemorating Ann Whitehead employs this trope in the manner described by Mack.[89] Domesticised notions of the mother in Israel lead to the observation that Ann 'Like a nursing Mother did cherish the good and reprove the contrary'.[90] In this instance, the testimony by Bridget Ford works by establishing oppositions, between the good and the contrary, and between the mother and her addressees. Veneration of Ann's godliness, then, is dependent on these oppositions for it to achieve significance.

---

[84] John Wilkinson (et al.), *The Memory of that Servant of God, John Story*, p. 38.

[85] William Rogers, *The Christian Quaker*, Book I, p. 66.

[86] Katherine Whitton, *An Epistle to Friends Everywhere* (London: Benjamin Clark, 1681), p. 6.

[87] On other roles for women see Mack, *Visionary Women*, p. 309.

[88] Mack, *Visionary Women*, p. 245. However, Mack also qualifies this statement pp. 291-292, p. 309.

[89] Ann Whitehead is referred to as a 'mother in Israel' in George Whitehead (et al.), *Piety Promoted [....] Ann Whitehead*, p. 19, p. 51, p. 73, pp. 87-88.

[90] George Whitehead (et al.), *Piety Promoted [. . .] Ann Whitehead*, p. 51.

In the dialectical representation of godly women, the testimony to Ann also follows the biblical account of Sarah, Abraham's wife. The biblical passage decrees that women of later ages can follow Sarah's propriety, so becoming daughters of Abraham: if they choose to put off 'outward adorning' they can behave as the holy women of old (1 Peter 3:1-6).[91] The word 'adornments' is given a religious charge here, but its other usage is in relation to a vain interest in clothing – something which, in the seventeenth century as well as the bible, had a female connotation[92] Vain women interested in clothes had a 'whorish' interest in entrapment and display, like the biblical whore of Babylon. By contrast, Friends increasingly used clothing as a symbol of their piety, adopting plain dress and reproving people who erred in matters of deportment.[93] Consequently, when William Ingram praised Ann Whitehead for her propriety, he showed her acceptance of Quaker dictates in addition to equating her with a venerable biblical model. Ingram defined her as 'a true Daughter of Abraham, adorned with those spiritual inward Ornaments of the hidden man of the Heart, as were the holy women of Old who trusted in God'.[94] The significance of this biblical model, for Ingram and others, is that it requires the other whorish woman to be repressed, and so points to righteous femininity.

The construction of feminine godliness is therefore dependent on an ungodly category; it is unsurprising, then, that for women involved in the women's meetings, moral instruction of others was a central task. Some of their observations on ungodly behaviour were specifically antifeminist: they condemned women for their vanity and gossiping which, inevitably in our period, carries with it suggestions of loose behaviour. The London 'Aged Women in the Truth' represented women's folly when they condemned '*Wanton Women, or Widows, that are Tale-Carriers and busie Bodies*'.[95] The passages being drawn upon here, 1 Timothy 5:11-13, are conflated by the women who notably bring together the most pejorative aspects of the women's behaviour, drawing attention to their sexuality and their vociferousness.[96] What is also made explicit is that particular care has to

---

[91] 1 Peter 3:3. The apostle Paul gives further advice on clothing: 'let it not be their outward adorning, of plaiting the haire, and of wearing of gold, or of putting on apparrell. But let it be the hidden man of the heart, in that which is not corruptible, even the ornament of a meeke and quiet spirit, which is in the sight of God of great price' (1 Peter 3:3-4).

[92] See Louis B. Wright, *Middle Class Culture in Elizabethan England* (Chapel Hill: The University of North Carolina Press, 1935), p. 478, p. 487, pp. 491-492; see also Ruth Kelso, *Doctrine for the Lady of the Renaissance* (Urbana: University of Illinois Press, 1956), pp. 47-48. On the whore's garments see Revelation 17: 4.

[93] Mack, *Visionary Women*, pp. 347-348. Patricia Crawford, *Women and Religion in England 1500-1720* (London and New York: Routledge, 1996), p. 191.

[94] William Ingram, 'His Testimony', in George Whitehead (et al.), *Piety Promoted [...] Ann Whitehead*, p. 74.

[95] Mary Forster (et al.), *A Living Testimony*, p. 5.

[96] After describing the good women who serve the community and God, the apostle Paul observes that 'the younger widowes refuse: for when they have begunne to waxe wanton against Christ, they will marry, having damnation because they have cast off their first faith'. It continues: 'And with all they learne to bee idle, and wandering about from house to

be taken if women are to be accepted as godly. Indeed, Mary Plumstead writes that women are to 'be careful, that we set no bad example to any, neither in our Habit or Behaviour'.[97] Likewise, the testimonies to Whitehead reinforce the admonitory stance of this venerable 'Mother in Israel' in relation to the young. Two writers confirm that Ann chastised young people's *'Pride* and *Vanity'*, during her final address to the London women, and she also seemingly used other meetings to exhort elder women to 'walk as good examples' to children.[98] At an abstract level, the representation of unworthy women in these texts by 'ancient women' serves as a point of contrast; linguistic oppositions between righteous and vain women enforce their own sobriety.

The act of both writing and meeting, however, challenges the essentially domesticated construction of women's power and, also, the notions that the home is the private sphere. Since the 'aged women' took Titus 2:4-5 as a role model, they could, with Ann Whitehead, declare that feminine duty involved 'Loving their own Husbands and Children, to be Discrete, Chaste, Sober, keeping at Home'.[99] However, the notion that this is a privatised task is undermined; training children, particularly, had a public function since it created the next generation of Quakers. Through these texts, which were conveyed both to the discrete audience in the particular women's meeting, and to a national readership, women extended their private duties into the public sphere.[100] Consequently, some of the admonitory tracts provide direct instructions for parents; when writers advise parents on good ways to bring up their children, they intrude into domestic settings. For instance, Mary Waite's observations, appended to a text by the York women's meetings, is a strongly worded attempt to fix patterns of child-rearing:

> Take heed of giving way or suffering them to get into the pride, and the vain and foolish fashions, which are a shame to the sober people, and a great inlet to many evils, for they are prone to that by nature, and it may be soon set up, but hard to get it down. So friends, keep the yoke upon the nature that is proud, stubborn, or disobedient to parents, break that will in them betimes which comes from the evil one, and bend them while they are young, lest when they grow up you cannot.[101]

---

house; and not only idle, but tattlers also, and busybodies, speaking things which they ought not' (1 Timothy 5:11-13).
[97] Mary Plumstead, 'A Testimony for Ann Whitehead', *Piety Promoted [. . .] Ann Whitehead*, by George Whitehead (et al.), p. 112.
[98] George Whitehead (et al.), *Piety Promoted [. . .] Ann Whitehead*, p.22; p. 106; p. 57. Theophila Townsend also criticises Friends' vanity and pride in apparel. See her *An Epistle of Love* (n. pl.: n. pr., n.d.), p. 2. In the same text, George Fox also reproves women who follow fashion (pp. 6-8).
[99] Anne [sic] Whitehead, *An Epistle for True Love*, p. 6.
[100] Katherine Whitton's text, for instance, is *An Epistle to Friends Everywhere: To be Distinctly Read in their Meetings*, (London: Benjamin Clark, 1681), title page.
[101] Mary Waite, 'A Warning to all Friends', in Katherine [Catherine] Whitton (et al.), *Epistle from the Womens Yearly Meeting at York*, pp. 16-17. Theophila Townsend also tells women to 'watch over' the young; see *An Epistle of Love to Friends*, p. 3; for a similar notion of child-rearing see Elizabeth Joscelin 'Manuscript Mother's Legacy', in *Women's Writing in Stuart England: The Mothers' Legacies of Dorothy Leigh, Elizabeth Joscelin, and Elizabeth*

Chillingly authoritarian in tone, this text nevertheless shows that Waite sought influence over the nation of Quaker parents, breaking them into her ideas in the same way that she required the obedience of children.

The contradictions within the emerging discourses defining women's public testimony demonstrate, perhaps, that the texts from the women's meetings simultaneously reinforced traditional roles, whilst also seeking to extend them. Whilst the texts demonstrably destabilise the notion that the endeavours of the women's meetings are private and separate, they also kowtow to traditional notions of pious femininity. This contradiction has been termed a 'double movement' wherein women are viewed as having accepted both 'deliberate self-enclosure within a limited and subordinate public role', and 'an equally deliberate definition of women's writing and public service as part of a new, highly expressive female identity'.[102] The negotiations in print are therefore finely balanced: they are notably circumscribed defences of women's activity, but are also resistant to some traditional aspects of sexual difference.

In the concluding part of this chapter, I will turn to issues relating to censorship and self-censorship, since the conventionalised and domestic emphasis of the texts examined so far requires further explanation. Through examining the minutes of the Quaker meetings, the relations between the writer and the wider Quaker body become clearer. And, by looking at the way that the prohibitions drove some women to seek elsewhere for support, we can begin to indicate the various ways in which community membership restricted women in post-Restoration Quakerism.

'Self' and Community in Post-Restoration Quakerism

When Susannah (Bateman) Blandford wrote an account of forty years spent serving the Quaker community, a principal factor underpinning her autobiographical observations was the attempt to separate the public from the private. Anxious to frame her writing around modest tropes, she observed, for instance, that the writing was not to exalt the self, but for the good of the community.[103] Such ideas immediately indicate an element of self-censorship that becomes increasingly pronounced as Blandford proceeds. The crucial caesura occurs, perhaps not unsurprisingly, in Blandford's comments on women's public speaking. Always an issue from the earliest days of the Quaker community, its reappearance here demonstrates the continuing appeal of the rejoinders to silence.

Richardson, ed. by Sylvia Brown (Thrupp, Gloucestershire: Sutton, 1999), pp. 106-139 (p. 107). On the historical and cultural context, see Stone, *The Family*, pp. 162-163.
[102] Mack, *Visionary Women*, p. 311.
[103] 'S. B.' [Susannah Bateman Blandford], 'A Small Account', in *HPS*, pp. 285-302. Blandford explains herself thus: 'whatever any may think of me, who look with an evil Eye, yet to my *Friends* that looks with an Impartial Eye, it will be received, as it is intended to all' (p. 286).

Bateman approvingly cites the Pauline epistles in which the apostle affirms that women should keep quiet in church (1 Corinthians 14:34-35; 1 Timothy 2:11-12), then criticises women whose ill-judged preaching revealed that they were 'not upon the right Ground'.[104] Evidently showing herself oblivious to the rights of her own sex, Blandford, however, praised a particular kind of female authority – the domestic:

> I know there is many Good and Vertuous [sic] *Women*, who are appointed for Good Examples in their Families, who in Modesty, Sobriety, Charity, and good Works, a good Life, and Conversation; with these I joyn.[105]

In commending a particular kind of femininity, Blandford was exerting a sense of the public/private divide which effectively both depoliticised the home – since it was seen as a site of private devotion – and denied women access to the more incontestably public sphere. However divided from her own gendered subjectivity this may appear, her use of the word 'joyn' implicitly suggests linkages between godly families, though surely this is not a dominant meaning.

The self-censoring discourse by Susannah Blandford leads us on to the more pronounced one of internal censorship, which operated through the Quakers' 'Second Day's Meeting', and the relation of writers to this body is significant even for the seemingly conventional texts we have been examining. From 1673 onwards, the 'Second Day's Meeting' appointed representatives whose responsibility it was to oversee texts before publication, and this included most of the Quaker texts I have discussed so far.[106] Internal censorship resulted, for instance, in the production of more doctrinal texts than prophetic pamphlets,[107] a focus that perhaps explains even the censorious response to Margaret Fell's resonantly apocalyptic text, *The Daughter of Zion Awakened* (1677).[108] Whilst Fell's prophetic strain jarred with post-Restoration Quaker attempts to represent their sobriety, the Second Day's Meeting found different things to criticise in the deathbed testimonials. Though the meetings usually passed the deathbed

---

[104] Blandford, in *HPS*, p. 294.
[105] Blandford, in *HPS*, p. 294.
[106] Thomas O'Malley, "'Defying the Power and Tempering the Spirit." A Review of Quaker Control over their Publications', *Journal of Ecclesiastical History*, 33:1 (1982), 72-88 (p. 77); D. J. Hall, "'The Fiery Tryall of their Infallible Examination": Self-control in the Regulation of Quaker Publishing in England from the 1670s to the mid-Nineteenth Century', in *Censorship and the Control of Print in England and France 1600-1910*, ed. by Michael Harris and Robin Myers (Winchester: St. Paul's Bibliographies, 1992), pp. 59-86; Braithwaite, *SPQ*, p. 280-284; p. 487, p. 495-496.
[107] Runyan, 'Appendix', in *EQW*, ed. by Barbour and Roberts, pp. 567-575, (pp. 568-572).
[108]*The Morning Meeting's Book of Records*. Quotations are taken from the transcript, and are given with the permission of the Librarian: 'A book of MFs entituled the daughter of Zion awakened &c Read and severall heads in it being objected against, John Burnyeat & Jasper Batt to write to MF & give the perticuler [sic] reasons why friends object against it and cannot print it, as it is, without it be Altered or Corrected', I. 17; Trans.15, 23rd 5th (July) 1677. See also Mack, *Visionary Women*, pp. 367-371.

testimonies without commenting that they needed alteration, they did demand revisions to a number of texts.[109] One problem with the comments of the censors, for our purposes, is that whilst they state that passages in the deathbed testimonies must be left out, they rarely make explicit the cause of their objections – little can be discerned about the agenda in relation to most of the deathbed censorship.

Where records detail the exact nature of the internal censorship, however, a particular pattern can begin to be discerned, particularly in relation to women's writing. Just as Margaret Fell was criticised for writing prophecy, so too were Barbara Blaugdone and Judith Boulbie. According to the opinion of the Second Day's Meeting, Blaugdone's paper 'beginning Thus saith the Lord' was 'not thought fit to be printed';[110] Judith Boulbie, too, was in trouble for writing 'A Warning to England' and, indeed, she seems to have been quite frequently admonished.[111] In both of these instances, the prophetic discourse was problematic to the censors, and we know that the works of at least one other woman has been lost to posterity as a result.[112] But though the censors had found little to criticise in the more domestic constructions given their figuration in the deathbed testimonies, they did criticise one text explicitly. In relation to *The Work of God in a Dying Maid*, by Rebecca Travers (et al.) the censors were critical of the mother of the deceased – Joan Whitrow. When objecting to Joan's text, the Second Day's Meeting states that 'what is chiefly to her owne praise be left out', and having criticised Joan's foregrounding of herself, the censors make a revealing statement about writing in the post-Restoration period. They assert that writers must accept the interventions of the censorial body to 'leave out what they see not of Service to the Truth'.[113]

---

[109] *The Morning Meeting's Book of Records*: Richard Samble's text was sent to the Devon meeting for correction: I. 49; Trans. 39, 6. 4 (June) 1681. Jane Whitehead's text was 'committed to Jasper Batt & William Gibson to correct the places marked & to leave out such things as this meeting in the Reading of it did judge meet to be omitted & being so corrected then sent to Press': I. 10, Trans. 9, 24. 11 (Jan) 1675-1676. Joseph Featherstone: 'the Friends Report that read them [the testimonies] that they will require some amendments before fit to be printed': I. 102, Trans. 93, 5.5 (July) 1689. The censors later observed that though Sarah (Featherstone) Brown's testimonies were acceptable, 'the other Testimonies of Thomas Brown concerning Grace and Hatherin [sic] Brown they think not meet to be printed as they are without some amendment nor his concerning Sarah Featherstone without Amendment': I. 104-105, Trans. 94; 9. 7 (Sept.) 1989. The case of Featherstone is referred to intermittently, beyond what is quoted here, see: I. 101-105, Trans. 92-94. Some of the testimonies to Isaac Pennington were also censored: some lines in 'C's text were underscored' and 'desired to be left out': I. 40, Trans. 36; 14. 12 (Feb.) 1680-1681.

[110] *The Morning Meeting's Book of Records*, I. 99, Trans. 90, 28.11 (Jan) 1688-1689.

[111] *The Morning Meeting's Book of Records*, I. 24, Trans 22, 26.3 (May) 1679; Boulbie is also referred to in: I. 29, Trans. 27, 16.12 (Feb) 1679-1680; I. 87, Trans.72, 25.5 (July) 1686; I. 98, Trans. 89, 7.11 (Jan) 1688-1689; a lengthy letter to her is reproduced in: I. 122, Trans. 103, 18.4 (June) 1690.

[112] A book by Isabel Easton was repressed, see *The Morning Meeting's Book of Records*: I. 73, Trans. 53, 19.11 (Jan) 1682-1683.

[113] *The Morning Meeting's Book of Records*, I.17, Trans. 15, 23.5 (July) 1677.

In terms of creating a collective consciousness and community image through print, the post-Restoration Quaker movement seems to have succeeded in using censorship to create a sense of greater uniformity. George Fox, as Larry Ingle has noted, became increasingly concerned with the concept of unity, though he did not necessarily involve himself in the disciplining of those who – as the phrase goes – would not 'submit to unity'.[114] The unity that emerged in the texts, though, could be a peculiar one. Ann Whitehead, for instance, criticising the detractors who challenged the women's meetings, stated that they should 'subdue that perverse wilful spirit' and be 'subject to unity'.[115] Silencing critics, Whitehead invoked the seemingly contradictory idea that unity is brought about through subjection. Moreover, a subtle echo of this sort of unifying idea can be heard in the declaration appended to Ann Whitehead's deathbed testimony. The women of the London women's meetings declare their public owning of the text by showing the importance of unanimity and concord:

> The said foregoing Testimonies are so concurrent in themselves, bespeaking one and the same Spiritual Sense and Judgement in many Witnesses, and so clearly agreeing with the general sence [sic] and Knowledg [sic] and Experience of our Womens Meeting in London, to whom the Faithfulness, Labour of Love, Care and Diligence of our said Sister was well known, that our said meeting doth unanimously own and recommend the same to all our Faithful Friends and Sisters in Christ, of other Womens-Meetings.[116]

The care taken to establish the text as a model for others, and the desire to represent sisterly companionship, indicates that, for women, establishing their legitimacy meant speaking from a place where unity had been transformed into uniformity.[117] The women try to define their own narratives as consistent, and so deny the plurality of the narrative structure – the multi-vocal deathbed testimony – and the heterogeneity of their own voices.

At the same time that the focus on community unity was being formalised through external censorship, there seems also to have been a decline in the kinds of multi-vocal writing that we earlier found to be so prominent within Quaker writing. In the deathbed testimonies, particularly, the multi-vocal biographies are constructed through personally observed testimonies. The deathbed testimonies might be seen to figure the community through their inclusion of testimonies from the many, and this might be seen as positive since they ranged from the most

---

[114] H. Larry Ingle, *First Among Friends*, pp. 189-285 (p. 209; pp. 257-258; p. 260, p. 280).

[115] Anne [sic] Whitehead, *An Epistle for True Love*, p. 9; p. 4.

[116] The Women of the London Meeting, in *Piety Promoted [. . .] Ann Whitehead*, by George Whitehead (et al.), pp. 119-120.

[117] See also the statements of George Whitehead on the Quaker community in the testimony to Giles Barnardiston for another model of community unity, this time perceived as masculine. *The Life of Christ Magnified [. . .] Giles Barnardiston*, by Samuel Cater, pp. 62-63.

public figures to one declaring herself 'one of the least'.[118] But though the texts themselves encode the voices of the many, only rarely is writing produced collectively. Collaborative writing, where it exists, usually occurs in instances either where members of the close family are bound together in a testimony, or where statements are given by the men's and women's meetings.[119] However, community writing need not be positive in this sense. To return to the relation between writers and the models of Quaker censorship, the censor's preference for the collective in the case of Joan Vokins' *God's Mighty Power* led to the omission of at least six personal testimonies.[120]

The deathbed testimonies arguably both create their biographies, and their sense of community, through individualised accounts where a new form of subjectivity might be apparent. Interpreting the deathbed testimonies, for instance, Phyllis Mack has observed that death is resonant 'not of bonding but of individuation and separation'.[121] The argument that the new sense of 'self' is manifest in autobiographies and biographies, which were produced in greater numbers during the early modern period than in earlier times, is apposite to our understanding of Quaker deathbed testimonies.[122] Like Ariès's contention that the collective forms of expression on the deathbed gave way, increasingly, to more bourgeoisified kinds of consciousness, the writing of the deathbed narratives might seem to point to a new emphasis on atomistic forms of selfhood. As Sidonie Smith observes in her study of autobiography, the idea of individualism developed as people began to write about themselves with greater frequency and intensity, and

---

[118] Anne Newman, in *A Handful After the Harvestman [. . .] Richard Samble*, by Thomas Salthouse (et al.), sig. B4^v.

[119] For familial testimonies see 'A Testimony from Margaret Fox's Children', in William Meade (et al.), *A Brief Relation of Remarkable Passages [. . .] Margaret Fell*; Henry Tounson (et al.) 'Post-script', in Christopher Cheesman (et al.), *Living Words [. . .] Francis Patchett*; John Beck (et. al), *A Certain True Relation [. . .] Sarah Wife of John Beck*. For the men's meetings see John Scantlebury (et al.), in *A Handful after the Harvest-Man [. . .] Richard Samble*, by Thomas Salthouse (et al.); John Tiffin (et al.), in *Some Testimonies Concerning [. . .] Hugh Tickell*, by Dorothy Tickell (et al.).

[120] *The Morning Meeting's Book of Records*, I. 143, Trans. 144, 27.3 (May) 1681. They observe that 'Martha Weston's testimony concerning Joan Vokins Read and John Buys, Mary Buys, and William Lambolles and Oliver Samsons and Mary Barbers laid by and they are desired to signe the Generall Testimony that was given forth by the Quarterly Meeting containing the substance of all the rest. And Oliver Samson is desired to get her Brothers and Childrens Testimonies Abstracted and the Substance of all of them put into one with all their Names to it. And to be printed with her Papers and Epistles'. Another reference to the text can be found in I. 141, Trans. 144, 4.3 (May) 1691.

[121] Mack, *Visionary Women*, p. 402.

[122] Paul Delany, *British Autobiography in the Seventeenth Century* (London: Routledge and Kegan Paul, 1969); *Studies in Autobiography*, ed. by James Olney (New York and Oxford: OUP, 1988). Luella M. Wright, *The Literary Life of Early Friends*, argues that the textual creation of subjectivity is 'the only claim that can be ascribed to Friends for bringing any new feature into English autobiography', (p. 218). See also Mary Anne Schofield, '"Women's Speaking Justified", Feminine Quaker Voice, 1662-1797', *Tulsa Studies in Women's Literature*, 6:1 (1987), 61-77.

as they challenged traditional ideas they foregrounded the speaking subject.[123] A bourgeoisified sense of 'self' as private and determinable, though, was compromised by the stratification structures of society, particularly those focussed on the gender hierarchy. As Catherine Belsey observes:

> In the definitions of power relations within the family their [women's] position was inconsistent and to some degree contradictory. While the autonomous subject of liberalism was in the making, women had no single place from which to define themselves as independent beings. In this sense, they both were and were not subjects.[124]

These abstract debates can only be considered here in relation to one writer's representation of her own subjectivity, because they extend far beyond the premises of this book and the post-Restoration historical moment. To conclude, therefore, I will examine the work of Joan Whitrow, a Quaker during the 1670s who chose to leave the movement and later wrote of her struggles to stand alone in the late 1680s.[125] When William of Orange became King in 1688, Whitrow addressed the monarch in several declarations of support; for Whitrow, the deferential relation to the monarch, expressed in her desire to 'humbly intreat the King, [to] take this counsel', was matched by another sense that she could command him.[126] Turning to the King's love of hunting, therefore, she points out the perils of engaging in this pastime whilst the nation was 'wallowing in their blood of uncleanness'.[127] Taking on this prophetic role, and showing that she was commanded by god to intervene in matters of state, Whitrow defined for herself a role that, as we have seen, was denied many women writing within the Quaker fold. The decline in prophetic writing in the later period, coupled to the censorial actions of the Second Day's Meeting meant that most female writing took a more domestic form.

However, despite the sense that Whitrow found greater authority by freeing herself of the increasingly regulated Quaker movement, she does not always conceive of the 'self' in autonomous terms. Whitrow's authority as a prophet required justification, and she has to protect herself from the charges levelled against herself and other inspired thinkers: 'They say, one is mad, and the other anything that the Angel of Darkness can invent; so great is their Malice to cover

---

[123] Sidonie Smith, *A Poetics of Women's Autobiography: Marginality and the Fictions of Self-Representation* (Bloomington and Indianapolis: Indiana University Press, 1987), pp. 25-26.

[124] Catherine Belsey, *The Subject of Tragedy*, pp. 149-150.

[125] For a detailed study of Joan Whitrow see Paula McDowell, *The Women of Grub Street: Press, Politics and Gender in the London Literary Market Place 1678-1730* (Oxford: Clarendon Press, 1998), pp. 156-190.

[126] Joan Whitrow [Whitrowe], *The Humble Salutation and Faithful Greeting* (n. pl.: n. pr., n. d). The text is signed 5th November 1690, p. 14.

[127] Joan Whitrow [Whitrowe], *The Humble Address of the Widow Whitrowe* (n. pl.: n. pr., 1689), p. 4.

the Good with so great an evil'.[128] Whereas Whitrow, standing alone, was able to address the King as a righteous prophet, she could no longer speak from a community position. However, the habits of collectivism remained, and this is evident in a couple of texts where she creates relations between herself and others. Though she was writing as 'one that is of no sect' at this point, she imagines herself in 'unity and fellowship with all that are in this [prophecy] throughout the universe'.[129] Earlier, though, this exalted position in relation to the universal prophets was figured in a more desperately individualised manner: declaring her 'fellowship' with others she describes this community as 'them that lived in Caves, and in Dens, and desolate places of the Earth'.[130] As this image of the prophet indicates, Whitrow figures herself as an outcast at this point. Perhaps her experience was similar to that of other inspired people who stood alone, claiming a right to speak in the public sphere against the trends of sectarian quietism. Neil Keeble observes, for instance, that 'nonconformist writing was consequently private in an age which was going public'.[131] For Whitrow, such circumscriptions were unacceptable.

The problems between Whitrow and the Quakers apparently began when she wrote a testimony to her son and daughter as part of a collective memorialisation of death. Indeed *The Work of God in a Dying Maid* perhaps best illustrates Mack's contention that death brought a sense of interiority, rather than community. The struggles for subjectivity in death are not usually a priority in Quaker deathbed testimonies, but *The Work of God in a Dying Maid* seems to thwart generic conventions by focussing on conflicts. This text, utterly atypical of the genre, departs from the usual conventions in two main ways. Firstly, it conveys a conversion that occurred on the deathbed – whereas most texts depict the joyful death of committed Quakers – and this context makes the sense of achieving salvation highly unstable. Secondly, marital disharmony is indicated in this text, in contradistinction to the usual depictions of the companionate marriage. True, in the drama of the period, marital conflict is a major theme, but it is rare in Quaker writing.[132] Moreover, the text, to which we will now turn, indicates an uneasy struggle towards self-expression taking place within its key subject – the dying Susannah Whitrow.

The formal elements of the text are very similar to other Quaker deathbed testimonies; however, the account of a deathbed conversion creates generic and

---

[128] Whitrow [Whitrowe], *The Humble Salutation*, p. 7.

[129] Whitrow [Whitrowe], *To King William and Queen Mary, Grace and Peace* (London: n. pr., 1692), p. 16.

[130] Whitrow [Whitrowe], *The Humble Address*, p. 13.

[131] N. H. Keeble, *The Literary Culture of Nonconformity in Later Seventeenth-Century England* (Leicester: Leicester University Press, 1987), p. 211. See also Christopher Hill, *The Experience of Defeat: Milton and Some Contemporaries* (London: Faber and Faber, 1984), p. 165.

[132] Catherine Belsey, *Shakespeare and the Loss of Eden: The Construction of Family Values in Early Modern Culture* (London: Macmillan, 1999), on marriage see chapters 2 and 3; p. 121.

theological complexities in other ways because it defies godly conventions. *The Work of God in a Dying Maid*, in common with other Quaker deathbed testimonies, shows that a number of witnesses were present, and the preferred focus is on spiritual rather than material issues. In terms of the testimonies from the family, Joan Whitrow is most prominent, but there are also other more distantly related observers such as Rebecca Travers and Sarah Ellis. Reading Susannah's life story, one learns that she died aged fifteen, that she had a failed romance, and that in life she was obsessed more with clothes than religion. Already, these details have a relevance greater than their immediate expression. For instance, if we look to the writing of a major commentator on godly dying, Jeremy Taylor, whose work was already in its ninth edition by the time Whitrow (et al.) were writing, we can see that the living of a godly life was perhaps becoming more important than a deathbed conversion. 'He that would die well', Taylor observes, 'must every day look for death, every day knocking at the gates of the grave'; and, accordingly, he dissuades his readership against making 'one general account' when at the gates of death.[133]

In contradistinction to the conventional narratives where the fatally ill Quaker had lived a pious godly life, the Whitrow text indicates the struggles that could befall those that had not properly prepared for death. One (anonymous) writer, commenting on Susannah's turmoils on the sickbed, states that 'for several days she had a very great conflict in soul and Spirit concerning the Tempter; and strong were the cries to the Lord for strength to overcome the Enemy'.[134] Such metaphysical doubts are absent from all of the texts we have considered so far, though they may be observed in some non-Quaker texts.[135] Furthermore, Susannah was apparently so fearful that she longed for life, rather than passively accepting death, and she is represented repeatedly asking that she might be freed to live longer.[136] Whereas the conventionalised subject, according to Jeremy Taylor at least, could be forgiven for some lapses of fortitude – Taylor more than the Quakers seems to accept that the physical pain of death was a trial in itself – he is nevertheless very clear on one point: that death is not fearful for those who have made their peace with god in their everyday life.[137] If people committed themselves to 'holy living', Taylor observes, 'it is certain that they could not be made miserable by chance and change, by sickness and death'.[138] Consequently, though it is the case that Susannah eventually envisaged herself embracing her godly creator

---

[133] Jeremy Taylor, *The Rule and Exercises of Holy Dying*, p. 37, p. 43. In *The Rule and Exercises of Holy Living* (London: R. Royston, 1650), Taylor states explicitly that 'a holy life is the onely perfection of Repentance' (p. 340).

[134] Anon, in Travers, *The Work of God*, p. 33.

[135] The classic is the account of Francis Spira: Nat. Bacon, *A Relation of the Fearful Estate of Francis Spira*.

[136] Joan Whitrow [witnessed by Ann Martin], in Travers, pp. 19-20.

[137] For lapses in fortitude see Taylor, *The Rule [. . .] of Holy Dying*, p. 108: 'I do not say it is a sin to be afraid of death'.

[138] Taylor, *The Rule [. . .] of Holy Dying*, p. 96.

as a bride of Christ, in accordance with the conventions of making a holy death, her spiritual narrative promotes anguish rather than peacefulness.[139]

The textuality of the deathbed narrative, as we have already observed, is a generic form wherein the experiences delineated are not only those of the dying person, but also those of the writers. Foremost, here, is Joan Whitrow who was a central contributor to the text and who seeks, both in this text and elsewhere, to find an explanation for Susannah's death. Whitrow's experiences were severe ones: she had lost her only son six months prior to Susannah, and seems also to have been at odds with her husband. Where the subjectivised position of Susannah differed from the usual accounts of a godly death, Joan Whitrow's authorial voice also refuses to represent the family as the site of domestic harmony. Almost ten years after the deaths of her children, Whitrow looked back on the events and found consolation, of a sort, in them. She masochistically accepts the decision of a providential god to take her children because, she insists, 'the LORD Commanded me to depart from the Multitude, and from all the concerns of this World, to seek him apart'.[140] Arguably, no such explicit statement would have been possible for Whitrow when writing within the Quaker community; giving voice to the emotions that, though seemingly resolved in her expression of loyalty to god, seem still to trouble her is possible only once she is alienated from the Quaker movement.

The sense of Whitrow's subjective anxieties, though, can also be projected backwards on to the 1677 text written to commemorate her daughter whilst Whitrow was still a Quaker. Most significant in this respect is the second interpretation that Whitrow put on the death of her children, when writing in 1689. Whitrow apparently believed that she lost her children before they reached maturity because her husband led an 'evil Life'.[141] Accordingly, *The Work of God in a Dying Maid* depicts considerable marital disharmony, particularly over the issues of salvation that we have seen frame the text. A binary is established where Whitrow's husband is equated with 'the world', and Joan herself is represented as godly – in one trope, for instance, she is compared to Mary of Bethany who chose the 'better part' by serving Jesus.[142] Questions of salvation are linked to questions of allegiance within the family, and though it is impossible to know for certain how involved Joan Whitrow was in the recording process, the bias of the account against Susannah's father at least raises the possibility that what is being presented is the damned state of Robert Whitrow. Susannah's dying aim apparently was to convert her father, and her call for him to reform has a painfully emotional tenor, the like of which I have observed in no other Quaker text. She pleads:

> Lord hear me; O Lord hear me; O lord let his mind be set on things above; Lord fix his mind upon thee; Lord let me never rest (unsatisfied) Lord, help him, turn him, Lord, and her will be turned.[143]

---

[139] Joan Whitrow [witnessed by Ann Martin], in Travers, p. 40.
[140] Whitrow, *The Humble Address*, p. 11.
[141] Whitrow, *The Humble Address*, p. 11.
[142] On the father see Travers, *The Work of God*, p.8; on Whitrow see p. 31.
[143] Robert Whitrow (et al.), in Travers pp. 8-9.

By way of contrast to Robert Whitrow's personal hell, Joan, the mother, is devotedly pious. Joan Whitrow writes of 'the Loving kindness of the Lord' in a text in which she masochistically embraces her suffering. Having lost both her children within six months, she nevertheless states that:

> Out of the willingness of my Heart have I offered up my Children unto the Lord, although my Children were as dear to me as my Life, and I could have laid down my life for theirs, if the Lord had required it. [144]

The contrast between these two narrative representations could hardly be greater in spiritual terms, and one might even understand the Quaker censors' view of Joan conveyed in their observation that in the narrative there was too much 'to her owne praise'. [145]

Self-evidently, the censorious attitudes to Whitrow did not in fact finally prohibit the text's publication, and the Quaker corpus was able to include such an atypical text despite the reservations against it; it seems, in fact, that *The Work of God in a Dying Maid* could function to fulfil some community values. In the first instance, it is a morality story: when Susannah Whitrow was struggling to experience salvation the text might seem to display a subject who was psychologically torn, but what was germane, as far as the Quaker commentators were concerned, was for 'a child that had Transgressed, to turn to the Lord'.[146] The writer of this moral overview, Rebecca Travers, shows how the text can be turned into something useful for others' salvation. Travers, who had established close connections to the Second Day's Meeting since it occasionally met at her own house, may possibly be the person who was responsible for the text's publication. In an expression of feminine sympathy, for instance, Travers defends the text in a way that privileges her own understanding above that of the men on the censorial board, observing 'none but a Tender mother can tell what it is to have Hopeful Children so soon taken from them'.[147] Textually speaking, a mother here defends the natural mother to the Quaker censors. Given the atypical aspects of this narrative, it is perhaps unsurprising that writers seek to formalise the conventions of the conversion narrative, and it is heartening to note that the female perspective finally triumphed.

Whereas my examination of Whitrow has centred on relatively individualised forms of subjectivity, post-Restoration writing clearly establishes a sense of the print community. There is a continuing sense that the writers address other Quakers, and establish textual relations that indicated the continuum between the writer and their community. This mutuality, for instance, could prompt Dorcas Dole to address Quakers in an effort to encourage their resistance to persecution, or could lead Margaret Fell to write of the Quakers in terms of the 'elect', 'saints' and

---

[144] Joan Whitrow, in Travers, *The Work of God*, p. 44.
[145] *The Morning Meeting's Book of Records*, I. 18, Trans. 15, 30. 5 (July) 1677.
[146] Travers, *The Work of God*, p. 2.
[147] Travers, *The Work of God*, p. 5; on motherhood see also p. 2.

'Israel'.[148] In the deathbed testimonies, also, writers might commonly construct their audience as sympathisers. The sense of the godly readership is conveyed, explicitly and implicitly, through inclusive language. George Fox, for instance, indicates that the readership will be familiar with his subject, writing in homely terms of 'our dear Friend and Brother Isaac Penington'.[149] William Bayly's life, furthermore, is commended to the 'Gentle Reader', and Elizabeth Smith's testimony to her husband opens by addressing 'Friends'.[150] Where the sense of audience is explicit, the inward focus of this kind of writing is even more evident; William Fortescue, for instance, declares 'I write to those have been convinced of the Truth'.[151] For writers in the Restoration period, therefore, the society that sometimes prohibited expression could also create a reading audience, and an active sense of the Quakers as an extended body.

If there is a sense, then, of an extended community framing itself around internal values, and if even the domestic participated in the shaping of the community, then self-society paradigms had not been lost, but had only shifted their emphasis. What seems to me to have changed, in these domesticised notions, is that they are no longer as collective or collaborative. The families are joined, to an extent, as Mary Forster shows when she declares that 'we above all the Families of the Earth, bear our Testimonies to Christ's Appearance in the spirit'.[152] However, the earlier petition of tithes, in which Mary Forster's contribution was central, extended notions of the public/private, the self and the community. If, as I think, identity was becoming less collective, then the pressures on the subject to find meaning were perhaps more pronounced. I think it is notable that in the main arena for women's collective activities, the separate meetings, women created roles for themselves that were individualised rather than communitarian. The 'Mother in Israel', the 'Aged woman in the Truth' and the 'Daughter of Abraham' are all extensions of personal roles – those of maids, wives and widows. Even in the collective expression, it seems, the models for public activity were both personalised and individual.

Instead of creating a format for collective activism, therefore, the models from the women's meetings created differences between Quakers; moreover, this was part of wider policies that imposed discipline within the ranks. Where Quakers were advised to protect themselves against moral censure, the writers' concerns seem to shrink. Writers turn inwards, and the guidance of god seems to be sought

---

[148] Dorcas Dole, *Once More a Warning* (n. pl.: n. pr., 1683); Dole, *A Salutation of my Endeared Love* (London: John Bringhurst, 1684); Margaret Fell, *The Daughter of Sion [sic]*, p. 11, p. 15, p. 18.
[149] George Fox, *The Works of [. . .] Isaac Penington*, sig. A2ʳ.
[150] John Crook, *A Collection of Several [. . .] William Bayly*, sig. B3ᵛ; Elizabeth Smith, in *Balm from Gilead [. . .] William Smith*, by Ellis Hookes (et al.) (n. pl.: n. pr., 1675), unpaginated.
[151] William Fortescue, *A Short Relation Concerning [. . .] William Simpson* (n. pl.: n. pr., 1671), p. 4.
[152] Mary Forster, *Some Seasonable Considerations*, pp. 10-11.

on moral issues: indeed Mary Forster, writing an address to her readership, declared 'let this, *my dear Friends*, engage our souls to all circumspection in our lives'.[153] Their relation to the world is figured in predominantly private terms. Certainly, the texts examined give little sense of the issues concerning the Stuart monarchy: the Exclusion Crisis, the Popish Plot, and the Glorious Revolution all go without comment in the texts I have examined. Whether or not the Quaker focus on internal politics created, as a result, a new kind of liberal humanist identity, or whether or not the relational, collectivised identity survived, is open to question. More work remains to be done on this issue. What seems clear, though, is that the self-society paradigms underwent considerable change in our period of study.

---

[153] Forster, *Some Seasonable Considerations*, p. 4. Forster's text was 'read and corrected' by Quaker censors. See *The Morning Meeting's Book of Records*, I. 79, Trans. 61, 9.4 (June) 1684.

Conclusion

Underpinning this book's analysis of Quaker women's published writing are a series of connected questions. How does the study of multiple-authorship increase our knowledge of women in the Quaker community? What did it mean to write *as a Quaker*? Was membership of this religious community empowering or constraining? These questions are the particular result of my feminist concern to analyse women's position in the Quaker movement, and this conclusion addresses each in turn.

Multiple-authorship is significant in that it shows that Quakerism sought to give voice to many 'ordinary' believers through its varied collective and collaborative modes of writing. Throughout the period of our study, the techniques that multiple-authorship employed allowed women to make their mark on the literature through the writing of passages to be embedded within larger texts, and through the signing of collectively authored messages. It also gave an opportunity for dual authorship, and for women's petitionary role to be acknowledged. The Quaker literature taking these varied forms produces a sense of the heterogeneity of the movement; women and men, leaders and followers, are numerously inscribed within these texts as signifiers of Quakerism's diversity. The collaborative approach produces a sense of the extended body of believers. There is a collectivist spirit to such writing, which is established through the implicit ties between Friends writing a text, or signing a statement, intended for the press.

Multiple-authorship is furthermore testament to Quaker attempts to give collectivity a positive image. Quaker works imply that a body of people standing alongside one another have more authority than an individual could usually expect when working alone. Potentially, the collective becomes a force to be reckoned with. As a political, lobbying force in 1659, the Quakers raised the profile of the anti-tithe campaign, for example. Quaker depictions of the mass activism of the body of believers show the movement working as an aggregate. Moreover, when Friends responded to persecution, they assumed that they were the victims of restrictive laws. Suffering willingly, they typically used their persecution to advance an argument for religious freedom of worship. These texts commonly speak of Quaker unity in suffering, as though their commitment to each other was greatest in adversity. A degree of commonality exists between the writers of a Quaker text: that is a given.

Yet multiply-authored pamphlets were not fully democratic, and both sufferings and deathbed narratives show that the community was fractured along gendered lines. Quakers, for instance, wrote of the shared experience of suffering whilst looking at male and female persecution through different lenses. Quaker women sufferers might be embodied and silenced in these texts, showing their androcentric formulation. We have seen that women were probably not involved in the compilation of multiply-authored sufferings narratives; the texts potentially inscribed the female author within an agenda over which she had no control. In later Quakerism, instructions came from the Second Day's Meeting, which 'corrected' the texts, showing the censors' intention was to 'leave out what they see not of Service to the Truth'.[1] The writer's work, then, was subject to outside influence: at worst, post-Restoration Quaker texts might give access only to women's edited opinions. At best, the multiply-authored deathbed testimonies from the 1680s might be female centred (when the writers or the subjects were mainly women), therefore establishing their worth – usually as mothers, wives, or daughters. Writing is only one part of the publishing process, and though women were a visible presence in the Quaker corpus, their voices were not autonomous.

What did it mean to write as a Quaker, then? The heterogeneity that is evident in early Quaker texts suggests a movement that was in the process of defining itself, rather than a body with a fixed sense of identity. The 1650s pamphlets show Quakers developing ideas, and revising them, as they responded to changing circumstances. They back-tracked from the most radical sense of the indwelling godhead post-1656 (after James Nayler's 'fall'), for instance, yet they spoke with renewed millenarian vigour when the commonwealth collapsed. With the added factor of the Quaker membership's varied social, religious, and geographical backgrounds taken into account, the lack of a fully shared conceptual structure for Quaker belief is explicable. This new religion was not only shaped by external, religio-political events, it was also diversified through its membership.

The absence of a 'central' ground might not be a disadvantage.[2] Where there is nothing so static as a set agenda, the discourse remains open to interpretation. Prophets, for instance, responded in different ways to the general Quaker belief that god spoke within them. The inner light is a fundamental idea in Quaker writing, but it is not one that is uniformly agreed upon; hence, there is no single prophetical mode. Prophets' tracts mark changes to the conceptualisation of that light that implicitly register what was going on, inside and outside the movement. Their works indirectly show the light to be a contentious and contradictory theory through the fluidity of the terminology. Even, and especially, in respect to its key tenets, Quakerism encodes plurality. Such malleability within key Quaker ideals opened up the public sphere of print to women, because the resulting writing was not rigidly pursuing a pre-empted agenda. Since women were present as writers from the earliest days of the Society, they helped to shape the public definitions of Quaker beliefs, even as they were emerging.

Quakers nevertheless wrote *for* and *to* their religious community. They wrote of concord, and 'fellowship'. When calling each other 'Friends', defending each other against the overbearing state, uniting to press for political and religious change, and travelling together in the ministry, Quakers experienced a sense of group membership. Theirs was a movement that collectivised the practice of faith. Friends wrote from the 'we' of discourse, constructing a sense of the

---

[1] *The Morning Meeting's Book of Records*, I.17, Trans. 15, 23.5 (July), 1677.

[2] Nigel Smith, 'Hidden Things Brought to Light: Enthusiasm and Quaker Discourse', in *Prose Studies*, 17:3 (1994), pp. 57-69 (p. 62). Smith explains the need for caution about using such terms as 'central' ground to refer to Friends' ideas.

communitarian spirit that can be glimpsed through the published texts. Furthermore, they saw their conversion (or, convincement) as an expression of commitment to the movement. In later Quakerism, writers of deathbed testimonies spoke of the movement as a family. Through such measures, they *write the community*.

Was Quakerism empowering or constraining for women? The Quaker leadership cannot be fully absolved of maintaining derisory attitudes to women, and particularly those who seemed to challenge authority too forwardly. Chapter one showed the treatment meted out to Martha Simmonds, a woman who was viewed as the chief actor in the Nayler affair. In her defence, Simmonds observed that 'being among the people called *Quakers* in *London,* I was moved to *declare to the world*, and often they would judge me exceedingly'.[3] She seems to have been conscious of leading Friends' desire to gag her, even before events came to a head, during Nayler's blasphemous entry into Bristol. Rebecca Travers and Sarah Blackborrow were also involved in the case, and each wrote prefaces to Nayler's late-1650s pamphlets.[4] Neither woman was alienated in the way that Simmonds was (Travers, for instance, continued to write into the Restoration period). Though the movement could forgivingly embrace individuals, the Nayler events certainly revealed incipient disciplinary codes, and tensions over acceptable practices. Martha Simmonds was victim to the movement's desire to find a scapegoat for the Nayler debacle. What is so important about these events is their exposure of a censorious strain that was rarely expressed so explicitly in print elsewhere. The Quaker movement (through its Foxian-led leadership) could close ranks against those deemed to be threatening to the collective's ultimate survival. The communitarian focus of early Quakerism, then, could work to the exclusion of women.

In principle, Quaker writers (including the movement's male leaders) held up values that were empowering, however. During the 1650s, the female ministry was defended by key figures, such as George Fox, in terms signifying the spiritual equality of all. Prophets could speak from the spirit, regardless of their gender. Quakerism was both individualist and communitarian in this respect; it valued the inner workings of the spirit within believers who were part of this Society. Many 1650s Quaker women were active in the fullest sense of being a present force within the ministry, as a result. They travelled, suffered, petitioned and prophesised alongside their brethren: early Quaker women were active in producing dynamic roles for themselves within the movement. They made early Quakerism follow egalitarian practices through their persistence, determination, and visibly public testimony.

Quaker women shaped the prophetical mode of writing by creating multi-vocal texts in which the voice of god, Christ, the light or the woman was merged. Hence, Suzanne Trill observes that 'to seek for a uniquely "female" voice in these texts

---

[3] Ralph Farmer, *Sathan Inthron'd* (London: Edward Thomas, 1657), p. 10.
[4] Sarah Blackborrow, 'Preface', in James Nayler, *How Sin is Strengthened* (London: Thomas Simmonds, 1657); Rebecca Travers, 'Preface', in James Nayler, *A Message From the Spirit of Truth* (London: Thomas Simmonds, 1658).

runs counter to the Quakers' aspiration to merge the "self" with God'.[5] These texts therefore cannot be said to represent an essentialised female position. If this is another limitation to Quaker practice, then it is one that is mostly perceived as such by some modern, twenty-first-century critics, rather than the writers themselves. 'The Lord hath put into my Heart; and I cannot forbear to write', explained Hester Biddle in her prophetic *The Trumpet of the Lord*.[6] Writing in god's name, through his voice, and at his imperative, gave women entry into the field of print, as well as religious authority. Rather than seeing this as a purely restrictive mode of writing, imposing masculine notions of authorship on the female writer, the openness of such discourse to women's varied understandings of their relationship to the godhead should be recognised. Quaker women negotiated entry into print on the basis that they were writing *for* god, and in so doing challenged the cultural restrictions against women's prophetical speaking. Rarely apologetic, Quaker women's approach assumed that the god within sanctioned their radical, often combative messages. They created a public role for themselves through these modes.

The Quaker texts produced during the Restoration period that have been examined here were more concerned to define traditional female roles for women. When compared to 1650s activism, later Quakerism seems far more limiting in the roles it provided. Collective female action was certainly espoused in writings produced by those involved in the separate women's meetings, but collectively held beliefs now included the need for women to act as models of domestic virtue. There was a shift from active testimony to more insular kinds of worship, as women accepted that they were to take a companionate role to men, as wives and mothers. Although women continued to express their close relationship to god, particularly in deathbed testimonies, this aspect of women's religious identity was also circumscribed. To speak on the deathbed was a qualified victory merely, since the position of authority it produced for the female subject was imminently curtailed by death. Memorialising writing ensured that women's speaking was, quite literally, a dying art. Concentration on the home, rather than active practice, also indicates that when women's words were made public, they were nevertheless firmly contained within the domestic sphere. These works therefore evidence that women's writing was less radical when it was more normatively feminine.

Quaker women's writing served a number of different purposes. In early Quakerism, it is clear that the works were distributed with the aim of enlarging the public understanding of this new movement, and that the readership was Quaker and non-Quaker alike. Quakers raised their profile by discussing their prophetical inspiration, their sufferings, and their political agendas. In the later period's commemorative writing the focus was more insular; similarly, this is also the case with statements from the women's meetings. The addressees, here, are commonly other Friends, almost exclusively. Back in 1655, in an anti-Quaker text that sought

---

[5] Suzanne Trill, 'Religion and the Construction of Femininity', in *Women and Literature in Britain, 1500-1700*, ed. by Helen Wilcox (Cambridge: CUP, 1996), pp. 30-55 (p. 47).
[6] Hester Biddle, *The Trumpet of the Lord [...] to These Three Nations* (London: n. pr., 1662), p. 20.

to show the errors of the movement, an intriguing response to pamphleteering suggests other possible uses for the literature. The anonymous *The Quacking Mountebank* takes issue with the proselytising actions of Martha Simmonds (who was, the writer believed, the 'chief *Virago*' of the sect).[7] In the process, it reveals her role in print culture. Simmonds, the writer explains, 'runs and gads up and down with *Missives,* and leaves Letters', she was, then, involved in the circulation of ideas. According to this critical writer, Simmonds was 'send[ing] them abroad to gain Disciples'. The anonymous anti-Quaker's fear of vocal women might produce a predisposition to overstate the case somewhat, but the impression that print extended the realms of women's spiritual authority does not seem exaggerated. Quaker women's engagement in Quaker print culture was extensive and involved; they were shaping Friends' radical discourse whilst they were *writing the community.*

---

[7] Anon., *The Quacking Mountebank* (London: E. B., 1655), p. 19. Thomason's date is 24 May 1655.

Appendix

Mary Forster, *These Several Papers* (London: Mary Westwood, 1659)

Overlap in the names in 'We who are the Seed of the Woman' (pp. 7-8) and Lancashire (pp. 8-13).

Note: because it was common for family members to be named after their parents, in this case the mother, the repetition of names does not necessarily represent an attempt to distort the figures (some are especially common: Mary, Anne and Elizabeth). However, the overlap between 'We who are the Seed' and the Lancashire petition is significant in one respect: that of the prominence of the Fell family of Swarthmore Hall, who can be identified with some certainty here.

Benson, Dorothy; Benson, Eliz /Elizabeth; Fell, Bridget; Fell, Margaret (sen.); Fell, Margaret (jun.) [2x Margaret Fell in the Lancashire Petition]; Fell, Mary Fell, Sarah; Johnson, Jane; Moor, Agnus; Smith, Margret/Margeret; Thomson, Jane; Thomson, Anne; Thomson, Elizabeth [3x in the Lancashire Petition]; Thomson, Margaret [2x in 'We who are the Seed']; Walker, Elizabeth/Eliz [2x in the Lancashire Petition]; Wharton, Margaret; Wilson, Isabel

Bibliography

A. Primary Texts

A.1. Manuscripts
The Morning Meeting's Book of Records, From the 15th of the 7th month 1673, to the 6th of the 4th month 1692, inclusive, Friends' House, London
The Swarthmore Manuscripts, Friends' House, London

A.2. Printed Books

This list is intended as a bibliographical resource, as well as a guide to the books cited in this book.

Conventions

All multiply authored texts are cross-referenced, with each contributor being listed as an individual in addition to being listed under the text's main contributor (the first writer to sign his/her name). The only exceptions to this practice are the women signing *These Several Papers*, which is here listed under the name of Mary Forster; Edward Burrough's *A Declaration of the Present Sufferings* (1659), and the signers of another non-Quaker petition, *The Husbandmans Plea Against Tithes*, which is not cross-referenced, though all the signatories can be seen by looking at the text's main entry. To aid the reader in the identification of the main writer of a deathbed testimony (who is not usually the deceased!), I have also included cross-references to the person who is the subject of the text.

Where an author is the first named contributor to one or more text, but is also a contributor to other writers' tracts, the principle has been to list all the texts under the author's name, and to subdivide them. The first titles to be listed are those where the author is the first named contributor; in library catalogues, this is usually the person whose name gives access to the text. The second titles to be listed are those where the writer is a contributor, rather than the author to whom the text is catalogued. These contributory addressees are arranged in alphabetical order of the main author's surname. (For an example of how this works, turn to George Whitehead).

For the approach taken to proper names, see 'A Note on the Quotation and Referencing of Seventeenth-Century Texts'.[1] Since standardization of names has been attempted only where identification can be checked against bibliographical and biographical sources, the reader who knows of variant spellings of proper names would be well advised to check all of the variations when using this bibliography.

---

[1] See pp. xi-xii above.

Key to Terminology

co-author: describes a text in which two authors write a single testimony.

'sigy': abbreviation for 'signatory'; used to identify a named contributor to a text, or passage, which has more than two named authors.

A.2.a) Quaker

A.2.a.i, Anonymous

Anon., *A Copie of a Paper Presented to the Parliament* (London: A.W. for Giles Calvert, 1659)

Anon., *A Declaration of the Marks and Fruits of the False Prophets* (n. pl.: n. pr., [1655])

Anon., *The Ungrateful Alms-men Rebuked [. . .] Geo. Begardner* (n. pl.: n. pr., 1674)
    Said to be by 'Certain Sober Women'.

A.2.a.ii) Named

A., T. in Margaret Fell, *False Prophets* (1655)

Abbott, Margaret, *A Testimony Against the False Teachers of this Generation* (n. pl.: n. pr., n. d.)

Abraham, Daniel, in William Mead, *A Brief Collection of Remarkable Passages [. . .] Margaret Fox* (1710)

Abraham, Rachel, in William Mead, *A Brief Collection of Remarkable Passages [. . .] Margaret Fox* (1710)

Adams, Robert, in James Parnell, *The Lambs Defence* (1656)

Addams, Elizabeth [sigy], in Oliver Sansom, *God's Mighty Power [. . .] Joan Vokins* (1691)

Addams, Richard, in Robert Wastfield, *A True Testimony of Faithful Witnesses* (1657)

Addamson, William, *A Persecution in Several Places in Lancashire* (n. pl.: n. pr. [1655])
    Other Writers: Leonard Addison, John Branthwait, Leonard Fell, Thomas Holmes, William Simpson, Isaac Yeats
    Non-Quaker: William Barret

Addison, Leonard, in William Addamson, *A Persecution in Several Places in Lancashire* [1655]

Aldam, Thomas, *False Prophets and False Preachers Described* (n. pl.: n. pr., 1652)
    Other Writers: Mary Fisher, Jane Holmes, Elizabeth Hooton, Benjamin Nicholson, William Pears

Allin, Abraham [sigy], in Jeremiah Haward, *Here Followeth a Relation of Some of the Sufferings [. . .] in Oxford* (n. d.)

Allin, Ralph [sigy], in Humphrey Norton, *New Englands Ensigne* (1659)

Allin, William [sigy], in Humphrey Norton, *New Englands Ensigne* (1659)

Anderton, Jane, in Theophila Townsend, *A Testimony Concerning [. . .] Jane Whitehead* (1676)

Anthony, Susanna [sigy], in George Whitehead, *Piety Promoted [. . .] Ann Whitehead* (1686)

Antrobus, Benjamin, in George Whitehead, *Piety Promoted [. . .] Ann Whitehead* (1686)

Antrubus, Mary [sigy], in George Whitehead, *Piety Promoted [. . .] Ann Whitehead* (1686)

Arch, Robert, in John Wilkinson, *The Memory of [. . .] John Story* (1683)

Ashfield, Patience [sigy], in George Whitehead, *Piety Promoted [. . .] Ann Whitehead* (1686)

Atkinson, Christopher, *The Standard of the Lord Lifted up* (London: Giles Calvert, 1653)

Other Writers: Elizabeth Bateman, Edward Burrough, Thomas Casley, Mary Colison, Margaret Gilpin, Miles Halhead, Thomas Holmes, Francis Howgill, Mary Howgill, Elizabeth Levens, Margaret Newby, Anne Thompson, Agnes Turner, Mabel Warriner, Jane Waugh, Alice Wilson

Atkinson, Thomas, in Dorothy Wilson, *The Memorial of [. . .] William Wilson* (1685)

Audland, Anne, *The Saints Testimony* (London: Giles Calvert, 1655)
Other writers; Walter Clement, Thomas Curtis, Thomas Gouldney, Edward Pyot, Robert Rich

——(later Camm) in Thomas Camm, *The Memory of the Righteous Revived* (1689)

Audland, John, in Thomas Camm, *The Memory of the Righteous Revived* (1689)
Subject of testimony and writer

——in Ralph Farmer (non-Quaker), *Sathan [sic] Inthron'd* (1657)

Austell, Mary [sigy], in Oliver Sansom, *God's Mighty Power [. . .] Joan Vokins* (1691)

Austell, William [sigy], in Oliver Sansom, *God's Mighty Power [. . .] Joan Vokins* (1691)

Austill, Bridget, in George Whitehead, *Piety Promoted [. . .] Ann Whitehead* (1686)

B., C. in Dewans Morey, *A True and Faithful Warning* [1665]

Badger, Abra [sigy], in Jeremiah Haward, *Here Followeth a Relation of Some of the Sufferings [. . .] in Oxford* (n. d)

Bailes, Thomas, in Samuel Cater, *The Life of [. . .] Giles Barnardiston* (1681)

Baker, Elizabeth [sigy], in George Whitehead, *Piety Promoted [. . .] Ann Whitehead* (1686)

Baker, Jacob, in Samuel Cater, *The Life of [. . .] Giles Barnardiston* (1681)

Baker, Mary [sigy], in Oliver Sansom, *God's Mighty Power [. . .] Joan Vokins* (1691)

Bales, William, in Mary Stout, *The Testimony of the Hartford Quakers* (1676)

Ball, Ann [sigy], in Oliver Sansom, *God's Mighty Power [. . .] Joan Vokins* (1691)

Ball, John, in William Penn, *Saul Smitten to the Ground* (1675)

Ballard, Jane [sigy], in Oliver Sansom, *God's Mighty Power [. . .] Joan Vokins* (1691)

Ballard, William [sigy], in Oliver Sansom, *God's Mighty Power [. . .] Joan Vokins* (1691)

Bangs, Benjamin, in Samuel Cater, *The Life of [. . .] Giles Barnardiston* (1681)

Barber, Anne, in Anne Martindall, *A Relation of [. . .] Alice Curwen* (1680)

Barker, John, in Anne Martindall, *A Relation of [. . .] Alice Curwen* (1680)

Barnardiston, Giles, in Samuel Cater, *The Life of [. . .] Giles Barnardiston* (1681)
Subject of deathbed testimony

Barrowe, Robert, in John Beck, *A Certain True Relation [. . .] of Sarah wife of John Beck* (1680)

Barwick, Grace, *To all the Present Rulers* (n. pl.: Mary Westwood, 1659)

Bateman, Elizabeth [sigy], in Christopher Atkinson, *The Standard of the Lord Lifted up* (1653)

Bateman, Susanna, 'I matter not how I appear to man' [first line] (n. pl.: n. pr., [1656/7]

Bathurst, Anne, in Elizabeth Bathurst, *An Expostulatory Appeal to the Professors of Christianity* [1679]

Bathurst, Charles, in George Whitehead, *Piety Promoted [. . .] Ann Whitehead* (1686)

Bathurst, Elizabeth, *An Expostulatory Appeal to the Professors of Christianity* (n. pl.: n. pr., [1679])
Other writer: Anne Bathurst

Bathurst, Grace, in George Whitehead, *Piety Promoted [. . .] Ann Whitehead* (1686)

Batt, Jasper, in Robert Ford, *A Testimony Concerning [. . .] George Russel* [1680]

——in Theophila Townsend, *A Testimony Concerning [. . .] Jane Whitehead* (1676)

——in Robert Wastfield, *A True Testimony of Faithful Witnesses* (1657)

Bayle, Thomas, in Samuel Cater, *The Life of [. . .] Giles Barnardiston* (1681)

Bayly, Mary, see Mary Fisher

Bayly, William, in John Crook, *A Collection of the Several Wrightings of [. . .] William Bayly* (1676)
    Subject of deathbed testimony

Bealing, Edward, in Thomas Salthouse, *A Handful After the Harvest-Man [. . .] Richard Samble* (1684)

Beaton, William [sigy], in Robert Wastfield, *A True Testimony of Faithful Witnesses* (1657)

Beauchamp, Loveday [sigy], in Benjamin Coales, *A Relation of the Last Words and Departure of [. . .] Loveday Hambly* (1683)

Beck, John, *A Certain True Relation of the Heavenly Enjoyments [. . .] Declared upon the Dying-bed of Sarah wife of John Beck* (n. pl.: n. pr., 1680)
    Other writers: Robert Barrowe, Elizabeth Corney, Elianor Dickinson, John Dickinson, Agnes Gardner, Isabel Gardner, Thomas Gardner, Elizabeth Ware

Beck, Sarah, in John Beck, *A Certain True Relation of the Heavenly Enjoyments [. . .] of Sarah wife of John Beck* (1680)
    Subject of deathbed testimony

Beckley, Rebecca [sigy], in Anne Martindall, *A Relation of [. . .] Alice Curwen* (1680)

Beckwith, Elizabeth, in Katherine Whitton, *An Epistle from the Womens Yearly Meeting at York* (1688)

Beer, Thomas, in Thomas Woodrowe, *A Brief Relation of the State of Man Before Transgression* (1659)

Begardner, George, in Anon., *The Ungrateful Alms-men Rebuked [. . .] Geo. Begardner* (1674)
    Subject of text

Bennet, William, in Samuel Cater, *The Life of [. . .] Giles Barnardiston* (1681)

Benson, Gervase, *The Cry of the Oppressed* (London: Giles Calvert, 1656)
    Other writer: George Fox

Benson, Mabel, in Thomas Camm, *The Memory of the Righteous Revived* (1689)

Bettris, Jeane, *A Lamentation for the Deceived People* (London: Thomas Simmonds, 1657)

Bewley, Elizabeth [co-author], in Robert Huntington, *The Memory of [. . .] Thomas Stordy* (1692)

Bewley, George [co-author], in Robert Huntington, *The Memory of [. . .] Thomas Stordy* (1692)

Biddle, Esther, *A Warning from the Lord God [. . .] Unto thee O City of London* (London: Robert Wilson, 1660)

——'Oh! Wo, wo, from the Lord' [first line] (London: Thomas Simmonds, 1659)

——*The Trumpet of the Lord* (London: n. pr., 1662)

——'Wo to thee City of Oxford' [first line] (n. pl.: n. pr., [1655])

——in John Crook, *The Cry of the Innocent for Justice* (n.d.)

——in Thomas Woodrowe, *A Brief Relation of the State of Man Before Transgression* (1659)

Biddle, Sarah [sigy], in John Cripps, *A True Account of the Dying Words of Ockanickon, an Indian King* (1682)

Birkhead, Christopher, in George Bishop, *The Cry of Blood* (1656)

Birkhead, Mary [sigy], in George Whitehead, *Piety Promoted [. . .] Ann Whitehead* (1686)

Bishop, George, *The Cry of Blood* (London: Giles Calvert, 1656)
    Other Quaker Writers: Christopher Birkhead, Thomas Goldney, Temperance Hignell, Dennis Hollister, Elizabeth Marshall, Benjamin Maynard, Edward Pyott, Henry Roe, John Smith, John Worring
    Non-Quaker Writers: William Cann, Henry Gibbs, John Gunning, George Hellier, John Jackson, John Lock, Gabriel Sherman, Richard Vickris

——*The Throne of Truth* (London: Giles Calvert, 1657)

Blackborrow, Sarah, *A Visit to the Spirit in Prison* (London: Thomas Simmonds, 1658)
——*Herein is Held forth the Gift* (London: Thomas Simmonds, 1659)
——*The Just and Equall Ballance[sic]* (London: M.W. [Mary Westwood], 1660)
——'Preface', in James Nayler, *How Sin is Strengthened* (1657)
Blackburne, Ann, in Peter Hardcastle, *Several Living Testimonies [. . .] Robert Lodge* (1691)
Blackburne, Christopher, in Peter Hardcastle, *Several Living Testimonies [. . .] Robert Lodge* (1691)
Blackburne, Rebeca, in Peter Hardcastle, *Several Living Testimonies [. . .] Robert Lodge* (1691)
Blackmore, John, in Edward Pyot, *The West Answering to the North* (1657)
Blakeley, James [sigy], in Edward Sammon, *A Discovery of the Education of the Schollars [sic] in Cambridge* (1659)
Blakely, Matthew [sigy], in Edward Sammon, *A Discovery of the Education of the Schollars [sic] in Cambridge* (1659)
Bols, Elizabeth, in Samuel Watson, *An Epistle [. . .] Mary Moss* (1695)
Bolton, John, *A Declaration from the Children of the Light* (London: Giles Calvert, 1655)
    Other writers: Rich. Davis, Simon Dring, Will Rayman
——in Amos Stodard, *Something Written in Answer to a Lying Scandalous Book* [1655]
Bonifield, Abraham [sigy], in Oliver Sansom, *God's Mighty Power [. . .] Joan Vokins* (1691)
Booth, Mary, 'Preface', in James Nayler, *Milk for Babes* (1665)
Boulbie, Judith, *A Testimony for Truth* (n. pl.: n. pr., [1665])
——in Katherine Whitton, *An Epistle from the Womens Yearly Meeting at York* (1688)
Braidley, Margaret, *Certain Papers which is the Word of the Lord* (n. pl.: n. pr., n. d)
    Other writers: Richard Hebson, Christopher Taylor
Braithwaite, John, in *A Brief Relation of [. . .] Elizabeth Braythwaite* [1684]
Branthwait, John, in William Addamson, *A Persecution in Several Places in Lancashire* [1655]
Brassey, Elizabeth [sigy], in George Whitehead, *Piety Promoted [. . .] Ann Whitehead* (1686)
Braythwaite, Elizabeth, in Anne Gardner, *A Brief Relation of the Life and Death of Elizabeth Braythwaite* [1684]
    Subject of deathbed testimony
Braythwaite, Edward [sigy], in Isabel Yeamans, *A Lively Testimony to [. . .] Robert Jeckell* (1676)
Braythwaite, John, in Anne Gardner, *A Brief Relation of the Life and Death of Elizabeth Braythwaite* [1684]
Broman, Will. [sigy], in James Parnell, *The Lambs Defence* (1656)
Brown, John [sigy], in Oliver Sansom, *God's Mighty Power [. . .] Joan Vokins* (1691)
Brown, Mary [sigy], in Oliver Sansom, *God's Mighty Power [. . .] Joan Vokins* (1691)
Brown, Sarah, see Featherstone
Brown, Thomas, in John Field, *Living Testimonies Concerning [. . .] Joseph Featherstone* (1689)
Browne, Anne [sigy], in George Whitehead, *Piety Promoted [. . .] Ann Whitehead* (1686)
——[sigy], in John Cripps, *A True Account of the Dying Words of Ockanickon, an Indian King* (1682)
Browne, George [sigy], in William Penn, *Saul Smitten to the Ground* (1675)
Brown[e], Grace, in John Field, *Living Testimonies Concerning [. . .] Joseph Featherstone* (1689)
    Subject of deathbed testimony

Brown[e], Katherine, in John Field, *Living Testimonies Concerning [. . .] Joseph Featherstone* (1689)
    Subject of deathbed testimony
Bryan, Hester [sigy], in George Whitehead, *Piety Promoted [. . .] Ann Whitehead* (1686)
Buce, Daniel, in Oliver Sansom, *God's Mighty Power [. . .] Joan Vokins* (1691)
Buce, Margery, in Oliver Sansom, *God's Mighty Power [. . .] Joan Vokins* (1691)
Budd, Thomas [sigy], in John Cripps, *A True Account of the Dying Words of Ockanickon, an Indian King* (1682)
——[sigy], in Robert Wastfield, *A True Testimony of Faithful Witnesses* (1657)
Bullock, Elizabeth [sigy], in Oliver Sansom, *God's Mighty Power [. . .] Joan Vokins* (1691)
Bunting, Will. [sigy], in James Parnell, *The Lambs Defence* (1656)
Burgis, Damaris [sigy], in Oliver Sansom, *God's Mighty Power [. . .] Joan Vokins* (1691)
Burgis, Hannah [sigy], in Oliver Sansom, *God's Mighty Power [. . .] Joan Vokins* (1691)
Burgis, Samuel [sigy], in Oliver Sansom, *God's Mighty Power [. . .] Joan Vokins* (1691)
Burr, Thomas, in Samuel Cater, *The Life of [. . .] Giles Barnardiston* (1681)
Burrough, Edward, *A Declaration of the Present Sufferings* (London: Thomas Simmonds, 1659); signed by 164 people.
——*A Declaration of the Sad and Great Persecution and Martyrdom* (London: Robert Wilson, [1660])
    Other writers: John Copeland, Mary Dyar, Jane Nicholson, Joseph Nicholson, Nicholas Phelps, John Rous, Samuel Shattock, Jastah Southwick
——*A Warning from the Lord to the Inhabitants of Underbarrow* (London: Giles Calvert, 1654)
——*Something in Answer to a Book Called Choice Experiences* (n. pl.: n. pr., 1654)
——*The Wofull Cry of Unjust Persecutions* (London: Giles Calvers [1657])
——*To the Parliament of the Common-wealth of England who are in Place of Authority to do Justice* (n. pl.: n. pr., [1659])
——in Christopher Atkinson, *The Standard of the Lord Lifted up* (1653)
——in Francis Howgill, *A Testimony Concerning [. . .] Edward Burroughs [sic]* (1662)
    Subject of deathbed testimony
Bussum, Joshua, in Humphrey Norton, *New Englands Ensigne* (1659)
Butcher, John, in A. Paterson, *The Testimony [. . .] John Matern* (1680)
Buy, John [sigy], in Oliver Sansom, *God's Mighty Power [. . .] Joan Vokins* (1691)
Buy, Mary [sigy], in Oliver Sansom, *God's Mighty Power [. . .] Joan Vokins* (1691)
Byrch, Henry, in Anne Martindall, *A Relation of [. . .] Alice Curwen* (1680)
C., J., in John Wilkinson, *The Memory of [. . .] John Story* (1683)
C., T., in Anne Gardner, *A Brief Relation of the Life and Death of Elizabeth Braythwaite* [1684]
Caipe, Elizabeth [sigy], in Thomas Fell, *A Short Testimony Concerning [. . .] Judith Fell* [1682]
Caipe, Matther [sigy], in Thomas Fell, *A Short Testimony Concerning [. . .] Judith Fell* [1682]
Camfield, Elizabeth, in George Whitehead, *Piety Promoted [. . .] Ann Whitehead* (1686)
Camm, Anne, in Thomas Camm, *The Memory of the Righteous Revived* (1689)
    Also see Anne Audland
Camm, John, in Thomas Camm, *The Memory of the Righteous Revived* (1689)
    Subject of testimony and writer
Camm, Thomas, *The Memory of the Righteous Revived [. . .] John Camm and John Audland* (London: Andrew Sowle, 1689)
    Other writers: John Audland, Mabel Benson, Anne Camm (formerly Audland), John Camm, George Fox, Charles Marshall

——in William Mead *A Brief Collection of Remarkable Passages [. . .] Margaret Fox* (1710)

Cape, John, in Thomas Fell, *A Short Testimony Concerning [. . .] Judith Fell* [1682]

Cartwright, Elizabeth [sigy], in George Whitehead, *Piety Promoted [. . .] Ann Whitehead* (1686)

Casley, Thomas [sigy], in Christopher Atkinson, *The Standard of the Lord Lifted up* (1653)

Cater, Samuel, *The Life of Christ Magnified in his Minister [. . .] Giles Barnardiston* (London: John Bringhurst, 1681)

    Other writers: Thomas Bailes, Jacob Baker, Benjamin Bangs, Thomas Bayle, William Bennet, Thomas Burr, John Cornwell, John Furly, Elizabeth Gibson, Mary Gridle, Jonathon Johnson, Edward Melsupp, Hester Melsupp, Samuel Wadenfield, William Welch, George Whitehead, John Willsford

Caton, William [sigy], in Margaret Fell, *A Declaration and an Information* (1660)

Cattle, Henry [sigy], in Robert Wastfield, *A True Testimony of Faithful Witnesses* (1657)

Cawse, John, in Edward Pyot, *The West Answering to the North* (1657)

Chandler, Margaret [sigy], in Oliver Sansom, *God's Mighty Power [. . .] Joan Vokins* (1691)

Cheeseman, Christopher, *Living Words through a Dying Man [. . .] Francis Patchett* (n. pl.: n. pr., 1678)

    Other writers: Elizabeth Cheesman, Ann Edmundson, Marabella Farnbury, Thomas Farnbury, Andrew Lund, Henry Toulnson, Rebecca Veal, Moses West

Cheesman, Elizabeth [co-author], in Christopher Cheesman, *Living Words through a Dying Man [. . .] Francis Patchett* (1678)

Childe, John [sigy], in James Parnell, *The Lambs Defence* (1656)

Childe, Zach. [sigy], in James Parnell, *The Lambs Defence* (1656)

Clark, George [sigy], in Edward Sammon, *A Discovery of the Education of the Schollars [sic] in Cambridge* (1659)

Clark, John, in John Crook, *A Collection of the Several Wrightings of [. . .] William Bayly* (1676)

——in Edward Sammon, *A Discovery of the Education of the Schollars [sic] in Cambridge* (1659)

Clarke, Alice, in Peter Hardcastle, *Several Living Testimonies [. . .] Robert Lodge* (1691)

Clarke, Katherine [sigy], in George Whitehead, *Piety Promoted [. . .] Ann Whitehead* (1686)

Clarke, Sarah [sigy], in George Whitehead, *Piety Promoted [. . .] Ann Whitehead* (1686)

Clement, Walter [sigy], in Anne Audland, *The Saints Testimony* (1655)

Clipsham, Margery, in Mary Ellwood, *The Spirit that Works Abomination* (1685)

Clothier, Samuel [sigy], in Robert Wastfield, *A True Testimony of Faithful Witnesses* (1657)

Coal, Benjamin, in John Wilkinson, *The Memory of [. . .] John Story* (1683)

Coal, Leonard, in John Wilkinson, *The Memory of [. . .] John Story* (1683)

Coale, Josiah, *The Last Testimony of [. . .] Richard Farnsworth* (London: n. pr., 1667)

——in Edward Pyot, *The West Answering to the North* (1657)

——in Francis Howgil, *A Testimony Concerning [. . .] Edward Burroughs [sic]* (1662)

Coales, Benjamin, *A Relation of the Last Words and Departure of [. . .] Loveday Hambly* (London: John Gain, 1683)

    Other writers: Loveday Beauchamp, Thomas Curtis, Anne Salthouse, Thomas Salthouse, Richard Tregenow

Coarse, Joseph [sigy], in Edward Sammon, *A Discovery of the Education of the Schollars [sic] in Cambridge* (1659)

Cobb, Alice, in Anne Martindall, *A Relation of [. . .] Alice Curwen* (1680)

Cobb, Thomas [sigy], in Anne Martindall, *A Relation of [. . .] Alice Curwen* (1680)

Cobbam, Elizabeth [sigy], in George Whitehead, *Piety Promoted [. . .] Ann Whitehead* (1686)

Cole, Josaiah, *The Last Testimony [...] Richard Farnworth* (London: n. pr., 1667)

Cole, Mary [co-author], in Priscilla Cotton, *To the Priests* (1655)

Coleman, Elizabeth, in Stephen Crisp, *A Backslider Reproved* (1669)

Colison, Mary [sigy], in Christopher Atkinson, *The Standard of the Lord Lifted up* (1653)

Collett, Elizabeth [sigy], in George Whitehead, *Piety Promoted [. . .] Ann Whitehead* (1686)

Colley, Francis, in Anne Martindall, *A Relation of [. . .] Alice Curwen* (1680)

Collins, John [sigy], in Robert Wastfield, *A True Testimony of Faithful Witnesses* (1657)

Colman, William [sigy], in John Wilkinson, *The Memory of [. . .] John Story* (1683)

Cook, Lucretia, in George Whitehead, *Piety Promoted [. . .] Ann Whitehead* (1686)

Cooper, Ann [sigy], in George Whitehead, *Piety Promoted [. . .] Ann Whitehead* (1686)

Cooper, Mary [sigy], in Oliver Sansom, *God's Mighty Power [. . .] Joan Vokins* (1691)

Cooper, William [sigy], in Oliver Sansom, *God's Mighty Power [. . .] Joan Vokins* (1691)

Coot, John, in James Parnell, *The Lambs Defence* (1656)

Copeland, John [sigy], in Edward Burrough, *A Declaration of the Sad and Great Persecution* [1660]

——in Humphrey Norton, *New Englands Ensigne* (1659)

Corney, Elianor [sigy], in John Beck, *A Certain True Relation [. . .] of Sarah wife of John Beck* (1680)

Cornwell, John, in Samuel Cater, *The Life of [. . .] Giles Barnardiston* (1681)

Cotton, Priscilla, *A Testimony of Truth* (n. pl.: M.W [Mary Westwood], n. d.)

——*A Visitation of Love unto all People* (London: Thomas Simmonds, 1661) Signed P. C.

——'As I was in the Prison-house' [first line] (n. pl.: n. pr., n. d)

——*To the Priests* (London: Giles Calvert, 1655) Co-authored by Mary Cole

Cottrell, John [sigy], in Oliver Sansom, *God's Mighty Power [. . .] Joan Vokins* (1691)

Cottrell, Mary [sigy], in Oliver Sansom, *God's Mighty Power [. . .] Joan Vokins* (1691)

Coveny, Thomas [sigy], in Margaret Fell, *A Declaration and an Information* (1660)

Cox, Ann [sigy], in George Whitehead, *Piety Promoted [. . .] Ann Whitehead* (1686)

Crabb, Thomas [sigy], in John Wilkinson, *The Memory of [. . .] John Story* (1683)

Creeke, Tho. [sigy], in James Parnell, *The Lambs Defence* (1656)

Cripps, John, *A True Account of the Dying Words of Ockanickon, an Indian King* (London: Benjamin Clark, 1682)

Other writers: Sarah Biddle, Anne Browne, Thomas Budd, Mary Cripps, Jane Noble Native American: Ockanickon, Jahkursoe, Matollinequay, Nemooponent, Tellinggrifee

Cripps, Mary [sigy], in John Cripps, *A True Account of the Dying Words of Ockanickon, an Indian King* (1682)

Crisp, Stephen, *A Back Slider Reproved [. . .] A Short Reply to [. . .] Robert Cobbet* (n. pl.: n. pr., 1669)

Other writers: Elizabeth Coleman, Anne Travers

Crook, John, *A Collection of the Several Wrightings of that True Prophet [. . .] William Bayly* (n. pl.: n. pr., 1676)

Other writers: Mary Bayly (formerly Fisher), John Clark, Jewell Guy, John Taylor, Rebecca Travers

Crook, John, *The Cry of the Innocent for Justice* (n.d)

Other author: Hester Biddle

[Text not seen by me: Wing reference T914]

Crouch, Ruth, in George Whitehead, *Piety Promoted [. . .] Ann Whitehead* (1686)

——in Mary Forster, *A Living Testimony from [. . .] Womens Meeting* [1685]

Cullcup, Elizabeth [sigy], in George Whitehead, *Piety Promoted [. . .] Ann Whitehead* (1686)

Curtis, Thomas [sigy], in Anne Audland, *The Saints Testimony* (1655)
——in Benjamin Coales, *A Relation of the Last Words and Departure of [. . .] Loveday Hambly* (1683)
——in John Wilkinson, *The Memory of [. . .] John Story* (1683)
Curwen, Alice, in Anne Martindall, *A Relation of [. . .] Alice Curwen* (1680)
  Subject of deathbed testimony and writer
Curwen, Thomas (sen.) [sigy], in Anne Martindall, *A Relation of [. . .] Alice Curwen* (1680)
Curwen, Thomas (jun), in Anne Martindall, *A Relation of [. . .] Alice Curwen* (1680)
Dando, John [sigy], in Robert Wastfield, *A True Testimony of Faithful Witnesses* (1657)
Davis, Rich. [sigy], in John Bolton, *A Declaration* (1655)
Dennis, Joan [sigy], in George Whitehead, *Piety Promoted [. . .] Ann Whitehead* (1686)
Dew, Susannah, in Mary Forster, *A Living Testimony from [. . .] Womens Meeting* [1685]
——in George Whitehead, *Piety Promoted [. . .] Ann Whitehead* (1686)
Dewsbury, William, *A True Testimony of what was done Concerning the Servants of the Lord [. . .] at Northampton* (London: Giles Calvert, 1655)
Dickinson, Elianor, in John Beck, *A Certain True Relation [. . .] of Sarah wife of John Beck* (1680)
Dickinson, John [sigy], in John Beck, *A Certain True Relation [. . .] of Sarah wife of John Beck* (1680)
Dixon, John, in Dorothy Wilson, *The Memorial of [. . .] William Wilson* (1685)
Docrey, Thomas, in William Mead *A Brief Collection of Remarkable Passages [. . .] Margaret Fox* (1710)
——in Dorothy Tickell, *Some Testimonies Concerning [. . .] Hugh Tickell* (1690)
Docwra, Anne, *A Looking-glass for the Recorder and Justices of the Peace* (n. pl.: n. pr., [1682])
——*An Epistle of Love and Good Advice* (n. pl.: n. pr., [1683])
Dogson, George, in John Wilkinson, *The Memory of [. . .] John Story* (1683)
Dole, Dorcas, *A Salutation of my Endeared Love*, 2nd edn (London: John Bringhurst, 1684)
——*Once More a Warning to thee O England* (n. pl.: n. pr., 1684)
Drewet, Mary, in Oliver Sansom, *God's Mighty Power [. . .] Joan Vokins* (1691)
Dring, Robert [sigy], in Amos Stodard, *Something Written in Answer to a Lying Scandalous Book* [1655]
Dring, Simon [sigy], in John Bolton, *A Declaration* (1655)
——[sigy], in Amos Stodard, *Something Written in Answer to a Lying Scandalous Book* [1655]
Drinkwell, Margaret [sigy], in George Whitehead, *Piety Promoted [. . .] Ann Whitehead* (1686)
Dyar, Mary, in Edward Burrough, *A Declaration of the Sad and Great Persecution* [1660]
Dymond, Philip, in A. Paterson, *The Testimony [. . .] John Matern* (1680)
Eccleson, Ann [sigy], in George Whitehead, *Piety Promoted [. . .] Ann Whitehead* (1686)
Edge, Sarah [sigy], in George Whitehead, *Piety Promoted [. . .] Ann Whitehead* (1686)
Edmundson, Ann, in Christopher Cheesman, *Living Words through a Dying Man [. . .] Francis Patchett* (1678)
Edmundson, Thomas [sigy], in Edward Sammon, *A Discovery of the Education of the Schollars [sic] in Cambridge* (1659)
Edward, Thomas, in Mary Stout, *The Testimony of the Hartford Quakers* (1676)
Ellis, Sarah, in Rebecca Travers, *The Work of God [. . .] Susannah Whitrow* (1677)
——[sigy], in George Whitehead, *Piety Promoted [. . .] Ann Whitehead* (1686)
Ellwood, Mary, *The Spirit that Works Abomination* (n. pl.: n. pr., 1685)
  Co-author: Margery Clipsham
Ellwood, Thomas, in George Fox, *The Works of [. . .]Isaac Penington* (1681)

Elsam, Elizabeth [sigy], in Ellis Hookes, *Balm for Gilead* (1675)

Elsam, Thomas, in Ellis Hookes, *Balm for Gilead* (1675)

Elson, Mary, in Mary Forster, *A Living Testimony from [. . .] Womens Meeting* [1685]

——in Ann Whitehead, *An Epistle for True Love* (1680)

——in George Whitehead, *Piety Promoted [. . .] Ann Whitehead* (1686)

Etheridge, Constant [sigy], in George Whitehead, *Piety Promoted [. . .] Ann Whitehead* (1686)

Everenden, Thomas, in George Fox, *The Works of [. . .]Isaac Penington* (1681)

Fairman, Richard, in Ralph Famer (non-Quaker), *Sathan [sic] Inthron'd* (1657)

Fallbery, Marvell [sigy], in Anne Martindall, *A Relation of [. . .] Alice Curwen* (1680)

Farnbury, Marrabella [sigy], in Oliver Sansom, *God's Mighty Power [. . .] Joan Vokins* (1691)

——in George Whitehead, *Piety Promoted [. . .] Ann Whitehead* (1686)

——[sigy], in Christopher Cheesman, *Living Words through a Dying Man [. . .] Francis Patchett* (1678)

Farnbury, Thomas [sigy], in Christopher Cheesman, *Living Words through a Dying Man [. . .] Francis Patchett* (1678)

Farnworth, Richard, *A Woman Forbidden to Speak in Church* (London: Giles Calvert, 1654)

——in Josiah Cole, *The Last Testimony of [...] Richard Farnworth*

    Subject of testimony

Featherstone, Sarah Brown, in John Field, *Living Testimonies Concerning [. . .] Joseph Featherstone* (1689)

Featherstone, Sarah (the younger), in John Field, *Living Testimonies Concerning [. . .] Joseph Featherstone* (1689)

    Subject of deathbed testimony

Fell, Anne [sigy], in Thomas Fell, *A Short Testimony Concerning [. . .] Judith Fell* [1682]

Fell, Anthony, in Thomas Fell, *A Short Testimony Concerning [. . .] Judith Fell* [1682]

Fell, Elizabeth [sigy], in Thomas Fell, *A Short Testimony Concerning [. . .] Judith Fell* [1682]

Fell, John [sigy], in Thomas Fell, *A Short Testimony Concerning [. . .] Judith Fell* [1682]

Fell, Judith, in Thomas Fell, *A Short Testimony Concerning [. . .] Judith Fell* [1682]

    Subject of deathbed testimony

Fell, Leonard, in William Addamson, *A Persecution in Several Places in Lancashire* (1655)

Fell, Lydia, *A Testimony and Warning given forth in the Love of Truth* (n. pl.: n. pr., [1676])

Fell, Margaret, *A Call unto the Seed out of Israel* (London: Robert Wilson [1668])

——*A Declaration and an Information from us the People of God Called Quakers* (London: Thomas Simmonds and Robert Wilson, 1660)

    Other writers: William Caton, Thomas Coveny, Samuel Fisher, George Fox, Joseph Fuce, Thomas Harte, Ellis Hookes, Richard Hubberthorne, Gerrard Roberts, Gobert Sikes, Amos Stodard, James Strut, John Stubbs

——*A Loving Salutation to the Seed of Abraham* (London: Thomas Simmonds, 1656)

——*A Paper Concerning Such as are made Ministers* (London: M. W. [Mary Westwood], 1659)

    Other writer: George Fox

——*A Testimonie of the Touchstone* (London: Thomas Simmonds, 1656)

——*An Evident Demonstration to God's Elect* (London: Thomas Simmonds, 1660)

——*False Prophets, AntiChrists [sic], Deceivers* (London: Giles Calvert, 1655)

    Other authors: 'T. A.', James Millner (on behalf of himself and his wife)

——*For Manasseth Ben Israel* (London: Giles Calvert, 1656)

——*The Daughter of Sion [sic] Awakened* (n. pl.: n. pr., 1677)

——*The Examination and Tryall of Margaret Fell and George Fox* (n. pl.: pr., 1664)

Other writer: George Fox

——*To the General Councel, and the Officers of the Army* (London: Thomas Simmonds, 1659)

——*Womens Speaking Justified* (London, 1666)

——in William Mead, *A Brief Collection of Remarkable Passages [. . .] Margaret Fox* (1710)

Subject of deathbed testimony

——in Dorothy Tickell, *Some Testimonies Concerning [. . .] Hugh Tickell* (1690)

Fell, Margaret [sigy], in Thomas Fell, *A Short Testimony Concerning [. . .] Judith Fell* [1682]

Not of Swarthmore

Fell, Matthew [sigy], in Thomas Fell, *A Short Testimony Concerning [. . .] Judith Fell* [1682]

Fell, Rachel [sigy], in Isabel Yeamans, *A Lively Testimony to [. . .] Robert Jeckell* (1676)

Fell, Ruth [sigy], in Thomas Fell, *A Short Testimony Concerning [. . .] Judith Fell* [1682]

Fell, Sarah (later Mead)[sigy], in Isabel Yeamans, *A Lively Testimony to [. . .] Robert Jeckell* (1676)

——[sigy], in William Mead *A Brief Collection of Remarkable Passages [. . .] Margaret Fox* (1710)

——[sigy], in George Whitehead, *Piety Promoted [. . .] Ann Whitehead* (1686)

Fell, Susanna [sigy], in Isabel Yeamans, *A Lively Testimony to [. . .] Robert Jeckell* (1676)

Fell, Thomas, *A Short Testimony Concerning the Death and Finishing of Judith Fell* (n. pl.: n. pr. [Andrew Sowle], [1682])

Other writers: Elizabeth Caipe, Matthew Caipe, John Cape, Anne Fell, Anthony Fell, Elizabeth Fell, John Fell, Margaret Fell, Matthew Fell, Ruth Fell

——in Robert Huntington, *The Memory of [. . .] Thomas Stordy* (1692)

——in Dorothy Tickell, *Some Testimonies Concerning [. . .] Hugh Tickell* (1690)

Field, John, *Living Testimonies Concerning the Death [. . .] of Joseph Featherstone* ([London]: Andrew Sowle, 1689)

Other writers: Sarah (Featherstone) Brown, Thomas Brown

Field, Margery [sigy], in George Whitehead, *Piety Promoted [. . .] Ann Whitehead* (1686)

Fisher, Abigail, in George Whitehead, *Piety Promoted [. . .] Ann Whitehead* (1686)

Fisher, Mary (later Bayly) [sigy], in Thomas Aldam, *False Prophets and False Preachers Described* [1652]

——in John Crook, *A Collection of the Several Wrightings of [. . .] William Bayly* (1676)

Fisher, Samuel [sigy], in Margaret Fell, *A Declaration and an Information* (1660)

Fletcher, Elizabeth, *A Few Words in Season* (London: Robert Wilson, 1660)

Fooks, Mary [co-author], in William Penn, *Saul Smitten to the Ground* (1675)

Ford, Bridget, in George Whitehead, *Piety Promoted [. . .] Ann Whitehead* (1686)

Ford, Robert, *A Testimony Concerning George Russel* (n. pl.: n. pr. [1680])

Other author: Jasper Batt

Forster, Mary, *A Living Testimony from the Power and Spirit of our Lord Jesus Christ in our Faithful Womens Meeting* (n. pl.: n. pr., [1685])

Other writers: Ruth Crouch, Susannah Dew, Mary Elson, Mary Plumstead, Anne Travice

——*Some Seasonable Considerations to the Young Men and Women* (London: Andrew Sowle, 1684)

——*These Several Papers* (London: Mary Westwood, 1659)

Collective petition signed by approximately 7,500 women

——in *A Declaration of the Bountifull [sic] Loving Kindness [. . .] Mary Harris*, Anon (n. pl.: n. pr., 1669)

——in Thomas Forster, _A Guide to the Blind_ (1671)
——in George Whitehead, _Piety Promoted [. . .] Ann Whitehead_ (1686)
Forster, Thomas, _A Guide to the Blind_ (repr. n. pl.: n. pr., 1671)
  Other writer: Mary Forster
Fortescue, William, _A Short Relation Concerning the Life and Death of [. . .] William Simpson_ (n. pl.: n. pr., 1671)
  Other writers: George Fox, Elizabeth Hooton, Oliver Hooton, William Simpson
Fox, George, _An Answer to Doctor Burgess his Book_ (London: Thomas Simmonds, 1659)
——_Saul's Errand to Damascus_ (London: Giles Calvert, 1653)
  Other writer: W. W. other subjects Jo. Lawson, James Nayler
——_The Woman Learning in Silence_ (London: Thomas Simmonds, 1656)
——_The Works of the Long-Mounfull and Sorely-Distressed Isaac Penington_ (London: Benjamin Clark, 1681)
  Other writers: Thomas Ellwood, Thomas Evernden, Samuel Jennings, Robert Jones, James Parke, Alexander Parker, Isaac Penington, John Penington, Mary Penington, William Penn, Ambrose Riggs, Christopher Taylor, George Whitehead, Thomas Zachary
——in Gervase Benson, _The Cry of the Oppressed_ (1656)
——in Thomas Camm, _The Memory of the Righteous Revived_ (1689)
——in Ralph Farmer (non-Quaker), _Sathan [sic] Inthron'd_ (1657)
——in Margaret Fell, _A Paper Concerning Such as are made Ministers_ (1659)
——[sigy] in Margaret Fell, _A Declaration and an Information_ (1660)
——in Margaret Fell, _The Examination and Tryall of Margaret Fell and George Fox_ (1664)
——in William Fortescue, _A Short Relation Concerning the Life and Death of [. . .] William Simpson_ (1671)
——in Peter Hardcastle, _Several Living Testimonies [. . .] Robert Lodge_ (1691)
——in Francis Howgill, _A Testimony Concerning [. . .] Edward Burroughs [sic]_ (1662)
——in Francis Howgill, _Caines Bloudy Race_ (1657)
——in Edward Pyot, _The West Answering to the North_ (1657)
——in Dorothy Tickell, _Some Testimonies Concerning [. . .] Hugh Tickell_ (1690)
——in Theophila Townsend, _An Epistle of Love_ [1680]
——in George Whitehead, _The Grounds and Causes of our Sufferings [. . .] in Suffolk_ (1656)
Freatwell, Ralph, in Anne Martindall, _A Relation of [. . .] Alice Curwen_ (1680)
Freatwell, Thomas, in Anne Martindall, _A Relation of [. . .] Alice Curwen_ (1680)
Freeman, Mary-Ann, in George Whitehead, _Piety Promoted [. . .] Ann Whitehead_ (1686)
Frost, Nicholas [sigy], in Edward Sammon, _A Discovery of the Education of the Schollars [sic] in Cambridge_ (1659)
Fry, John [sigy], in John Wilkinson, _The Memory of [. . .] John Story_ (1683)
Fuce, Joseph [sigy], in Margaret Fell, _A Declaration and an Information_ (1660)
Fulbrook, Margaret [sigy], in Oliver Sansom, _God's Mighty Power [. . .] Joan Vokins_ (1691)
Fullove, Elizabeth [sigy], in George Whitehead, _Piety Promoted [. . .] Ann Whitehead_ (1686)
Furly, John, in Samuel Cater, _The Life of [. . .] Giles Barnardiston_ (1681)
Gandye, Tho. [sigy], in James Parnell, _The Lambs Defence_ (1656)
Gardner, Agnes, in John Beck, _A Certain True Relation [. . .] of Sarah wife of John Beck_ (1680)
Gardner, Anne, _A Brief Relation of the Life and Death of Elizabeth Braythwaite_ (n. pl.: n. pr., [1684])
  Other writers: John Braithwaite, T. C., Thomas Gardner
  Wing C128; Smith I, 315

Harding, Prudence [sigy], in William Smith, *A Real Demonstration of the True Order in the Spirit of God* (1663)

Harlow, Abigail [sigy], in George Whitehead, *Piety Promoted [. . .] Ann Whitehead* (1686)

Harper, Robert [sigy], in Humphrey Norton, *New Englands Ensigne* (1659)

Harris, Charles, in John Wilkinson, *The Memory of [. . .] John Story* (1683)

Hart, John, in Ellis Hookes, *Balm for Gilead* (1675)

Hart, Priscilla [sigy], in George Whitehead, *Piety Promoted [. . .] Ann Whitehead* (1686)

Harte, Thomas [sigy], in Margaret Fell, *A Declaration and an Information* (1660)

Harwood, John, in George Whitehead, *The Grounds and Causes of our Sufferings [. . .] in Suffolk* (1656)

Haward, Jeremiah, *Here Followeth a Relation of Some of the Sufferings [. . .] in Oxford* (n. pl.: n. pr., n. d.)
> Other writers: Abraham Allin, Abra Badger, Alex Green, Thomas Ryland, Thomas Swank, Henry Traine, Lawrence Willyer

Hawarth, William, in Mary Stout, *The Testimony of the Hartford Quakers* (1676)
> Subject of deathbed testimony

Haynes, Elizabeth, in George Whitehead, *Piety Promoted [. . .] Ann Whitehead* (1686)

Head, Peter [sigy], in Dorothy Tickell, *Some Testimonies Concerning [. . .] Hugh Tickell* (1690)

Hebson, Richard, in Margaret Braidley, *Certain Papers which is the Word of the Lord* (n. d)

Heywood, Elizabeth [sigy], in George Whitehead, *Piety Promoted [. . .] Ann Whitehead* (1686)

Hide, Elizabeth [co-author], in William Penn, *Saul Smitten to the Ground* (1675)

Hide, Matthew, in William Penn, *Saul Smitten to the Ground* (1675)
> Subject of deathbed testimony

Hignell, Temperance, in George Bishop, *The Cry of Blood* (1656)

Hill, Ruth, in Ralph Farmer (non-Quaker), *Sathan [sic] Inthron'd* (1657)

Hincks, Elizabeth, *The Poor Widdows [sic] Mite* (n. pl.: n. pr., 1671)

Hodgshone, R., in Humphrey Norton, *New Englands Ensigne* (1659)

Hodgson, David, in Robert Huntington, *The Memory of [. . .] Thomas Stordy* (1692)

Holder, Christopher, in Humphrey Norton, *New Englands Ensigne* (1659)

Hollister, Dennis, in George Bishop, *The Cry of Blood* (1656)

Holmes, Jane [sigy], in Thomas Aldam, *False Prophets and False Preachers Described* [1652]

Holmes, Thomas, in William Addamson, *A Persecution in Several Places in Lancashire* [1655]

——in Christopher Atkinson, *The Standard of the Lord Lifted up* (1653)

Hookes, Ellis, *The True Light Discovered [. . .] in Several Treatises by Stephen Smith* (London: n. pr., 1679)
> Other writers: William Lickfold, Susanna Smith, Stephen Smith, George Whitehead

——*Balm for Gilead: A Collection of the Living Divine Testimonies [. . .] William Smith* (n. pl.: n. pr, 1675)
> Other writers: Elizabeth Elsam, Thomas Elsam, John Hart, John Reckless, Ann Shaw, Robert Shaw, Elizabeth Smith, William Smith, John Theaker, John Whitehead, John Willsford

——[sigy], in Margaret Fell, *A Declaration and an Information* (1660)

Hooton, Elizabeth, in Thomas Taylor, *To the King* [1670]

——in Thomas Aldam, *False Prophets and False Preachers Described* [1652]

——in William Fortescue, *A Short Relation Concerning the Life and Death of [. . .] William Simpson* (1671)

Hooton, Oliver, in William Fortescue, *A Short Relation Concerning the Life and Death of [. . .] William Simpson* (1671)

Hopper, Elizabeth [co-author], in Isabel Yeamans, *A Lively Testimony to [. . .] Robert Jeckell* (1676)

Houland, Henry, in Humphrey Norton, *New Englands Ensigne* (1659)

Howell, Mary [sigy], in George Whitehead, *Piety Promoted [. . .] Ann Whitehead* (1686)

Howgill, Francis, *A Testimony Concerning the Life, Death, Trials [. . .] Edward Burroughs [sic]* (London: William Warwick, 1662)
    Other writers: Josiah Cole, George Fox, George Whitehead

——*Caines Bloudy Race* (London: Thomas Simmonds, 1657)
    Signed by F. H; Smith makes Anthony Hutchins the main author
    Other writers: George Fox, Anthony Hutchins, Richard Sale

——*One of Anti Christs Voluntiers Defeated* (London: Thomas Simmonds, 1660)

——in Christopher Atkinson, *The Standard of the Lord Lifted up* (1653)

Howgill, Mary, *A Remarkable Letter of Mary Howgill to Oliver Cromwell* (n. pl.: n. pr., 1657)

——*A Vision of the Lord of Hosts* (n. pl.: n. pr., 1662)
    Signed M. H.

——[sigy], in Christopher Atkinson, *The Standard of the Lord Lifted up* (1653)

Hubbard, Ann [sigy], in George Whitehead, *Piety Promoted [. . .] Ann Whitehead* (1686)

Hubberthorne, Richard, *A True Testimony of the Zeal of Oxford Professors* (London: Giles Calvert, 1654)

——*The Immediate Call to the Ministry* (London: Giles Calvert, 1654)
    Other Quaker writers: James Parnell
    Non-Quaker writers: Will. Pickering

——*The Real Cause of the Nations Bondage* (London: Thomas Simmonds, 1659)

——[sigy], in Margaret Fell, *A Declaration and an Information* (1660)

Hull, Martha [sigy], in George Whitehead, *Piety Promoted [. . .] Ann Whitehead* (1686)

Huntington, Robert, *The Memory of that Faithful Man of God, Thomas Stordy* (London: T. Sowle, 1692)
    Other writers: Elizabeth Bewley, George Bewley, Thomas Fell, David Hodgson, William Jonson, John Robinson, Mary Stordy, Thomas Stordy

Hutchins, Anthony, in Francis Howgill, *Caines Bloudy Race* (1657)

Hutchins, Grace [sigy], in Oliver Sansom, *God's Mighty Power [. . .] Joan Vokins* (1691)

Hutson, Thomas in A Paterson, *The Testimony [. . .] John Matern* (1680)

Ingram, Susan [sigy], in William Mead *A Brief Collection of Remarkable Passages [. . .] Margaret Fox* (1710)

Ingram, Susanna [sigy], in George Whitehead, *Piety Promoted [. . .] Ann Whitehead* (1686)

Ingram, William, in George Whitehead, *Piety Promoted [. . .] Ann Whitehead* (1686)

Isacke, John [sigy], in James Parnell, *The Lambs Defence* (1656)

Jagger, John [sigy], in Oliver Sansom, *God's Mighty Power [. . .] Joan Vokins* (1691)

Jeckell, Robert, in Isabell Yeamans, *A Lively Testimony to [. . .] Robert Jeckell* (1676)
    Subject of deathbed testimony

Jelly, Isabel [sigy], in George Whitehead, *Piety Promoted [. . .] Ann Whitehead* (1686)

Jenner, Grace [sigy], in George Whitehead, *Piety Promoted [. . .] Ann Whitehead* (1686)

Jennings, John, in John Wilkinson, *The Memory of [. . .] John Story* (1683)

Jennings, Mary [sigy], in George Whitehead, *Piety Promoted [. . .] Ann Whitehead* (1686)

Jennings, Samuel, in George Fox, *The Works of [. . .]Isaac Penington* (1681)

Johnson, Jonathan, in Samuel Cater, *The Life of [. . .] Giles Barnardiston* (1681)

Johnson, William, in Robert Huntington, *The Memory of [. . .] Thomas Stordy* (1692)

Jones, Robert, in George Fox, *The Works of [. . .] Isaac Penington* (1681)

Jones, Sarah, *This is the Lights Appearance in the Truth* (n. pl.: n. pr., n.d)

Kerby, Richard [sigy], in Humphrey Norton, *New Englands Ensigne* (1659)

Keyes, Leonard, in John Wilkinson, *The Memory of [. . .] John Story* (1683)

Killam, Margaret [co-author], *A Warning from the Lord to the Teachers and People of Plymouth* (London: Giles Calvert, 1656)
    Co-author: Barbara Patison; in text, Killin.

Kinch, Margaret [sigy], in George Whitehead, *Piety Promoted [. . .] Ann Whitehead* (1686)

Knowles, John, in Oliver Sansom, *God's Mighty Power [. . .] Joan Vokins* (1691)

Laity, Mary [sigy], in George Whitehead, *Piety Promoted [. . .] Ann Whitehead* (1686)

Lambole, William [sigy], in Oliver Sansom, *God's Mighty Power [. . .] Joan Vokins* (1691)

Langhorn, Dorothy [sigy], in George Whitehead, *Piety Promoted [. . .] Ann Whitehead* (1686)

Laurence, Benjamin [sigy], in John Wilkinson, *The Memory of [. . .] John Story* (1683)

Lavor, Henry [sigy], in Robert Wastfield, *A True Testimony of Faithful Witnesses* (1657)

Lawrence, Adam [sigy], in Oliver Sansom, *God's Mighty Power [. . .] Joan Vokins* (1691)

Lawrence, Sarah [sigy], in Oliver Sansom, *God's Mighty Power [. . .] Joan Vokins* (1691)

Laythes, Thomas [sigy], in Dorothy Tickell, *Some Testimonies Concerning [. . .] Hugh Tickell* (1690)

Letchworth, Robert [sigy], in Edward Sammon, *A Discovery of the Education of the Schollars [sic] in Cambridge* (1659)

Levens, Elizabeth [sigy], in Christopher Atkinson, *The Standard of the Lord Lifted up* (1653)

Lickfold, William, in Ellis Hookes, *The True Light Discovered [. . .] in Several Treatises by Stephen Smith* (1679)

Lindley, Mary, in Katherine Whitton, *An Epistle from the Womens Yearly Meeting at York* (1688)

Lockley, Edw. [sigy], in Oliver Sansom, *God's Mighty Power [. . .] Joan Vokins* (1691)

Lockley, Mary [sigy], in Oliver Sansom, *God's Mighty Power [. . .] Joan Vokins* (1691)

Lodge, Robert, in Perter Hardcastle, *Several Living Testimonies [. . .] Robert Lodge* (1691)

Loosvelt, William, in A. Paterson, *The Testimony of [. . .] John Matern* (1680)

Loscombe, Thomas, in Robert Wastfield, *A True Testimony of Faithful Witnesses* (1657)

Lower, Mary [sigy], in William Mead *A Brief Collection of Remarkable Passages [. . .] Margaret Fox* (1710)

Lower, Thomas [sigy], in William Mead *A Brief Collection of Remarkable Passages [. . .] Margaret Fox* (1710)

Ludgater, Robert [sigy], in James Parnell, *The Lambs Defence* (1656)

Lund, Andrew [sigy], in Christopher Cheesman, *Living Words through a Dying Man [. . .] Francis Patchett* (1678)

Mackett, Ann, in George Whitehead, *Piety Promoted [. . .] Ann Whitehead* (1686)

Man, Elizabeth [sigy], in George Whitehead, *Piety Promoted [. . .] Ann Whitehead* (1686)

Mardin, Mary [sigy], in George Whitehead, *Piety Promoted [. . .] Ann Whitehead* (1686)

Marshall, Charles, in Thomas Camm, *The Memory of the Righteous Revived* (1689)

Marshall, Elizabeth, in George Bishop, *The Cry of Blood* (1656)

Marshall, Henry, in George Whitehead, *The Grounds and Causes of our Sufferings [. . .] in Suffolk* (1656)

Martin, Ann [sigy], in Rebecca Travers, *The Work of God [. . .] Susannah Whitrow* (1677)

Martin, Richard, in Mary Stout, *The Testimony of the Hartford Quakers* (1676)

Martindall, Anne, *A Relation of the Labour, Travel and Suffering of [. . .] Alice Curwen* (n. pl.: n. pr., 1680)
    Other writers: Anne Barber, John Barker, Rebeca Beckley, Henry Byrch, Alice Cobb, Thomas Cobb, Francis Colley, Alice Curwen, Thomas Curwen [sen.], Thomas Curwen

[jun], Ralph Freatwell, Thomas Freatwell, Marvell Fallbery, Elizabeth Gretton, Mary Milles, Mary Nelson, Matthew Pryar, John Reader, John Readman, Stephen Richards, Patience Story, Robert Thorpe, John Todd, R. T. [Rebecca Travers], Jasper Tregouse, Mary Tyllton, Edward Wright

Matern, J., in A. Paterson, *The Testimony [. . .] John Matern* [1680]
    Subject of deathbed testimony

Matern, Rosina, in A. Paterson, *The Testimony [. . .] John Matern* [1680]

Matthew, Deborah [sigy], in Oliver Sansom, *God's Mighty Power [. . .] Joan Vokins* (1691)

Matthew, Jamer [sigy], in Oliver Sansom, *God's Mighty Power [. . .] Joan Vokins* (1691)

Matthews, Martha [sigy], in George Whitehead, *Piety Promoted [. . .] Ann Whitehead* (1686)

May, John [sigy], in Oliver Sansom, *God's Mighty Power [. . .] Joan Vokins* (1691)

Maylin, Abigail [sigy], in George Whitehead, *Piety Promoted [. . .] Ann Whitehead* (1686)

Maynard, Benjamin, in George Bishop, *The Cry of Blood* (1656)

Mead, Sarah, see Sarah Fell

Mead, William, *A Brief Collection of Remarkable Passages [. . .] Margaret Fox* (London: Tace Sowle, 1710)
    Other writers: Daniel Abraham, Rachel Abraham, Thomas Camm, Thomas Dockrey, Susan Ingram, Mary Lower, Thomas Lower, Sarah Mead, George Whitehead

Meekings, Margaret, in George Whitehead, *Piety Promoted [. . .] Ann Whitehead* (1686)

Melsupp, Edward, in Samuel Cater, *The Life of [. . .] Giles Barnardiston* (1681)

Melsupp, Hester, in Samuel Cater, *The Life of [. . .] Giles Barnardiston* (1681)

Metreuers, John, in John Wilkinson, *The Memory of [. . .] John Story* (1683)

Meurs, Susanna [sigy], in Rebecca Travers, *The Work of God [. . .] Susannah Whitrow* (1677)

Mileman, Sarah [sigy], in George Whitehead, *Piety Promoted [. . .] Ann Whitehead* (1686)

Milles, Mary, in Anne Martindall, *A Relation of [. . .] Alice Curwen* (1680)

Milner, James, in Margaret Fell, *False Prophets* (1655)
    Written on behalf of himself and his wife

Moon, James, in William Smith, *A Real Demonstration of the True Order in the Spirit of God* (1663)

Morey, Dewance, *A True and Faithful Warning from the Lord God* (n. pl.: n. pr., n. d)
    Other author: C. B.

Moss, Elizabeth [sigy], in George Whitehead, *Piety Promoted [. . .] Ann Whitehead* (1686)

Moss, Mary, in Samuel Watson, *An Epistle [. . .] Mary Moss* (1695)
    Subject of deathbed testimony

Mudd, Anne, *A Cry, A Cry; A Sensible Cry* (London: n. pr., 1678)
——in John Pennyman, *The Following Words* (1670)

Nash, William [sigy], in Rebecca Travers, *The Work of God [. . .] Susannah Whitrow* (1677)

Nayler, James, *A Discovery of the Man of Sin* (London: Giles Calvert, 1654)
    Other author: Jane Withers
——*A Message from the Spirit of Truth* (London: Thomas Simmonds, 1658)
    Other author: Rebecca Travers
——*How Sin is Strengthened* (London: Thomas Simmonds, 1657)
    Other author: Sarah Blackborrow
——*Milk for Babes*, 2nd edn. (n. pl.: n. pr., 1665)
    Other author: Mary Booth
——*O England, Thy Time is Come* (n. pl.: n. pr., n. d.)
    Other authors, Martha Simmonds, Hannah Stranger, W. T.

Nelson, Mary [sigy], in Anne Martindall, *A Relation of [. . .] Alice Curwen* (1680)

Newby, Margaret [sigy], in Christopher Atkinson, *The Standard of the Lord Lifted up* (1653)

Newman, Anne, in Thomas Salthouse, *A Handful After the Harvest-Man [. . .] Richard Samble* (1684)

Newman, Elizabeth [sigy], in George Whitehead, *Piety Promoted [. . .] Ann Whitehead* (1686)

Newman, Paul [sigy], in Oliver Sansom, *God's Mighty Power [. . .] Joan Vokins* (1691)

Newton, Elizabeth, in William Smith, *A Real Demonstration of the True Order in the Spirit of God* (1663)

Nicholls, Rachel [sigy], in Oliver Sansom, *God's Mighty Power [. . .] Joan Vokins* (1691)

Nicholson, Benjamin [sigy], in Thomas Aldam, *False Prophets and False Preachers Described* [1652]

Nicholson, Jane [sigy], in Edward Burrough, *A Declaration of the Sad and Great Persecution* [1660]

Nicholson, Joseph [sigy], in Edward Burrough, *A Declaration of the Sad and Great Persecution* [1660]

Noble, Jane [sigy], in John Cripps, *A True Account of the Dying Words of Ockanickon, an Indian King* (1682)

Norton, Humphrey, *New Englands Ensigne* (London: T. L. for Giles Calvert, 1659)

Other writers: Ralph Allin, William Allin, Joshua Bussum, John Copeland, Thomas Greenfield, Robert Harper, R. Hodgshone, Christopher Holder, Henry Houland, Richard Kerby, Edward Perry, Nicholas Phelps, John Rous, Katherine Scott, Samuel Shattock, William Shattock

Non-Quaker: Edward Rawson

Norton, Rich. [sigy], in James Parnell, *The Lambs Defence* (1656)

Oade, Cotten [sigy], in William Penn, *Saul Smitten to the Ground* (1675)

Oades, Mary [sigy], in George Whitehead, *Piety Promoted [. . .] Ann Whitehead* (1686)

Ockanickon, in John Cripps, *A True Account of the Dying Words of Ockanickon, an Indian King* (1682)

Subject of deathbed testimony. Native American.

Oddy, Miles, in Peter Hardcastle, *Several Living Testimonies [. . .] Robert Lodge* (1691)

Ormandy, Agnes [sigy], in Isabel Yeamans, *A Lively Testimony to [. . .] Robert Jeckell* (1676)

Orpwood, Joan [sigy], in Oliver Sansom, *God's Mighty Power [. . .] Joan Vokins* (1691)

P., M., in John Penyman, *The Quakers Rejected* (1676)

According to Foxton possibly Penyman's wife, Mary Penyman

Parish, Alexander [sigy], in Edward Sammon, *A Discovery of the Education of the Schollars [sic] in Cambridge* (1659)

Parke, James, in George Fox, *The Works of [. . .]Isaac Penington* (1681)

Parker, Alexander, in George Fox, *The Works of [. . .]Isaac Penington* (1681)

Parker, Martha [sigy], in George Whitehead, *Piety Promoted [. . .] Ann Whitehead* (1686)

Parnell, James, *The Lambs Defence* (London: Giles Calvert, 1656)

Other writers: Robert Adams, Will. Broman, Will. Bunting, John Childe, Zach Childe, John Coot, Tho. Creeke, Tho. Gandye, Ed. Grant, Francis Hanwick, John Isacke, Robert Ludgater, Rich. Norton, Thomas Shortland, Tho. Sparrow, Sam Stillingham, Will. Talcott, Dorothy Waugh

Non-Quakers: John Gerl, Jude Taylor, Joseph Smith

——in Henry Glisson (non- Quaker), *A True and Lamentable Relation of the Most Desperate Death of James Parnell* (1656)

——in Richard Hubberthorne, *The Immediate Call to the Ministry* (1654)

Pask, James, in Dorothy Wilson, *The Memorial of [. . .] William Wilson* (1685)

Pate, Elizabeth [sigy], in George Whitehead, *Piety Promoted [. . .] Ann Whitehead* (1686)

Paterson, A., *A Testimony of [. . .] John Matern [. . .] With Several Testimonies of Sensible Children* (London: Ben Clark, 1680)
Other writers: John Butcher, John Crouch, Philip Dymond, , Thomas Green, Thomas Hutson, William Loosvelt, John Matern, Rosina Matern, Edward Penington, William Penington, Margaret Rouse, C. T., Frances Taylor, Mary Taylor, Ezekiel Wooley, John Wolley

Patison, Barbara [co-author], in Margaret Killin, *A Warning from the Lord to the Teachers and People of Plymouth* (1655)

Paxton, Ann [sigy], in George Whitehead, *Piety Promoted [. . .] Ann Whitehead* (1686)

Peace, John [sigy], in Edward Sammon, *A Discovery of the Education of the Schollars [sic] in Cambridge* (1659)

Pears, William [sigy], in Thomas Aldam, *False Prophets and False Preachers Described* [1652]

Pearson, Anthony, *The Great Case of Tithes Truly Stated*, 7th edn (London: Edward Couchman, 1835); first published 1657
——*To the Parliament of the Common-wealth of England* (n. pl.: n. pr., [1653])

Peel, George [sigy], in Dorothy Tickell, *Some Testimonies Concerning [. . .] Hugh Tickell* (1690)

Penington, Edward, in A. Paterson, *The Testimoy [. . .] John Matern* (1680)

Penington, Isaac, in George Fox, *The Works of [. . .]Isaac Penington* (1681)
Subject of deathbed testimony and author

Penington, John, in George Fox, *The Works of [. . .]Isaac Penington* (1681)

Penington, Mary, in George Fox, *The Works of [. . .]Isaac Penington* (1681)

Penington, William, in A. Paterson, *The Testimony [. . .] John Matern* (1680)

Penn, William, *Saul Smitten to the Ground: Being a Brief, but Faithful Narrative of [. . .] Matthew Hide* (n. pl.: n. pr., 1675)
Other writers: John Ball, George Browne, Mary Fooks, Elizabeth Hide, Cotton Oade, George Whitehead
——in George Fox, *The Works of [. . .]Isaac Penington* (1681)

Pennyman, John, *The Quakers Rejected* (n. pl.: n. pr., 1676)
Signed by J. P.
Other writer: M. P. [possibly Mary Penyman]
——*The Following Words the Lord Required a Servant of his to Write* (n. pl.: John Pennyman, 1670)
Other writer: Anne Mudd

Pennyman, Mary, see P., M.

Perry, Edward [sigy], in Humphrey Norton, *New Englands Ensigne* (1659)

Perkins, Joan [sigy], in George Whitehead, *Piety Promoted [. . .] Ann Whitehead* (1686)

Perrie, Hannah [sigy], in George Whitehead, *Piety Promoted [. . .] Ann Whitehead* (1686)

Peterm, Ellen [sigy], in George Whitehead, *Piety Promoted [. . .] Ann Whitehead* (1686)

Peters, John, in Thomas Salthouse, *A Handful After the Harvest-Man [. . .] Richard Samble* (1684)

Phelps, Nicholas [sigy], in Edward Burrough, *A Declaration of the Sad and Great Persecution* [1660]
——in Humphrey Norton, *New Englands Ensigne* (1659)

Phillips, Ann [sigy], in George Whitehead, *Piety Promoted [. . .] Ann Whitehead* (1686)

Pinder, Bridget [co-author], in Isabel Yeamans, *A Lively Testimony to [. . .] Robert Jeckell* (1676)

Pinder, Grace [sigy], in George Whitehead, *Piety Promoted [. . .] Ann Whitehead* (1686)

Pitman, John [sigy], in Robert Wastfield, *A True Testimony of Faithful Witnesses* (1657)

Pittard, Christopher [sigy], in Robert Wastfield, *A True Testimony of Faithful Witnesses* (1657)

Platts, Martha [sigy], in William Smith, *A Real Demonstration of the True Order in the Spirit of God* (1663)

Plumley, Sarah, in George Whitehead, *Piety Promoted [. . .] Ann Whitehead* (1686)

Plumstead, Edward, in Mary Stout, *The Testimony of the Hartford Quakers* (1676)

Plumstead, Mary, in Mary Forster, *A Living Testimony from [. . .] Womens Meeting* [1685]

——in George Whitehead, *Piety Promoted [. . .] Ann Whitehead* (1686)

Plumsted, Clement, in George Whitehead, *Piety Promoted [. . .] Ann Whitehead* (1686)

Pool, Agnes [sigy], in George Whitehead, *Piety Promoted [. . .] Ann Whitehead* (1686)

Potter, James [sigy], in Oliver Sansom, *God's Mighty Power [. . .] Joan Vokins* (1691)

Potter, Margery [sigy], in Oliver Sansom, *God's Mighty Power [. . .] Joan Vokins* (1691)

Pryar, Matthew, in Anne Martindall, *A Relation of [. . .] Alice Curwen* (1680)

Pyot, Edward, *The West Answering to the North* (London: Giles Calvert, 1657)

    Other Quaker writers: John Blackmore, John Cawse, Joseph Coale, George Fox, William Salt

    Non-Quakers: Edw. Aiscot, Peter Ceely, John Copplestone, Henry Fitz-William, John Page, Richard Spurwell

——in Anne Audland, *The Saints Testimony* (1655)

——in George Bishop, *The Cry of Blood* (1656)

Quare, Mary [sigy], in George Whitehead, *Piety Promoted [. . .] Ann Whitehead* (1686)

Raunce, John, in John Wilkinson, *The Memory of [. . .] John Story* (1683)

Rawes, William, in Dorothy Wilson, *The Memorial of [. . .] William Wilson* (1685)

Rayman, Will. [sigy], in John Bolton, *A Declaration* (1655)

Readar, John, in Anne Martindall, *A Relation of [. . .] Alice Curwen* (1680)

Readman, John, in Anne Martindall, *A Relation of [. . .] Alice Curwen* (1680)

Reckless, Hannah [sigy], in William Smith, *A Real Demonstration of the True Order in the Spirit of God* (1663)

Reckless, John, in Ellis Hookes, *Balm for Gilead* (1675)

——[sigy], in William Smith, *A Real Demonstration of the True Order in the Spirit of God* (1663)

Rich, Robert in Anne Audland, *The Saints Testimony* (1655)

——[sigy], in Amos Stodard, *Something Written in Answer to a Lying Scandalous Book* [1655]

Richards, Stephen, in Thomas Salthouse, *A Handful After the Harvest-Man [. . .] Richard Samble* (1684)

——in Anne Martindall, *A Relation of [. . .] Alice Curwen* (1680)

Rigg, William, in Dorothy Wilson, *The Memorial of [. . .] William Wilson* (1685)

Riggs, Ambrose, in George Fox, *The Works of [. . .] Isaac Penington* (1681)

Roberts, Gerrard [sigy], in Margaret Fell, *A Declaration and an Information* (1660)

——[sigy] in Amos Stodard, *Something Written in Answer to a Lying Scandalous Book* [1655]

Robinson, John, in Robert Huntington, *The Memory of [. . .] Thomas Stordy* (1692)

Roe, Henry, in George Bishop, *The Cry of Blood* (1656)

Rogers, John [sigy], in John Wilkinson, *The Memory of [. . .] John Story* (1683)

Rogers, William, *The Christian Quaker* (London: n. pr., 1680)

Rose, George [sigy], in George Whitehead, *The Grounds and Causes of our Sufferings [. . .] in Suffolk* (1656)

Rous, John [sigy], in Edward Burrough, *A Declaration of the Sad and Great Persecution* [1660]

——in Humphrey Norton, *New Englands Ensigne* (1659)

Rouse, Margaret, in A. Paterson, *The Testimony [. . .] John Matern* (1680)

Russel, George, in Robert Ford, *A Testimony Concerning George Russel* [1680]

Rutt, Abraham, in Mary Stout, *The Testimony of the Hartford Quakers* (1676)

Ryland, Thomas [sigy], in Jeremiah Haward, *Here Followeth a Relation of Some of the Sufferings [. . .] in Oxford* (n. d.)

Sale, Richard, in Francis Howgill, *Caines Bloudy Race* (1657)

Salt, William [co-author], in Edward Pyot, *The West Answering to the North* (1658)

Salthouse, Anne [sigy], in Benjamin Coales, *A Relation of the Last Words and Departure of [. . .] Loveday Hambly* (1683)

Salthouse, Thomas *A Handful After the Harvest-Man, Or a Loving Salutation [. . .] Richard Samble* (London: Andrew Sowle, 1684)

Other writers: Edward Bealing, Anne Newman, John Peters, Stephen Richards, Jane Samble, John Scantlebury, Abigail Shepherd, John Shillson, John Tregallas, William Trethowan

——in Benjamin Coales, *A Relation of the Last Words and Departure of [. . .] Loveday Hambly* (1683)

——in Robert Wastfield, *A True Testimony of Faithful Witnesses* (1657)

Samble, Jane, in Thomas Salthouse, *A Handful After the Harvest-Man [. . .] Richard Samble* (1684)

Samble, Richard, in Thomas Salthouse, *A Handful After the Harvest-Man [. . .] Richard Samble* (1684)

Subject of deathbed testimony

Sammon, Edward, *A Discovery of the Education of the Schollars [sic] in Cambridge* (London: Giles Calvert, 1659)

Other writers: James Blakeley, Matthew Blakeley, George Clark, John Clark, Joseph Coarse, Thomas Edmondson, Nicholas Frost, Mary Godfrey, Robert Letchworth, Alexander Parish, John Peace

Sanders, Mary [sigy], in George Whitehead, *Piety Promoted [. . .] Ann Whitehead* (1686)

Sandilans, Mary [sigy], in Oliver Sansom, *God's Mighty Power [. . .] Joan Vokins* (1691)

Sansom, Jane [sigy], in Oliver Sansom, *God's Mighty Power [. . .] Joan Vokins* (1691)

Sansom, Oliver, *God's Mighty Power Magified [. . .] Joan Vokins* (London: Thomas Northcott, 1691)

Other writers: Elizabeth Addams, Mary Austell, William Austill, Mary Baker, Ann Ball, Jane Ballard, William Ballard, Abraham Bonifield, John Brown, Mary Brown, Daniel Buce, Margery Buce, Damaris Burgis, Hannah Burgis, Samuel Burgis, Elizabeth Bullock, John Buy, Mary Buy, Margaret Chandler, Mary Cooper, William Cooper, John Cotterell, Mary Cotterell, Mary Drewet, Marabillia Farmborough, Margaret Fulbrook, John Gidden, Alice Glover, Grace Hutchings, John Jagger, John Knowles, William Lambole, Addam Lawrence, Sarah Lawrence, Edw. Lockley, Mary Lockley, Deborah Matthew, James Matthew, John May, Paul Newman, Rachel Nicholls, Joan Orpwood, James Potter, Margery Potter, Mary Sandilans, Jane Sansom, William Speakman, Theophilla Townsend, Ann Truss, Jane Tull, Elizabeth Vokins, Hopeful Vokins, Joan Vokins, Richard Vokins, Richard Vokins [jun], Elizabeth Weightwick, Martha Weston, Frances Wren

Scantlebury, John [co-author], in Thomas Salthouse, *A Handful After the Harvest-Man [. . .] Richard Samble* (1684)

Scott, Katherine [sigy], in Humphrey Norton, *New Englands Ensigne* (1659)

Scott, Thomas [sigy], in Dorothy Tickell, *Some Testimonies Concerning [. . .] Hugh Tickell* (1690)

Scotting, Hannah [sigy], in George Whitehead, *Piety Promoted [. . .] Ann Whitehead* (1686)

Sealy, John [sigy], in John Wilkinson, *The Memory of [. . .] John Story* (1683)

Shattock, Samuel, [sigy], in Edward Burrough, *A Declaration of the Sad and Great Persecution* [1660]
——in Humphrey Norton, *New Englands Ensigne* (1659)
Shattock, William, in Humphrey Norton, *New Englands Ensigne* (1659)
Shaw, Ann [sigy], in Ellis Hookes, *Balm for Gilead* (1675)
Shaw, Robert [sigy], in Ellis Hookes, *Balm for Gilead* (1675)
Shepherd, Abigail, in Thomas Salthouse, *A Handful After the Harvest-Man [. . .] Richard Samble* (1684)
Shillson, John, in Thomas Salthouse, *A Handful After the Harvest-Man [. . .] Richard Samble* (1684)
Shortland, Thomas, in James Parnell, *The Lambs Defence* (1656)
Sikes, Gobert [sigy], in Margaret Fell, *A Declaration and an Information* (1660)
Simmonds, Martha, *A Lamentation for the Lost Sheep of the House of Israel* (repr. London: Giles Calvert, 1655)
——'When the Lord Jesus Came' [first line] ([London]: n.p., [1655])
——in James Nayler, *O England, Thy Time is Come* (n. d.)
——in Ralph Farmer (non-Quaker), *Sathan [sic] Inthron'd* (1657)
Simmonds, Thomas, in Ralph Farmer (non-Quaker), *Sathan [sic] Inthron'd*
Simms, Mary [sigy], in George Whitehead, *Piety Promoted [. . .] Ann Whitehead* (1686)
Simpson, William, in William Fortescue, *A Short Relation Concerning the Life and Death of [. . .] William Simpson* (1671)
    Subject and author
——[co-author], in William Addamson, *A Persecution in Several Places in Lancashire* [1655]
Skinner, Elizabeth [sigy], in George Whitehead, *Piety Promoted [. . .] Ann Whitehead* (1686)
Smith, Elizabeth, in Ellis Hookes, *Balm for Gilead* (1675)
——[sigy], in George Whitehead, *Piety Promoted [. . .] Ann Whitehead* (1686)
Smith, Humphrey, *Something Further Laid Open of the Cruel Persecution [. . .] by the Magistrates and People of Evesham* (London: n. pr., 1656)
Smith, John, in George Bishop, *The Cry of Blood* (1656)
Smith, Stephen, in Ellis Hookes, *The True Light Discovered [. . .] in Several Treatises by Stephen Smith* (1679)
    Subject of deathbed testimony and author
Smith, Susanna, in Ellis Hookes, *The True Light Discovered [. . .] in Several Treatises by Stephen Smith* (1679)
Smith, William, *A Real Demonstration of the True Order in the Spirit of God* (London: n. pr., 1663)
    Other writers: Prudence Harding, John Moon, Elizabeth Newton, Martha Platts, Hannah Reckless, John Reckless, Sarah Watsone
——in Ellis Hookes, *Balm for Gilead* (1675)
    Subject of deathbed testimony and author
Smith, Willmot [sigy], in George Whitehead, *Piety Promoted [. . .] Ann Whitehead* (1686)
Southwick, Jastah [sigy], in Edward Burrough, *A Declaration of the Sad and Great Persecution* [1660]
Sowle, Jane, in George Whitehead, *Piety Promoted [. . .] Ann Whitehead* (1686)
Sparrow, Tho. [sigy], in James Parnell, *The Lambs Defence* (1656)
Speakman, William [sigy], in Oliver Sansom, *God's Mighty Power [. . .] Joan Vokins* (1691)
Staplo, Grace [sigy], in George Whitehead, *Piety Promoted [. . .] Ann Whitehead* (1686)
Staplo, John, in George Whitehead, *Piety Promoted [. . .] Ann Whitehead* (1686)

Stealy, John, in *The Memory of [. . .] John Story* (1683)
Stedman, Elizabeth [sigy], in Katherine Whittton, *An Epistle from the Womens Yearly Meeting at York* (1688)
Stilingham, Sam. [sigy], in James Parnell, *The Lambs Defence* (1656)
Stoakes, Elizabeth [sigy], in George Whitehead, *Piety Promoted [. . .] Ann Whitehead* (1686)
Stodard, Amos, *Something Written in Answer to a Lying Scandalous Book* (n. pl.: n. pr., [1655])
　　Other writers: John Bolton, Robert Dring, Simon Dring, Robert Rich, Gerrard Roberts
——[sigy], in Margaret Fell, *A Declaration and an Information* (1660)
Stordy, Mary, in Robert Huntington, *The Memory of [. . .] Thomas Stordy* (1692)
Stordy, Thomas, in Robert Huntington, *The Memory of [. . .] Thomas Stordy* (1692)
Story, John, in John Wilkinson, *The Memory of [. . .] John Story* (1683)
　　Subject of deathbed testimony and writer
Story, Patience, in Anne Martindall, *A Relation of [. . .] Alice Curwen* (1680)
Stott, Mary [sigy], in George Whitehead, *Piety Promoted [. . .] Ann Whitehead* (1686)
Stout, H., in Mary Stout, *The Testimony of the Hartford Quakers* (1676)
Stout, Mary, *The Testimony of the Hartford Quakers [. . .] William Hawath* (n. pl.: n. pr., 1676)
　　Other writers: William Bales, Thomas Edward, Richard Martin, Edward Plumstead, Abraham Rutt, H. Stout, H. Sweeting, Richard Thomas
——in George Whitehead, *Piety Promoted [. . .] Ann Whitehead* (1686)
Stranger, Hannah, in James Nayler *O England, Thy Time is Come* (n. d.)
——in Ralph Farmer (non-Quaker), *Sathan [sic] Inthron'd* (1657)
Stranger, John, in Ralph Farmer (non-Quaker), *Sathan [sic] Inthron'd* (1657)
Strut, James [sigy], in Margaret Fell, *A Declaration and an Information* (1660)
Stubbs, John [sigy], in Margaret Fell, *A Declaration and an Information* (1660)
Swank, Thomas [sigy], in Jeremiah Haward, *Here Followeth a Relation of Some of the Sufferings [. . .] in Oxford* (n. d.)
Sweeting, H., in Mary Stout, *The Testimony of the Hartford Quakers* (1676)
T., C., in A. Paterson, *The Testimony [. . .] John Matern* (1680)
T., W., in *O England, Thy Time is Come* (n. d.)
Talcott, Will., in James Parnell, *The Lambs Defence* (1656)
Tayler, Edward [sigy], in Robert Wastfield, *A True Testimony of Faithful Witnesses* (1657)
Tayler, Hannah [sigy], in George Whitehead, *Piety Promoted [. . .] Ann Whitehead* (1686)
Taylor, Christopher, in Margaret Braidley, *Certain Papers which is the Word of the Lord* (n. d.)
——in George Fox, *The Works of [. . .]Isaac Penington* (1681)
Taylor, Frances [sigy], in Katherine Whitton, *An Epistle from the Womens Yearly Meeting at York* (1688)
——in A. Paterson, *The Testimony [. . .] John Matern* (1680)
Taylor, George [sigy], in Robert Wastfield, *A True Testimony of Faithful Witnesses* (1657)
Taylor, John, in John Crook, *A Collection of the Several Wrightings of [. . .] William Bayly* (1676)
Taylor, Mary, in A. Paterson, *The Testimony [. . .] John Matern* (1680)
Taylor, Thomas, *To the King and both Houses of Parliament* (n. pl.: n. pr., [1670])
　　Other writer: Elizabeth Hooton
Theaker, John [sigy], in Ellis Hookes, *Balm for Gilead* (1675)
Thomas, Richard, in Mary Stout, *The Testimony of the Hartford Quakers* (1676)
Thompson, Anne [sigy], in Christopher Atkinson, *The Standard of the Lord Lifted up* (1653)
Thorpe, Elizabeth [sigy], in George Whitehead, *Piety Promoted [. . .] Ann Whitehead* (1686)

Thorpe, Robert, in Anne Martindall, *A Relation of [. . .] Alice Curwen* (1680)

Tickell, Dorothy, *Some Testimonies Concerning the Life and Death of Hugh Tickell* (London: Thomas Northcott, 1690)
Other writers: Thomas Docrey, Margaret Fell, Thomas Fell, George Fox, Peter Head, Thomas Laythes, George Peel, Thomas Scott, John Tiffin

Tickell, Hugh, in Dorothy Tickell, *Some Testimonies Concerning [. . .] Hugh Tickell* (1690)
Subject of deathbed testimony

Tiffin, John [sigy], in Dorothy Tickell, *Some Testimonies Concerning [. . .] Hugh Tickell* (1690)

Todd, John, in Anne Martindall, *A Relation of [. . .] Alice Curwen* (1680)

Toulnson, Henry [sigy], in Christopher Cheesman, *Living Words through a Dying Man [. . .] Francis Patchett* (1678)

Townsend, Theophila, *A Testimony Concerning the Life and Death of Jane Whitehead* (London: n. pr., 1676)
Other writers: Jane Anderton, Jasper Batt, Thomas Whitehead

——*An Epistle of Love to Friends in the Womens Meetings in London* (n. pl.: n. pr., [1680])
Other writer: George Fox

——in Oliver Sansom, *God's Mighty Power [. . .] Joan Vokins* (1691)

Traine, Henry [sigy], in Jeremiah Haward, *Here Followeth a Relation of Some of the Sufferings [. . .] in Oxford* (n. d.)

Travers, Anne, in Stephen Crisp, *A Backslider Reproved* (1669)

——in George Whitehead, *Piety Promoted [. . .] Ann Whitehead* (1686)

Travers, Rebecca, *For those that Meet to Worship at the Steeplehouse* (London: n. pr., 1659)

——*Of that Eternal Breath* (n. pl.: n. pr., n. d.)

——*The Work of God in a Dying Maid [. . .] Susannah Whitrow* (n. pl.: n. pr., 1677)
Other writers: Sarah Ellis, Ann Martin, Susanna Meurs, William Nash, Joan Whitrow, Robert Whitrow

——*This is for any of that Generation* (n. pl.: Mary Westwood, 1659)

——in John Crook, *A Collection of the Several Wrightings of [. . .] William Bayly* (1676)

——in Anne Martindall, *A Relation of [. . .] Alice Curwen* (1680)
Signed R. T.

——in James Nayler, *A Message from the Spirit of Truth* (1658)

——in George Whitehead, *Piety Promoted [. . .] Ann Whitehead* (1686)

Travice, Anne, in Mary Forster, *A Living Testimony from [. . .] Womens Meeting* [1685]

Tregellas, John [co-author], in Thomas Salthouse, *A Handful After the Harvest-Man [. . .] Richard Samble* (1684)

Tregenow, Richard [sigy], in Benjamin Coales, *A Relation of the Last Words and Departure of [. . .] Loveday Hambly* (1683)

Tregouse, Jasper, in Anne Martindall, *A Relation of [. . .] Alice Curwen* (1680)

Trethowan, William, in Thomas Salthouse, *A Handful After the Harvest-Man [. . .] Richard Samble* (1684)

Truss, Ann [sigy], in Oliver Sansom, *God's Mighty Power [. . .] Joan Vokins* (1691)

Tucker, Edward, in Thomas Woodrowe, *A Brief Relation of the State of Man Before Transgression* (1659)

Tull, Jane [sigy], in Oliver Sansom, *God's Mighty Power [. . .] Joan Vokins* (1691)

Turner, Agnes [sigy], in Christopher Atkinson, *The Standard of the Lord Lifted up* (1653)

Tyllton, Mary, in Anne Martindall, *A Relation of [. . .] Alice Curwen* (1680)

Vaughton, Elizabeth [sigy], in George Whitehead, *Piety Promoted [. . .] Ann Whitehead* (1686)

Veal, Rebecca [sigy], in Christopher Cheesman, *Living Words through a Dying Man [. . .] Francis Patchett* (1678)

Vokins, Elizabeth [sigy], in Oliver Sansom, *God's Mighty Power [. . .] Joan Vokins* (1691)
Vokins, Hopeful [sigy], in Oliver Sansom, *God's Mighty Power [. . .] Joan Vokins* (1691)
Vokins, Joan, in Oliver Sansom, *God's Mighty Power [. . .] Joan Vokins* (1691)
    Subject of deathbed testimony and writer
Vokins, Richard, in Oliver Sansom, *God's Mighty Power [. . .] Joan Vokins* (1691)
Vokins, Richard [jun.] [sigy], in Oliver Sansom, *God's Mighty Power [. . .] Joan Vokins* (1691)
W., I., in John Wilkinson, *The Memory of [. . .] John Story* (1683)
W., W., in George Fox, *Saul's Errand to Damascus* (1653)
Wadenfield, Samuel, in Samuel Cater, *The Life of [. . .] Giles Barnardiston* (1681)
Waite, Mary, in Katherine Whitton, *An Epistle from the Womens Yearly Meeting at York* (1688)
Ware, Elizabeth [sigy], in John Beck, *A Certain True Relation [. . .] of Sarah wife of John Beck* (1680)
Warriner, Mabel [sigy], in Christopher Atkinson, *The Standard of the Lord Lifted up* (1653)
Wass, Mary [sigy], in George Whitehead, *Piety Promoted [. . .] Ann Whitehead* (1686)
Wastfield, Robert, *A True Testimony of Faithful Witnesses* (London: Giles Calvert, 1657)
    Other writers: Richard Addams, Jasper Batt, William Beaton, Thomas Budd, Henry Cattle, Samuel Clothier, John Collins, John Dando, Arthur Gundry, Henry Gundry, Henry Lavor, Thomas Loscombe, John Pitman, Christopher Pittard, Thomas Salthouse, Edward Tayler, George Taylor
    Non-Quakers: John Cary, Rob. Hunt
Watson, Samuel, *An Epistle by Way of Testimony to the Friends of Manchester [. . .] Mary Moss* (London: Thomas Northcott, 1695)
    Other writer: Elizabeth Bols
Watsone, Sarah [sigy], in William Smith, *A Real Demonstration of the True Order in the Spirit of God* (1663)
Waugh, Dorothy, in James Parnell, *The Lambs Defence* (1656)
Waugh, Jane [sigy], in Christopher Atkinson, *The Standard of the Lord Lifted up* (1653)
——(later Whitehead) see Theophila Townsend, *A Testimony Concerning [. . .] Jane Whitehead* (1676)
    Subject of deathbed testimony
Weightwick, Elizabeth [sigy], in Oliver Sansom, *God's Mighty Power [. . .] Joan Vokins* (1691)
Welch, William, in Samuel Cater, *The Life of [. . .] Giles Barnardiston* (1681)
West, Moses, in Christopher Cheesman, *Living Words through [. . .] Francis Patchett* (1678)
Weston, Martha [sigy], in Oliver Sansom, *God's Mighty Power [. . .] Joan Vokins* (1691)
Wheeler, Joan [sigy], in George Whitehead, *Piety Promoted [. . .] Ann Whitehead* (1686)
White, Dorothy, *A Call from God out of Egypt* (London: n. pr., 1662)
——*A Diligent Search Amongst the Rulers* (n. pl.: n. pr., [1659])
——*A Lamentation unto this Nation* (London: Robert Wilson, 1660)
——*A Salutation of Love to all the Tender Hearted* (n. pl.: n. pr., [1684])
——*A Visitation of Heavenly Love unto the Seed of Jacob* (London: Robert Wilson, 1660)
——*An Epistle of Love and of Consolation* (London: Robert Wilson, 1661)
——*This to be Delivered to the Counsellors that are Sitting in Counsel* (London: Thomas Simmonds, 1659)
——*To all those that Worship in Temples Made with Hands* (n. pl.: n. pr., 1664)
——*Unto all Gods Host in England* (n. pl.: n. pr., [1660])
Whitehead, Ann, *An Epistle for True Love, Unity, and Order in the Church of Christ* (London: Andrew Sowle, 1680)

Other writer: Mary Elson
——in George Whitehead, *Piety Promoted [. . .] Ann Whitehead* (1686)
Subject of deathbed testimony and writer
Whitehead, George, *Piety Promoted by Faithfulness Manifested by Several Testimonies Concerning [. . .] Ann Whitehead* (n. pl.: n. pr., 1686)
Other writers: Benjamin Antrobus, Bridget Austill, Charles Bathurst, Grace Bathurst, Elizabeth Camfield, Lucretia Cook, Ruth Crouch, Susanna Dew, Mary Elson, Abigail Fisher, Bridget Ford, Mary Forster, Mary-Ann Freeman, Elizabeth Haynes, William Ingram, Ann Mackett, Margaret Meekings, Sarah Plumley, Mary Plumstead, Clement Plumsted, Jane Sowle, John Staplo, Mary Stout, Ann Travers, Rebecca Travers, Ann Whitehead, Mary Woolley
Women signing on behalf of the women's meeting: Susanna Anthony, Mary Antrobus, Patience Ashfield, Elizabeth Baker, Mary Birkhead, Elizabeth Brassey, Ann Browne, Hester Bryan, Elizabeth Cartwright, Katherine Clarke, Sarah Clarke, Elizabeth Cobbam, Elizabeth Collett, Ann Cooper, Ann Cox, Elizabeth Cullcup, Joan Dennis, Margaret Drinkwell, Ann Eccleson, Sarah Edge, Sarah Ellis, Constant Etheridge, Marrabella Farmbury, Margery Field, Elizabeth Fullove, Elizabeth Gibson, Elizabeth Gouldney, Elizabeth Grice, Mary Gritten, Margaret Hallowfield, Abigail Harlow, Priscilla Hart, Elizabeth Heywood, Mary Howell, Ann Hubbard, Martha Hull, Susanna Ingram, Isabel Jelly, Grace Jenner, Mary Jennings, Margaret Kinch, Mary Laity, Dorothy Langhorn, Elizabeth Man, Mary Mardin, Martha Matthews, Abigail Maylin, Sarah Mead, Sarah Mileman, Elizabeth Moss, Elizabeth Newman, Mary Oades, Martha Parker, Elizabeth Pate, Ann Paxton, Joan Perkins, Hannah Perrie, Ellen Peterm, Ann Phillips, Grace Pinder, Agnes Pool, Mary Quare, Mary Sanders, Hannah Scotting, Mary Sims, Elizabeth Skinner, Elizabeth Smith, Willmot Smith, Grace Staplo, Elizabeth Stoakes, Mary Stott, Hannah Tayler, Elizabeth Thorpe, Elizabeth Vaughton, Mary Wass, Joan Wheeler, Mary Whitpane, Mary Wilson, Rebecca Zachary
——*The Grounds and Causes of our Sufferings [. . .] in Suffolk* (London: Thomas Simmonds, 1656)
Other writers: George Fox, John Harwood, Henry Marshall, George Rose
——in Samuel Cater, *The Life of [. . .] Giles Barnardiston* (1681)
——in George Fox, *The Works of [. . .] Isaac Penington* (1681)
——in Ellis Hookes, *The True Light Discovered [. . .] in Several Treatises by Stephen Smith* (1679)
——in Francis Howgill, *A Testimony Concerning [. . .] Edward Burroughs [sic]* (1662)
——in William Mead *A Brief Collection of Remarkable Passages [. . .] Margaret Fox* (1710)
——in Willaim Penn, *Saul Smitten to the Ground* (1675)
Whitehead, Jane, see Jane Waugh
Whitehead, John, in Ellis Hookes, *Balm for Gilead* (1675)
Whitehead, Thomas, in Theophila Townsend, *A Testimony Concerning [. . .] Jane Whitehead* (1676)
Whiting, John, *Early Piety Exemplified in the Life and Death of Mary Whiting* (n. pl.: n. pr. [1681])
Other writer: Mary Whiting
Whiting, Mary, in John Whiting, *Early Piety Exemplified in the Life and Death of Mary Whiting* [1681]
Subject of deathbed testimony and writer
Whitpane, Mary [sigy], in George Whitehead, *Piety Promoted [. . .] Ann Whitehead* (1686)
Whitrow, Joan, *The Humble Address of the Widow Whitrowe to King William* (n, pl.: n. pr., 1689)

——*The Humble Salutation and Faithful Greeting of Widow Whitrowe to King William* (n. pl.: n. pr., [1690])
——*The Widow Whitrows Humble Thanksgiving for the Kings Safe Return* (London: D. Edwards for J. B., 1694)
——*To King William and Queen Mary, Grace and Peace* (London: n. pr., 1692)
——in Rebecca Travers, *The Work of God [. . .] Susannah Whitrow* (1677)
Whitrow, Robert [sigy], in Rebecca Travers, *The Work of God [. . .] Susannah Whitrow* (1677)
Whitrow, Susannah, in Rebecca Travers, *The Work of God [. . .] Susannah Whitrow* (1677)
    Subject of deathbed testimony
Whitton, Katherine, *An Epistle to Friends Everywhere to be Distinctly Read in their Meetings* (London: Benjamin Clark, 1681)
——*An Epistle from the Womens Yearly Meeting at York* (n. pl.: n. pr., 1688)
    Other writers: Elizabeth Beckwith, Judith Boulbie, Mary Lindley, Elizabeth Stedman, Frances Taylor, Mary Waite, Deborah Winn
Whitton, Thomas, in Peter Hardcastle, *Several Living Testimonies [. . .] Robert Lodge* (1691)
Wilkinson, John, *The Memory of that Servant of God, John Story* (London: John Gain, 1683)
    Other writers: Robert Arch, J. C., Benjamin Coal, Leonard Coal, William Colman, Thomas Crabb, Thomas Curtis, George Dogson, John Fry, Charles Harris, John Jennings, Leonard Keyes, Benjamin Laurence, John Metreuers, John Raunce, John Rogers, John Stealy, John Story, I. W.
Willsford, John, in Samuel Cater, *The Life of [. . .] Giles Barnardiston* (1681)
——in Ellis Hookes, *Balm for Gilead* (1675)
Willyer, Lauwrence [sigy], in Jeremiah Haward, *Here Followeth a Relation of Some of the Sufferings [. . .] in Oxford* (n. d.)
Wilson, Alice, in Christopher Atkinson, *The Standard of the Lord Lifted up* (1653)
Wilson, Dorothy, *The Memorial of the Just Shall not Rot [. . .] William Wilson* (London: Thomas Northcott, 1685)
    Other writers: Thomas Atkinson, John Dixon, James Pask, William, Rawes, William Rigg, Michael Wilson, Rebeca Wilson, Ruth Wilson, William Wilson
Wilson, Mary [sigy], in George Whitehead, *Piety Promoted [. . .] Ann Whitehead* (1686)
Wilson, Michael, in Dorothy Wilson, *The Memorial of [. . .] William Wilson* (1685)
Wilson, Rebecca, in Dorothy Wilson, *The Memorial of [. . .] William Wilson* (1685)
    Signed 'Rebecca', but she describes herself as the deceased's daughter
Wilson, Ruth, in Dorothy Wilson, *The Memorial of [. . .] William Wilson* (1685)
Wilson, William, in Dorothy Wilson, *The Memorial of [. . .] William Wilson* (1685)
    Subject of deathbed testimony and author
Winn, Deborah, in Katherine Whitton, *An Epistle from the Womens Yearly Meeting at York* (1688)
Winn, Katherine, in Thomas Hardcastle, *Several Living Testimonies [. . .] Robert Lodge* (1691)
Withers, Jane, in James Nayler, *A Discovery of the Man of Sin* (1654)
Woodcock, Jane, in Ralph Farmer (non-Quaker), *Sathan [sic] Inthron'd* (1657)
Woodrowe, Thomas, *A Brief Relation of the State of Man Before Transgression* (London: T. W. and Thomas Simmonds, 1659)
    Other writers: Bartholemew Beer, Hester Biddle, Edward Tucker
Wooley, Ezeiel, in A. Paterson, *The Testimony [. . .] John Matern* (1680)
Wooley, John, in A. Paterson, *The Testimony [. . .] John Matern* (1680)
Wooley, Mary, in George Whitehead, *Piety Promoted [. . .] Ann Whitehead* (1686)

Woring, John, in George Bishop, *The Cry of Blood* (1656)
Wray, Charles, in John Field, *Living Testimonies Concerning [. . .] Joseph Featherstone* (1689)
    Subject of deathbed testimony
Wren, Frances [sigy], in Oliver Sansom, *God's Mighty Power [. . .] Joan Vokins* (1691)
Wright, Edward, in Anne Martindall, *A Relation of [. . .] Alice Curwen* (1680)
Yeamans, Isabel, *A Lively Testimony to the Living Truth Given Forth by Robert Jeckell* (London: n. pr., 1676)
    Other writers: Edward Braythwaite, Rachel Fell, Sarah Fell, Susanna Fell, Ed.
    Haiswittle, Elizabeth Hopper, Agnes Ormandy, Bridget Pinder
——*An Invitation of Love to all who Hunger and Thirst After Righteousness* (n. pl.: n. pr., 1679)
Yeats, Isaac, in William Addamson, *A Persecution in Several Places in Lancashire* [1655]
Zachary, Rebecca [sigy], in George Whitehead, *Piety Promoted [. . .] Ann Whitehead* (1686)
Zachary, Thomas, in George Fox, *The Works of [. . .]Isaac Penington* (1681)

A.2.b) Non-Quaker

A.2.b.i) Anonymous

Anon., *A Few Words Offered in Humility [. . .] for the Removing of Tythes* (London: L. Chapman, 1659)
Anon., *A Sad Caveat to all Quakers* (London: W. Gilbertson, 1659)
    Thomason E 1645 (5)
Anon., *A Spirit Moving in the Women Preachers* (London: Henry Shepheard, 1646)
    Thomason E 324 (10)
Anon., *A True Copie of the Petition of the Gentlewomen, and Tradesmens Wives* (London: R. O. and G. D. for John Bull, 1641)
    Thomason E 134 (17)
Anon., *The Humble Petition of Divers Inhabitants of the County of Hertford who have Faithfully Adhered to the Good Old Cause* (London: Thomas Brewster, 1659)
Anon., *The Husbandmans Plea Against Tithes*
    See Nathaniel Humphrey
Anon., *The Quakers Quaking* (London: W. Gilbertson, 1657)
Anon., *The Quaking Mountebank* (London: E. B., 1655)
Anon., *The Womens Petition*
    See K. Frese
Anon., *To the Parliament of the Common-wealth of England* (n. pl.: n. pr., [1653])
    Thomason 669.f.17(26); Leveller women
Anon., *To the Supream Authority of this Nation [. . .] the Humble Petition of Divers Wel-Affected Women* (London: n. pr., 1649)
    Thomason E 551 (14); Leveller women
Anon., *To the Supreme Authority of England the Commons Assembled in Parliament* (n. pl.: n. pr., [1649])
    Thomason 669.f.14 (27); Leveller women
Anon., *Unto Every Individual Member of Parliament* (n. pl.: n. pr., [1653])
    Thomason 669.f.17 (36); Leveller women

A.2.b.ii) Named

Aiscot, Edw., in Edward Pyot (Quaker), *The West Answering to the North* (1657)
Aldridge, Susanna, in Mary Ellwood (Quaker), *The Spirit that Works Abomination* (1685)
  Subject of denunciation
Alleine, Richard, in Richard Baxter, *The Life and Death [. . .] Joseph Alleine* (1672)
  Subject of deathbed testimony and writer
Alleine, Theodosia, in Richard Baxter, *The Life and Death [. . .] Joseph Alleine* (1672)
Atkinson, Elizabeth, *Brief and Plain Discovery of the Labourers in Mistery, Babylon, Generally Called by the Name of Quakers* (n. pl.: P. L., 1669)
Bacon, Nat., *A Relation of the Fearful Estate of Francis Spira* (London: T. Ratcliff and N. Thompson, for Edward Thomas, 1662)
  Other writer: M. N.
Barret, William, in William Addamson, *A Persecution in [. . .] Lancashire* (Quaker) [1655]
Bassfield, E., in K. Frese, *The Womens Petition* (1652)
Baxter, Richard, *The Life and Death of that Excellent Minister of Christ Joseph Alleine* (n. pl.: n. pr., 1672)
  Other writers: Richard Alleine, Theodosia Alleine, Richard Fairclough, George Newton
Bedsfield, E., in K. Frese, *The Womens Petition* (1652)
Bunyan, John, *A Vindication of the Book Called Some Gospel Truths* (Newport: Matthias Cowley, 1657)
  Other writers: John Burton, John Child, Richard Spencly
Burton, John [sigy], in John Bunyan, *A Vindication of the Book Called Some Gospel Truths* (1657)
C., R., *A Godly Form of Householde Government* (London: Thomas Creede for Thomas Man, 1598)
Cann, William, in George Bishop (Quaker), *The Cry of Blood* (1656)
Canne, John, *An Indictment Against Tythes* (London: Livewel Chapman, 1659)
Cary, Joh [sic], in Robert Wastfield (Quaker), *A True Testimony of Faithful Witnesses* (1657)
Ceely, Peter, in Edward Pyot (Quaker), *The West Answering to the North* (1657)
Child, John, in John Bunyan, *A Vindication of the Book Called Some Gospel Truths* (1657)
Cole, E., in K. Frese, *The Womens Petition* (1652)
Cole, Thomas, in Ralph Farmer, *Sathan [sic] Inthron'd* (1657)
Cole, Will., in Thomas Weld, *The Perfect Pharise [sic]* (1654)
Collier, Thomas, *A Looking Glasse for the Quakers* (London: Thomas Brewster, 1657)
——in Thomas Weld, *The Perfect Pharise [sic]* (1654)
Copplestone, John, in Edward Pyot (Quaker), *The West Answering to the North* (1657)
Cranfield, James, in Thomas Edwards, *Gangraena* (1646)
Durant, Will., in Thomas Weld, *The Perfect Pharise [sic]* (1654)
Edwards, Thomas, *Gangraena* (London: Ralph Smith, 1646)
  Other writer James Cranfield plus other unnamed contributors
Fairclough, Richard, in Richard Baxter, *The Life and Death [. . .] Joseph Alleine* (1672)
Farmer, Ralph, *Sathan [sic] Inthron'd* (London: Edward Thomas, 1657)
  Other Quaker writers: John Audland, Richard Fairman, George Fox, Ruth Hill, Martha Simmonds, Thomas Simmonds, Hannah Stranger, John Stranger, Jane Woodcock
  Other non-Quakers: Thomas Cole, Thomas Perkins, Thomas Prince
Fitz-William, Henry, in Edward Pyot (Quaker), *The West Answering to the North* (1657)
Frese, K., *The Womens Petition* (n. pl.: n. pr., 1652)
  Other writers: E. Bassfield, E. Cole, D. Trinhale
  Leveller women
  Thomason: 669.f.16 (26)

Gael, John, in Henry Glisson, *A True and Lamentable Relation of the Most Desperate Death of James Parnell* (1656)

Gardner, John, in Jane Turner, *Choice Experiences* (1653)

Gibbs, Henry, in George Bishop (Quaker), *The Cry of Blood* (1656)

Gilpin, John, *The Quakers Shaken* (London: Simon Waterson, 1653)

Glisson, Henry, *A True and Lamentable Relation of the Most Desperate Death of James Parnell* (London: T. C. for William Gilbertson, 1656)

    Quaker writers: James Parnell

    Non-Quakers: John Gael, Joseph Smith, Jude Taylor

Gunning, John, in George Bishop, *The Cry of Blood* (1656)

Hall, Ralph, *Quakers Principles Quaking* (London: R. I., 1656)

Hammond, Sam., in Thomas Weld, *The Perfect Pharise [sic]* (1654)

Hellier, George, in George Bishop, *The Cry of Blood* (1656)

Higginson, Francis, *A Brief Relation of the Irreligion of the Northern Quakers* (London: T. R. and H. R., [1653])

Howet, Henoch, *Quaking Principles Dashed in Pieces* (London: Henry Hills, 1655)

Humphrey, Nathaniel [sig], *The Husbandmans Plea Against Tithes* (London: n. pr., 1647) Thomason E 389 (2)

    Other signatories: Henry Adeane, Samuel Aston, William Babble, Henry Ball, William Beale, John Beech, John Belfield, Thomas Berchmore, Robert Blackwett, Joseph Bovenden, John Browne, Edward Chandler, Giles Child, Richard Child, Thomas Clarke, Thomas Dover, Thomas Downes, Robert Edlin, John Foster, John Garret, Thomas Gate, John Gibson, Thomas Goodson, Thomas Gould, William Gr[os]ingham, James Grover, Edward Halsey, John Halsey, John Halsey, John Halsey [there are three], Joseph Halsey, Joshua Halsey, Thomas Halsey, Thomas Halsey [sen], William Halsey, William Hammond, James Harding, John Harding, Matthew Harding, John Hawse, Thomas Heyward, Jeremie Hill, John Hill, John Hill [there are two], William Hill, Francis How, John How, John Humphrey, Nathaniel Humphrey, Uhomas [Thomas ?] Ivor, Faustene Knight, Francis Knight, John Knight, William Knight, William Lasley, John Leaper, Thomu [sic] Leaperd, Peter Medwes [jun], John Monk, Robert Nash, Thomas Nash, Richard Norwood, Edward Nowell, John Paice, Richard Parrat, Thomas Peppitt, Henry Perger, Nathaniel Picket, Robert Pitkin, Peter Redowes [sen.], Thomas Robins, James Rolfe, Edward Rose, George Rose, George Rose [sen], John Rose, John Rutland, Jos[ias] Rutland, William Sanders, Hugh Smith, Robert Smith [jun.], Robert Smith [sen], William Soule, Anthony Story, Thomas Suell, Edmund Sybley, Ralph Trumper, Foster Wallis, Walter Warris, Timothy Weeden, William Wells, Jerom Weston, John Wheeler, Thomas Wight, Richard Young

Hunt, Rob., in Robert Wastfield (Quaker), *A True Testimony of Faithful Witnesses* (1657)

Jackson, Joseph, in George Bishop (Quaker), *The Cry of Blood* (1656)

Lock, John, in George Bishop (Quaker), *The Cry of Blood* (1656)

Miller, Joshua, *Anti Christ in Man the Quakers Idol* (London: J Macock for L. Lloyd, 1655)

N., M., in Nat. Bacon, *A Relation of the Fearful Estate of Francis Spira* (1548)

Newton, George, in Richard Baxter, *The Life and Death [. . .] Joseph Alleine* (1672)

Norton, John, *The Heart of New England Rent* (London: J. H. for John Allen, 1660)

Ockanickon, in John Cripps (Quaker), *A True Account of the Dying Words of Ockanickon, an Indian King* (1682)

Page, John, in Edward Pyot (Quaker), *The West Answering to the North* (1657)

Pagit, Ephriam, *Herisiography*, 6th edn (London: W. L., 1661)

Perkins, Thomas, in Ralph Farmer, *Sathan [sic] Inthron'd* (1657)

Pickering, Will., in Richard Hubberthorne (Quaker), *The Immediate Call to the Ministry* (1654)

Prideaux, Rich., in Thomas Weld, *The Perfect Pharise [sic]* (1654)
Prince, Thomas, in Ralph Farmer, *Sathan [sic] Inthron'd* (1657)
Prynne, William, *A True and Perfect Narrative of what was done* (n. pl.: n. pr., 1659)
——*Ten Considerable Quaeries* (London: Edward Thomas, 1659)
——*The Quakers Unmasked*, 2nd edn (London: Edward Thomas, 1655)
Rawson, Edward, in Humphrey Norton (Quaker), *New Englands Ensigne* (1659)
Selden, John, *The History of Tythes* (n. pl.: n. pr., 1618)
Sherman, Gabriel, in George Bishop (Quaker), *The Cry of Blood* (1656)
Smith, Joseph, in Henry Glisson, *A True and Lamentable Relation of the Most Desperate Death of James Parnell* (1656)
Spencly, Richard, in John Bunyan, *A Vindication of the Book Called Some Gospel Truths* (1657)
Spilsbery, John, in Jane Turner, *Choice Experiences* (1653)
Spurwell, Richard, in Edward Pyot (Quaker), *The West Answering to the North* (1657)
Taylor, Jeremy, *The Rule and Exercises of Holy Dying*, 9th edn (London: Roger Norton for Richard Royston, 1670)
——*The Rule and Exercises of Holy Living* (London: R. Royston, 1650)
Taylor, Jude, in Henry Glisson, *A True and Lamentable Relation of the Most Desperate Death of James Parnell* (1656)
Toldervy, John, *The Snare Broken* (London: N. Brooks, 1656)
Trinhale, D., in K. Frese, *The Womens Petition* (1652)
Turner, Jane, *Choice Experiences* (London: H. Hils [sic], 1653)
    Other writers: John Gardner, John Spilsbery, John Turner
Turner, John, in Jane Turner, *Choice Experiences* (1653)
Underhill, Thomas, *Hell Broke Loose* (London: Simon Miller, 1660)
Vickris, Richard, in George Bishop (Quaker), *The Cry of Blood* (1656)
Weld, Thomas, *The Perfect Pharise [sic]* (London: Richard Tomlins, 1654)
    Other writers: Will. Cole, Thomas Collier, Will. Durant, Sam. Hammond, Rich. Prideaux

B. Modern Editions of Seventeenth Century Texts

Aughterson, Kate, *Renaissance Women: A Sourcebook: Constructions of Femininity in England* (London and New York: Routledge, 1995)
Barbour, Hugh, and Arthur O. Roberts (eds), *Early Quaker Writing 1650-1700* (Grand Rapids, Michigan: William B. Eerdmans, 1973)
Bacon, Francis, *The Essays 1625* (Yorkshire: Scolar Press, 1971)
Beaumont, Agnes, *The Narrative of the Persecution of Agnes Beaumont in 1674*, ed. by G. B. Harrison (Glasgow: The University Press, n. d.)
Brown, Sylvia (ed.), *Women's Writing in Stuart England: The Mothers' Legacies of Dorothy Leigh, Elizabeth Joscelin and Elizabeth Richardson* (Stroud, Gloucestershire: Sutton Publishing, 1999)
Bunyan, John, *Grace Abounding to the Chief of Sinners and The Pilgrims Progress from this World to that which is to Come*, ed. by Roger Sharrock (London: OUP, 1966)
Donne, John, *The Oxford Authors*, ed. by John Carey (Oxford and New York: OUP, 1990)
Erskine-Hill, Howard, and Graham Story, *Revolutionary Prose of the English Civil War* (Cambridge: CUP, 1983)
Extracts from the Minutes and Proceedings of the Yearly Meeting of Friends (London: Office of the Society of Friends), vol. 1857, vol. 1897-1901, vol. 1902

Fell, Margaret, *A Sincere and Constant Love: An Introduction to the Work of Margaret Fell*, ed. by Terry S. Wallace (Richmond, Indiana: Friends United Press, 1992)

———*Women's Speaking Justified, Proved and Allowed by the Scriptures*, ed. by Christine Trevett (London: Quaker Home Service, 1985)

Fox, George, *The Journal*, ed. by Nigel Smith (London and New York: Penguin, 1998)

Foxe, John, *Foxe's Book of Martyrs*, ed. and abridged by G. A. Williamson (London: Secker and Warburg, 1965)

Garman, Margery, and others, (eds), *Hidden in Plain Sight: Quaker Women's Writings 1650-1700* (Wallingford, Pennsylvania: Pendle Hill Publications, 1996)

Graham, Elspeth, and others (eds), *Her Own Life: Autobiographical Writings by Seventeenth-Century Englishwomen* (London and New York: Routledge, 1989)

Greer, Germaine, and others (eds), *Kissing the Rod: An Anthology of 17th Century Women's Verse* (London: Virago, 1988)

Haller, William, Godfrey Davies (eds), *The Leveller Tracts 1647-1653* (repr. New York: Columbia University Press, 1964)

Haller, William (ed.), *Tracts on Liberty in the Puritan Revolution 1638-47*, 3 vols (New York: Octagon Books, 1979)

Higginson, Frances, *Extracts from A Brief Relation of the Northern Quakers*, ed. by Emlyn Warren (Willow Close, Garsington, Oxford, 1999); available from Friends' Book Centre, Euston Road, London

Hobbes, Thomas, *Leviathan*, introduced by K. R. Minogue (repr. London and New York: Everyman, 1973)

Howgill, Francis, and others, *Caine's Bloudy Race*, ed. by F. Sanders, in 'The Quakers in Chester Under the Protectorate', *Journal of the Chester and North Wales Archaeological Society*, 4 (1908), 29-84

Hutchinson, Lucy, *Memoirs of the Life of Colonel Hutchinson*, ed. by N. H. Keeble (London and Rutland, Vermont: Everyman, 1995)

Milton, John, *The Complete Poems*, ed. by John Leonard (London and New York: Penguin, 1998)

Milton, John, *Complete Prose Works of John Milton*, ed. by Robert Ayers (New Haven and London: York University Press, 1980), VII

Morril, John (ed.), *The Revolt of the Provinces: Conservatives and Radicals in the English Civil War 1630-1650* (London: George Allen and Unwin, 1976)

Pepys, Samuel, *The Diary of Samuel Pepys*, ed. by Robert Latham and William Matthews (London: George Bell, 1971), V

Raymond, Joad (ed.), *Making the News: An Anthology of the Newsbooks of Revolutionary England 1641-1660* (Moreton-in-Marsh: The Windrush Press, 1993)

Shakespeare, William, *The Merchant of Venice*, ed. and introduced by Jay L. Halio (Oxford: Clarendon Press, 1993)

Smith, Nigel (ed.), *A Collection of Ranter Writings from the Seventeenth Century* (London: Junction Books, 1983)

Smith, Sir Thomas, *De Republica Anglorum* (York: Scolar Press, 1970)

Winstanley, Gerrard, *The Law of Freedom and other Writings*, ed. by Christopher Hill (Harmondsworth, Middlesex: Penguin, 1973)

Woodhouse, A. P. (ed.), *Puritanism and Liberty: Being the Army Debates 1647-9 from the Clarke Manuscripts with Supplementary Documents*, 2nd edn (repr. London: J. M. Dent and Sons, 1974)

Woods, T. P. S. (ed.), *Prelude to Civil War 1642* (Great Britain: Michael Russell, 1980)

C. Secondary Sources

Achinstein, Sharon, 'Texts in Conflict: The Press and the Civil War', in *The Cambridge Companion to Writing of the English Revolution*, ed. by Neil Keeble (Cambridge: CUP, 2001), pp. 50-68
——'The Politics of Babel in the English Revolution', in *Pamphlet Wars: Prose in the English Revolution*, ed. by James Holstun (London: Frank Cass, 1992), pp. 14-44
Allen, Richard, C., 'The Society of Friends in Wales: The Case of Monmouthshire c. 1654-1836' (Unpublished doctoral thesis, University of Wales, Aberystwyth, 1999)
Amussen, Susan Dwyer, *An Ordered Society: Gender and Class in Early Modern England* (New York and Oxford: Basil Blackwell, 1988)
Anderson, Bonnie S., and Judith P. Zinsser, *A History of their Own*, 2 vols (London and New York: Penguin, 1988)
Anselment, Raymond A., '"The Tears of Nature": Seventeenth-Century Parental Bereavement', *Modern Philology*, 91 (1993-1994), 26-53
Ariès, Phillippe, *Western Attitudes Toward Death from the Middle Ages to the Present* (Baltimore and London: The Johns Hopkins University Press, 1974)
Aylmer, G. E., 'Did the Ranters Exist?', *Past and Present*, 117 (1987), 208-219
Bailey, Richard, *New Light on George Fox and Early Quakerism: The Making and Unmaking of God* (San Francisco: Mellen Research University Press, 1992)
Bakhtin, *The Bakhtin Reader: Selected Writings of Bakhtin, Medvedev, Voloshinov*, ed. by Pam Morris (London and New York: Edward Arnold, 1994)
Barbour, Hugh and J. William Frost, *The Quakers* (Richmond Indiana: Friends United Press, 1988)
Barbour, Hugh, 'Quaker Prophetesses and Mothers in Israel', in *Seeking the Light: Essays in Quaker History in Honour of Edwin B. Bronner*, ed. by J. William Frost and John M. Moore (Wallingford and Haverford: Pendle Hill and Friends' Historical Association, 1986), pp. 41-60
——*The Quakers in Puritan England* (New Haven and London: Yale University Press, 1964)
Bauman, Richard, *Let Your Words be Few: Symbolism of Speaking and Silence among Seventeenth-Century Quakers*, 2nd edn (London: Quaker Home Service, 1998)
Beaty, Nancy Lee, *The Craft of Dying: A Study in the Literary Tradition of the Ars Moriendi in England* (New Haven and London: Yale University Press, 1970)
Beckett, 'Land Tax or Excise: The Levying of Taxation in Seventeenth and Eighteenth-Century England', *English Historical Review*, 395 (1985), 285-308
Bell, Maureen, and others, *A Biographical Dictionary of English Women Writers 1580-1720* (New York: Harvester Wheatsheaf, 1990)
Bell, Maureen, 'Elizabeth Calvert and the "Confederates"', *Publishing History*, 32 (1992), 5-50
——'"Her Usual Practices": The Later Career of Elizabeth Calvert, 1664-75', *Publishing History*, 35 (1994), 5-64
——'Mary Westwood – Quaker Publisher', *Publishing History*, 23 (1988), 5-66
——'Women Publishers of Puritan Literature in The Mid Seventeenth-Century: Three Case Studies' (unpublished doctoral thesis, Loughborough University of Technology, 1987)
Belsey, Catherine, *Shakespeare and the Loss of Eden: The Construction of Family Values in Early Modern Culture* (Basingstoke: Macmillan, 1999)
——*The Subject of Tragedy: Identity and Difference in Renaissance Drama* (London: Routledge, 1985)

Bennett, H. S., *English Books and Readers 1603 to 1640: Being a Study of the History of the Book Trade in the Reigns of James I and Charles I* (Cambridge: CUP, 1970)

Bennett, Martyn, *The Civil Wars in Britain and Ireland: 1638-1651* (Oxford and Cambridge, Massachusetts: Blackwell, 1997)

Berry, Philippa, and Berg, Christine, 'Spiritual Whoredom: An Essay on Female Prophets in the Seventeenth Century', in *Literature and Power in the Seventeenth Century: Proceedings of the Essex Conference on the Sociology of Literature*, ed. by Frances Barker, and others (Colechester, University of Essex, 1991), pp. 37-54

Besse, Joseph, *A Collection of the Sufferings of the People Called Quakers*, 2 vols (London: Luke Hinde, 1753)

Boose, Linda, E., 'Scolding Brides and Bridling Scolds: Taming the Woman's Unruly Member', *Shakespeare Quarterly*, 42:2 (1991), 179-213

Brace, Laura, *The Idea of Property in Seventeenth-Century England: Tithes and the Individual* (Manchester and New York: Manchester University Press, 1998)

Brailsford, H. N., *The Levellers and the English Revolution*, 2nd edn (Nottingham: Spokesman, 1983)

Brailsford, Mabel Richmond, *Quaker Women 1650-1690* (London: Duckworth, 1915)

Braithwaite, William C., *The Beginnings of Quakerism*, 2nd edn (York: William Sessions, 1981)

——*The Second Period of Quakerism*, 2nd edn (York: William Sessions, 1979)

Breay, John, *Light in the Dales: Volumes II and III: The Agrarian Background to the Rise of Political and Religious Dissent in the Northern Dales in the Sixteenth and Seventeenth Centuries* (Norwich: The Canterbury Press, 1996) [vols II and III are combined]

Brigden, Susan, 'Tithe Controversy in Reformation London', *Journal of Ecclesiastical History*, 32: 3 (1981), 285-301

Burt, Richard, and John Michael Archer, eds, *Enclosure Acts: Sexuality, Property, and Culture in Early Modern England* (Ithaca and London: Cornell University Press, 1994)

Butler, David M., 'Friends' Sufferings 1650-1688: A Comparative Study', *JFHS*, 55: 6 (1988), 180-184

Cadbury, Henry J., 'Friends at the Inquisition at Malta', *JFHS*, 53 (1974), 219-225

Cameron, Deborah, *Feminism and Linguistic Theory*, 2nd edn (Basingstoke: The Macmillan Press, 1992)

Capp, Bernard, *The Fifth Monarchy Men: A Study in Seventeenth-Century English Millenarianism* (London: Faber, 1972)

Carroll, Kenneth L., 'American Quakers and their London Lobby', *Quaker History*, 70:1 (1981), 22-39

——'Early Quakers and Going Naked as a Sign', *Quaker History*, 67: 2 (1978), 69-87

——'Martha Simmonds, a Quaker Enigma', *JFHS*, 53:1 (1972), 31-52

——'Quaker Attitudes towards Signs and Wonders', *JFHS*, 54:2 (1977), 70-84

Clair, Colin, *A History of Printing in Britain* (London: Cassell, 1965)

Clark, Alice, *Working Life of Women in the Seventeenth Century* (London and Boston: Routledge and Kegan Paul, 1982)

——*Working Life of Women in the Seventeenth Century*, 3rd edn (London and New York: Routledge, 1992)

Clarke, Danielle and Elizabeth Clarke (eds), *'This Double Voice': Gendered Writing in Early Modern England* (Basingstoke: Macmillan, 2000)

Cohn, Norman, *The Pursuit of the Millenium* (London: Secker and Warburg, 1957)

Cole, Alan, 'The Quakers and the English Revolution', in *Crisis in Europe 1560-1660: Essays from Past and Present*, ed. by Trevor Aston (London: Routledge and Kegan Paul, 1969), pp. 341-358

——'The Social Origins of the Early Friends', *JFHS*, 48:3 (1957), 97-118

Coleman, Linda, S. (ed.), *Women's Life Writing: Finding a Voice/Building Community* (Ohio: Bowling Green State University Popular Press, 1997)

Collinson, Patrick, *The Religion of the Protestants: The Church in English Society 1559-1629* (Oxford: Clarendon Press, 1982)

Cope, Jackson I, 'Seventeenth-Century Quaker Style', *PMLA*, 76 (1956), 725-754

Corns, Thomas N., '"No Man's Copy": The Critical Problems of Fox's *Journal*', *Prose Studies*, 17:3 (1994), 99-111

——'The Freedom of Reader Response: Milton's *Of Reformation* and Lilburne's *The Christian Mans Triall*', in *Freedom and the English Revolution: Essays in History and Literature*, ed. by R. C. Richardson and G. M. Ridden (Manchester: MUP, 1986), pp. 93-110

——*Uncloistered Virtue: English Political Literature, 1640-1660* (Oxford: Clarendon Press, 1992)

Coward, Barry, *The Stuart Age: A History of England 1603-1714* (London and New York: Longman, 1992)

Cranfield, G. A., *The Press and Society From Caxton to Northcliffe* (London and New York: Longman, 1978)

Crawford, Patricia, 'Women's Published Writings 1600-1700', in *Women in English Society 1500-1800*, ed. by Mary Prior (London: Methuen, 1985), pp. 211-232

——*Women and Religion in England 1500-1720* (London and New York: Routledge, 1996)

Creasey, Maurice A., '"Inward" and "Outward": A Study in Early Quaker Language', *JFHS*, supplement 30 (1962), 3-24

Cressy, David, *Birth, Marriage, and Death: Ritual, Religion, and the Life-Cycle in Tudor and Stuart England* (Oxford and New York: OUP, 1997)

——*Literacy and the Social Order: Reading and Writing in Tudor and Stuart England* (Cambridge: CUP, 1980)

Cross, Clare, '"He-goats before the Flocks": A Note on the Part Played by Women in the Founding of Some Civil War Churches', *Studies in Church History*, 8 (1972), 195-202

Cust, Richard, 'News and Politics in Early Seventeenth-Century England', *Past and Present*, 112 (1986), 60-69

Damrosch, Leo, *The Sorrows of the Quaker Jesus: James Nayler and the Puritan Crackdown on the Free Spirit* (Cambridge, Massachusetts and London: Harvard University Press, 1996)

Davies, Adrian, *The Quakers in English Society 1655-1725* (Oxford: Clarendon Press, 2000)

Davies, K. M., '"The Sacred Condition of Equality": How original were Puritan Doctrines of Marriage?', *Social History*, 5 (1977), 563-580

Davies, Stevie, *Unbridled Spirits: Women and the English Revolution 1640-1660* (London: The Women's Press, 1998)

Davies, Tony, *Humanism* (London and New York: Routledge, 1997)

Davis, J. C., *Fear Myth and History: The Ranters and the Historians* (Cambridge, London and New York: Cambridge University Press, 1986)

Davis, Natalie Zemon, 'Boundaries and the Sense of Self in Sixteenth-Century France', in *Reconstructing Individualism: Autonomy, Individuality, and the Self in Western Thought*, ed. by Thomas C. Heller, and others, (Stanford, California: Stanford University Press, 1986), pp. 53-63

——*Society and Culture in Early Modern France* (London: Duckworth, 1975)

Delaney, Paul, *British Autobiography in the Seventeenth Century* (London: Routledge and Kegan Paul, 1969)

Dolan, Frances E. '"Gentlemen, I have one thing more to say": Women on Scaffolds in England, 1563-1680', *Modern Philology*, 92 (1994-1995), 157-178

Durston, Christopher, 'Puritan Rule and the Failure of Cultural Revolution 1645-1660', in *The Culture of English Protestantism, 1560-1700*, ed. by Christopher Durston and Jackqueline Eales (Basingstoke: Macmillan, 1996), pp. 210-233

——*The Family in the English Revolution* (Oxford and New York: Basil Blackwell, 1989)

Durston, Christopher, and Jacqueline Eales (eds), *The Culture of English Puritanism 1560-1700* (Basingstoke: Macmillan, 1996)

Earle, Peter, 'The Female Labour Market in London in the Late Seventeenth and Early Eighteenth Centuries', *Economic History Review*, 42:3 (1989), 328-353

Edwards, George W., 'The London Six Weeks Meeting: Some of its Work and Records over 200 Years', *JFHS*, 50:4 (1964), 228-245

Edwards, Irene L., 'The Women Friends of London: The Two-Weeks and Box Meetings', *JFHS*, 47:1 (1955), 3-21

Edwards, Karen L., 'Susannas Apologie and the Politics of Privity', *Literature and History*, 6:1 (1997), 1-16

Erickson, Amy Louise, *Women and Property in Early Modern England* (London and New York: Routledge, 1993)

Ezell, Margaret, J. M., *The Patriarch's Wife: Literary Evidence and the History of the Family* (Chapel Hill and London: The University of North Carolina Press, 1987)

——'The Posthumous Publication of Women's Manuscripts and the History of Authorship', in *Women's Writing and the Circulation of Ideas: Manuscript Publication in England, 1500-1800*, ed. by George L. Justice and Nathan Tinker (Cambridge: CUP, 2002), 121-136

——*Writing Women's Literary History* (Baltimore and London: The Johns Hopkins University Press, 1993)

Fergusson, Moira, 'Seventeenth-Century Quaker Women: Displacement, Colonialism, and Anti-Slavery Discourse', in *Culture and Society in the Stuart Restoration*, ed. by Gerald Maclean (Cambridge: CUP, 1995), 221-240

Fletcher, Anthony, *The Outbreak of the English Civil War* (London: Edward Arnold, 1981)

Foxton, Rosemary, *'Hear the Word of the Lord': A Critical and Bibliographical Study of Quaker Women's Writing 1650-1700* (Melbourne: The Bibliographical Society of Australia and New Zealand, 1994)

Fraser, Antonia, *The Weaker Vessel* (London: Weidenfeld and Nicholson, 1984)

Friedman, Jerome, *Miracles and the Pulp Press during the English Revolution: The Battle of Frogs and Fairford's Flies* (London: UCL, 1993)

Friest, Dagmar, 'The King's Crown is the Whore of Babylon: Politics, Gender and Communication in Mid-Seventeenth Century England', *Gender and History*, 7:3 (1995), 457-481

Frost, William, 'The Dry Bones of Quaker Theology', *Church History*, 39 (1970), 503-523

Galt-Harpham, Geoffrey, 'Conversion and the Language of Autobiography', in *Studies in Autobiography*, ed. by James Olney (New York and Oxford: OUP, 1988), pp. 42-50

Gardiner, Judith Kegan, 'Margaret Fell Fox and Feminist Literary History: A "Mother in Israel" Calls to the Jews', *Prose Studies*, 17:3 (1994), 42-56

Gowing, Laura, 'Gender and the Language of Insult in Early Modern London', *History Workshop*, 35 (1993), 1-21

Graham, Elspeth, '"Lewed, Profane Swaggerers" and Charismatic Preachers: John Bunyan and George Fox', in *Sacred and Profane: Secular and Devotional Interplay in Early Modern British Literature*, ed. by Helen Wilcox, Richard Todd and Alasdair MacDonald (Amsterdam: V. U. University Press, 1996), pp. 307-318

——'"Oppression Makes a Wise Man Mad": The Suffering of the Self in Autobiographical Tradition', in *All By Myself: Literary Representations of the Self in Early-Modern*

Autobiography, ed. by Henk Dragsta, Sheila Otway and Helen Wilcox (Macmillan, 1998)

——'Women's Writing and the Self', in *Women and Literature in Britain 1500-1700*, ed. by Helen Wilcox (Cambridge: CUP, 1996), pp. 209-233

Greaves, Richard L., *Deliver us from Evil: The Radical Underground in Britain 1660-1663* (New York and Oxford: OUP, 1986)

Greaves, Richard L., and Robert Zaller (eds), *Biographical Dictionary of British Radicals in the Seventeenth Century*, 3 vols (Sussex: The Harvester Press, 1983)

Greenblatt, Stephen, *Renaissance Self-Fashioning from More to Shakespeare* (Chicago and London: The University of Chicago Press, 1980)

Gregory, Anne, 'Witchcraft, Politics and Good Neighbourliness', *Past and Present*, 133 (1991), 31-66

Grubb, Isabel, *Quakerism and Industry before 1800* (London: Williams and Northgate, 1930)

Guibbory, Achsah, 'Conversation, Conversion, Messianic Redemption: Margaret Fell, Menasseh ben Israel, and the Jews', in *Literary Circles and Cultural Communities in Renaissance England*, ed. by Claude J. Summers and Ted-Larry Pebworth (Columbia and London: University of Missouri Press, 2000), pp. 210-234

Hall, D. J., '"The Fiery Tryal of their Infallible Examination": Self-Control and the Regulation of Quaker Publishing in England from the 1670s to the mid Nineteenth Century', in *Censorship and the Control of Print in England and France 1600-1910*, ed. by Michael Harris and Robin Myers (Winchester: St. Paul's Bibliographies, 1992), pp. 59-86

Haller, William, 'Hail Wedded Love', *Journal of English Literary History*, 13:2 (1946), 79-97

Haller, William, and Malleville Haller, 'The Puritan Art of Love', *Huntington Library Quarterly*, 5:2 (1941-1942), 235-272

Hamm, Thomas D., 'George Fox and the Politics of Late Nineteenth-Century Quaker Historiography', in *New Light on George Fox*, ed. by Michael Mullett (York: William Sessions and Ebor Press, 1991)

Hazelton, Meiling, '"Mony Choaks": The Quaker Critique of the Seventeenth-Century Public Sphere', *Modern Philology*, 98:2 (2000), 251-270

Hess, Ann Giardina, 'Midwifery Practice among the Quakers in Southern Rural England in the late Seventeenth Century', in *The Art of Midwifery: Early Modern Midwives in Europe*, ed. by Hilary Marland (London and New York: Methuen, 1993), pp. 49-76

Higgins, Patricia, 'The Reactions of Women, with Special Reference to Women Petitioners', in *Politics, Religion and the English Civil War*, ed. by Brian Manning (London: Edward Arnold, 1973), pp. 179-222

Hill, Christopher, *Change and Continuity in Seventeenth-Century England* (London: Weidenfield and Nicholson, 1974)

——*Economic Problems of the Church, from Archbishop Whitgift to the Long Parliament* (Oxford: Clarendon Press, 1968)

——'God and the English Revolution', *History Workshop*, 17 (1984), 19-32

——*Milton and the English Revolution* (London: Faber and Faber, 1977)

——*A Nation of Change and Novelty: Radical Politics, Religion and Literature in Seventeenth-Century England* (London and New York: Routledge, 1990)

——*Puritanism and Revolution* (London: Secker and Warburg, 1958)

——*Society and Puritanism in Pre-Revolutionary England* (London: Panther; Manchester: The Philips Press, 1969)

——*The English Bible and the Seventeenth Century Revolution* (London and New York: Penguin, 1994)

——*The Experience of Defeat: Milton and Some Contemporaries* (London: Faber and Faber, 1984)

——'The Lost Ranters? A critique of J. C. Davis', *History Workshop Journal*, 24 (1987), 134-140

——*The World Turned Upside Down* (Harmondsworth, Middlesex: Penguin, 1975)

——'Till the Converstion of the Jews', in *Millenarianism and Messianism in English Literature and Thought 1650-1800: Clark Library Lectures 1981-1982*, ed. by Richard H. Popkin (London and New York: E. J. Brill, 1988), pp. 12-36

——*A Tinker and a Poor Man: John Bunyan and his Church 1628-1688* (New York: Alfred A. Knopf, 1988)

Hinds, Hilary, *God's Englishwomen: Seventeenth-Century Radical Sectarian Writing and Feminist Criticism* (Manchester: Manchester University Press, 1996)

Hirst, Derek, *Authority and Conflict: England 1603-1658* (London: Edward Arnold, 1986)

——'Concord and Discord in Richard Cromwell's House of Commons', *English Historical Review*, 103 (1988), 339-359

——*England in Conflict 1603-1660: Kingdom, Community, Commonwealth* (London and Sidney: Arnold; New York: OUP, 1999)

——'The Failure of Godly Rule in the English Republic', *Past and Present*, 131 (1991), 33-67

Hobby, Elaine, '"Come to Live a Preaching Life": Female Community in Seventeenth-Century Radical Sects', in *Female Communities 1600-1800: Literary Visions and Cultural Realities*, ed. by Rebecca D'Monté and Nichole Pohl (London: Macmillan Press, 2000), pp. 76-92

——'"Discourse so Unsavoury": Women's Published Writings of the 1650s', in *Women, Writing, History*, ed. by Isobel Grundy and Susan Wiseman (London: B. T. Batsford, 1992), pp. 16-32

——'Handmaids of the Lord and Mothers in Israel: Early Vindications of Quaker Women's Prophecy', *Prose Studies*, 17:3 (1994), 88-98

——'"O Oxford thou art full of Filth": The Prophetical Writings of Hester Biddle', in *Feminist Criticism: Theory and Practice*, ed. by Susan Sellers (Hemel Hempsted: Harvester Wheatsheaf, 1991), pp. 157-169

——'The Politics of Gender', in *The Cambridge Companion to English Poetry: Donne to Marvell*, ed. by T. N. Corns (Cambridge, New York, Melbourne: CUP, 1993), pp. 31-52

——'The Politics of Women's Prophecy in the English Revolution', in *Sacred and Profane: Secular and Devotional Interplay in Early Modern British Literature*, ed. by Helen Wilcox, Richard Todd, Alasdair MacDonald (Amsterdam: V. U. University Press, 1996), pp. 295-306

——*Virtue of Necessity: English Women's Writing 1649-88* (London: Virago, 1988)

Hodgkin, L. V., *A Quaker Saint of Cornwall: Loveday Hambly and her Guests* (London: Longmans, 1927)

Holstun, James (ed.), *Pamphlet Wars: Prose in the English Revolution* (London: Frank Cass, 1992)

Horle, Craig, *Quakers and the English Legal System 1660-1688* (Philadelphia: University of Pennsylvania Press, 1988)

Houlbrooke, Ralph, 'The Puritan Death-bed, c. 1560-1700', in *The Culture of English Puritanism 1560-1700*, ed. by Christopher Durston and Jacqueline Eales (Basingstoke: McMillan, 1996), pp. 122-144

——ed., *Death, Ritual, and Bereavement* (London and New York: Routledge, 1989)

——*The English Family* (London: Longman, 1984)

Hughes, Ann, 'Gender and Politics in Leveller Literature', in *Political Culture and Cultural Poetics in Early Modern England: Essays Presented to David Underdown*, ed. by Susan D. Amussen and Mark A. Kishlansky (Manchester: Manchester University Press, 1995), pp. 162-188
——'Public Disputations, Pamphlets and Polemic', *History Today*, 41 (1991), 27-33
——*The Causes of the English Civil War* (London: Macmillan Education, 1991)
Hull, Susanne, *Chaste, Silent and Obedient: English Books for Women 1475-1640* (repr. San Marino, California: The Huntington Library, 1988)
Hutton, Ronald, *The Restoration: The Political and Religious History of England and Wales 1658-1667* (Oxford: Clarendon Press, 1985)
Ingham, Martyn, '"Scolding Women Cucked or Washed": A Crisis of Gender Relations in Early Modern England', in *Women, Crime and the Courts in Early Modern England*, ed. by Jennifer Fermode and Garthine Walker (Chapel Hill and London: The University of North Carolina Press, 1994), 44-80
——'Ridings, Rough Music and Popular Culture in Early Modern Europe', *Past and Present*, 105 (1984), 79-113
Ingle, H. Larry, *First Among Friends: George Fox and the Creation of Quakerism* (New York and Oxford: OUP, 1994)
——'Richard Hubberthorne and History: The Crisis of 1659', *JFHS*, 56: 3 (1992), 189-200
Jackson, Stevi, 'Towards a Historical Sociology of Housework: A Materialist Feminist Analysis', *Women's Studies International Forum*, 15:2 (1992), pp. 153-172
James, Margaret, 'The Political Importance of the Tithes Controversy in the English Revolution, 1640-60', *History*, 26 (1941), 1-18
Jenkins, Geraint H., *Protestant Dissenters in Wales, 1639-1689* (Cardiff: University of Wales Press, 1992)
Jones, R. Tudur, *Congregationalism in England 1662-1962* (London: Independent Press, 1962)
Keeble, Neil, '"The Colonel's Shadow": Lucy Hutchinson, Women's Writing and the Civil War', in *Literature in the English Civil War*, ed. by Thomas Healy and Jonathan Sawday (Cambridge and New York: CUP, 1990), pp. 227-247
——*The Literary Culture of Non-Conformity in Later Seventeenth-Century England* (Leicester: Leicester University Press, 1987)
——(ed.), *Writing of the English Revolution* (Cambridge: CUP, 2001)
Kelso, Ruth, *Doctrine for the Lady of the Renaissance* (Urbana: University of Illinois Press, 1956)
Kibbey, Ann, *The Interpretation of Material Shapes in Puritanism: A Study of Rhetoric, Prejudice and Violence* (Cambridge and elsewhere: CUP, 1986)
Knott, John R., *Discourses of Martyrdom in English Literature 1563-1694* (Cambridge: CUP, 1993)
——'Joseph Besse and the Quaker Culture of Suffering', *Prose Studies*, 17:3 (1994), 126-141
Kunze, Bonnelyn Young, *Margaret Fell and the Rise of Quakerism* (New York: Macmillan, 1994)
——'Religious Authority and Social Status in Seventeenth-Century England: The Friendship of Margaret Fell, George Fox, and William Penn', *Church History*, 57 (1988), 170-186
La Courege Blecki, Catherine, 'Alice Hayes and Mary Penington: Personal Identity within the Tradition of Quaker Spiritual Autobiography', *Quaker History*, 65 (1976), 19-31
Lambert, Sheila, 'State Control of the Press in Theory and Practice: The Role of the Stationer's Company before 1640', in *Censorship and the Control of Print in England*

and France 1600-1910, ed. by Michael Harris and Robin Myers (Winchester: St. Paul's Bibliographies, 1992), 1-23

Lamont, William, *Godly Rule: Politics and Religion 1603-60* (London: Macmillan, 1969)

Lang, Amy Schrager, *Prophetic Woman: Anne Hutchinson and the Problem of Dissent in the Literature of New England* (Berkeley, Los Angeles and London: University of California Press, 1987)

Larner, Christina, *Enemies of God: The Witchhunt in Scotland* (London: Chatto and Windus, 1981)

Laslett, Peter, *The World We Have Lost Further Explored*, 3rd edn (Cambridge: University Printing House, 1983)

Laurence, Anne, 'Godly Grief: Individual Responses to Death in Seventeenth-Century Britain', in *Death, Ritual and Bereavement*, ed. by Ralph Houlbrooke (London and New York: Routledge, 1989), pp. 62-76

Leachman, Caroline L., 'From an "Unruly Sect" to a Society of "Strict Unity": The Development of Quakerism in England c. 1650-1689' (unpublished doctoral thesis: University College London, 1997)

Leedham-Green, E. S. (ed.), *Religious Dissent in East Anglia* (Cambridge: Cambridge Antiquarian Society, 1991)

Lindley, Keith, 'London and Popular Freedom in the 1640s', in *Freedom and the English Revolution: Essays in History and Literature*, ed. by R. C. Richardson and G. M. Ridden (Manchester: Manchester University Press, 1986), pp. 111-150

Lovejoy, David S., *Religious Enthusiasm in the New World: Heresy to Revolution* (Cambridge, Massachusetts and London: Harvard University Press, 1985)

Lowenstein, David, *Representing Revolution in Milton and his Contemporaries: Religion, Politics, and Polemics in Radical Puritanism* (Cambridge: CUP, 2001)

——'The War of the Lamb: George Fox and the Apocalyptic Discourse of Revolutionary Quakerism', *Prose Studies*, 17:3 (1994), 25-41

Ludlow, Dorothy, 'Shaking Patriarchy's Foundations: Sectarian Women in England 1641-1700', in *Triumph Over Silence: Women in Protestant History*, ed. by Richard L. Greaves (Westport and London: Greenwood Press, 1985), pp. 93-123

Lunger-Knoppers, Laura, ' "This so Horrid Spectacle": *Samson Agonistes* and the Execution of the Regicides', *English Literary Renaissance*, 20: 3 (1990), 487-504

Macek, Ellen, 'The Emergence of a Feminine Spirituality in *The Book of Martyrs*', *Sixteenth Century Journal*, 19:1 (1988), 63-80

Mack, Phyllis, *Visionary Women: Ecstatic Prophecy in Seventeenth-Century England* (Berkeley, Los Angeles, London: University of California Press, 1994)

Maclean, Gerald (ed.), *Culture and Society in the Stuart Restoration* (Cambridge: CUP, 1995)

Malcolmson, Cristina and Mihoko Suzuki (eds), *Debating Gender in Early Modern England, 1500-1700* (New York and Basingstoke: Palgrave Macmillan, 2002)

Manning, Brian, *The English People and the English Revolution* (London: Heinemann, 1976)

Matar, Nabil I., 'George Herbert, Henry Vaughan, and the Conversion of the Jews', *SEL*, 30:1 (1990), 79-92

Matchinske, Megan, *Writing, Gender and State in Early Modern England: Identity Formation and the Female Subject* (Cambridge: CUP, 1998)

McArthur, Ellen A., 'Women Petitioners and the Long Parliament', *English Historical Review*, 24 (1909), 698-709

McCray-Beire, Lucinda, 'The Good Death in Seventeenth-Century England', in *Death, Ritual and Bereavement*, ed. by Ralph Houlbrooke (London and New York: Routledge, 1989), pp. 43-61

McDowell, Paula, *The Women of Grub Street: Press, Politics and Gender in the London Literary Marketplace 1678-1730* (Oxford: Clarendon Press, 1998)

McEntee, Ann Marie, '"The [Un]Civill-Sisterhood of Oranges and Lemons": Female Petitioners and Demonstrators, 1642-53', *Prose Studies*, 14.3 (1991), 92-111

McFarlane, Alan, *Witchcraft in Tudor and Stuart England* (London: Routledge and Kegan Paul, 1970)

McGregor, J. F., 'Seekers and Ranters', in *Radical Religion in the English Revolution*, ed. by Barry Reay and J. F. McGregor (repr. Oxford: OUP, 1986), pp. 121-139

McGregor, J. F, and Barry Reay (eds), *Radical Religion in the English Revolution*, (repr. Oxford: OUP, 1986)

McKeon, Michael, *The Origins of the English Novel 1600-1740* (Baltimore and London: The Johns Hopkins University Press, 1987)

McKerrow, Ronald B., *An Introduction to Bibliography for Literary Studies*, 2nd edn (Oxford: The Clarendon Press, 1928)

Moore, Rosemary Anne, 'The Faith of the First Quakers: The Development of their Beliefs and Practices up to the Restoration, (unpublished doctoral thesis, The University of Birmingham, 1993)

——*The Light in their Consciences: Early Quakers in Britain 1646-1666* (University Park, Pennsylvania: The Pennsylvania State University Press, 2000)

——'Reactions to Persecution in Primitive Quakerism', *JFHS*, 57:2 (1995), 123-131

Morgan, Nicholas, *Lancashire Quakers and the Establishment 1760-1830* (Halifax: Ryburn Publishing, 1993)

Morrill, J. S., *Cheshire 1630-1660: County Government and Society During the English Revolution* (London: OUP, 1974)

Mortimer, Russell S., 'The First Century of Quaker Printers', *JFHS*, 40 (1948) continued in *JFHS*, 41:2 (1949), 37-49

——'The First Century of Quaker Printers', *JFHS*, 41 (1949), 74-84

Mullett, Michael, 'George Fox and the origins of Quakerism', *History Today*, 41 (1991), 26-31

——(ed.), *New Light on George Fox 1624-1691* (York: William Sessions, The Ebor Press, 1991)

Nadel, Ira B., 'The Biographer's Secret', in *Studies in Autobiography*, ed. by James Olney (New York and Oxford: OUP, 1988)

Nevitt, Marcus, '"Blessed, Self-denying, Lambe-Like"? The Fifth Monarchist Women', *Critical Survey*, 11: 1 (1999), 83-97

Norbrook, David, *Poetry and Politics in the English Renaissance* (London: Routledge, 1984)

Nuttall, Geoffrey, *The Holy Spirit in Puritan Faith and Experience*, 2nd edn (Chicago and London: University of Chicago Press, 1992)

O'Faolin, Julia, and Laura Martines (eds), *Not in God's Image* (London: Temple Smith, 1973)

O'Malley, Thomas, '"Defying the Powers and Tempering the Spirit" A Review of Quaker control over their Publications 1672-1689', *Journal of Ecclesiastical History*, 33:1 (1982), 72-82

——'The Press and Quakerism 1653-1659', *JFHS*, 54:4 (1979), 169-184

Olney, James (ed.), *Studies in Autobiography* (New York and Oxford: OUP, 1988)

Pacheco, Anita (ed.), *A Companion to Early Modern Women's Writing* (Oxford: Blackwell, 2002)

Parish, Debra L., 'The Power of Female Pietism: Women as Spiritual Authorities and Religious Role Models in Seventeenth-Century England', *The Journal of Religious History*, 17:1 (1992), 33-46

Parry, Graham, *The Seventeenth Century: The Intellectual and Cultural Context of English Literature 1603-1700* (London: Longman, 1989)

Patrides, C. A., and Joseph Wittriech (eds), *Apocalypse in English Renaissance Thought and Literature* (Manchester: Manchester University Press, 1984)

Patterson, Annabel, *Reading Between the Lines* (London: Routledge, 1993)

Penny, N., *First Publishers of Truth* (London: Headley Brothers, 1907)

Pestana, Carla Gardina, *Quakers and Baptists in Colonial Massachussetts* (Cambridge and New York: CUP, 1991)

Peters, Kate, 'Patterns of Quaker Authorship 1652-1656', *Prose Studies*, 17:3 (1994), 6-24

——'Quaker Pamphleteering and the Development of the Quaker Movement 1652-1656' (unpublished doctoral thesis, Cambridge University, 1996)

Poole, Kristen, *Radical Religion from Shakespeare to Milton: Figures of Nonconformity in Early Modern England* (Cambridge: CUP, 2000)

Pooley, Roger, '*Grace Abounding* and the New Sense of Self', in *John Bunyan and his England 1628-88*, ed. by Anne Laurence, W. R. Owens and Stuart Sim (London and Ronceverte: The Hambledon Press, 1990), pp. 105-114

Powell, Chilton Lathan, *English Domestic Relations 1587-1653: A Study of Matrimony and Family Life* (New York: Columbia University Press, 1917)

Purkiss, Diane, 'Producing the Voice, Consuming the Body: Women Prophets of the Seventeenth Century', in *Women, Writing, History 1640-1740*, ed. by Isobel Grundy and Susan Wiseman (London: B. T. Batsford, 1992), pp. 139-158

——*The Witch in History* (London and New York: Routledge, 1996)

Radford-Ruether, Rosemary, 'Prophets and Humanists: Types of Religious Feminism in Stuart England', *Journal of Religion*, 70 (1990), 1-18

Raymond, Joad, *Pamphlets and Pamphleteering in Early Modern Britain* (Cambridge: CUP, 2003)

Reay, Barry, 'Popular Hostility towards Quakers in Mid Seventeenth Century England', *Social History*, 5 (1980), 387-407

——'Quaker Opposition to Tithes (1652-1660)', *Past and Present*, 86 (1980), 98-220

——*The Quakers and the English Revolution* (London: Maurice Temple Smith, 1985)

——'The Quakers, 1659, and the Restoration of the Monarchy', *History*, 63 (1978), 193-213

Richey, Esther Gilman, *The Politics of Revelation in the English Renaissance* (Columbia and London: University of Missouri Press, 1998)

Rickman, Lydia L. 'Esther Biddle and her Mission to Louis XIV', *JFHS*, 53 (1974), 38-45

Rivkin, Julie, and Michael Ryan (eds), *Literary Theory: An Anthology* (Oxford and Malden, Massachusetts: Blackwell, 1998)

Roberts, Stephen, 'The Quakers in Evesham 1655-1660: A Study in Religion, Politics and Culture', *Midland History*, 16 (1991), 63-85

Roper, Lyndal, *Oedipus and the Devil: Witchcraft, Sexuality and Religion in Early Modern Europe* (London and New York: Routledge, 1994)

Rose, Judith, 'Prophesying Daughters: Testimony, Censorship, and Literacy Among Early Quaker Women', *Critical Survey*, 14:1 (2002), 93-110

Rose, Mary Beth, 'Gender, Genre, and History: Seventeenth-Century English Women and the Art of Autobiography', in *Women in the Middle Ages and the Renaissance: Literary and Historical Perspectives*, ed. by Mary Beth Rose (Syracuse: Syracuse University Press, 1986), pp. 245-278

Ross, Isabel, *Margaret Fell Mother of Quakerism*, 3rd edn (York: The Ebor Press, 1996)

Rowbotham, Shelia, *Hidden From History: 300 Years of Women's Oppression and the Fight Against it* (repr. London: Pluto Press, 1992)

Roy, Ian, 'England Turned Germany? The Aftermath of the Civil War in its European Context', *Transactions of the Royal Historical Society*, fifth series, 28 (1978), 172-244

Runyan, David, 'Types of Quaker Writings by Year: 1650-1699', in *Early Quaker Writings 1650-1700*, ed. by Hugh Barbour and Arthur O. Roberts (Grand Rapids, Michigan: William B. Eerdmans, 1973), pp. 567-576

Rusche, Henry, 'Prophecies and Propaganda 1641-51', *English Historical Review*, 84 (1969), 752-770

Rutty, John, *A History of the Rise and Progress of the People Called Quakers in Ireland* (Dublin: L. Jackson, 1751)

Sawday, Jonathan, *The Body Emblazoned: Dissection and the Human Body in Renaissance Culture* (London and New York: Routledge, 1995)

Scarry, Elaine, *The Body in Pain: The Making and Unmaking of the World* (New York and Oxford: OUP, 1985)

Schofield, Mary Anne, '"Women's Speaking Justified": The Feminine Quaker voice, 1662-1797', *Tulsa Studies in Women's Literature*, 6:1 (1987), 61-77

Scholz, Suzanne, *Body Narratives: Writing the Nation and Fashioning the Subject in Early Modern England* (Basingstoke: Palgrave Macmillan, 2000)

Scrager-Lang, Amy, *Prophetic Woman: Anne Hutchinson and the Problem of Dissent in the Literature of New England* (Berkeley, Los Angeles and London: University of California Press, 1987)

Serraino Luecke, Marilyn, 'God Hath Made no Difference Such as Men Would: Margaret Fell and the Politics of Women's Speech', *Bunyan Studies*, 7 (1997), 73-95

Sewel, William, *The History of the Rise, Increase, and Progress of the Christian People Called Quakers*, 6th edn, 2 vols (London: Darton and Harvey, 1834)

Sharpe, J. A., *Early Modern England: A Social History 1550-1760* (London and Baltimore: Edward Arnold, 1987)

—'"Last Dying Speeches": Religion, Ideology and Public Execution in Seventeenth-Century England', *Past and Present*, 107 (1995), 144-167

Sharpe, Kevin, '"An Image Doting Rabble" The Failure of Republican Culture in Seventeenth-Century England', in *Refiguring Revolutions: Aesthetics and Politics from the English Revolution to the Romantic Revolution*, ed. by Kevin Sharpe and Steven N. Zwicker (Berkeley, Los Angeles and London: University of California Press, 1998), pp. 25-56

—*Reading Revolutions: The Politics of Reading in Early Modern England* (New Haven and London: Yale University Press, 2000)

Sharpe, Pamela, 'Literally Spinsters: A new Interpretation of Local Economy and Demography in Colyton in the Seventeenth and Eighteenth Centuries', *Economic History Review*, 44:1 (1991), 46-65

Siebert, Fredrick Seaton, *Freedom of the Press in England 1476-1776: The Rise and Decline of Government Control* (Urbana: University of Illinois Press, 1965)

Skerpan, Elizabeth, *The Rhetoric of Politics in the English Revolution 1642-1660* (Columbia and London: University of Missouri Press, 1992)

Smith, Joseph, *A Descriptive Catalogue of Friends' Books*, 2 vols (London: Barrett and Sons, 1867)

Smith, Nigel, 'Hidden Things Brought to Light: Enthusiasm and Quaker Discourse', *Prose Studies*, 17:3 (1994), 57-69

—*Literature and Revolution in England 1640-1660* (New Haven and London: Yale University Press, 1994)

—*Perfection Proclaimed: Language and Literature in English Radical Religion 1640-1660* (Oxford: Clarendon Press, 1989)

Smith, Sidonie, *A Poetics of Women's Autobiography: Marginality and the Fictions of Self-Representation* (Bloomington and Indianapolis: Indiana University Press, 1987)

Spraggs, Gillian, 'Rogues and Vagabonds in English Literature 1552-1642' (unpublished doctoral thesis, University of Cambridge, 1980)

Spufford, Margaret, *Contrasting Communities: English Villagers in the Sixteenth and Seventeenth Centuries* (Cambridge: CUP, 1974)

Spufford, (ed.), *The World of Rural Dissenters 1520-1725* (Cambridge: CUP, 1995)

Spurr, John, 'Rational Religion in Restoration England', *Journal of the History of Ideas*, 49:4 (1988), 563-585

Stachniewski, John, *The Persecutory Imagination: English Puritanism and the Literature of Religious Despair* (Oxford: Clarendon Press, 1991)

Stanley, Liz, 'Feminist Auto/Biography and Feminist Epistemology', in *Out of the Margins: Women's Studies in the Nineties*, ed. by Jane Aaron and Sylvia Welby (London: Falmer, 1991), pp. 204-219

Stevenson, Bill, 'The Social and Economic Status of Post-Restoration Dissenters, 1660-1725', in *The World of Rural Dissenters 1520-1725*, ed. by Margaret Spufford (Cambridge: CUP, 1995), pp. 332-359

Stevenson, William, 'Sectarian Cohesion and Social Integration 1640-1725', in *Religious Dissent in East Anglia*, ed. by E. S. Leedham-Green (Cambridge: Cambridge Antiquarian Society, 1991), pp. 69-86

Stillinger, Jack, *Multiple Authorship and the Myth of Solitary Genius* (New York and Oxford: OUP, 1991)

Stone, Lawrence, *The Family, Sex and Marriage in England 1500-1800* (London: Weidenfield and Nicholson, 1977)

Tarter, Michele Lise, 'Nursing the New Wor(l)d: The Writings of Quaker Women in Early America', *Women and Language*, 16:1 (1993), 22-6

——'Quaking in the Light', in *Centre of Wonders: The Body in Early America*, ed. by Janet Moore Mindman and Michele Lise Tarter (Ithaca and London: Cornell University Press, 2001), 145-162

Thomas, Keith, *Religion and the Decline of Magic: Studies in the Popular Beliefs in Sixteenth and Seventeenth-Century England* (repr. London and New York: Penguin, 1991)

——'Women and the Civil War Sects', *Past and Present*, 13 (1958), 42-62

Todd, Barbara J., 'The Remarrying Widow: A Stereotype Reconsidered', in *Women in English Society 1500-1800*, ed. by Mary Prior (London and New York: Methuen, 1985), pp. 54-92

Todd, Janet (ed.), *A Dictionary of British and American Women Writers 1660-1800* (London: Methuen, 1987)

——*Women, Writing and Fiction 1660-1800* (London: Virago, 1989)

Todd, Margo, 'Humanists, Puritans and the Spiritualised Household', *Church History*, 49:1 (1980), 18-34

Trevett, Christine, *Women and Quakerism in the Seventeenth Century* (York: The Ebor Press, 1995)

Trill, Susan, 'Religion and the Construction of Femininity', in *Women and Literature in Britain 1500-1700*, ed. by Helen Wilcox (Cambridge: CUP, 1996), pp. 30-55

Trubowitz, Rachel, 'Female Preachers and Male Wives: Gender and Authority in Civil War England', in *Pamphlet Wars: Prose in the English Revolution*, ed. by James Holstun (London: Frank Cass, 1992), pp. 112-133

Truman, James, C. W., 'John Foxe and the Desires of Reformation Martyrology, *ELH*, 70:1 (2003), 35-66

Tuana, Nancy, 'The Weaker Seed: The Sexist Bias of Reproductive Theory', in *Feminism and Science*, ed. by Nancy Tuana (Bloomington and Indianapolis: Indiana University Press, 1989), pp. 147-171

Underdown, David, *Pride's Purge: Politics in the Puritan Revolution* (Oxford: The Clarendon Press, 1971)

——*Revel, Riot and Rebellion: Popular Politics and Culture in England 1603-1660* (Oxford: Clarendon Press, 1985)

—— 'The Taming of the Scold: The Enforcement of Patriarchal Authority in Early Modern England', in *Order and Disorder in England*, ed. by Anthony Fletcher (Cambridge: CUP, 1985), pp. 116-136

Underwood, T. L., *Primitivism, Radicalism and the Lamb's War: Baptist – Quaker Conflict in Seventeenth-Century England* (New York and Oxford: OUP, 1997)

Vann, Richard T., 'Diggers and Quakers – A Further Note', *JFHS*, 50:1 (1962), 65-68

—— 'Quakerism and the Social Structure in the Interregnum', *Past and Present*, 43 (1969), 71-91

——*The Social Development of English Quakerism 1655-1755* (Cambridge, Massachusetts: Harvard University Press, 1969)

Vipont, Elfrida, *George Fox and the Valiant Sixty* (London: Hamish Hamilton, 1975)

Wallach-Scott, Joan, *Gender and the Politics of History* (New York: Columbia University Press, 1988)

Watkins, Owen, *The Puritan Experience* (London: Routledge and Kegan Paul, 1972)

Watts, Michael R., *The Dissenters* (Oxford: Clarendon Press, 1978)

Weber, Max, *The Protestant Ethic and the Spirit of Capitalism*, trans. by Talcott Parsons (repr. London and New York: Routledge, 1992)

Wilcox, Catherine M., *Theology and Women's Ministry in Seventeenth-Century English Quakerism: Handmaids of the Lord* (New York: The Edwin Mellen Press, 1995)

Wilcox, Helen, 'Private Writing and Public Function: Autobiographical Texts by Renaissance English Women', in *Gloriana's Face*, ed. by S. P. Cerasano and Marion Wynne-Davies (New York and London: Harvester Wheatsheaf, 1992), pp. 47-62

Williams, Ethyn Morgan, 'Women Preachers in the English Civil War', *Journal of Modern History*, 1 (1926), 561-569

Williams, Raymond, *Marxism and Literature* (Oxford: OUP, 1977)

Wiseman, Susan, 'Unsilent Instruments and the Devil's Cushions: Authority in Seventeenth-Century Women's Prophetic Discourse', in *New Feminist Discourses*, ed. by Isabel Armstrong (London and New York: Routledge, 1992), pp. 176-196

Woolrych, Austin, *Commonwealth to Protectorate* (Oxford: Clarendon Press, 1982)

—— 'Historical Introduction (1659-1660)', in *Complete Prose Works of John Milton*, ed. by Robert W. Ayers, 8 vols (rev. edn, New Haven and London: Yale University Press, 1980), VII, pp. 1-228

—— 'Last Quests for a Settlement 1657-1660', in *The Interregnum: The Quest for Settlement 1646-1660*, ed. by G. E. Aylmer (London: Macmillan, 1972), pp. 183-204

—— 'The Good Old Cause and the Fall of the Protectorate', *The Cambridge Historical Journal*, 13: 2 (1957), 133-161

Worden, Blair, *The Rump Parliament 1648-1653* (London and Cambridge: CUP, 1974)

Worrall, Arthur J., *Quakers in the Colonial Northeast* (Hanover, New Hampshire and London: University Press of New England, 1980)

Wright, Louis B., *Middle Class Culture in Elizabethan England* (Chapel Hill, The University of North Carolina Press, 1935)

Wright, Luella M., *The Literary Life of the Early Friends 1650-1725* (New York: Columbia University Press, 1932)

Wrightson, Keith, and Joan Walter, 'Dearth and the Social Order in Early Modern England', *Past and Present*, 71 (1976), 22-42

Wrightson, Keith, *English Society 1580-1680* (London: Hutchinson, 1982)

Zaret, David, *Origins of Democratic Culture: Printing, Petitions, and the Public Sphere in Early-Modern England* (Princeton: Princeton University Press, 2000)

Index